Poetry, Providence, and Patriotism

Princeton Theological Monograph Series

K. C. Hanson, Charles M. Collier, and D. Christopher Spinks,
Series Editors

Recent volumes in the series:

Roger A. Johnson
*Peacemaking and Religious Violence: From Thomas Aquinas
to Thomas Jefferson*

Ilsup Ahn
*Position and Responsibility: Jürgen Habermas, Reinhold Niebuhr,
and the Co-Reconstruction of the Positional Imperative*

Poul F. Guttesen
*Leaning Into the Future: The Kingdom of God in the Theology
of Jürgen Moltmann and the Book of Revelation*

Chris Budden
Following Jesus in Invaded Space: Doing Theology on Aboriginal Land

L. Paul Jensen
*Subversive Spirituality: Transforming Mission through the Collapse
of Space and Time*

Eliseo Pérez-Álvarez
A Vexing Gadfly: The Late Kierkegaard on Economic Matters

Scott A. Ellington
Risking Truth: Reshaping the World through Prayers of Lament

Jerry Root
*C. S. Lewis and a Problem of Evil: An Investigation
of a Pervasive Theme*

Poetry, Providence, and Patriotism
Polish Messianism in Dialogue with Dietrich Bonhoeffer

Joel Burnell

◦PICKWICK *Publications* · Eugene, Oregon

POETRY, PROVIDENCE, AND PATRIOTISM
Polish Messianism in Dialogue with Dietrich Bonhoeffer

Princeton Theological Monograph Series 123

Copyright © 2009 Joel Burnell. All rights reserved. Except for brief quotations in critical publications or reviews, no part of this book may be reproduced in any manner without prior written permission from the publisher. Write: Permissions, Wipf and Stock Publishers, 199 W. 8th Ave., Suite 3, Eugene, OR 97401.

Pickwick Publications
An Imprint of Wipf and Stock Publishers
199 W. 8th Ave., Suite 3
Eugene, OR 97401

www.wipfandstock.com

ISBN 13: 978-1-60608-042-9

Cataloguing-in-Publication data:

Burnell, Joel.

    Poetry, providence, and patriotism : Polish messianism in dialogue with Dietrich Bonhoeffer / Joel Burnell.

    xxvi + 294 p. ; 23 cm. — Includes bibliographical references.

    Princeton Theological Monograph Series 123

    ISBN 13: 978-1-60608-042-9

    1. Messianism, Political — Poland. 2. Bonhoeffer, Dietrich, 1906–1945. I. Title. II. Series.

BX4827.B57 B93 2009

Manufactured in the U.S.A.

To Renata

Contents

Preface / ix

Acknowledgments / xi

List of Abbreviations / xii

An Introduction to Polish Messianism / xiii

The Birth Pains of Polish Messianism / 1

The Foundation of Polish Messianism: Jan Paweł Woronicz—Patriotic Priest / 34

The Flowering of Polish Messianism: Adam Mickiewicz—Patriotic Pilgrim / 68

The Polish Reception of Bonhoeffer / 122

Bonhoeffer on Christ, Providence, and Responsibility / 175

Bonhoeffer and Polish Messianism / 218

A Post-Messianic, Bonhofferian Polish Alternative to Secularism and Fundamentalism / 258

Bibliography / 285

Preface

IN 1989 THE WORLD LOOKED WITH BAITED BREATH AT EVENTS UNFOLDing in Poland, as Tadeusz Mazowiecki was chosen as Prime Minister of the newly elected Solidarity government. After a 200-year long struggle, Poland had regained its right to national self-determination, setting in motion a chain of events that led to sweeping changes throughout Central and Eastern Europe. The issues the Poles wrestled with during their long battle for independence, and the lessons they learned regarding patriotism, civil society, pluralism, and dialogue between diverse ethnic, religious and national groups, all speak with surprising relevance to today's world. Yet apart from students of Polish history and literature, or close observers of the social and political transformations that took place in this region in the second half of the twentieth century, few outside of Poland understand the historical background, intellectual traditions or social processes leading up to these changes. Despite the growing number of articles and books dealing with these subjects, there are still many areas requiring further study.

This study makes its contribution in two such areas; an analysis of Polish messianism from a theological perspective,[1] and a survey of the Polish reception of Bonhoeffer[2] by the Polish opposition movement, which leads to the use of Bonhoeffer's thought to critique both historic and contemporary expressions of Polish messianism. Since these topics are largely unexplored and undocumented, the original six chapters of my PhD dissertation are published here in full, with only minor editing. Though the text thus retains its academic character, I have been told it reads well, and non-specialists are invited to enter the colorful, multi-

---

1. Literary analyses of course abound, and many of these touch on theological issues intrinsic to messianism, such as providence, theodicy, and eschatology. Among articles and books that discuss the theology of Polish messianism, the section by Masłowski entitled "Wiara i historia" (Faith and History) in *Gest, Symbol i rytuały polskiego teatru romantycznego*, 259–342, is worthy of note. For a philosophical study on messianism, see Walicki, *Philosophy and Romantic Nationalism*, 1982.

2. Cf. Melhorn, "Na marginesie recepcji Bonhoeffera w Polsce", 246–50.

faceted world of Polish messianism and civil society without getting bogged down in the footnotes. To bring the study up to date and suggest appropriate application, the original brief conclusion has been expanded into a final, seventh chapter. In particular, that chapter proposes the outline and building blocks of what I have called a "A Post-Messianic, Bonhoefferian, Polish Alternative to Secularism and Fundamentalism."

Within Poland itself the ongoing academic debates over messianism seldom trickle down to public consciousness. Although messianism itself is part and parcel of Polish history, culture and experience, and has continued to exert its influence[3] long past the twilight of the romantic era, it is commonly misunderstood by Poles today, or regarded as a curious relic of the past. Furthermore, while works by or about Bonhoeffer appear from time to time in Polish, they reach a limited audience, and few are aware of his influence on the Polish opposition movement, or appreciate what his legacy has to offer for Polish culture and society, including political and religious life, in the twenty-first century. Polish history includes moments both noble and petty, events grand and tragic, ideas that are troubling and inspiring. For readers within and without Poland, it is my hope that this study captures some of the passion, pathos and promise of Poland's rich history, intertwined as it is with messianism and more recently the life and witness of Dietrich Bonhoeffer.

In recent years a heated debate has raged over the legacy of Solidarity, the "Round Table," and the leaders of the Polish opposition movement. Many have questioned or denied outright the myths of Solidarity, and attacked such legendary figures as Lech Wałęsa, Adam Michnik, Tadeusz Mazowiecki, and the late Jacek Kuroń and Bronisław Geremek. As these leaders themselves admit, they made numerous mistakes to go along with their remarkable victories. Much work remains to be done in the study and interpretation of both their mistakes and victories. Yet it is my opinion that history will in the end vindicate them rather than their detractors.

---

3. E.g., through Polish literary, religious, and political traditions, through (often subconsciously-held) values, or through the continued use of images and metaphors drawn from the canon of messianic literature.

Acknowledgments

I would like to express my gratitude to Professor Stephen Williams of Queens University, Belfast, whose guidance and critique helped keep me on course to the completion of this project. I am also grateful for the encouragement and insight I have received from my colleagues and friends in the International Bonhoeffer Society. Special thanks are due to Prof. Dr. hab. Jacek Kolbuszewski of the University of Wrocław, Poland, who served as my early guide to Polish messianism, and whose suggestions for selected literature provided a solid foundation for my further research. Needless to say, responsibility for any and all shortcomings in the final product is mine alone.

Abbreviations

The following abbreviations of selected works by Dietrich Bonhoeffer includes those of his major works that proved particularly fruitful in the dialogue with Polish messianism.

AB	*Act and Being*, Dietrich Bonhoeffer Works English (hereafter DBWE) 2
C	*Christology*
CD	*The Cost of Discipleship*
CF	*Creation and Fall*, DBWE 3
D	*Discipleship*, DBWE 4
E	*Ethics*, DBWE 6
LPP	*Letters and Papers from Prison*
LT/P	*Life Together and Prayerbook of the Bible*, DBWE 5
SC	*Sanctorum Communio*, DBWE 1

An Introduction to Polish Messianism

The Purpose, Method, and Structure of the Book

THIS BOOK IS A CONTEXTUAL STUDY OF POLISH MESSIANISM, WITH special attention given to its contribution to the theory and practice of patriotism and civil responsibility. After examining the influence of Dietrich Bonhoeffer on the Polish opposition movement's creative appropriation of messianism, Bonhoeffer's theology is then employed to critique messianism and to suggest positive contributions it offers for today.

This book aims at an independent reading of Polish messianism, which is neither revisionist nor epigonic, and which remains faithful to its spirit while reflecting current scholarship. Translations from the Polish, unless otherwise noted, are my own. Regarding key anthropological concepts, "myth" is defined functionally as an "organizing belief," while "nation" is treated as a sociological and not metaphysical entity. The approach to both concepts follows their common usage in Polish cultural anthropology and literary criticism.[1] "Citizens' society" refers to the program for an independent civil society,[2] as described in chapter 4, "Citizens' Society," which was developed by the Polish opposition movement following 1968.[3]

The Introduction discusses the role of historical myths, introduces the main ideas of Polish messianism, and addresses the choice of Bonhoeffer as a dialogue partner. Furthermore, it explains the Polish

---

1. Polish academicians are widely read; their approach to these subjects reflects their acquaintance with and contribution to contemporary international scholarship.

2. In this book, the context determines if the more general term "civil society" refers to "citizens' society." This is generally the case when civil society is described as "independent," i.e., from the ruling socialist government.

3. Although each situation was unique, dissident leaders and groups in other countries such as Czechoslovakia and Hungary also shared in developing the theory and practice of citizens' society.

distinction between patriotism and nationalism, as well as the impact of eschatology or the philosophy of history on respective visions of Poland's national identity. Chapter 1 provides a survey of Polish messianism, while chapters 2 and 3 examine its quintessential expressions in the poetry of Jan Pawel Woronicz and Adam Mickiewicz. Woronicz was recognized by classicists, sentimentalists, and romantics alike as the one who developed Polish messianism into a coherent philosophy of history. Mickiewicz in turn was the most influential and eloquent of Poland's romantic poets. Building on Woronicz's work, he delineated the messianic system others would subsequently try to emulate, modify or replace. His work, which contains a rich expression of the biblical and humanistic ideals of Polish messianism, is also a classic example of romantic epistemology and historiosophy. The interpretation in these chapters, while original, is primarily descriptive in nature; the critique of messianism is largely reserved for chapter 6.

The Polish opposition movement that arose after 1968 was a continuation of the Polish struggle for independence. The program and postulates of this struggle were originally formulated by messianism. Chapter 4 traces Bonhoeffer's influence on members of the opposition and their efforts to create an independent civil society. The Polish reception of Bonhoeffer affected the opposition's critical adaptation of Poland's messianic tradition, and facilitated the rapprochement between the secular and progressive Catholic wings of the Polish intelligentsia that led to their ensuing cooperation in such endeavors as the Committee for the Defense of Workers (KOR) and the Solidarity movement. Nevertheless, the Polish reception of Bonhoeffer, undertaken in the historical context of resistance to Poland's communist regime, was not radical enough in its appropriation of Bonhoeffer's Christological center, or in its critique of Poland's underlying messianic legacy. Therefore chapter 5 surveys Bonhoeffer's theology, with an eye towards themes relevant to messianism. In chapter 6 Bonhoeffer's theology of sociality, his Christocentric ethics, his understanding of divine providence and human responsibility, and his programmatic response to the "crisis of modernity" are applied to a theological critique of Polish messianism.[4] Finally, chapter 7 offers a constructive proposal for Christian engagement with Polish

---

4. Citizens' society will also be critiqued at several critical points where it adopts, develops, or modifies key aspects of Polish messianism.

society in the twenty-first century, as an alternative to secularism and the resulting fundamentalist reaction.

The Underlying Themes of the Book

Historical Myths

Although deconstructionism has revised the truism that "winners write the history books," historians still have a conscious if often unstated agenda in their selection, organization, and description of historical events. Together with anthropologists, they now acknowledge that history is at the mercy of those who describe it. Some even go so far as to declare that, "All history is myth." What then is myth? Samsonowicz recounts a fellow historian's presumably tongue-in-cheek reply to this question: "[Myth] is a wrong thesis presented by my antagonists."[5] Kolbuszewski proposes a more functional definition of myth as "a pronouncement expressing and organizing a belief of a given society."[6] Norman Davies, who has devoted the bulk of his career to the study of Polish history, explains the function of and need for myths.

> Everyone needs myths. Individuals need myths. Nations need myths. Myths are the sets of simplified beliefs, which may or may not approximate reality, but which give us a sense of our origins, our identity, and our purposes. They are patently subjective, but are often more powerful than the objective truth—for the truth can be painful.[7]

Historians, regardless of how objective they aim or claim to be, are themselves part of the story, influenced by the categories and biases they bring to the process of observation, analysis, and synthesis. The subjectivity of historical perception encourages one to make judgments cautiously and hold them with humility. However, subjectivity does not imply complete relativity in analyzing and interpreting history. Neither is the influence of a given historical-mythical account necessarily related to its degree of factual historicity. Rather, as Kolbuszewski writes, "the strength of a work's literary expression is not uncommonly linked with

---

5. Samsonowicz, O "historii prawdziwej," 6.
6. Kolbuszewski, *Literatura wobec historii*, 17.
7. Davies, "Polish National Mythologies," 141.

the unverified nature of its enormously convincing generalizations."[8] Truth[9] and goodness can be communicated by means of myth, while historical "facts" are often manipulated to promote falsehood and evil.

A dynamic interplay exists between history and myth, appearing in a cultural form of the hermeneutical spiral that moves from (1) act-event, to (2) reflection-interpretation, to (3) expression-plan. Noteworthy political and cultural events capture the society's imagination and remain in its collective memory. There they serve as the occasion for reflection on national character traits, being reinterpreted according to the need of the hour and their interpreter's agenda. Finally, these interpretations are turned into myth and used to construct a social, economic, religious, and political program. The spiral continues, for with the reception of these myths and programs by society they themselves become a mythical act-event that leads in turn to further reflection. History also has its say, for myths are accepted or rejected partially on the basis of their effectiveness in achieving the society's vision or goals or explaining its fate. Myths take their revenge however, for they often outlive their usefulness, or are misappropriated by a society that seeks to apply them in the wrong manner or in inappropriate circumstances.

Polish messianism is a patently mythical construction, a structured narrative rooted in the nation's history, set in its nineteenth-century geo-political context, and linked to its developing self-consciousness. Its authors believed that the past held the key to understanding the nation's present identity and calling.[10] For the myth-makers who crafted it, messianism was a vision of what Poles must become if they were to survive as a nation. All agree that messianism has shaped the Polish people and impacted their history for 200 years, though opinions vary on whether its influence was positive or negative, or whether it has anything to offer today. Regardless, myths will continue to both reflect and shape the nation's changing situation, needs, and self-perception. As Davies writes,

> All myths serve a purpose. As the purposes change, the myths change with them. The critical question in Poland today, there-

---

8. Kolbuszewski, *Literatura wobec historii*, 99.

9. While this book is not devoted to epistemology or the question of truth, romantic epistemology is described in chapter 1 and critiqued in chapter 6.

10. As Moltmann writes, "Only when there is something in the past that points beyond itself to the future is there any point in remembering the past." Moltmann, *On Human Dignity*, 105.

fore, is whether any of the traditional myths can be revived or modified to match the conditions of life in the "Third," post-communist, Republic. [...] We shall see. One thing is certain. If the old myths do not suffice, then new ones will be invented.[11]

Polish Messianism

Polish messianism was born in the wake of the final partition of Poland in 1795. The loss of independence forced the Poles to reassess their national identity, reflect on their nation's suffering, and reformulate their expectations of Polish citizens and patriots. Poland was christened "the Christ of the Nations" by its patriots and poets, and its sufferings were endowed with a dual significance. In addition to the goal of national renewal and recovered independence, messianism held that the "resurrection" of an independent, democratic Poland would demonstrate the triumph of freedom and justice over tyranny and oppression, and usher in a new era of peace, justice, and international brotherhood among the nations of Europe. This form of messianism took shape in the late classicist[12] period in the writings of Jan Paweł Woronicz (1757–1829), and reached its peak during the romantic period (1822–1863)[13] in the poetry of Adam Mickiewicz (1798–1855).

Woronicz and Mickiewicz understood the importance of myths. Consciously selecting certain elements of Polish legend and history, they crafted their own versions of the Polish national myth. Their immediate purpose was to shape Poles' awareness of their national identity, as an essential step towards the goal of reestablishing a sovereign Polish state. But they also believed Poland was destined to share her dream of democracy, freedom, pluralism, and tolerance with other nations.

While Polish messianism drew heavily on the biblical messianism of Judaism and Christianity, it was part of the broader messianic movement that appeared in Europe around the turn of the eighteenth and

---

11. Davies, "Polish National Mythologies," 156–57.

12. Polish classicism adopted the literary forms of the great writers of antiquity, and more recently those of France, as its own artistic canon. Arising in the eighteenth century as part of the effort to revive the sagging fortunes of the Polish State, following the partitions classicism strove to maintain Polish identity by preserving the nation's language and literary treasures.

13. The publication in 1822 of Adam Mickiewicz's first volume of poetry marks the traditional beginning of the romantic period in Poland, which ended in 1863 with the downfall of the January Uprising.

nineteenth centuries, in the context of political ferment, social injustice, religious crisis, and growing national self-awareness. Sensing that great changes were just beyond the horizon, messianism sought hope for the future in the relationship between the spiritual and historical worlds. As Siwicka explains, "Romantic messianism was born from the feeling of the crisis of the age and the global downfall of Christian culture and religion . . . [It] became a religious-political movement, which would both renew Christianity, as well as change the political face of Europe."[14] In atheistic and panentheistic forms of messianism, belief in a personal deity was replaced with faith in history, progress, or various incarnations of the "World Spirit." Jürgen Moltmann describes modern political forms of messianism:

> Nationalism declared the nation to be the messiah; Italian fascism spoke of the Duce of the end time; German National Socialism worshipped the Fuhrer of a Third, or Thousand Year, Reich; Saint Simon called the machine messiah because it would liberate us from toil and work; and in early Marxism the proletariat who freed themselves became the "redeemed redeemer" of the world.[15]

Messianism displays a characteristic passion to relate religious belief to socio-political involvement, perceived either as proactive engagement in social and political affairs, or as the passive acceptance of suffering, understood to have redemptive significance. Polish romanticists agonized over which form of action, active or passive, was appropriate or possible at any given historical moment. Hence, messianism's critics accuse it both of inciting rash, senseless sacrifices, and of encouraging an attitude of passive martyrdom.

Messianism's political action is grounded in hope for the coming messianic kingdom. According to Andrzej Walicki, messianism is "first of all, a type of *religious* consciousness closely bound up with millenarianism, i.e., with the quest for total, imminent, ultimate, this-worldly, collective salvation."[16] "Messianism," argues Janion, "allowed for hope for the supernatural end of history, which is the basis of messianic optimism; the Kingdom of God would free mankind from everything

---

14. Siwicka, *Romantyzm*, 90.
15. Moltmann, *On Human Dignity*, 100–101.
16. Walicki, *Philosophy and Romantic Nationalism*, 240.

that made history hard to bear."[17] This hope was especially significant for nineteenth-century Poles, who found history to be unbearable. As Siwicka writes, "The national defeats and misfortunes ... were part of the providential plan of God, a plan which must lead to the renewal of humanity, the liberation of all nations, and universal brotherhood. This happy end of history was universally conceived as the imminent, it was believed, victory of the 'Polish idea': the love of holy law for freedom."[18] Janion summarizes the hope Polish romanticists sought in the concept of redemptive suffering for the salvation of Poland and all humanity:

> Polish messianism, acknowledged by all as the most classical among the messianisms of the nineteenth century, lived by the conviction that human history reproduces the course of holy history and that the post-partition history of Poland must repeat the passion and resurrection of Christ. A nation that drew upon itself the persecution of the tyrants could only be regarded as an innocent victim—her martyrdom and resurrection begin a new era of freedom in human history.[19]

Why Messianism? Why Bonhoeffer? Why Together?

The 1918 collapse of imperial Germany and czarist Russia, together with successful Polish uprisings in the West and a hard-won armistice with the Red Army in the East, allowed Poland to briefly regain its independence. In 1939 Hitler's *Wehrmacht* and Stalin's Red Army invaded Poland. During the war, Poland's multi-ethnic society was deeply scarred by Nazi genocide, which began with the Jewish Holocaust, and included plans for the gradual extermination of the Polish nation. Following World War II Poland, consigned by the Yalta agreements to the Soviet sphere of influence, experienced 45 years of life under the communist regime of the People's Republic of Poland.

In 1989 Poland recovered its right to self-determination, initiating events that led to the fall of the Berlin Wall and the end of the Cold War. Poland became a leader in the non-violent transition from Soviet-backed socialism to democracy and a free-market economy among the former satellite countries of Central and Eastern Europe. Crucial to

---

17. Janion and Żmigrodzka, *Romantyzm i historia*, 30.
18. Siwicka, *Romantyzm*, 91.
19. Janion and Żmigrodzka, *Romantyzm i historia*, 30–31.

this victory were the efforts of the Polish opposition movement to create an independent civil society (1968–1989). Polish activists drew on their nation's messianic legacy, as viewed through the prism of Poland's turbulent history and current geopolitical realities, to forge the ethos and strategies of the opposition movement. Their reading of Bonhoeffer aided them in their struggle against communism. To date the scope of Bonhoeffer's influence on the opposition has been largely underestimated not only by observers in the West, but by many commentators in Poland as well.

Today, after their freedom has been won, Poles ask whether Mickiewicz and romanticism have anything to offer their nation today. Though many would answer in the negative, a careful observer recognizes many outward signs of the messianic thought and values that underlie Polish culture and character. Some of messianism's grandchildren remain true to its original spirit, while others draw on its mythical power in ways quite at odds with that vision. Some even count Mickiewicz as a source of the xenophobic, authoritarian, anti-Semitic nationalism of the National Democrats,[20] which has reappeared in the reactionary political broadcasts of *Radio Maryja*, the rhetoric and policies of the League of Polish Families, and the reactivated youth organization *Młodzież Wszechpolski*. These claims will be addressed below. For now we may cite Porter's judgment, that while "the ideological framework of nationalism contained points of tension that could be pushed in a number of directions . . . no clear causal explanation for radical right nationalism can be found [. . .] Nothing about either the intellectual or social history of nineteenth century Poland compelled the National Democrats to think as they did."[21] Porter cites Andrzej Bryk, who writes that, "Polish culture has the luxury of choosing from a wide variety of streams. One of the most powerful and appealing, albeit a little forgotten, is the tradition of tolerance and pluralism."[22] Porter ambitiously argues that the revival of Polish messianism can aid in the "imagining of a Poland—indeed a Europe—for the twenty-first century, within which the nation-state will no longer be equated with cultural homogeneity."[23]

20. Cf. Eile, *Literature and Nationalism in Partitioned Poland*, 49.
21. Porter, *When Nationalism Began to Hate*, 237.
22. Bryk, cited in ibid., 237.
23. Ibid., 238. Porter's work focuses on developments following the heyday of Polish romantic messianism. Nevertheless, it supports the interpretation of messianism presented in this book.

An Introduction to Polish Messianism xxi

Returning to Bonhoeffer, many are surprised to discover the widespread appeal of this German Lutheran pastor and theologian among both secular and Catholic Poles during the 1970s and 80s. They would be even more surprised at the attempt made in this book to confront Woronicz and Mickiewicz with Bonhoeffer, especially when this is treated as a dialogue between friends and not a clash of worldviews. However, the phenomenon of Bonhoeffer's reception in Poland is more readily understood when one compares the challenges faced by Christians and "people of good will" in Nazi Germany to those faced by Christians and "people of good will" in partitioned Poland and in the Peoples' Republic of Poland. His insistence on responsible action in the world matched well the romantic insistence on the congruence between word and deed, to which even those Poles who rejected the romantic legacy remained true. The very fact that he was used widely and well by Polish opposition leaders suggests a deep resonance waiting to be explored between Bonhoeffer and the "Polish spirit," which remains after all romantic.[24] The recent publication of certain of Bonhoeffer's works[25] is a sign that Poles still look to him for insight and inspiration at the beginning of the twentieth century.

Patriotism vis-à-vis Nationalism

Patriotism is a complex interweaving of attitudes, and actions, which function as shared values that provide criteria for citizens' involvement in the life of their nation. The patriotic attitudes characteristic of the members of a given nation, ethnic group or political party influence what patriotic actions they undertake in its behalf. A nation's patriotic myths both explain and influence its history, and Poland is no exception in this regard. Davies writes,

> Imperial nations invent myths in order to justify their rule over other peoples. Defeated nations invent myths to explain their misfortune and assist in their survival. Poland may well have belonged to this latter category, as political adversity over many

---

24. Adam Michnik is one who proclaims his lasting debt to Bonhoeffer, and who identifies strongly with the poetry of Mickiewicz. The terms romantic, romanticism, classicist, classicism, positivist, positivism and messianism are used in the lower case throughout.

25. These publications include *Discipleship, Life Together,* and *Prayerbook of the Bible.*

generations seems to have created the sort of imaginative climate in which myths can flourish. Polish culture, and in particular literature, art, and historiography, is full of instances where the national imagination triumphs over realism.[26]

Patriotism has acquired a bad name, due to such aberrations as militant nationalism, imperialism, fascism, Nazism, Stalinism,[27] and ethnic cleansing. Traditionally, patriotism is viewed positively and nationalism negatively in Polish literature and political thought. "In Poland," Walicki explains, "the term 'nationalism' is . . . a pejorative term, meaning, approximately, the same as chauvinism, narrow national egoism, state expansionism, intolerant attitudes towards national minorities. Already in nineteenth-century Poland the word 'nationalism' was used as a synonym for national egoism, and was sharply distinguished from 'patriotism,' i.e., from the legitimate and humanitarian manifestations of the love of one's own nation."[28]

In the West patriotism and nationalism are often considered roughly synonymous. In academic literature, many employ nationalism as a neutral term descriptive of any nation's efforts towards self-identification and realization. The Polish historian Walicki therefore argues for the use of adjectives to qualify "nationalism," settling on a description of Polish messianism as "progressive, romantic nationalism."[29] Nevertheless, Porter argues that such distinctions may lead to considering various types of nationalism as distinct and hermetic.[30] Porter therefore follows Duara's more nuanced view, in which "nationalism marks the site where different representations of the nation contest

---

26. Davies, "Polish National Mythologies," 141.

27. Marxism, though ideologically opposed to nationalism, often falls to its lure, e.g., through continuity with national tradition such as led to the replacement of imperial Russia by the Soviet Union. More cynically, Poland's communist regime, plagued by a failed ideology and flagging economy, appealed to national-chauvinism in an effort to recruit popular support.

28. Walicki, "National Messianism and the Historical Controversies," 5.

29. Ibid., 6.

30. Porter cites Gauri Viswanathan, who writes that adjectival classifications of nationalism "assume a seamless unity of aspirations, goals, and agendas, a selection and filtering that irons out the contradictions embedded in the construction of a national identity from the fragments of religious, racial, cultural and other forms of self-identification." Porter, *When Nationalism Began to Hate*, 14.

and negotiate with each other."³¹ In the end, despite his appreciation of Polish linguistic conventions, Porter employs the term nationalism in his discussion of Polish "patriotism."

With full appreciation for Porter's position, since the early chapters of this book devoted to Polish messianism are heavily based on primary and secondary literature in the Polish language, the Polish convention will be adopted throughout. Patriotism is thus understood to have positive connotations and nationalism negative connotations. This distinction also proves useful in chapters 4 through 6, where Bonhoeffer's patriotism stands in contrast to the nationalism of the Third Reich.

Patriotism, National Identity, and Eschatology

Patriotism is closely tied to the question of national identity, which is itself perplexing and controversial. When a nation's members become conscious of their identity as distinct from other nations, such self-perception shapes their social and political stance in respect to those who are "other." But what is a nation? Here we face the same difficulties that social anthropology has in defining ethnicity, tribes, tribal groups, race, civilizations, etc. This book uses the term "nation" in a non-technical, pragmatic sense to describe the Polish people, their characteristics, aspirations, ideals, and "national spirit."

During the last 200 years the term "nation" took on a personalist connotation in Polish literature. Poland was metaphorically endowed with its own consciousness, character traits, mind, emotions, spirit, aspirations, and calling. At times the nation was granted ontological being, understood either metaphysically or structurally as a socio-political entity. This view of the nation was paired with a philosophy of history that grants nations a specific role in world history, understood either as the realization of divine Providence or the Hegelian World-Spirit. This trend is evident in the discussion of "Polish National Philosophy" initiated by Maurycy Mochnacki (1803–1834).

Of the various definitions suggested for the Polish nation, two have particular significance. "Jagiellonian" Poland views the nation as an open, inclusive, ethnically, and religiously diverse society, such as existed in the Polish Commonwealth following the union of Poland and

---

31. Prasenjit Duara, cited in ibid., 13.

Lithuania.³² "Piast" Poland envisions the nation as a closed, exclusive, ethnically Polish, and religiously Catholic homogeneous society.³³ The struggle between advocates of these competing views has reemerged at the beginning of the twenty-first century, with scarcely less passion but considerably less clarity than one hundred years ago. An alternative approach is suggested by Porter, who distinguishes between Poland envisioned as either an *enacted* or an *embodied* community. These categories, which roughly correspond to the distinction between Jagiellonian (enacted) and Piast (embodied) Poland, bring out a crucial aspect of each vision. Writing of the romantic era, Porter declares that,

> The most striking aspect of the nationalism of the day was that it did not necessarily entail the description (or creation) of an ethnically and culturally homogeneous social collective. The Polish patriot of the early nineteenth century *enacted* the nation rather than *embodying* it ... One participated in the nation by striving to realize its principles and fulfill its historical mission, and the nation thrived when enough people acted in its name.³⁴

Porter correctly contends that messianism conceived of Poland as an *enacted* community, as an ideal to identify with and to strive for. Moreover, he argues persuasively that this vision of Poland remained characteristic of Polish positivism, and following 1880 of the leftist, socialist parties. It was only with the rise ca. 1880 of the National Democrats (*endecja*) that some came to see Poland as an *embodied* nation. The *endecja*, more consistently applying the social Darwinism they inherited from positivism, believed in a national "survival of the fittest"; if Poland was to survive as a nation, it must therefore compete with and defeat its neighbors. For the National Democrats, "... national conflict became a force of nature, ever present and irredeemable. In their world, cultural unity had to be *made*, since it would never develop on its own [...] The only answer was to make the new Poland, even if doing so

---

32. Władysław Jagiełło, Grand-Duke of Lithuania, married Queen Jadwiga of Poland in 1386. The ensuing Polish-Lithuanian union encompassed Poland, Lithuania, Belarus and the Ukraine. Religiously, inhabitants of the Commonwealth were Catholic, Orthodox, Protestant, and Jewish, with a scattering of Moslem Tatars pledged to the Polish crown.

33. The Piast dynasty was the first Polish dynasty, which united several Slavic tribes into the Polish nation, in a geographical area roughly equivalent to present-day Poland.

34. Porter, *When Nationalism Began to Hate*, 16.

required the same techniques of denationalization (polonization, in this case), against which the Poles themselves had protested for so long."[35] Here patriotism, in the Polish sense of the word, has long since crossed over into nationalism.

In order to fight with one's enemies, one must know who they are. Germans and Russians became Poland's mortal enemies, while White Russians and Ukrainians were considered potential Poles. Protestants were counted as heretics, and the Jews perceived as an internal fifth column. These boundaries, the *endecja* claimed, must be established and enforced. Where polonization did not succeed, other harsher measures would be brought to bear. Thus the language and politics of struggle, aggression, xenophobia, authoritarianism, and anti-Semitism entered into the Polish intellectual and political mainstream. While those who subscribe to this ideology have always remained a minority, they have again become vocal and aggressive, and are making their presence known far beyond their relatively small numbers.

Romanticism shared the strong penchant for historiosophy prevalent in the early nineteenth century. Porter argues that behind the shift to an embodied vision of Piast Poland, and the adoption of an authoritarian, exclusivist ideology whose task it was to realize that vision, lay the loss of eschatology, understood as the belief that history is going somewhere and has a purpose.

> I argue that those intellectuals (mainly socialists) who managed to retain their faith in historical time could also imagine a world in which the boundaries between ethnic groups were porous and not necessarily of critical importance. Those who renounced their faith in historical time, however, perceived a world populated by mutually hostile and competing communities surrounded by high walls of inclusion and exclusion. The way people positioned themselves in historical time, therefore, enabled—perhaps on one level caused—the development of exclusionary and disciplinary forms of nationalism.[36]

Porter's thesis concerning Polish political history at the turn of the nineteenth and twentieth centuries is convincingly argued. If he is

---

35. Ibid., 234–35. Denationalization refers to attempts by the partitioning powers to Germanize or Russify their new newly acquired Polish "citizens," e.g., by barring the use of the Polish language in government offices and schools.

36. Ibid., 9.

correct, the rejection of eschatology was a causal factor leading to the rise of national-chauvinism in Poland. "The secret," suggests Porter, "to recovering this older style of national imagining, this idea of a multicultural Poland, is to look for the point at which the old dreams began to disintegrate, when it became hard to imagine a world of harmony among the nations and diversity within the nations."[37] Though one suspects there is more to the matter, Porter's thesis is correct: to understand the background and roots of contemporary enacted and embodied versions of Polish identity, we must examine the original, messianic myth of enacted, Jagiellonian Poland. This task is undertaken in chapters 1 through 3 of this book.

---

37. Ibid., 238.

The Birth Pains of Polish Messianism

The Historical Roots of Polish Messianism

THE HISTORY OF THE FIRST POLISH COMMONWEALTH BEGAN IN 966 AD with the baptism of Grand Duke Mieszko I, and ended in 1795 when Poland was partitioned by Prussia, Russia, and Austria. The nation's proud patriots, who saw Poland as an island of democracy in a continental sea of absolutism, perceived its loss of independence as a deathblow to freedom. Przybylski contrasts the Polish State, which had evolved into a parliamentary monarchy, with the authoritarian rule of the Prussian, Russian, and Austrian sovereigns:

> Beneath this arch of tyranny—enlightened and only just waiting for enlightenment—there bloomed a strange garden of parliamentarianism, the glory and curse of our fatherland. For the Most-Enlightened Commonwealth[1] guaranteed the preeminence of society over the government and the rulers, owing to the participation of citizens in government. The representatives of the nation had the right to control the king, and ... the entire lawmaking activity fell to the parliament.[2]

Parliamentarianism was indeed Poland's glory and curse. The stagnation of Polish society throughout the seventeenth and eighteenth centuries, due largely to the gentry's abuse of their freedoms, weakened Poland's political will, economic competitiveness, and military might. The dominance of agricultural magnates hindered the industrialization

---

1. Poland was called "Najjaśniejsza Rzeczypospolita," meaning "Most Enlightened" or "Brightest" Commonwealth. Przybylski's play on words makes clear which European country he believes was truly enlightened.
2. Przybylski, *Klasycyzm, czyli prawdziwy koniec Królestwa Polskiego*, 110.

of the economy, and the tax-paying nobles in parliament resisted the levies needed for defense. According to the right of *liberum veto*, if a member of parliament cried out "I object," the entire session of Parliament was annulled together with the laws it had passed. With time certain of the nobles placed their personal welfare above the good of the nation. Some sold their votes and their veto to neighboring states.

In the midst of this crisis King Stanisław August Poniatowski came to power. The republic's leading citizens eagerly joined his attempts to reform the Polish Commonwealth, which were crowned by the adoption by the "Great Parliament" of the May 3rd Constitution of 1791. Przybylski argues that this constitution "was a true rebirth of the country, because it was deduced from its entelechy, from parliamentarianism[3] ... Drawn from the sovereign rights of the nation, it established balance and order between the individual and government, guaranteeing in equal measure the right of the citizen and the power of government."[4]

Poland had produced the first modern democratic republic on the European continent. But before its new constitution could be implemented, the Polish State was erased from Europe's political map by the "Unholy Trinity"[5]: the German Kaiser, the Russian Czar, and the Austrian Emperor. Prince Adam Czartoryski's (1770–1861) eloquent, heart-rending lament, *The Polish Bard*,[6] captured the Poles' initial despair. In this poem a young poet, in the company of the Bard,[7] travels throughout a Poland ravaged by war and subjugated by foreign powers. At the end of their journey, the poet's pen runs dry, and the bard's voice cracks and falls silent. His harp is cast aside on the nation's grave, much as the nation has been cast on the rubbish heap of history. It is the Bard's heart, not his harp that is broken. The problem is not his ability to sing,

---

3. Przybylski supplies Aristotle's definition of entelechy, defined as "the force inherent in every being as potentiality, which leads to the realization of that being in its truest form." Przybylski, *Klasycyzm, czyli prawdziwy koniec Królestwa Polskiego*, 110.

4. Ibid., 111. As Przybylski notes, this was a democracy of the gentry. 15 percent of the Commonwealth's population belonged to the gentry, and this figure reached 25 percent in Poland's traditional heartland.

5. Reconstructing Europe after the Napoleonic wars, these monarchs divided the nations of Eastern Europe according to the terms of the Treaty of Vienna (1815).

6. First published in 1841, *The Polish Bard* was written in 1797.

7. Cf. Kleiner, *Sentymentalizm i preromantyzm*, 13–17, on the blind Celtic folk-singer Ossian in MacPherson's works *Fingal* and *Temora*. In Poland and Germany the bard assumed the role of a national prophet or seer.

but whether there is anyone left to sing for. Is God still there to hear his people's cry? If he hears, why does he not answer? As Chlebowski explains,

> . . . against their will the question arises, "How can one reconcile the experience of wrong and defeat with the concept of the justice and providence of God? Why have they fallen on Poland in the very moment when, having shaken off its errors, it began to correct its old injustices, [and] embarked on the road of hard work, order, and the uniting of brotherly classes[8] in the struggle for the common good?"[9]

Poles in the nineteenth century found themselves in circumstances quite distinct from those experienced by citizens of more favored European nations. The nation's suffering shook their faith in an ordered, predictable world. In light of Poland's historical catastrophe, Janion writes, "romantics could not share the linear faith of the enlightened in the automatic progress of history, nor did reason, deified by the Enlightenment, serve any longer for them as an adequate guarantee of justice, and hence of freedom."[10] Poland's historical crisis forced the streams of Polish cultural, intellectual, and spiritual life into new channels that left their lasting mark on the national landscape. As Chlebowski explains, "Polish poetry and art became at once a powerful, immortal protest of the nation against the act of political extermination and the ensuing application of the means of denationalization to which it was subjected, and the primary testimony to the society's vitality and its ongoing ability to produce cultural works."[11]

Poles had lost their independence, and many would lose their lives and their loved ones in subsequent uprisings. Yet many refused to accept their loss as the result of blind fate or the vagaries of chance. Instead, they looked deep into the nation's collective "soul," either to confess Poland's guilt or to defend its innocence. Above all, they sought a basis for hope in their nation's future. Humanly speaking, there was

---

8. An allusion to the May 3rd Constitution, which granted city dwellers full rights as citizens, gave peasants legal protection and aimed at their increasing integration into the life of the nation.

9. Chlebowski, *Literatura Polska Porozbiorowa jako Główny Wyraz Życia Narodu po Utracie Niepodległości*, 14.

10. Janion and Żmigrodzka, *Romantyzm i Historia*, 19.

11. Chlebowski, *Literatura Polska Porozbiorowa jako Główny Wyraz Życia Narodu po Utracie Niepodległości*, 15.

little to be found. As Kleiner writes, "One could not expect salvation from normal, everyday means; there was time for that as long as the Polish state existed—now those who did not want to resign had to seek and desire extraordinary paths."[12] Those paths often led to the hidden secrets of Providence. In their agony and despair Poles clung to their belief in the benevolent rule of God in history.[13]

Out of despair came hope. Out of suffering came a sense of calling. Poland was envisioned as the champion of freedom, the bulwark of Christianity, the innocent victim of tyranny, "the Christ of the nations" whose political life had been sacrificed for their redemption. Poland would rise again to lead the nations into a new era of Christianity, not claiming superiority over them but living with them as equals and serving them as brothers. In this new era the gospel ethic, which governed interpersonal relationships, would rule international relationships as well. The Law of Christ would become the law of society. Nations would consider other nations as higher than themselves, and learn that it is more blessed to give than to receive—and certainly than to take. This vision is the heart of Polish messianism, which interpreted the past, gave meaning to the present, and shaped the future. Helping Poles maintain their belief in providence, it moved from theodicy to ethics and eschatology, prescribing how to live as citizens of the Kingdom of God, and how that Kingdom would be brought to Earth. Messianism was at once a movement of spiritual renewal, a nation-building myth, and a sociopolitical program.

Polish Messianism as a Spiritual Journey

While Polish representatives of deism and libertarianism can be found, messianism reached its full stature in more biblically literate circles. Following the Commonwealth's downfall, Woronicz, a Catholic priest and poet identified with King Stanisław's reform movement, found comfort and inspiration in the writings of the Old Testament prophets, particularly those addressed to Israel during the exile. As Kolbuszewski

---

12. Kleiner, *Sentymentalizm i preromantyzm*, 23.

13. Chlebowski exclaims: "The souls of the time ... not daring to protest against the (to them) incomprehensible decrees of Providence, that allowed such wrongs to take place, strove to penetrate those decrees, in order to draw from them a basis for the hope that had not deserted them." Chlebowski, *Literatura Polska Porozbiorowa jako Główny Wyraz Życia Narodu po Utracie Niepodległości*, 223.

writes, "the unusually complicated, many-faceted phenomenon of Polish messianism, . . . already achieved the measure of its authority from the pen of Jan Paweł Woronicz by virtue of—out of necessity simplifying things here to the maximum—his biblical roots."[14] Woronicz crafted a messianic vision that described the past, present, and future of the Polish nation within the framework of a covenant relationship with God.

Woronicz's classical[15] form of messianism was passed on to the next, romantic generation. Polish messianism became so closely associated with romanticism that the two words are often used interchangeably. Romanticism prevailed over classicism largely through the literary genius of its chief representatives. Yet artistic superiority alone cannot account for the triumph of romanticism. Classicism was accused, by virtue of its allegiance to the poetic regulations and literary genre of foreign cultures, of betraying the Polish national spirit.[16] As Mickiewicz's contemporary Siemieński declares, "the spring rain of that [romantic] poetry, warm and renewing, at once rinsed away the impurities of the long winter, and the golden ray of inspiration lit such a fire, that those words, those [classical] forms imposed and made respectable, in which until now one had to think and express his feelings, were no longer adequate for the enthused."[17]

Romanticism was a religious reaction to Enlightenment rationalism. Janion writes that, "Romanticism may be understood as the rebirth of religious thought following the philosophical polemics of the ideologists of the Enlightenment, who—equally in the materialistic and deistic version—undermined Christian providentialism, with the aim of abolishing faith in the intervention of Providence in the course of human affairs."[18] In the fervent language of a disciple, Siemieński relates the impact of Mickiewicz upon his generation: "Youthful fantasy awakened . . . and turned at once to the higher tasks of life; spiritual-

---

14. Kolbuszewski, *Literatura wobec historii*, 32.

15. Classical in the dual sense of belonging to the literary tradition of classicism, and being the quintessence of messianism.

16. As Siwicka writes, ". . . the conviction appeared among young critics and poets that the hitherto existing model of Polish literature and the picture of the world it proposed no longer adequately described the current reality." Siwicka, *Romantyzm*, 65.

17. Siemieński, *Religijność i mistyka w życiu i poezjach Adama Mickiewicza*, 7.

18. Janion and Żmigrodzka, *Romantyzm i historia*, 20.

ism began to gain precedence over shallow materialism, feeling over scoffing frivolity—minds directed towards the spiritual depths became visibly more earnest."[19] Romantic messianism held several presuppositions that served as its point of departure for the exploration of the spiritual world. To begin with, it assumed that the spiritual world exists, and subscribed to the ultimate unity of spiritual and material reality. Furthermore, the romantics believed that truth exists. This is not the same as claiming sole possession of the truth, nor does it grant a license to impose one's beliefs upon others. Rather, it directed the romantic journey towards a goal. Finally, the romantics assumed that some travelers get closer to truth than others.[20] The recognition that all attempts to discover and live in the truth are subjective and incomplete does not imply that all such efforts are of equal quality or worth. Rather, it should foster true dialogue between fellow-travelers, who expect to learn from each other's experiences.

Philosophically, romanticism was an epistemological reaction to rationalism. McGrath aptly summarizes the consensus view: "Romanticism found itself equally unhappy with both traditional Christian doctrines and the rationalist moral platitudes of the Enlightenment; both failed to do justice to the complexity of the world, in an attempt to reduce the 'mystery of the universe'—to use a phrase found in the writings of August William Schlegel—to neat formulae."[21] This reaction was even more intense in Poland, where historical events had shown traditional formulas, whether political, religious or literary, to be grossly inadequate. Like his fellow romantic Schleiermacher, Mickiewicz called upon feeling (*czucie*) to describe direct religious experience of reality that precedes all reflection, dogma, and evidence. Throughout his life Mickiewicz remained true to his early conviction that the spiritual and material worlds are closely interrelated and that they influence each other. As his early convert wrote, "The poet . . . having chosen this course, could not then separate the matters of this world and that which is, or rather should be its spirit, its life task, stimulated by higher longings. You felt that a different current blows from the world that he discovered . . ."[22] Many found find their first entry into that world through his poetry.

19. Siemieński, *Religijność i mistyka w życiu i poezyach Adama Mickiewicza*, 16.
20. For the romantics, poets, of course, get closest of all.
21. McGrath, *Historical Theology*, 227.
22. Siemieński, *Religijność i mistyka w życiu i poezyach Adama Mickiewicza*, 13.

Polish Messianism as Myth

Myth as Historiosophy, Prophecy, Poetry, Propaganda, and Psychology[23]

Polish romantic historiosophy interpreted historical events as providential. The romantics believed that God reveals himself in history, which by virtue of his presence and purpose becomes *sacred history*.[24] Romantic messianism looked for salvation through the appearance of the promised Messiah, who would renew humanity and usher in the millennial kingdom. Whereas the Enlightenment saw history as a straight, unerring path of unending progress, romanticism combined Hellenic cyclical time with Hebraic linear time to form a spiral concept of human history, which though continually repeating itself yet led inexorably upward.[25] At the same time, romantic eschatology was chiliastic and apocalyptic. As Janion explains, the apocalyptic consummation of history "results from divine intervention and will announce the birth of a new world, [which is] no longer historical."[26] Romanticism thus sought to reconcile two conflicting views of history and the messianic Kingdom: the continual if tortured upward process of salvation history, and the apocalyptic end of the world brought about by God's dramatic breaking into history.

Building on its historiosophy, romanticism awarded myth a prophetic role. For the Enlightenment, myths were the superstitious product of primitive mankind's attempts to explain the world, seen at best as "allegorical tales of a philosophical or moral nature," at worst as the "conscious invention of priests, striving for control of the darkened mass of the faithful."[27] Polish romanticism on the other hand understood myth "as the prophetic revelation of the essence of truth,"[28] containing

---

23. This section is based on Janion and Żmigrodzka, *Romantyzm i historia*, 27–42; as well as Kolbuszewski, *Literatura wobec historii*, 14–36.

24. Cf. Janion: "History ... ceased being history—an unintelligible chaos, destruction and downfall, but became the place of fulfillment of higher purposes, goals, intentions. The sacredness of history in this concept took away its aspect of human frailty and transferred it into the domain of the sacrum, and thus of myth." Janion and Żmigrodzka, *Romantyzm i historia*, 29.

25. Ibid., 32.
26. Ibid., 30.
27. Ibid., 33.
28. Ibid., 26.

a divine message received either through a prophet or directly from the people, who were perceived as "childlike, untainted by civilization, close to nature, and capable of spontaneous contact with the higher world."[29] This belief helps to explain the romantics' fascination with legends and folklore, and the passion with which they sought to recover, interpret, and mold myth to their own use. When accepted as prophecy, myths supply an unassailable basis for future hope and a "directive for action" in the present.[30]

Myth as prophecy served as "the model of poetic creativity."[31] Responding to the call of Schlegel, who considered the lack of mythology to be the downfall of contemporary poetry, romantic poetry understood its task to be the creation of a "new mythology."[32] Myth and poetry, it was believed, shared a common source of divine inspiration; hence the poetic myths created by Polish messianism were considered as the revelation of truth, and the great Polish romantic poets took on the mantle of the prophets. That which was revealed to them in the spiritual world must come to pass in the visible world. As Stanisław Kolbuszewski writes, "A vision was for them something in the manner of platonic ideas, of which reality must become the reflection."[33] Poets became prophets, and contemporary events were turned into myth. To paraphrase J. Kolbuszewski: (1) Myths are formed from contemporary events or ancient legends. (2) Romantic poetic inspiration is equated with divine revelation, and poets are granted power to create a prophetic vision of the coming Kingdom. (3) Myth, accepted as revealed truth, is placed into the realm of faith.[34] Such myths become the carrier of a society's core values, passed from generation to generation. When accepted *a priori* at a subconscious level, they lie beyond the reach of both rational critique and the need for or possibility of verification.

The reception of poetry as prophecy led to its utilization as propaganda. Polish poets and politicians quickly grasped the potential of myth as a political instrument. This does not imply that the political use of myth is always or in itself improper. Rather, it recognizes the

29. Ibid., 33.
30. Ibid., 10.
31. Ibid., 33.
32. Ibid., 34.
33. S. Kolbuszewski, cited in J. Kolbuszewski, *Literatura wobec historii*, 26.
34. Kolbuszewski, *Literatura wobec historii*, 27.

power of myth to mobilize society. Accordingly, romantic poetry was translated into social and political programs. Myths were used in an increasingly utilitarian manner to further the ideas and ideologies of their propagators, ranging from the conservative to the radical.[35] The metastory of Polish messianism galvanized the nation and mobilized its youth, who as Norwid wrote, "redeemed with blood and tears the pages of the poetry they read."[36]

Myth's use in propaganda suggests its role as psychology, for what is propaganda but a form of mass psychology? Here the reception of myths comes to the forefront. Among several factors that Kolbuszewski points to as contributing to the remarkable longevity of Polish romanticism, together with the virtual monopoly it held over the national imagination,[37] only the literary genius of the romantic poets, and the charismatic, prophetic nature of their works relate to myth-creation. Three additional factors point instead to the nation's reception of romantic poetry. To begin with, Poles recognized these poet-seers as their socio-political as well as moral leaders, and promoted their "cult" long after their death. Furthermore, the people readily accepted these romantic myths, which not only met their emotional needs, but also offered answers for their spiritual and political needs. The last factor is what Kolbuszewski calls "the compensatory function of these myths." While already evident in the creativity of Mickiewicz,[38] this became central to such popular propagators of romantic myths as Sienkiewicz and Orzeszkowa, and scores of lesser epigones, who sought to treat Poles' inferiority complex psychologically by raising their sense of worth. Thus these myths passed into the general consciousness of the nation where, reduced though they were to the level of symbols and stereotypes, they continued to shape the nation's self-perception.

---

35. Janion writes, "Myths could be employed as an argument for regressive, conservative utopias, which glorify a theocratic model of society ruled by religious law and priestly authority. But mythical accounts were also often interpreted in the spirit of democracy and radical socio-political ideas, for example by emphasizing the equality of the alleged original society." Ibid., 36.

36. Norwid, "O Juliuszu Słowackim w sześciu publicznych posiedzeniach," from *Dzieła wybrane*, vol. 4, *Proza*, 297.

37. Kolbuszewski, *Literatura wobec historii*, 28–35.

38. Cf. especially the *Books of the Polish Nation and the Polish Pilgrimage*.

Mythical Poles

In old Polish and Enlightenment literature two views of Polish identity vied for supremacy; an idyllic picture of Poles as landed gentry, and another of Poles as valiant warrior-knights. The latter view, called *sarmatism*, was based on the belief that the Slavs were descended from the biblical figure of Assarmot. The idyllic and Sarmatian myths were often combined into a picture of peaceful farmers who bravely defended their tribe or nation against foreign invaders. In 1587 Sarnicki claimed that only those of noble blood had Sarmatian ancestry.[39] Henceforth many considered the gentry ethnically distinct from and superior to the peasants. Nonetheless, Sarnicki included both the Polish and Lithuanian gentry in one Sarmatian "nation." This made excellent political sense, for the two countries were joined in 1386 by a personal union, and the resulting "Commonwealth of Two Nations" was declared an "indivisible body" in 1499 by the *Unia Lubelska*. While ethnic Poles constituted the more dominant culture, the Lithuanian gentry were, theoretically at least, considered their equals.[40] Although *sarmatism* on the whole is a colorful but negative myth,[41] it contains certain positive elements. While peasants, merchants,[42] and city dwellers could not qualify as Poles by virtue of speech or religion, neither did ethnic or religious differences serve as the criteria of citizenship or a means of distinction between nobles. Had such a multi-national Commonwealth survived until the end of the nineteenth century, full citizenship might have been granted to all who lived within its borders. This open, inclusive aspect of the Sarmatian myth was a pillar supporting the myth of "Jagiellonian Poland," discussed below, as a religiously, ethnically, and linguistically pluralistic society.

In 1821, Brodziński argued that Slavs "will not be what they can be without comprehending who they were."[43] His claim that the essence of Slavic character is found in idyllic country life was not new. Far more

---

39. Cf. Davies, "Polish National Mythologies," 143.

40. Although polonization of the Lithuanian gentry was largely voluntary, it is difficult to quantify the subtle pressure exerted by the dominant Polish culture.

41. *Sarmatism* came to describe the colorful customs, dress and lifestyle of the Polish gentry, full of zest for battle and revelry, but short on hard work and careful planning.

42. Germans and Jews made up a large portion of the merchant class.

43. Brodziński, cited in Kolbuszewski, *Literatura wobec historii*, 113.

significant was the manner in which he linked Poland's hopes for independence to its understanding of its own national character. His reconstructed myth of Poland's past glory was elevated to a program for her future that was considered obligatory for all Poles, and provided a sense of permanence and purpose to a nation whose existence was threatened by the loss of statehood. Brodziński's idyllic past-future myth formed the ideological basis for the minimalist program of the classicists, which stressed education, strove to maintain the Polish language and culture, and glorified the country life of the gentry.

Mickiewicz's polemical caricature of country life[44] soon discredited Brodziński's myth as a description of Polish national character. The problem, the romantics believed, was that Poland's partition made the idyllic vision impossible to implement. Politically, they called on Poles to resist the occupying powers by all means, including civil disobedience, conspiracy, and armed uprising. Since this required a national myth that idealized heroism and sacrifice, they declared that being Polish means to place the national good above one's own personal happiness. Siwicka writes, "Romantic literature therefore created new heroes and new models of behavior. The figures of medieval warriors revived the dreams of knightly armed combat. The loner-individualist, remaining on a collision course with the world and hiding his activities beneath a cloak of secrecy, easily became a contemporary conspirator."[45] Ironically, as Siwicka notes, the moral ambiguities of such works as Mickiewicz's *Konrad Wallenrod*, whose protagonist wrestled with the ethical dilemmas raised by the use of conspiracy and treachery to fight for one's country, were lost to a generation that read this tale as a one-dimensional call to arms.

The romantic myth did not define the Polish nation in ethnic terms. Instead, Polishness was conceived as a principle, i.e., the idea of universal freedom, national self-determination, and international brotherhood. As Porter argues, true Poles were those who acted on behalf of this idea:

> Poland, which was said to exist in the hearts of all Poles, embodied an ethical principle and acted as a moving force in history

---

44. Mickiewicz, *Dziady*, 204.
45. Siwicka, *Romantyzm*, 76.

... It did not push anybody outside of its ranks solely on the basis of language, cultural practices, religion or ethnicity.[46]

In relationship to other nations, Poland's goal was not conquest or revenge, but friendship and peaceful coexistence. Commenting on the cry of Polish legionnaires, "For your freedom and for ours!" Janion asserts that, "*ours* and *theirs* could thus be understood in terms of the brotherhood of the nations, the 'fellowship of believers' of Mickiewicz, as opposed to traditionalistic xenophobia."[47] In this spirit, Brodziński adapted his own idyllic myth following the collapse of the November Uprising. In his May 3, 1831 speech "On the Nationality of Poles," Brodziński proclaimed the concept of the "Christ-like sacrifice of Poland,"[48] which subsequently appears in Polish romantic literature and philosophy. While Polish romantic literature played an enormous role in overthrowing the idyllic myth, this marked change in Brodziński's position suggests that the November Uprising of 1830, and in particular its downfall, put the nails in its coffin.

Polish positivists (ca. 1863–1880) considered armed uprisings against the occupying powers unrealistic, irresponsible, and destructive. They accused romanticism of creating a nation of dreamers, primed for rash heroic deeds, but unprepared for the grinding discipline needed to strengthen the nation. They discouraged the romantic "deed" (i.e., conspiracy and insurrection), arguing instead for the need for "organic work" that would strengthen the nation intellectually, culturally, and economically. Convinced that a hard-nosed critique of Poland's geopolitical situation was essential to forging a program for its national survival, positivist writers positioned themselves as "modern" and "rational," drawing heavily on Spencer's humanism while downplaying the more brutal mechanisms implied by his social Darwinism. Nevertheless, the positivist Pole began to take on the distinctly ethnic characteristics that were lacking in romantic messianism.[49] Rejecting divine Providence and the messianism of the "seers," positivists yet held to the inevitability of "progress." Thus, according to Porter's thesis that the loss of eschatology

---

46. Porter, *When Nationalism Began to Hate*, 20.
47. Janion and Żmigrodzka, *Romantyzm i historia*, 55.
48. Brodziński, cited in Kolbuszewski, *Literatura wobec historii*, 120–21.
49. Porter writes of the positivists: "their nation would be a community of Polish speakers, inhabiting a specific territory and cultivating certain customs and norms." Porter, "Marking the Boundary of the Faith," 9.

or "historical time" led to the rise of national-chauvinism in Poland,[50] "this new [i.e., positivistic] way of talking about the nation ... did not necessarily lead to exclusionary identities or disciplinary politics, because these tendencies were held in check by a vision of progressive time..."[51]

As Michnik explains, most positivists rejected the irredentist goal of national independence, or couched it so nebulously that it became a distant hope. It was left to the émigré community in the West to keep alive the goal of national sovereignty.[52] However, around 1880 there emerged the generation of the "indomitable" [*niepokorni*], who reasserted the goal of independence and the imperative to act to achieve that goal, if necessary by conspiracy and armed resistance. The indomitables rejected positivism's faith in progress, and reasserted the voluntary deed over the fatalism of Spencerian liberalism. They soon split into several parties, including the influential Polish Socialist Party (PPS) and the National Democrats (*endecja*).[53] The emerging leftist[54] parties adopted socialism's eschatological vision. In contrast, the *endecja*'s consistent rejection of historical time opened the door to its increasingly nationalistic, authoritarian policies. Porter asserts that Polish nationalists had long wedded their patriotism to a revolutionary agenda of social emancipation and international harmony, and it was not particularly hard to sustain this. Only in the 1880's, when trust in the promise of dynamic historical time began to wane, was this linkage between the nation and the left strained, leading to a deep split in the once unified "generation of the *niepokorni*."[55] Thus were born the rival visions of socialist and *eńdek*[56] Poles.

Whereas the PPS sought to restore pluralistic Jagiellonian Poland, the *endecja*'s social Darwinism believed in the international "survival of the fittest," and promoted the creation of "Piast Poland," an ethni-

---

50. Cf. the discussion in the Introduction.

51. Ibid.

52. Cf. Michnik, "Dispute over Organic Work," *Letters from Prison and Other Essays*, 223–48.

53. Porter, *When Nationalism Began to Hate*, 188.

54. "Leftists" ranged from devoted Marxists to democrats with a social conscience.

55. Ibid., 234.

56. In Polish, *Endek* is short for "National Democrat," i.e., a supporter of the *endecja*.

cally pure, religiously Catholic society. Positivism had considered ethnic Polishness a goal to pursue; the *endecja* recast it as a condition to impose. Ethnic (Polish) and religious (Catholic) boundaries were set about the nation that must be established and enforced. In the ideology of social Darwinism, national conflict became a force of nature, ever present and irredeemable. As Davies writes, "the message was clear. All patriotic Poles had a duty to unite and drive all foreigners from their native soil."[57]

The socialists were appalled by the *endek* vision of a world that had "no moral laws other than survival, and no social cohesion without authoritarianism."[58] As Porter elaborates, the socialists "soon realized that they had to believe in progress—in history—in order to remain on the left."[59] Marxism's promise of a better future enabled them to endure the tension between the real and ideal worlds. The National Democrats, who refused all replacements for their lost belief in providence, messianism, and progress, "could find no such comfort . . . In their world, cultural enemies had to be destroyed, because conflict would never be transcended by time or by the spread of humanitarian ideals."[60]

By a process described in chapter 6,[61] the *endecja*'s Darwinian social ethics became wedded to the *Polak-Katolik*[62] myth.[63] Davies, tracing this myth in part to the highly embellished account[64] of the defense of the Częstochowa monastery during the Swedish invasion of 1655, notes its ties to the myth of the "Black Madonna," and the enthronement in 1656 of Mary as the "Queen of Poland."[65] The conflict with Lutheran Sweden

---

57. Cf. Davies, "Polish National Mythologies," 152.

58. Porter, *When Nationalism Began to Hate*, 234.

59. Ibid.

60. Ibid.

61. Cf. section in chapter 6 entitled "National Chauvinism: From Darwin to 'God is on Our Side!'"

62. I.e., "to be Polish is to be Catholic."

63. Velikonja, comparing the "immanent Catholicism" of Slovenes and Poles, writes that "in both religio-national mythologies, religious and national identities are simply equated and both nations are seen as Catholic." Velikonja, "Slovenian and Polish Religio-National Mythologies," 246.

64. Popularized by Sienkiewicz in *The Deluge* (*Potop*).

65. Davies writes: "Here was a key moment in the growth of the myth of the *Polak-Katolik*, 'the Catholic Pole'—the belief that if you weren't a Roman Catholic, you somehow didn't qualify to be a true Pole." Davies, "Polish National Mythologies," 146.

fanned patriotic-religious fervor and further eroded Poland's official religious tolerance, already weakened by the Counter-Reformation.[66] In 1658, just three years after the Swedish "Deluge," the equal status granted in 1572 to all religions was officially revoked. Although there was little religious bloodshed compared to other European countries,[67] Protestants, Orthodox, and Jews came under increasing social pressure and discrimination.

In contrast, two other Polish myths sought to expand the inclusive definition of the nation contained in the vision of Jagiellonian Poland. Politically, many attributed the failure of the November Uprising to the exclusion of peasants and Jews from those fighting for the national cause. Hopes for a successful popular uprising required a new definition of the nation that included these groups. The myth of the noble peasant, which recalled the participation of the *kosynierzy*[68] in the Kościuszko' Uprising of 1793–1794, held a special attraction for romantics, who interpreted it "in the spirit of democracy and radical socio-political ideas, emphasizing for example the equality of the alleged original society."[69] Corresponding to the noble peasant myth was the myth of "Poles of the faith of Moses." There had always been assimilated Jews, now there was a growing acceptance of Jews as Jews. Porter declares that by the 1850s "we find Poles willing to accept Jews as compatriots without any presumption of cultural assimilation."[70] The myth of "Poles of the faith of Moses" reached its peak with the death of several Jews in the demonstrations of 1861. The Jews, it was proclaimed, had identified themselves with the Polish nation through their spilling of blood for the national cause. As Porter explains, "membership in the nation required action, not political change. It was no longer what the Jews were *like*—it was what they had *done* that counted."[71] Unfortunately, things would soon

---

66. After some Protestant nobles sided with Sweden, suspicion fell upon all Protestants, who were considered by many a real or potential fifth column.

67. The pogroms which occurred were occasional and local.

68. I.e., peasants wielding *kosy* (scythes).

69. Janion and Żmigrodzka, *Romantyzm i historia*, 35–36.

70. Porter continues: "The idea of the transcendent Polish nation had pushed ethnicity so far into the background that it became possible to imagine cultural diversity within the national community . . . Public spaces were reserved for 'Poles,' while 'Jews' (and 'Christians') were exiled to the world of 'faith.'" Porter, "Marking the Boundary of the Faith," 38–39.

71. Ibid., 42.

get worse, with the rise of organizations that were programmatically anti-Semitic.

It is unfair to judge either the classicists' realism or the romantics' mysticism too harshly. For well over a century, there was no program, either realistic or mystical, that could lead to regaining Polish independence. Accordingly, classicist attempts to preserve and rebuild failed to satisfy the Poles' national aspirations. The romantics, seeking stronger weapons in the spiritual world, erred in mistaking their personal or corporate visions for the decrees of divine providence. In a changing world pregnant with new possibilities, socialists affirmed the revolutionary claims for social justice inherent in the messianic vision, while National Democrats practised their version of *Realpolitik*. Each new program required its own myths, thus the understanding of patriotism, the definition of a hero, and the perceived national spirit were subject to ongoing modification. However, in each case the goal remained the same: (1) to shape convictions and character, (2) which would issue in patriotic action/deeds, (3) which would lead to independence.

Mythical Poland

If, speaking metaphorically, nation is to country what spirit is to body, when the Polish nation lost its state its spirit began an out-of-body experience. The myth of Poland as a spiritual community is manifest in the Polish Legionnaires' hymn *Mazurka Dąbrowskiego*,[72] which begins with the words, "Poland has not yet died, while we yet live."[73] Yet the classicists did not stop at singing Dąbrowski's *Mazurka*. They undertook the ambitious task of passing the literary, cultural, religious, and political heritage of the deceased Commonwealth on to their spiritual heirs,[74] i.e., to Mickiewicz and his fellow romantics, who further developed the myth of Poland as a spiritual homeland. Jacek Kolbuszewski writes, "In the face of the impossibility of developing full life as a

---

72. Wybicki, "Mazurek Dąbrowskiego," 103–4. The hymn, written by Józef Wybicki, was named after Henryk Dąbrowski, the leader of the Polish Legions organized abroad under Napoleon's aegis.

73. Of this song, now Poland's national anthem, Porter writes, "as long as Poles are alive, Poland would continue to exist. [. . .] To be a Pole, therefore, meant to retain the nation in one's heart and to fight for independence; it implied both a sense of identity and a plan of action." Porter, "Marking the Boundary of the Faith," 18–19.

74. Cf. Przybylski, *Klasycyzm, czyli prawdziwy koniec Królestwa Polskiego*, 9.

nation and a state, the evolution of spiritual life under the partitions ... led toward the end of the nineteenth century, particularly in light of the lack of clear perspectives for regaining independence, to the conceptual, 'dematerialized' understanding of Poland as an idea."[75] It was among the writers of the 'Young Poland' period (1890–1918), also called neo-romanticism, that this vision both reached its apogee and was at last overcome. In the play *Wyzwolenie* (*Deliverance*), Wyspiański has his hero Konrad[76] exclaim:

> I know what you want: that Poland is to be a myth, a national myth, a country above countries, surpassing all such republics and governments; of course unattainable, imaginary. It is to be a dream—yes, an ideal. Yes, and it is never to BECOME, never to BE, never to come true.[77]

As Kolbuszewski argues, Wyspiański removed Poland from the land of spirit and myth, and insisted on making it a political and historical entity.[78] Here the process comes full circle—the myth that replaced the lost historical state is not enough, the nation must once again become an independent country. Although the romantics also demanded the restoration of Polish sovereignty, Wyspiański, with his vision of a "normal country, just like any other," surpassed them not by his patriotism, but by bringing a demythologized Poland back to earth.

There is probably no such thing as a post-mythical nation, for a nation cannot long survive the death of its myths. However, since 1989 Poland is now post-mythical in the sense that the spiritual community has once again become a political entity. After 200 years of captivity, exile, and occupation, the Polish people once again live in a normal country, with normal problems and normal opportunities. Today, twenty years after the first Solidarity government took power, the words of a novel written by Wyspiański during the brief period of independence following World War I are just as appropriate:

> We are at last citizens, like everyone in the world—responsible, fighting, guilty. No longer just a victim—already a trespasser.

75. Kolbuszewski, *Literatura wobec historii*, 65.

76. A clear allusion to the romantic hero Gustav—Konrad from Mickiewicz's *Forefather's Eve*, who Wyspiański wants to replace as a model of patriotism.

77. Wyspiański, *Wyzwolenie*, cited in Kolbuszewski, *Literatura wobec historii*, 68–69.

78. Kolbuszewski, *Literatura wobec historii*, 69.

> Nothing justifies us, there are no longer any ways out. Neither the "Christ of the nations," nor the "chains of Siberia," nor the czarist oppressors. Nothing! Nothing! We are what we can be—like a throng always is.[79]

Poles today, however, are suffering a national identity crisis. The national myths that sustained the nation during the partitions and under communist rule have fragmented into many competing sub-myths. These include post-solidarity versus post-communist myths, social-justice versus liberal-capitalist myths, and *Polak-Katolik* versus ethnic diversity and religious toleration myths. Behind many of these myths lie the competing visions of inclusive Jagiellonian Poland and exclusive Piast Poland. Just as in Wyspiański's day, many Poles prefer their ideal or mystical dream of spiritual Poland to this real, concrete, and considerably-less-than perfect society. More dangerously, there are those who would impose their ideological vision upon the nation in ways that threaten democracy and civil rights. Which vision of Poland gains the upper hand depends largely on the degree to which nationalist, populist, and integrist-Catholic groups gain power or influence over the nation's citizens and government. The most effective defense against such groups may well prove to be a reaffirmation and contemporary restatement of the Christian humanism that characterized Polish messianism.[80]

Polish Messianism as a Social and Political Agenda

Poetry and Praxis

Polish romanticism shared much in common with the worldview and literary style of its European counterparts. Yet in Poland romanticism moved decisively from aesthetics to ethics, from theory to action. Król enquires rhetorically: ". . . Was not and is not romanticism for Poles a form of the revelation of truth, if by this we understand a method of knowing reality, of perceiving it and then—if possible—of changing it?"[81] Thus romanticism progressed from artistic beauty and religious belief to a social and political program. Romantic epistemology and

---

79. Wyspiański, *Romans Teresy Hennert*, cited in Kolbuszewski, *Literatura wobec historii*, 69–70.

80. Such a restatement is found in chapter 7.

81. Król, *Romantyzm*, 3.

ontology existed to serve romantic historical goals and romantic praxis. Polish romantic patriots tied Poland's freedom and happiness to the general European movement towards freedom, social justice, equality, and democracy, and sought concrete strategies and actions to achieve this aim.

As a form of idealism, romanticism held to the priority of spirit over matter. However, philosophy *per se* had little attraction for Polish romantic poets—neither the abstract philosophy of enlightenment rationalism, nor even the idealism of the German romantics, whose remarkable spiritual freedom failed on the whole to transfer into engagement with social and political realities. Poles found historical reality unacceptable; therefore it must be brought into conformity with their ideals, or rather with a higher, *spiritual* reality. God's Kingdom must come to earth, and while that coming is ultimately God's doing, his people are called to take part. Porter thus explains that, "as Poles spoke the language of idealism, the concept of the 'deed' (*czyn*) became an integral part of their definition of the nation: to be a Pole, one had to join in the enactment of the nation's historical mission, one had to both recognize and contribute to the fulfillment of the nation's destiny."[82]

Treating romanticism as a social and political program highlights the particularity of its historical expression in the life of the Polish nation and the self-consciousness of Polish patriots. To cite Król again, "between wonder at great poetry and 'revealed truth' lies our whole imagination, the entire heaven and hell of Poles."[83] One can admire "great poetry" from a distance, but "revealed truth" requires a personal response. That said, the relationship between literature and life was far from one-sided, for living myths and current history exist in a dynamic, dialectical relationship. Life and literature joined hands in the struggle for independence; the pen and the sword both belonged to the arsenal of approved weapons. The fight for freedom belonged to the poet and the partisan. Better yet if poet and partisan were one and the same.

Although the May 3rd Constitution of 1791 was classicism's legitimate if late offspring, romanticism, its fierce rival for the "rule of souls," adopted the Constitution as its own step-child. Among the building blocks romanticism drew from the Constitution to construct its vision

---

82. Porter, "Marking the Boundary of the Faith," 23.

83. Król, *Romantyzm*, 3–4. The suggestion is that "hell" is what results from treating "great poetry" (i.e. "heaven") as "revealed truth."

of freedom and national independence, Kolbuszewski lists the goal of independence, the concept of Poland's unity and territorial integrity, self-sacrificial dedication for the nation, and the belief that "by God's help 'knights of the nation' would arise 'from the ashes.'"[84] Romanticism also found a basis in the Constitution for its program of social reform. Although in its final version the Constitution maintained distinctions between the gentry, freemen, and peasantry, both the latter classes were granted significant rights. True, the nation was still gendered, yet the trend was clearly set towards the eventual enfranchisement of all members of society. Janion in turn considers the Constitution to be an "act of spiritual liberation," which promised the liberation of the peasantry and expiated, at least in part, the sins of the gentry.[85]

The Kościuszko Uprising, which broke out in 1793 after Catherine the Great intervened to prevent the implementation of the May 3rd Constitution, was a national uprising with significant participation by the peasants. Kościuszko granted them new rights and removed many restrictions. A new myth of the solidarity between the gentry and peasants was born, which continued in the Polish legions.[86] Following the final partition in 1795, a growing number of Poles, notably members of the minor gentry that formed the basis of the Polish intelligentsia, concluded that members of all socio-economic classes should be granted full rights of citizenship. Furthermore, these rights were to be extended to all those living within the former boundaries of the Polish Commonwealth, including Lithuanians, White Russians, Ukrainians, Tatars, Germans, and Jews. Such a program called for radical social reforms, beginning with the abolition of serfdom and statute-labor and including wide scale land reform. Among those who recognized that independence could only be regained through the joint efforts of the entire society, and that only those who stood to gain from the fruits of victory would be willing to join the struggle, these issues were seen as integral to the fight for freedom.

84. Ibid., 44–45.
85. Janion and Żmigrodzka, *Romantyzm i historia*, 89–96.
86. Ibid., 104–8.

Poetry, Plots, and Partisans

Following the Congress of Vienna in 1815, most classicists took a conciliatory stance towards the partitioning powers. While a few acted out of opportunism, and some simply resigned themselves to the actual state of affairs, most were attempting by conciliation, mediation, and preservation to rescue what could be saved of Polish life and culture. Nevertheless, the new romantic generation considered all these attempts, regardless of motivation, as acts of treachery and betrayal, and held classicism as a literary style to be in service to the Czar. Thus, as Siwicka writes, "the formation of romanticism in Poland was more clearly linked with political conflict and aspirations of freedom than in other countries, and by the same token was defined to a greater extent by the concrete historical situation of the 1820s."[87]

The confluence of romanticism and history had enormous implications for Polish society. Poles, confronted by their nation's greatest historical challenge, experienced a political vacuum resulting from the liquidation of the Polish parliament and other institutions of national government. Lacking these normal centers of political expression, nineteenth century Polish culture looked to poetry for guidance. The political aspirations of Polish poets and their reception by the general population arose out of the existing political vacuum. Janion declares that Polish society "submitted itself to the rule of literature, which desired to impose literary forms upon history as directives for historical understanding and action."[88] Thus the Polish version of the romantic revolution passed from a literary confrontation to armed conflict. By the 1820s, patriotism demanded resistance to the occupying powers, and the romantic poets became the heralds of revolution.[89] Poland's history, particularly her nineteenth-century uprisings, demonstrates the ability that Poland's poets had to mobilize their followers.[90]

87. Siwicka, *Romantyzm*, 67.

88. Janion and Żmigrodzka, *Romantyzm i historia*, 10. Cf. Kolbuszewski, who writes: "When leaders were lacking ... then poets took power, not so much by creating political programs ... as much as by delineating a vision, whose power and meaning depended on ... explaining the prophetic significance of historical events (the national suffering)." Kolbuszewski, *Literatura wobec historii*, 28.

89. Cf. Janion and Żmigrodzka: "Mickiewicz and Słowacki wrote the screenplays of Polish plots, patriotic manifestations and finally uprisings." Ibid., 11.

90. Kolbuszewski writes of the November Uprising: "It was the triumph of Mickiewicz's 'Ode to Youth', seeing that during its early days the words 'Greetings to

If the November Uprising (1830–1831) can be called the ultimate romantic deed, then the January Uprising (1861–1863) served a different purpose. Its citizen-warriors were willing to fight and to die in order to awaken the sleeping nation, believing that during sixty-five years of foreign occupation the nation had grown accustomed to bondage. In their minds, the acceptance of the status quo posed a greater threat to Poland's continued existence than the armies of the occupying powers. Perhaps their sacrifices were too great. Nonetheless, Janion argues that while the Polish people suffered terribly as a result of its national uprisings, without them the nation that regained its independence in 1918, and again in 1989, would be a different nation, lacking the collective experience that freedom is a priceless commodity. It is this conviction, inherited from the Polish nobility, which romanticism passed on to the entire nation.[91]

Poetry and Parliament

In 1821, Shelley declared that, "Poets are the unacknowledged legislators of the world."[92] If attributing such power to poetry seems foreign today, Shelley felt it necessary even in nineteenth century England to defend his thesis in a polemical essay. Nevertheless, his words meant more to his fellow citizens than to their contemporaries in Germany or Russia, not because the British had a greater respect for poetry, but because their country boasted a long parliamentary tradition in which legislators shaped the course of their nation's social, economic, and foreign policy.

Poets influence politics, not by casting votes but by casting visions; that is, by creating, adapting and propagating the myths that communicate and shape the nation's values. In Shelley's England, the influence of poet-politicians was powerful but indirect; thus Shelley christens them "unacknowledged legislators." In partitioned Poland, where poets had no parliament to compete with, they were in practice "acknowledged legislators." Poles looked to them for leadership in formulating and realizing their nation's aspirations for freedom and self-determination. Like

---

the dawn of freedom, following you there comes the sun of salvation' were written on the walls of Warsaw." Kolbuszewski, *Literatura wobec historii*, 46. "Ode to Youth" is discussed in chapter 3.

91. Janion and Żmigrodzka, *Romantyzm i historia*, 9–10.
92. Shelley, "A Defense of Poetry," 1055.

political parties in a democracy, poets often represented conflicting political points of view, as they competed with each other for the "rule of souls." In Kolbuszewski's description of their literary "shadow government," Polish writers "fulfilled the functions and divided the ministerial posts of politics, war, economy, social affairs, education, and culture ... representing and proclaiming at times quite dissimilar visions, concepts, views, and ideas."[93]

One should not take the political roles of the poets too literally. In many cases their influence derived more from the reception of their poetry than their conscious intent. The boundaries between poetry, prophecy, politics, and propaganda became increasingly blurred.[94] Although the diverse forms of messianism, romantic historiosophy, and political programs proposed by the poet-seers were debated in politically active circles, such nuances were lost to average Poles. At the popular level romantic messianism shaped people more than programs, by engaging Poland's historical-mythical past to motivate its citizens to action in the present. As Kolbuszewski writes, "the national functionality of this literature depended on this, that it was able by virtue of its 'fatal force' to change ordinary bread-winners, not into angels but into plotters, conspirators, and soldiers of the uprisings, capable of fighting and suffering."[95]

Poetry, Patriotism, and Religion

Classicism and romanticism both viewed Poland as a spiritual community, which possessed a divine and not merely political right to independence.[96] Although the romantics rejected classicism's aesthetics, idyllic myth, and historiosophy, they learned their patriotism from the classicists, many of whom fought under Kościuszko or in the Polish Legions. The heroic tradition that originated with classicism and reached its apogee in romanticism made it every Pole's patriotic duty to fight for the nation's independence, regardless of the personal cost. Women were

---

93. Kolbuszewski, *Literatura wobec historii*, 38.

94. Kolbuszewski warns that, "... paying no attention to the fact that it was above all [romantic] poetry and for this reason utilized visions, far too often the attempt was made to concretize it ... while trying to read poetic metaphors and symbols in the categories of a specific political program." Ibid., 52.

95. Ibid., 53–54.

96. Ibid., 44–45.

also called to heroic deeds and sacrifice. It became their patriotic duty to send their husbands and lovers off to war, and to raise their orphaned children to become patriots and freedom fighters. Where classicism and romanticism parted ways was over the question of tactics. Since an uprising was judged unlikely to succeed, Classicism aimed at ensuring that Poles survived to fight another day. Romanticism's more immediate demands required heroes, not farmers or laborers. Each camp resolved the tension between heroism and hard work, between "reform or revolution," by elevating one form of patriotism over the other.

Kolbuszewski terms the readiness of Polish patriots to accept sacrifice, suffering, torture, and death, "romantic maximalism." According to this ethical standard, "departure from the road of martyrdom is treated virtually as the betrayal of the holiest national ideals."[97] Martyrdom and participation in armed uprising became the two most important moral deeds imposed upon Polish patriots. Messianism created its own pantheon of heroes and martyrs, including such figures as Tadeusz Kościuszko,[98] Józef Poniatowski,[99] Captain Ordon,[100] and Emilia Plater.[101] The cult of these "secular saints," as Kolbuszewski calls them,[102] was propagated in poetry and practised in everyday life; the burial mounds of slain partisans were carefully maintained and became the site of regular family pilgrimages. To further its maximalist demands, and enlist the entire nation in the struggle for independence, romanticism expanded the ranks of heroes to include soldiers and conspirators, together with all who were imprisoned, deported, exiled or killed by the occupying powers.

Poland's messianic mission became intrinsically linked to the religiousness of its people. Although romanticism throughout Europe was a religious reaction to the Enlightenment, this element in Poland was

---

97. Kolbuszewski, *Literatura wobec historii*, 47.

98. A Polish general, who fought under George Washington prior to leading an uprising against Russia (1793–1794).

99. Prince Józef, the nephew of King Stanisław, served under Napoleon. He chose to perish with his troops rather than surrender.

100. In Mickiewicz's poem, Ordon blows himself up along with the tower he is defending, rather than surrender it to attacking Russian troops. In real life Ordon, though a genuine hero, survived the battle.

101. Emilia Plater disguised herself as a man to fight during the November Uprising. The incident, while true, was embellished.

102. Cf. Kolbuszewski, *Literatura wobec historii*, 33.

particularly strong. The Polish Enlightenment lacked the anti-clerical character it possessed in the West.[103] Neither did Polish romanticism take the form of an anti-clerical revolution, such as took place in France. Instead, as Chlebowski affirms, the romantic poets expected Slavs, by virtue of their religiousness, to inaugurate ". . . the moral renewal of humanity, through the realization of the principles of Christianity in social and international relationships."[104] Kolbuszewski concurs that Polish religiousness profoundly influenced nineteenth-century Polish patriotism;[105] nevertheless, he describes that religiousness as "ostentatious" and "shallow,"[106] recalling the incongruous picture of colorful, swashbuckling "Sarmatian" nobles kneeling to pray earnestly before an altar or Marian shrine. While such a separation of faith from everyday behavior seems contradictory, it is not at odds with Chlebowski's own definition of Polish religiousness as "sensing the close relationship of human affairs with the supernatural world that influences them."[107] Rather, it indicates that while many Poles did indeed separate personal faith from everyday behavior, in the life of the nation faith and politics became closely intertwined. The partitioning of Poland was understood religiously as a moral crime against God's law and a subversion of divine justice.[108] Janion writes of the "marriage" of Polish politics and morality, and Siwicka considers "the conviction of the necessary union of politics and morals" the most significant trait of Polish messianism.[109]

John Paul II's pilgrimages to his native Poland elevated patriotic-religious attitudes to the stature of a spiritual-political manifestation. During his first pilgrimage in 1979 the Pope turned Psalm 104:30 into a prayer: "Let your Spirit descend and renew the land . . . *this land!*," thus reaffirming the biblical and romantic belief that God is at work in this world, that justice will prevail, and that true freedom begins with spiritual deliverance and renewal at the personal and national level. Solidarity, which non-coincidentally arose the following year, was as

---

103. Romanticism in the West was often religious and anti-clerical.

104. Chlebowski, *Literatura Polska Porozbiorowa jako Główny Wyraz Życia Narodu po Utracie Niepodległości*, 49.

105. Kolbuszewski, *Literatura wobec historii*, 45.

106. Kolbuszewski does not imply that all Polish religiousness is shallow.

107. Chlebowski, *Literatura Polska Porozbiorowa jako Główny Wyraz Życia Narodu po Utracie Niepodległości*, 49.

108. Cf. Ibid., 45.

109. Siwicka, *Romantyzm*, 91.

much a political-religious movement as a trade union. In 1983, alluding to the outlawed movement, the Pope declared: "There is no freedom without solidarity." In 1999, commenting on the bickering among the movement's heirs, he proclaimed: "There is no solidarity without love."[110] These words capture well the marriage of politics, social ethics, and religion characteristic of Poland's patriotic tradition.

The conviction that freedom has a spiritual as well as economic and political dimension is rooted deep in Polish romanticism. Król considers Polish romanticism, through its emphasis on "positive" freedom that promotes spiritual growth, to provide a stronger moral and religious foundation for society than liberalism's "negative" freedom from restrictions. Michnik, whose vision of civil society is considered "liberal"[111] by integrist Catholics located far to the right of Król, agrees that society needs a moral basis. As he declared in 2000, "economic values are not sufficient to sustain a society and its harmonious development ... other values must function, which support the society and provide life with meaning."[112] Differences exist between Michnik and Król, and between progressive, mainstream, and integrist Catholicism over what "other values" are needed, and whether they should be promoted by dialogue, legislation or divine *fiat*. Yet messianism's diverse heirs agree that spiritual values must "support the society and provide life with meaning."

The religious nature of Polish romanticism raises many questions about its relationship to institutional Christianity. To begin with, who was included in the messianic vision? Woronicz was a Catholic priest, yet his vision of the Polish nation was broadly ecumenical, and he freely recognized the contributions made by Protestants and Jews to the national culture. The "List of Rules" that Mickiewicz wrote in 1848 for his Polish Legion, intended as the proto-constitution of a revived Polish State, was even more inclusive, declaring that "Poland ... gives freedom to all confessions of God, all rites and congregations . . ." Messianism had room for all forms of the Christian and Jewish traditions, even if this was an envisioned trajectory rather than an accomplished fact.

Secondly, were the romantics orthodox in their beliefs? The leading representatives of Polish romanticism never left the Catholic Church,

---

110. Karol Wojtyła, "Homilia Jana Pawła II podczas Mszy św. W Sopocie," *VII pielgrzymka Jana Pawła II do ojczyzny*, 25.

111. I.e., immoral, un-Polish and anti-Catholic.

112. Michnik, "George, fajny chłop," *Gazeta Wyborcza*, 1.

nor were they excommunicated. As Przybył comments, "Mickiewicz, Słowacki or Cieszkowski[113] never regarded themselves as heterodox, although their contemporaries, for example the Resurrectionists,[114] had not the least doubts in the matter."[115] Compared to the Catholicism of their day, many of the romantics' views do appear unorthodox. However, their work is better understood as an early form of political theology, and Masłowski claims that Mickiewicz's theology prefigures Catholic modernism and the teachings of the Vatican II Council.[116]

Thirdly, what was the brunt of the romantics' criticism of the institutional Church? As Przybył explains, "Catholic practices or beliefs were not attacked ... That which at first glance one could regard as anti-Rome or anti-papal content, was as a rule criticism of concrete policies of the Vatican ..."[117] Janion makes clear what policies came under fire: "Of no little importance are the charges leveled against the churches of being in league with tyranny, of betraying the divine matter of the freedom of the people and the nations, of slowing the progress of history."[118] Romanticism's heaviest guns were thus aimed at the Church's stance towards movements of liberation and social justice. Throughout the nineteenth century, the Church hierarchy largely supported the *status quo* established by the Congress of Vienna (1815). While efforts were made to maintain Polish culture and religion, the Vatican opposed attempts to resurrect an independent Polish state, particularly by armed uprisings. Pope Gregory XVI declared that "submission to rulers established by God is an unwavering principle from which one cannot be released..."[119] As a result, Catholic patriots were forced to choose between obedience to their Pope and allegiance to their nation.

Fourthly, did the romantics want to overthrow or reform the Church? Here the answer is complex. Alongside sharp criticism of

113. A Polish romantic philosopher.

114. A Polish religious order that Mickiewicz helped found, who later became his most vocal critics.

115. Przybył, "Romantyzm, Katolicyzm, antyklerykalizm," *Rocznik Teologiczny*, 87.

116. Cf. the discussion in chapter 6, under "Providence, Freedom and Responsibility."

117. Przybył, "Romantyzm, Katolicyzm, antyklerykalizm," 90–91.

118. Janion and Żmigrodzka, *Romantyzm i historia*, 20–21.

119. Pope Gregory XVI, "CUM PRIMUM ...," a June 1832 encyclical condemning the November Uprising. In Makowski, Watykan "wobec powstania listopadowego," in *Kordian Juliusza Słowackiego*, 124–26.

the Roman Church, Mickiewicz's writings contain strongly pro-Catholic passages, ample devotion to the Virgin Mary, and the sacramental images of *Forefathers' Eve, Part III*. Furthermore, in the *Paris Lectures*, Mickiewicz blames Protestants for the decline of the Polish Commonwealth. Many therefore hold Mickiewicz co-responsible for disseminating the *Polak-Katolik* myth. Yet claims that Mickiewicz was anti-Protestant or anti-Catholic err if either position is understood primarily in terms of doctrine. Mickiewicz criticized the Reformation for breaking the unity of Christianity, and thereby weakening its spiritual and temporal power. Przybył argues that the romantics wanted to renew and reform the Church, not destroy it, concluding: "Słowacki and Mickiewicz, August Cieszkowski, Zygmunt Krasiński... did not intend in the least to leave the Church; they wanted to reform it."[120]

The crux of the issue lies in what the Church was to become. Mickiewicz envisioned a renewed, reunited Church that could speak with one voice and act decisively to defend Europe's cultural and spiritual unity. The romantic longing for an idea or institution that would reunite a fractured Europe often turned to an idealized, mythological conception of the medieval *christianitas*.[121] Nevertheless, the messianic vision did not entail a mere restoration of apostolic Christianity or medieval Christendom. Rather, the romantics waited "expectantly for new revelation, which would thrust Christianity forward and transform it."[122]

The realization of messianic visions requires messianic change agents. In biblical as in extra-biblical messianism, the messiah may be either an individual or a collective group, e.g., a nation or a given social class. Over time, Mickiewicz and Słowacki both moved from seeing Poland as a corporate messiah to expecting the appearance of an individual messianic figure. Some of their contemporaries placed their messianic hopes in a particular class, while others foretold the uniting of the commoners and gentry; seers expected a hero, conservatives looked to the nobility for leadership, and democrats stressed the role of the people.[123] Ultimately, it was the union of the individual and the community, like the marriage of politics and religion, which came to

---

120. Cf. Przybył, "Romantyzm, Katolicyzm, antyklerykalizm," 88.
121. Cf. Ibid., 96–97.
122. Janion and Żmigrodzka, *Romantyzm i historia*, 20–21.
123. Cf., Ibid., 23–24.

mark Polish romanticism. Janion provides an excellent summary of the resulting "romantic cult of the charismatic leader":

> And yet the ideas: God—the individual—the community, so basic to the romantic understanding of the historical process, remained in an indivisible union, creating the dialectic of Polish romanticism. [. . .] The nation understands itself and finds its path in the action of heroes, the condition and measure of the greatness of the individual is his relationship with the feelings, dreams, and aspirations of the fellowship, with the "thought of the people," with the consciousness and memory of the nation.[124]

Poetry and Political Ethics

Romanticism's insistence on morality in politics implies that when a given regime becomes oppressive, the church must decide whether to side with the rulers or the people. Since the church is on God's side, who does God support? If kings rule by divine right, then the church must endorse government efforts to suppress the people's struggle for self-rule. On the other hand, if God has granted people the right to freedom and self-expression, Christians should align themselves with the forces of liberation, democracy, and social justice. Polish romantics agreed with the classicists who framed the May 3rd Constitution that the government's right to rule comes from the people. The opposition of both classical and religious camps to the doctrine of "divine right" was not a claim to human autonomy or a revolt against divine providence. The supporters of democracy within Polish romanticism believed themselves to be on God's side. Most perceived true Christianity as their ally in the fight for freedom. When the institutional Church opposed the socio-political aspirations of oppressed classes and emerging nations, the romantics proposed their own interpretation of biblical Christianity.

Although the May 3rd Constitution was spiritually akin to the American "Declaration of Independence," it was no cultural import from the New World. It drew on Poland's long parliamentary tradition, where the king was the elected representative of the nation's enfranchised classes. The romantic poets' claim that valid political order must

---

124. Ibid.

arise from the "internal truth" or "essence" of the nation was a declaration of war against autocratic and tyrannical governments.[125] God is the ally of the people, whose prerogative it is to select their own form of government and to appoint their own rulers. God granted the nations both dignity, and the authority to oppose rulers whose claim to power is supported by force of arms rather than the principles of freedom and justice.

The Polish uprisings of 1831 and 1846 were interpreted throughout Europe as the harbingers of the 1848 "Spring of Nations." The failed November Uprising made it clear to Poles that the only hope to overthrow the czar was the anti-royalist movement gaining strength throughout Europe. Poland's heroic, sacrificial fight for freedom was integrated into the European-wide struggle for freedom. Poland led the way, but freedom would only come when all the oppressed peoples would join to throw off the shackles of tyranny.

In Poland the battle was directed primarily against the Russian czar, variously called "a wild beast," "satan," and "the antichrist." Kolbuszewski notes that this identification of the czar with the devil ". . . sanctified the battle with the tyrant, and so justified the rejection of ethical—i.e., knightly—forms of battle."[126] The hopeless struggle towards a just end seemed to justify means that under normal circumstances are immoral or unethical. Poles were ethically torn between the desire for revenge against the partitioning powers, and the moral obligation of Christ's command to love one's enemies. Janion adds that, this "unending internal conflict" became one of romanticism's "most notable ethical antinomies."[127]

To the ethical tension between hate and love there was added the practical tension between thought and deed. Striving to surmount this tension, romanticism viewed history as something that can be changed. Things were not as they should be, but neither must they remain as they are. Polish romantics chose neither stoicism, nor quietism, nor mysticism. They understood political activity as living poetry, as the incarnation of the national spirit.[128] Kolbuszewski declares that, "the

125. Cf. Siwicka, *Romantyzm*, 76.
126. Kolbuszewski, *Literatura wobec historii*, 47.
127. Ibid., 61–62.
128. During the Uprising Mochnacki wrote, "We have improvised the most beautiful poem of the National Uprising! Our life is already poetry.—The clash of arms and

November Uprising ... as the most explicit realization of the idea of independence—constituted the most perfect of all romantic deeds."[129]

Poland's poets sought to actively shape history. Seeking to bring this world into conformity with the ideal, spiritual world, they demanded congruence between the prophetic word and the patriotic deed. The romantic "man of the word" became the romantic "man of action." The reader was expected to emulate the romantic hero, to labor to reduce the gap between the ideal and the real. Poetry was consigned to the service of politics. Art for art's sake was treated as irresponsible, unpatriotic frivolity.[130] It became a patriotic imperative to be doers of the word, and not hearers only.

One of the first to supply Polish poetry with political aims was Brodziński, who declared that nations should live for the good of humanity. He proclaimed that while the Polish astronomer Copernicus had discovered that planets revolve around the sun, the Polish people had discovered that nations revolve around the international human community. Poland's messianic calling was to proclaim this "second Copernican Revolution" to the world's rulers and oppressed peoples alike.[131] The "three Seers" turned this idea into a confession of faith for the Polish nation.

The People's Republic of Poland claimed Mickiewicz as a socialist, titling their national newspaper "The People's Tribune," after the journal Mickiewicz had edited in Paris. They convinced few that Poland's national seer was a Marxist, although such insipid propaganda discouraged generations of school children from reading Mickiewicz. In real life, though Mickiewicz never espoused socialism as an ideology, he was sympathetic to socialist ideals; he criticized England's parliamentary system for serving the interests of business and not the people, and championed the cause of freedom and social justice. One cannot deny the revolutionary content of the messianic vision. The romantics' love

---

the roar of guns.—From now on this will be our rhythm and our melody." Cited in Siwicka, *Romantyzm*, 73.

129. Kolbuszewski, *Literatura wobec historii*, 45.

130. Kolbuszewski writes: "Romanticism ... radically cancelled out the classicist notion of literature as a form of entertainment ... Literature became an obligation, a necessity both for the creator himself as well as for his readers." Kolbuszewski, *Literatura wobec historii*, 26.

131. Cf. Brodziński, "O narodowości Polaków," cited in Janion and Żmigrodzka, *Romantyzm i historia*, 458–59. Mickiewicz republished this in *Pielgrzym Polski*.

for freedom and their revolt against tyranny led them by an internal logic to join the cause for social justice. They realized that the peoples of Europe could only win their freedom by acting together.[132] Furthermore, the peoples' revolution could only succeed if all the members of the nation joined its cause and shared in its benefits. Janion argues that "the process of economic-social change and the need to fight to regain independence led to a new model of the nation . . . the people replaced the nobility as the most important class . . ."[133] while Porter adds that the appeal to the people led to the "infusion of revolutionary content into the nationalist agenda."[134]

The traditional linkage of politics and religion in Polish society provided messianism with a moral justification of the nation's struggle for independence. If Poland was the innocent victim of immoral politics, the nation's resistance to the partitioning powers' tyranny proclaimed the political gospel of freedom and justice, leading to Siwicka's claim that, "romantic messianism was therefore above all a thought concerning the necessity of moralizing and Christianizing all political activities."[135] Messianism's political gospel was seen as the natural development of personal salvation, as the next stage in salvation-history, as the furtherance of God's divine plan to bring his Kingdom to earth. The gospel of love and brotherhood was to rule among the nations as well as in individual hearts. The following excerpt from John Paul II's 1999 sermon in Gdańsk on the heritage of the Solidarity movement demonstrates the continuing vitality of the romantic vision.

> Nineteen years ago in this place Solidarity was born. It was a turning point in the history of our nation, of ours and also the history of Europe. "Solidarity" opened the door of freedom in countries enslaved by totalitarian systems, it pulled down the Berlin Wall, and contributed to the unification of Europe that since the time of the Second World War had been divided into two blocks. We must never blot this from our memory. This event belongs to our national heritage. I heard from you then in Gdańsk: "There is no freedom without solidarity." Today we must say: "There is no solidarity without love." [. . .] We are thus

---

132. In "A Pilgrim's Prayer," Mickiewicz's called for "the universal war of the peoples." Cf. discussion in chapter 3.

133. Janion and Żmigrodzka, *Romantyzm i historia*, 16–18.

134. Porter, "Marking the Boundary of the Faith," 29.

135. Siwicka, *Romantyzm*, 91.

called to build a future founded on the love of God and neighbor. To build a *civilization of love* [italics his].[136]

These words declare that freedom's victory over totalitarianism must be defended and expanded upon if it is to accomplish its true end, which is a "civilization of love." They also echo the messianic belief concerning the vital, indispensable role that Poland continues to play in furthering the freedom and unity of Europe. In the Polish mind, Solidarity's workers, through their courage, faith, and sacrifice, led the way spiritually and politically to the dismantling of the Iron Curtain.

136. Wojtyla, "Homilia."

2

The Foundation of Polish Messianism
Jan Paweł Woronicz: Patriotic Priest

The Poet and the Polish National Spirit[1]

Jan Paweł Woronicz (1757–1829) was the consummate Polish patriot. Prior to Poland's final partition in 1795, he supported the program of national renewal associated with King Stanisław August Poniatowski.[2] In Poland's parliamentary monarchy, the king was more a Prime Minister than a ruling monarch, yet he remained the visible symbol of the Commonwealth. To this day the crown remains the symbol of free democratic Poland.[3] Two poems predating the king's abdication in 1795 demonstrate the extent to which Woronicz identified the Polish State with its monarch. The first, *On the New Rooms in the Royal Palace*,[4] compares Stanisław August to Casimir the Great, who restored Poland's fallen fortunes during his long reign (1333–1370). Woronicz considered it Stanisław's destiny to lead Poland back to greatness, just as Casimir had done centuries before. Woronicz likens the king's presence amidst the nation to the statue of *Pallada*[5] in ancient Troy; Athena's presence

---

1. This chapter draws heavily on two recent, seminal works on Woronicz: *Klasycyzm, czyli prawdziwy koniec Królestwa Polskiego* by Ryszard Przybylski, and *Jan Paweł Woronicz* by Zofia Rejman.

2. Poniatowski ruled from 1764 to 1795.

3. The communist government that ruled Poland after 1945 removed the crown from the head of the Polish eagle, for obvious ideological reasons. The Solidarity government formed in 1989 quickly restored the crown.

4. Woronicz, "Na pokoje nowe w Zamku Królewskim," 84–105.

5. I.e., Athena in armor.

guaranteed the city's safety, and her loss[6] led to its downfall. The poem's message is clear: there is hope for the nation while the king still rules.

Another verse, On the Entrance of Michał Jerzy Ciołek Poniatowski,[7] both links the fate of the nation with its king, and reflects the traditional Polish union of cross and crown. Michał Jerzy, the newly elected Primate[8] of Poland, had come to Warsaw to meet with his uncle King Stanisław and the Parliament. Only by working together, Woronicz declares, in cooperation with the nation as represented by parliament, could they lead the country back to greatness. Woronicz could little imagine that Poland would soon face the question of the nation's political viability when king and parliament are no more. As Reyman writes,

> That which Woronicz had learned from the old Polish historiographers, and that which he also observed in enlightened Europe, formed a basic maxim—we exist as long as the country and its symbol, the king, exist. The question arises—what will the poet call upon, when all hope to sustain the country that is leaning towards its fall has failed, when the third partition liquidates that country.[9]

It is a maxim that the nineteenth century marks the birth of modern nations and nationalism. The French Revolution of 1789 changed the way in which people thought about the nation. The established social order, already shaken to its core by the Revolution, was turned upside down by the king-slaying of Louis XVI and his bride Marie Antoinette. The *ancien regime* had fallen, the divine right of kings had suffered a violent death, the unquestioned primacy of the noble class was a thing of the past, and the people had arrived on the stage of history. The nation was now destined to include all of its citizens, not just the privileged few.

The French Revolution captured the imagination of Poles, who critically adored or categorically condemned it, depending upon their political convictions. Prior to 1795, they were too absorbed with their own struggle for survival to reflect upon it in depth, yet it influenced the course of debate on the May 3rd Constitution adopted in 1791. It

---

6. She was stolen by Odysseus and Diomedes.
7. Ibid., 77–83
8. I.e., head of the Roman Catholic Church in Poland.
9. Rejman, *Jan Paweł Woronicz*, 28.

took on greater significance following the final partition of Poland. The Commonwealth was no more, the king languished in a Russian prison, and parliament was dissolved. Yet Poles felt in their hearts that Poland lived on. What does it mean then to be Polish? In their efforts to construct a viable model for a restored state, Poles looked to the "Great" Revolution, both to learn from its achievements and to avoid its mistakes. Interpretations varied but one principle seemed clear; the people make up the nation, not the king. This conclusion came to the aid of Polish patriots and romantic poets, who followed Woronicz in arguing that what constitutes Poland is the nation, not the state. As Rejman declares, Woronicz "was the first to formulate the thesis that a nation deprived of its state lives not only in culture—as a new Troy—but also in the political events of the world, in history. For its essence is not comprised by institutions—the king, parliament, ministries—but by the awareness of cultural identity."[10]

The conviction that a nation's essence is found in its cultural identity had profound implications for Poles, whose emerging self-consciousness was conducted in an institutional vacuum,[11] and under the yoke of foreign rule. Their self-reflection became at times became all-consuming. As Wincenty Lutosławski wrote, "All of Polish art focused on one theme, which is the drive for independence, of which the nation had been deprived. In no other country did the passionate love of freedom find such a diverse expression."[12] Although widowed by the loss of statehood, Poland's spirit continued its metaphorical existence, growing in prison cells, the furtive gatherings of conspirators, partisans' forest camps, and the lonely exile of the Polish emigration. It was nourished in homes where parents, wives, and children awaited the return of their sons, husbands, and fathers, or mourned their violent, untimely death.

Poland was not alone in its search for the national spirit, for nineteenth century European nations faced a general identity crisis. Already rocked by the French Revolution, they sensed the rising storm of economic, social, and political pressures that led to the Spring of

---

10. Rejman *Jan Paweł Woronicz*, 185.

11. The Roman Catholic Church, the one major Polish institution that survived the partitions, was instrumental in maintaining Polish language, culture and traditions. This contributed to the replacement of "Church and state" by the new formula "Church and nation." The linkage between patriotism, politics and religion is expressed in the Polish phrase, "God, Honor and the Fatherland."

12. Lutosławski, "Filozofia narodowa," 436.

Nations, toppled governments, and transformed the face of Europe. In the background there lingered the "barbarian complex"[13] common to Europeans who were, for the most part, descendants of the tribes that sacked Rome. On what basis could they establish their right to exist? As the divine right of kings crumbled, some nations turned to Hegelian philosophy to validate their national pedigree. Others stressed their intellectual and artistic achievements, or pointed to their mythical origins in antiquity. In anticipation of Darwin, the most persuasive argument was that they had endured the test of time. The strong survived and the weak perished. According to this last criterion, the downfall of the Polish state served to confirm that it had failed the test of historical survival, and thus forfeited its right to exist.

Traditional views of Providence had also fallen on hard times. Already in the 18th century Volney[14] had denied determinism, and taught that people are responsible for their own fate. Furthermore, he held that nations and empires fall because of internal decay, not outward attacks. According to this thesis, Poland lost her statehood because her vital strength, her driving force or *entelechy*,[15] was consumed from within by despotism and religion.[16] Poland was left with no one to blame but herself, and no God to call on for help. What hope remained of regaining independence? Woronicz's *Temple of Sybil*, constructed on the motifs of Volney's *Les ruines ou Meditations sur les revolutions des empires*, presents an alternative explanation for Poland's calamities, combined with a defense of the divine Providence that Volney denied. For Woronicz, Poland's entelechy was parliamentary democracy, which assumed historical expression in the Polish *Sejm* or parliament. Parliament, which embodied the essence of the Polish nation, was the historical realization of the principles of freedom, equality, and democracy implicit in the term "Commonwealth."[17]

---

13. Rejman, *Jan Paweł Woronicz*, 113.

14. Kleiner, *Sentymentalizm i preromantyzm*, 26.

15. Entelechy can be defined as a "vital principle." The vitalists of the XIX and XX centuries, drawing on Aristotle, believed in a vital force or principle that gives life to all living things and directs them towards the realization of their essential nature.

16. Przybylski, *Klasycyzm, czyli prawdziwy koniec Królestwa Polskiego*, 227–28. The argument here follows Przybylski.

17. Ibid., 230.

Volney held that nations fall due to the twin cancers of despotism and religion. Woronicz replied by asserting that Poland's genius was freedom and equality. While the gentry, nobles, and magnates had at times placed their own interests above those of the nation, such actions were regarded as a betrayal of the national spirit. Regarding religion, Woronicz responded that the problem was not religion but its lack. Poland had been unfaithful to her God, and to her divinely appointed task. Renewal and rebirth could therefore only come through a renewal of her true essence, her spiritual *entelechy*, which included love of freedom, love for God, and the readiness to serve both in life and by death. Woronicz believed that Poland had proven its right to exist through its valiant attempts at religious and political reforms under King Stanisław, crowned by the May 3rd Constitution. It was in parliament, as the expression of the national spirit, that Poland continually renewed itself and its entelechy from within.

The lessons of the French Revolution were not lost on Poland's powerful, autocratic neighbors, who could not permit this oasis of freedom to exist in their midst, for fear that their own citizens would catch the virus of freedom.[18] Catherine the Great in particular perceived this constitution, and the freedom loving Polish people who produced it, to pose a serious threat to her authority and rule. Failing to control the Polish parliament through agitation, threats, and her bought agents, she finally put a stop to the reforms by force. Russian troops invaded Poland in 1792, leading to the final partition of Poland in 1795. As Przybylski notes, Poles perceived their loss of statehood as the "murder of the holy idea of democracy."[19] This tragic act was not the last in the war between democracy and autocracy. The leaders of the Soviet Union continued the repressive tactics of the czars that they deposed. Once again, Poland was considered particularly dangerous, due to its size, its love of freedom, and its tradition of resistance to tyranny.

The Poet as a Storyteller

Woronicz, a providentialist, realized that the defense of the Polish nation required an explanation of how evil had defeated good, a task made

---

18. Less ideological motives included the Poland's rich natural resources, and the opportunity afforded the powers to enlarge their own territory and influence by the annexation of Polish territory.

19. Przybylski, *Klasycyzm, czyli prawdziwy koniec Królestwa Polskiego*, 230.

more difficult by the fact that the good was in the process of cleansing and self-renewal prior to its defeat. Before looking in more depth at his answer, we must consider his understanding of history and his view of poetry.

Woronicz believed that if Poland was to endure, it must be made conscious of its national identity and calling. Furthermore, this knowledge must be passed on to each succeeding generation. Other nations boasting a long history but who failed in that task had long since passed away and been forgotten. The nation that forgets or lightly regards its past is doomed to perish. Woronicz declared: "Only that nation perishes forever, which does not know how to appreciate its national spirit."[20] Poland's national memory must be awakened, nourished, and kept alive. But the past could not remain the property of the elite, a vast treasure house to which only scholars have access. The nation would endure or perish in the hearts and homes of its people. It became the life calling of Woronicz to tell the story of Poland's glory and suffering to patriotic fathers and mothers who would pass the account along to their children.

In 1800 Poland's surviving statesmen and scholars formed the "Society of the Friends of Learning."[21] Believing the Polish nation to be dead, the Society's first president Jan Albertrand articulated its program as the preservation and propagation of Polish culture and learning. In his mind Poland's task, like that of ancient Greece when conquered by Rome, was to pour Polish culture into the nations of which it was now a part. In this way its legacy would endure, and it would prove in the end to be the nobler and more lasting culture.[22] Woronicz would not accept Albertrand's vision. Appearing before the Society on May 15, 1803, Woronicz proposed the creation of a "Polish national Pentateuch" that would serve as the "Bible of the national memory."[23] This pentateuch would consist of three sections, encompassing religious, cultural,[24] and historical songs, which taken together constituted for Woronicz the heritage of a civilized nation. While the first two sections were conceived of as an anthology of past literature, Woronicz himself undertook the

20. Woronicz, "First Discourse on Polish Songs," 88.
21. I.e., *Towarzystwo Przyjaciół Nauk*.
22. Rejman, *Jan Paweł Woronicz*, 59.
23. Woronicz, "First Discourse on Polish Songs," 213–39. Woronicz returned to this theme in the *Discourses* of 1805, 1806, and 1807.
24. I.e., relating to customs and morals.

writing of the third section, which would establish the ancient genealogy and historical greatness of the Polish nation. His self-described goal was 'to paint and picture the Poles', and thus provide a definition of their unique national traits.

In hand-picking the elements from Poland's historical and legendary past that served his purpose, Woronicz drew from three main sources. First there came the Biblical tradition of Assarmot, followed by the writers of antiquity, who themselves were often quoted by medieval Polish chroniclers. Here Woronicz paid special attention to Ptolemy's description of the many tribes of European Sarmatia, believed by many to descend from Assarmot, and traditionally linked with the Slavic peoples. Finally, he studied the Polish chronicles, which contained the oldest accounts of the origins and deeds of legendary Polish rulers. Rejman notes that Woronicz made up nothing: every name, place, and event he mentions can be found in these sources.[25] After choosing what he found useful, he ordered the selected elements in accordance with his own historical-philosophical vision. She writes:

> The outline that he presented to the Society testifies to the fact that he placed great importance on the Slavic origins of the Poles. He attempts to mark out [their] own circle from the entire history of the world, which will progressively narrow until it makes possible the setting apart of the Polish nation and the definition of its individual characteristics.[26]

Woronicz envisioned the national pentateuch as a prophetic work, not merely an historical one.[27] The separation of the history[28] of the Polish nation from the history of the Polish State[29] allowed him to proclaim that the partitions were not the end of Poland's national existence. He finished a long poem called *Assarmot*, which traces Poland's origin to Assarmot, the biblical son of Seth the son of Noah, through the Sarmatians who were considered the ancestors of the Slavic peoples. In this poem Assarmot himself prophesies of one hundred more Polish rulers following the division of Poland. Woronicz also wrote major portions of *Lech*, which brought the tale up to founding of the Polish

---

25. Rejman, *Jan Paweł Woronicz*, 113.
26. Ibid., 85.
27. Ibid., 112–13.
28. I.e., mythical beginnings.
29. The recorded history of Poland begins ca. 966 AD.

nation. It describes the coming of the first legendary king of Poland to Gniezno, where he founded the Polish state and became the ancestor of the Piast dynasty. In *Sejm Wiślicki* Woronicz described a gathering of nobles that was the forerunner of the Polish parliament. Woronicz also dreamed of writing a great national epic, the *Jagiellonidy*, in praise of Władysław Jagiełło, the king who united Lithuania and Poland into one Commonwealth. Only the plan of this proposed epic has survived.

In the midst of a heated contemporary debate over whether Lech and his Sarmatian-Slavic-Polish cohorts should be granted a place in Polish history, Woronicz argued for their inclusion on the basis of their role as mythical characters. He thus employed today's modern understanding of myths as stories that are foundational for a nation's self-awareness and moral convictions. According to this view, the truth contained in myths comes from the lasting moral and ethical values they present, regardless of whether the things they describe actually happened that way in history. At the same time, Woronicz defended the truth of even the most legendary parts of his tale, if only on the grounds that the chroniclers insisted on them so unanimously. In the end, he concluded with a certain ambivalence that since legends date from prehistoric times before the Slavs learned to write, it was neither possible nor necessary to verify their authenticity. Their true and lasting value is to aid in reflection upon the nation.

Woronicz was convinced that the past held the key to the present and to the future. By showing his generation who the Poles had been and what they had done, he was reminding them of their identity and calling. As Rejman notes, "Woronicz's concept, which is entirely modern, grows out of the geneticism typical of his thought, from the conviction that the essence of every being lies in its origins."[30] Such geneticism can be traced to the thought of Rousseau (the primeval is good, ideal), to the "myth of our honorable ancestors" found in old Polish legends, and the concept of the progressive degeneration of the world. Perhaps most influential was Herder.[31] In contrast to the theory of Polish origins that held them to be a nation of valiant warriors descended from the

---

30. Rejman, *Jan Paweł Woronicz*, 111.

31. Herder wrote: "it is essential to get to the source of those things which one desires to fully understand ... just as a tree grows from its roots, so the development and flowering of art must be drawn from its beginnings. They contain within themselves the entire essence of their product, just as the entire plant with all its parts lies hidden within a seed of grain." Herder, cited in: Rejman, *Jan Paweł Woronicz*, 111.

ancient Sarmatians, Herder believed the Poles to be a "farming people, marked by simplicity of customs, gentleness, hospitality, merriment, and love of music."[32] As noted in chapter 1, Sarnicki combined these views into a composite theory of the "pastoral" common people and the "knightly" (Sarmatian) gentry. Woronicz chose to combine the two myths in a different manner, which included all Poles in the nation regardless of class. Thus the Poles, descendants of a Sarmatian tribe, are courageous and victorious in war, but they only fight in self-defense when attacked by non-Slavic tribes. Among themselves the Slavic (i.e., Sarmatian) peoples live as brothers. This of course made the tragedy of 1795 all the greater, for Poland's Slavic brother Russia became its enemy and occupier.

Besides bolstering Poland's damaged self-confidence and establishing her historical pedigree, these myths aimed to equip the Polish people to reclaim their place among the nations of Europe. Each major part of the unfinished national pentateuch focused on one deed of the Polish people, and each deed revealed one trait essential to the Poles' national character.[33] These traits were not arbitrary but were carefully selected for their perceived value in the nation's fight for survival. *Assarmot* taught that Poles naturally live in peace as equals with their fellow-Poles and their Slavic brothers. However, when they must fight Poles ably defend their land against foreign attacks. The prophetic elements in *Lech*, which relate for example to the establishment of the Piast dynasty, reveal the nation's special role in God's plan. In *Sejm Wiślicki*, Poland's ethical greatness is demonstrated by the actions of parliament, which made laws for itself. Poland thus became a nation ruled by law. Finally, *Jagiellonidy* was to provide an account of the nation's growth in military might and prowess.

In addition to identifying Poland's essential national characteristics, Woronicz set out to demonstrate her greatness. A nation may consider itself great because of the scope of its military victories and the size of its realm, or on account of the magnitude of its sufferings. Poland could boast on both counts. In *Assarmot*, Woronicz traced the meaning of Slav (*sławian*) to the Polish word for fame and glory (*sława*).[34]

32. Cf. Rejman, *Jan Paweł Woronicz*, 86.

33. Following: Ibid., 86.

34. Romantic etymology more often derived Slav (*słowian*) from "word" (*słowo*), emphasizing the creative power of God word (Word?), with obvious messianic and

Rejman summarizes the reasons Woronicz provides for Poland's claim to fame: the Slavs are glorious by virtue of their expansion throughout the entire ancient world; the Slavs and particularly the Poles were glorious through what they built;[35] the Poles were great even in the scope of their calamity, i.e., the partition of Poland; the Poles would be great in the future restoration of their State. In the prophecy of Assarmot, the word for fame or glory also means virtue. By linking glory with virtue, Woronicz turned Assarmot's prophecy of Poland's national revival into a commandment for moral renewal. This was a key step in the "socialization" of virtue—love for the Fatherland now becomes the supreme value, by which other virtues are measured.[36]

Though never completed, Woronicz's attempt to create the national pentateuch was understood as the birth of a truly Polish national literature. Across generations, Poles from all literary, philosophical, and political persuasions recognized that Woronicz had attempted something new and important. As Juliusz Kleiner wrote, "Woronicz was the first who understood the national calling of poetry."[37] In the hour of crisis, Woronicz knew that the nation's most lasting testimony was her literature. In the *First Discourse* he wrote, "Not everyone can have costly drawings and works of art, and every enemy can tear and destroy them. Therefore that is more certain, which on the lips of undying generations does not fear the fire and the sword."[38] Mickiewicz later picked up this theme in *Konrad Wallenrod*, when the bard sings,

> Fire consumes paintings,
> Thieves devastate treasures with their swords,
> The song escapes untouched . . .[39]

Although songs and poems may be best, sometimes artifacts must do. In the pre-partition poem mentioned above, *On the New Rooms in the Royal Palace*, Woronicz interpreted the paintings and artifacts con-

---

eschatological overtones.

35. When Lech, the legendary founder of the Polish State, arrived in Gniezno, he found his fellow Sarmatians (the Vandals), who welcomed him as one of their own. Rejman writes, "This is the Pan-Slavic legend—Slavic brothers meeting in peace and unity in Slavic lands."

36. Rejman, *Jan Paweł Woronicz*, 121–22.

37. Kleiner, *Sentimentalism and Pre-Romanticism*, 25.

38. Woronicz, cited in Rejman, *Jan Paweł Woronicz*, 88 .

39. Mickiewicz, *Konrad Wallenrod*, 101.

tained in the Knight's Room, built at the direction of King Stanisław August Poniatowski. The King had a dual purpose for each object and painting placed in the room: "to awaken the patriotic spirit through bringing to mind the wondrous pages of the nation's history, and to support the ruler's reform efforts."[40] Woronicz's interest in material objects may appear strange for one who considered the written word to be a nation's most effective and lasting heritage. Yet in his day poems were often written describing various souvenirs or memorials. Such poems focused not on the artifacts themselves, but on the values and virtues they represented, thereby encouraging the reader/viewer to follow the example set by their ancestors. As Rejman notes, "the Polish Enlightenment ... believed that material objects, things, have the power to immortalize and preserve [deeds and events] in memory ... The thing and the word complemented and explained each other."[41] The same approach appears in *The Temple of Sybil*,[42] written in 1802 following the downfall of the Polish state. Later in life, as the Archbishop of Kraków, Woronicz created his own museum of national remembrance. Like the Knight's Room in the Royal Palace, and the Temple of Sybil[43] at Isabel Czartoryska's country estate, this museum did not endure the onslaughts of time and war, and its artifacts were scattered or lost. It is fitting irony that Woronicz's poems are all that remains of these "temples" dedicated to Poland's past glory and greatness.

Though the purpose and nature of his later poems would vary somewhat, they all follow the method proposed in *On the New Rooms in the Royal Palace*: we study the past, in order to understand the present, and to influence the future. By reflecting on past deeds and heroes, the nation learns what made it great. It recognizes its own virtues and strengths, and its weaknesses. To remember your national past is to understand who you are in the present, and to grasp the purpose for which you exist. The self-knowledge gained equips the nation to respond appropriately to its present-day challenges. Woronicz's poem, however, is more than a history lesson, for the retelling of Poland's story becomes a recording of sacred history. The work ends with a vision—the paintings

---

40. Rejman, *Jan Paweł Woronicz*, 22.
41. Ibid., 21.
42. Discussed below.
43. Many of the artifacts Isabela gathered were taken to France, and later returned to Poland. They are now housed in the Czartoryski museum in Kraków.

in the hall depicting the great warriors, statesmen, and writers of the past come to life and speak. As Rejman explains, "The voices from beyond the grave reveal the proper meaning of the meditations on the nation's past written on the walls of the Knights' Hall."[44] This sign signifies that the message of the past has been read correctly, and marks the unbreakable ties between the past and the present generations. Woronicz often turned to this device in his later poems,[45] in which the voices from the spiritual world return to explain the significance of material objects, confirm that one's understanding of historical signs is correct, and lay a divine calling upon the readers.

The Poet as a Prophet[46]

Woronicz carried a Bible with him everywhere. Given his knowledge of Scripture, and his convictions regarding the divine inspiration of poetry, he naturally made wide use of Biblical images, drawing especially upon the Old Testament prophets. Following the lead of Jesuit preacher Piotr Skarga,[47] Woronicz took up the OT picture of God as a potter. Another of his favorite passages was the prophecy of Ezekiel 37, where Israel's "dry bones" come back to life. Woronicz believed that true poetry not only looks to the Bible for inspiring thoughts and images, but is itself inspired by Scripture's divine Author.[48] That this belief somehow survived the eighteenth century's deification of reason was due in large part to the intuitive experience of those poets who felt, as Isaac Watts put it, the "celestial fire" within.

The classicists' return to Scripture and frequent appeal to its imagery was also related to their fascination with origins. They believed that the primeval world and the people who inhabited it were closer to the original, untainted creation, thus their imagination was formed by

---

44. Ibid., 25. As Masłowski argues, Mickiewicz uses the same device in *Forefathers' Eve*.

45. E.g., *The Vision of Emilka, The Temple of Sybil*.

46. This section follows Przybylski, *Klasycyzm, czyli prawdziwy koniec Królestwa Polskiego*, 199–209.

47. Skarga was a sixteenth-century Jesuit priest, famous for his sermons and his patriotism.

48. Przybylski declares that the seventeenth century, "discovered that poetry is in its essence a religious phenomenon, for God himself, the meta-author of the Holy Scripture, inspires it." Przybylski, *Klasycyzm, czyli prawdziwy koniec Królestwa Polskiego*, 201.

their wonder at things new and marvelous. Fortunately, what humanity lost over the centuries is still accessible to those entrusted with, or rather possessed by the poetic gift. As Przybylski explains, "the poet to Woronicz was a 'primeval' man, wandering about in a civilized society. He has received a gift that the classicists rated unusually high: enthusiasm, i.e., the ability to react personally and emotionally to the world. Due to this ability he is able to penetrate the true essence of things."[49]

Epistemologically, this appeal to poetic "enthusiasm" implies that true knowledge is found by the poet and not, as Enlightenment rationalists claimed, by the philosopher. Poetic imagination is thereby related directly to, if not equated with divine inspiration.[50] Woronicz, arguing for the acceptance of this view of prophetic poetry before the Society of the Friends of Learning, asked: "Who is able to speak of this higher and indescribable inspiration, which like fire that consumes and devours everything in thunder and flashes of lightning, allows itself to be perceived and honored, but not comprehended by an amazed creation?"[51] By comparing poetry to fire, Woronicz alludes to the prophetic gift that elevates poetry to the level of God's word. Przybylski concludes that, "on that same day the classicists[52] accepted [prophetic poetry] as the program of national culture."[53]

In the *Second Discourse on National Songs*, delivered to the Friends of Learning on May 15, 1805, Woronicz argued that the poet-prophet is above all a singer. Here the harmony of poetry becomes a musical harmony, owing its contact with eternity to its non-material qualities.[54] The classical and romantic poets, including Mickiewicz in *Konrad Wallenrod* and *Forefathers' Eve*, often followed this pattern. Taking his own advice to heart, Woronicz closed his *Second Discourse* with perhaps

---

49. Ibid., 201–2.

50. Przybylski writes: "The great battle over the Christianization of Plato's thesis regarding the divine origin of poetry... ended after all with the clear and simple conclusion, that poetry is not so much... 'the language of the gods,' as much as 'the language of God himself.'" Ibid., 202–3.

51. Woronicz, *First Discourse on National Songs*, cited in Przybylski, *Klasycyzm, czyli prawdziwy koniec Królestwa Polskiego*, 209–10.

52. I.e., the members of the Society of the Friends of Learning.

53. Ibid., 209.

54. Ancient prophets often spoke or sang to the accompaniment of music, a practice caricatured by the image of Nero fiddling while Rome burns.

his most outstanding work, *Hymn to God*,[55] which was modeled on the Psalms and presented in the form of a national requiem.

Ambitious goals are reached by personal commitment and hard work, not the acclaim of the crowd. With Rejman, we may question how serious the Friends of Learning were about Woronicz's plan for creating a new psalter of national songs to add to the national pentateuch. Busy with other tasks, few assisted in the actual compilation and writing of the pentateuch. Happy as they were for someone else to do the work, they did not consider Woronicz the poet the one for the job, despite their respect for him as a patriot and priest. Ironically, although a classicist proposed the program of poetic prophecy, it was left to the romantics to adopt it as their sacred model. Like Woronicz, their search for hope following Poland's partition took the form of a philosophy of history. Woronicz's historiosophy thus served as the starting point for romantic messianism.

Woronicz's historiosophy makes its debut in the poem, *The Temple of Sybil*.[56] Like his earlier work, *On the New Rooms,* it describes a museum tour, this time of the Temple of Sybil, which Princess Isabella Czartoryska built in her family's gardens to commemorate the nation's greatness. Three visions come to the author as he reflects upon the artifacts in the Temple. In the first vision, the statue of Casimir the Great comes to life to recount the greatness of the Polish Commonwealth under the reigns of the Piast and Jagiellonian dynasties. In the second vision, King Jan Casimir describes Poland's distress and foretells its impending fall. The idea of the covenant between God and Poland that became prominent in *Hymn to God* leads here to the conclusion that God has withdrawn his blessing in order to test and purify the nation.[57] Finally, in the third vision Sybil herself appears. Asked by the narrator if all that visitors to her temple will take away are memories of Poland's former greatness, the prophetess answers that the fate of the nation is in the hand of God, and part of his plan. Przybylski, arguing correctly that our view of providence is determined largely by our image of God, suggests that when Woronicz looked at God, he saw the face of a loving

---

55. Discussed below.

56. The widespread belief that Sybil prophesied to Caesar of Christ's coming allowed for the Christianization of this pagan prophetess, supposed author of the *Books of Sybil.*

57. Rejman, *Jan Paweł Woronicz*, 39.

Father. Since God cares for his creation, "every event, even those that seem senseless and monstrous, must have some meaning, for it has its place in God's plan. Whatever has taken place, whether good or bad, happened by the will of God."[58]

Despite Woronicz's confidence in God's goodness and sovereignty, he does not proceed at this point to enumerate the reasons for Poland's fall, or predict the manner of its resurrection. Rather his providentialism provides the interpretive context for understanding the nation's crisis. This leads Rejman to conclude that the "voice from heaven" makes the nation aware that it erred "by not sufficiently trusting in the goodness and omnipotence of God."[59] The purpose of Poland's suffering was to call the Polish nation, which had broken its covenant with God, back to faith in God and faithfulness to his calling. Viewed from this perspective, the conclusion was clear. As Siwicka, quoting *The Temple of Sybil*, explains, "The nation bears the guilt: 'When the fault does not fall on the Father and Ruler, the source and the cause must be found among you.' Consistently, hope is brought in by the idea of renewing the covenant."[60]

The Poet As A Priest

National Liturgy: Calling the Nation to Repentance

Along with a national philosophy, and a renewed belief in Providence, Poland found itself in need of a national theodicy. Woronicz would provide all of these in what is regarded as his greatest work, *Hymn to God*, which further developed the concept of Poland as God's covenant people. Woronicz was generally a mediocre poet, yet on this occasion his passion for Poland carried his poetry to unusual heights. Rejman describes *Hymn to God* as "a liturgical rite," through which "the congregation, led by the choir director,[61] touches on mystery, achieves self-knowledge, and matures to the act of repentance."[62] She

---

58. Przybylski, *Klasycyzm, czyli prawdziwy koniec Królestwa Polskiego*, 214.

59. Rejman, *Jan Paweł Woronicz*, 44.

60. Ibid., 44.

61. I.e., Woronicz.

62. Ibid., 45. This use of poetry prefigures Mickiewicz's *Forefathers' Eve, Part III*, in which the nation as audience becomes a participant in the drama.

compares the choir director's role to that of Jeremiah, who was both a prophet and a priest.⁶³

Priesthood came naturally to Woronicz, who felt the weight of his country's sins and called on the nation to repent. The model of poetic priesthood he established also characterized the later poetry of the romantics. Proud Konrad, Mickiewicz's literary alter-ego, would stand before God and challenge him to act on behalf of the nation. His predecessor Woronicz knelt before God and led the nation in a corporate act of repentance.⁶⁴ Despite such differences, the romantics, who were far better poets, were nevertheless indebted to Woronicz for establishing "the priesthood of poetry." Kleiner writes:

> Woronicz, though far from all fanaticism and full of toleration, though not underscoring his Catholicism, is above all a priest-preacher, to a much greater degree than a writer ... But in that he desired to carry out his service to ideas with his poetical works, that in [fulfilling that service] he still felt himself a priest, that through his reliance on strong faith in God he gave [that priestly service] its proper character, by this he in fact initiated the priesthood of poetry.⁶⁵

*National Theology: I Have Made A Covenant with My People.*⁶⁶

Woronicz believed that the nation is at heart a spiritual community. This view was grounded in his post-1795 conviction that a nation's essence is found in the national spirit, not in the state. This in turn allowed him to argue for Poland's continued viability, since God's concern and providential care concerns the nation and not the state.⁶⁷ While every nation has its place in God's plan, Woronicz held that this relationship can take

---

63. Ibid., 46.

64. Rejman, *Jan Paweł Woronicz*, 46, who writes: "we have to do here with a process: from the affirmation of God and the confession of faith, through the description of defeat and the confession of guilt, up to the joint lamentation, which foretells the mending of one's ways."

65. Kleiner, *Sentymentalizm i preromantyzm*, 26.

66. This section follows Przybylski, *Klasycyzm, czyli prawdziwy koniec Królestwa Polskiego*, 221–27.

67. Ibid., 221.

the form of a covenant between God and his people. Potentially, the Biblical history of Israel is a type of the history of any nation.

As *The Temple of Sybil* makes clear, the Old Testament covenants provide the religious and theological background of *Hymn to God*. Woronicz viewed the Mosaic covenant established on Mount Sinai as a bilateral covenant, which stipulated the obligations placed on God and on Israel, and delineated the consequences for the latter if they failed to keep their word.[68] The stone tablets upon which God inscribed the Ten Commandments were the visible sign of this Mosaic covenant, which Woronicz took as the type of the covenant between God and the Polish nation. In *Hymn to God* Woronicz argued that Poland's covenant with God was established at the conversion of Poland's ruler Duke Mieszko I, with baptism as its sign and seal.[69] Thus when Mieszko I, the historical founder of the Polish State, was baptized as a Christian in 966 AD, the nation that he represented made a willing choice to become God's people, to enjoy his favor, and to submit to his rule. As Przybylski explains, "In Woronicz's opinion the very act of baptism, which is after all an act of free choice, transformed Poles into a chosen nation."[70] Woronicz writes,

> 1,000 years now near the end of their irreversible road,
> From when you befriended our fathers,
> And tearing them from the hand of their hewn gods,
> Lit their land with the holy visage of truth
> And let it be known amidst the error of confusion,
> That you are their God and they are your children.[71]

In *Hymn to God*, Poland now became the vassal of Almighty God. God, as feudal lord, obligated himself to protect and care for his people. For their part, the Poles took upon themselves the responsibility to serve their liege Lord and to obey his will. As the "Bulwark of Christianity,"[72]

---

68. Rejman: "The covenant on Mount Sinai is a legal act, in which the nation takes upon itself clearly defined responsibilities, whose fulfillment guarantees it the care and grace of God." Rejman, *Jan Paweł Woronicz*, 46.

69. Rejman agrees, declaring that for Woronicz "the establishment of the covenant took place therefore at the moment that Poland received baptism." Ibid., 47.

70. Przybylski, *Klasycyzm, czyli prawdziwy koniec Królestwa Polskiego*, 222.

71. Woronicz, *Hymn to God*, lines 7–12.

72. Poles understood their "calling" to be the defense of Christian Europe against the Mongol, Tatar, and Turkish hordes.

the nation was given a cause to defend and a battlefield on which to fight, i.e., the extensive lands of the Polish-Lithuanian Commonwealth. In return, God promised to lead them to greatness and glory. As Woronicz declares,

> These same burial halls, overgrown with gray moss,
> Looked upon the covenant you made with our fathers,
> As they, acknowledging you to be the true God,
> Were to serve you loyally with faith unwavering,
> And you in return swore in grace
> To lead them into greatness and fame.[73]

One may marvel today at the length Woronicz went to develop this idea of the covenant. Yet God's continued good favor and Poland's status as his "chosen people" seemed to him the only guarantee of national survival. Viewed sacramentally, Poland's baptism left a spiritual mark or chrism on the personalized spirit of the nation. As the sign of the nation's covenant with God, baptism elevated Poland to existence on a higher, spiritual plane.[74]

Hymn to God presents an idealized vision of Sarmatian Poland, which stands in sharp polemical contrast to the vilified partitioning powers. Woronicz contrasts the *un*just attacks of the czars to Poland, which fought only just wars. Przybylski, who highlights the use in the *Hymn* of the prefix of negation to describe the Sarmatians' *un*tarnished armor, *un*checked sword, *ir*resistible weapons, *un*failing fruit, *un*wavering faith, and *un*erring deeds, comments:

> As the denial of frailty and limitation, all these adjectives with the prefix of negation gave a glimpse of a perfect and infinite being. Thus they made it possible to touch the essence of the national spirit, just as in theology a system of negative statements made it possible to sense the nature of God.[75]

This "perfect and infinite being" refers of course to the "chosen nation," not as it appears in its concrete historical form, but as seen in its transcendent, eternal, spiritual relationship with God. All this of course was the result of God's blessing his people:

73. Woronicz, *Hymn to God*, lines 13–18.

74. As Przybylski explains, "When Mieszko I made a pact with Yahweh, Poland became God's brother in eternity." Przybylski, *Klasycyzm, czyli prawdziwy koniec Królestwa Polskiego*, 223.

75. Ibid., 225.

> You filled their land, as once [you filled] the land of Jordan,
> With blessings, with milk and honey,
> And harnessed teams of domestic beasts in its service
> And enriched all [their] labors with unfailing fruit,
> So that they asked nothing from their neighbors,
> But fed them with their own fullness.[76]

Woronicz was not the first to suggest the idea of a covenant between God and the Polish nation. Yet he was the one who wove this and other elements of Polish culture, history and literature into an integrated, consistent messianic system. It was in the form supplied by Woronicz that the tradition was passed on to the next, romantic generation.[77]

National Theodicy: The Judgment, Cleansing, and Renewal of the Nation[78]

Hymn to God explains the consequences delineated by the Old Testament prophets of breaking the covenant with God. Woronicz describes Polish territory as a paradise on earth. Like Israel in Palestine (Joshua 21:43–45), the Polish nation occupied its promised land. There it enjoyed peace and prosperity, and God gave it victory over its enemies. Then suddenly—God turned his back on the Poles.

> When you, o God, were the God of the Poles,
> Her neighbor dared not become her crafty enemy.
> What happened then with their later descendants!
> You turned your face away—and we—fell into dust![79]

For Woronicz, Poland after 1795 was threatened by more than the loss of independence. A nation that breaks its covenant with God risks losing its status as his covenant people, and is threatened with ultimate extinction.[80] Since God's covenant with the nation was contingent

---

76. Woronicz, *Hymn to God*, lines 37–42.

77. Szczypa writes, "In the history of Polish literature the conviction reigns that those who came after Woronicz—Brodziński, Mickiewicz, Krasiński, Słowacki—began their reflections on the history of the nation from an already prepared point of departure, which consisted among others of the views of Woronicz." Szczypa, *Jan Paweł Woronicz*, 71–72.

78. The following discussion is indebted to Przybylski.

79. Woronicz, *Hymn to God*, lines 137–40.

80. Przybylski writes: "Woronicz therefore presents the matter unequivocally and sharply: faithfulness towards God or annihilation. To betray God means to lose the

on Poland's faithfulness to its liege Lord and to its mission, Woronicz sought the reason for God's judgment in Poland's own guilt.

> Neither blind chance, nor the vicissitudes of life rule the nations,
> In your hands are born both times and fates.
> And since you cannot punish without reason,
> Our fate must be the fruit of our own treason.[81]

Poland had come to exist in the spiritual realm as "the chosen people of God."[82] But it had broken the covenant, forgotten its identity, betrayed its purpose, and proved unfaithful to God. As a result, like Israel of old, the nation suffered ignominy and exile.[83] Rejman summarizes the effects of God's judgment.

> The nation's holy ground was desecrated, the people scattered, history degraded. It is no longer the stage for the realization of God's care but of the divine curse. All efforts here were negated, for the nation fell from the state of grace ... The guilt lies on the side of the nation.[84]

Simply acknowledging Poland's past guilt and present shortcomings, however, did not in itself provide a satisfactory theodicy. If Poland had continued on the downward spiral that became visible in the seventeenth century, its fate would be deserved. But during the second half of the eighteenth century Poles had undertaken sweeping efforts at reform. Woronicz, a providentialist, had to explain why God allowed Poland to perish from without when the nation was renewing itself from within.[85] Woronicz supplied two answers to this question. The first was spiritual and related to Poland. The second was political and related to the nations.

Employing Old Testament imagery, Woronicz affirmed that God the potter can do what he wants with his pots. Yet some of the pots on God's shelf come under His special care. What is punishment for one nation becomes a test for God's chosen people. Woronicz understood God's judgment as an act of grace, proof that the individual or nation

nation." Przybylski, *Klasycyzm, czyli prawdziwy koniec Królestwa Polskiego*, 226.
81. Woronicz, *Hymn to God,* lines 189–92.
82. This claim is not exclusive. Woronicz does not deny this role to other nations.
83. Woronicz compared the nation's loss of statehood to exile.
84. Rejman, *Jan Paweł Woronicz*, 49.
85. Przybylski, *Klasycyzm, czyli prawdziwy koniec Królestwa Polskiego*, 229.

belongs to God's family. As Solomon writes in Proverbs 3:11–12, "the Lord disciplines those he loves, as a father the son he delights in." When God declares his people guilty, he does not abandon them. Rather, his discipline reaffirms the covenant relationship. Woronicz believed that God had smashed the pot of the Polish state to end the spiritual blindness that led the nation to its moral downfall. The partitioning Powers were his tools to call the nation to repentance.[86]

Although the nation's guilt also touched the economic and political life of the community, Woronicz proclaimed that Poland's fundamental problem was moral. Repentance was required, not mere economic or political reforms. Sin and punishment, if properly responded to, are not the end of the nation's spiritual pilgrimage but the first stage of its renewal. Poland's suffering has a purpose. Through it the nation can remember that it belongs to God, repent of its sins, rediscover its identity, and regain its commission. The nation's tears following the loss of statehood are proof that it has acknowledged its guilt, and confessed its sins. By testifying to the nation's repentance, those tears give hope for the renewal of its covenant with God.

> Our tears are the witnesses of our error and redress,
> Neither can you gaze on the streams of human tears
> Nor renounce your children, o gracious Parent![87]

Woronicz provides a second reason for Poland's suffering. He viewed the partitions as a political crime, and proclaimed the eschatological role a revived Poland would play in the history of the nations. For this Polish patriot, Poland's dramatic rise and fall took place on the center stage of European history. For 800 years the nations and their rulers witnessed how God had blessed the Polish people.

> The ink on those sacred treaties had not dried,
> When our fathers, by virtue of that agreement[88]
> Rose from the errant ranks of the scattered tribes,
> To take an honored place among the nations;

---

86. As Rejman writes, "the repentance of Israel ... as a nation was the fruit of two things: the teaching of the prophets and the experiences associated with the captivity. Captivity itself was a providential opportunity for [the nation] to become aware of its sins and to sincerely confess them." Rejman, *Jan Paweł Woronicz*, 49.

87. Woronicz, *Hymn to God*, lines 193–95.

88. 'Those sacred treaties' and 'that agreement' both refer to God's covenant with Poland.

And those who had proudly scorned them,
Sought their kinship and favor.[89]

This account of the beginning of Poland's pilgrimage with God is reprised near the end of the poem, immediately preceding the verses where God turns his back on his beloved people.

Such a wonder, that before them the peoples bowed,
Neighboring monarchs, princes, and kings
Their advice, kinship, and friendship sought,
The poor came for support, the wise for understanding.
When you, o God, were the God of the Poles,
Her neighbor dared not become her crafty enemy.

What happened then with their later descendants!
You turned your face away—and we—fell into dust![90]

God the potter has smashed the clay pot (i.e., the state) that contained the nation.

Our honorable memory, known throughout the world,
As the potsherds shattered by a rock,
Are trampled on and scorned by the jeering traveler.
Who gazing upon our blackened gates,
Shakes his head and asks in astonishment:
"And where now is this God they called out to?"[91]

As Przybylski notes, the phrase "the God they called out to" (*Bóg zawołany*) is an allusion to Jan Kochanowski's[92] Polish translation of the Psalter. Verse eleven of Psalm 42 declares, "my foes taunt me, saying to me all day long, 'where is your God?'" Kochanowski translates these lines with well-earned poetic license:

And where now, o exiled wretch,
Is your God, whom you called out to?

Reading David's lament, Woronicz recalled Poland's present circumstances. Like ancient Israel, the nation had become the laughingstock of the nations, and its enemies mocked the God who would not

---

89. Ibid., lines 19–24.
90. Ibid., lines 133–40.
91. Ibid., lines 180–86.
92. Kochanowski, the outstanding poet of renaissance Poland, wrote both in Latin and in Polish.

or could not prevent such a horrible fate. According to this scenario, the restoration of an independent Poland signifies the return of God's covenant people to the promised land, and vindicates God before the scoffers. God will act, for the good of his people and the glory of His own name. Woronicz ends the *Hymn* with an allusion to the vision of Ezekiel (Ezek 37:11–12). The dry bones of the Polish Commonwealth will arise. God will restore the nation's spirit, body, and strength, his people will live with him in peace and harmony (Ezek 36:26–28).[93] The 33rd and last stanza of *Hymn to God* gives hope for the rebirth of the Polish state.

> Our tears are the witnesses of our error and redress,
> Neither can you gaze on the streams of human tears
> Nor renounce your children, O gracious Parent!
> What is left for you to do? Utter your ancient words:
> "Dry bones! Arise from your burial mounds,
> Take on spirit, and flesh, and strength!"[94]

Woronicz also ties the hope of national renewal to the New Testament account of Christ, for stanza number 33 is symbolic of the year of Christ's death and resurrection. This combination of the story of Christ and belief in the political significance of Poland's national crisis anticipates the romantic poets, who rejected Woronicz's thesis regarding Poland's guilt[95] but agreed that the partitions of Poland were international crimes against freedom. They also shared his belief in the divine purpose behind historical events, and saw the partitions as a new beginning for Poland, which would become a blessing to the nations. Yet Poland must pass the test, not by repentance as Woronicz taught, but through faith and spiritual labor. In order to regain its independence, and thereby to pass the torch of freedom on to the nations, Poland must itself become free spiritually.

Woronicz repeatedly interpreted contemporary events as signs of Poland's imminent deliverance by God's hand. He placed his faith in a series of political and military leaders, whom he hoped would reestablish an independent Polish state. Nevertheless, as a student of Scripture he

---

93. Rejman, *Jan Paweł Woronicz*, 50.

94. Woronicz, *Hymn to God*, 33rd stanza, lines 193–98.

95. Janion and Żmigrodzka, *Romantyzm i historia*, 68: "[The romantic poets] started from the presupposition that Poland is an innocent, Christlike offering for the freedom of the world, and not a sinner who must severely do penance for her transgressions."

knew that one can never fully grasp the mind of God. Neither his confidence that God is at work in history, nor his belief that everything has a place and a purpose in his divine plan, could be shaken by the recurring collapse of his overly optimistic readings of salvation history. As Janion concludes, Woronicz, by returning "faith in the far-reaching wisdom of the divine decrees," laid the foundation for romantic messianism.[96]

The Poet as a Preacher

The Polish National Kerygma

Woronicz was known as a powerful preacher, and he took this responsibility seriously.[97] Just as his religious convictions marked his poetic works, so his concept of culture impacted his preaching. Considering culture "a form of capital that demands to be exploited,"[98] he knew that dusty tomes on a library shelf would do little good for the national cause. If his stories and myths were to help Poland survive and regain its independence, they must instruct the nation's mind and baptize its heart. Accordingly Woronicz, continuing Poland's rich tradition of political sermons, drew on the Biblical stories concerning Israel to construct a national kerygma. Dismayed by Poland's ongoing political tragedy, which he linked to the increasing secularization of Polish society, Woronicz refused to accept either as irreversible or final. The Hebrew prophets provided him with a wealth of examples that, interpreted figuratively, spoke to contemporary events and placed the nation's downfall in the context of a story leading to its future rebirth.[99] As his biographer Rejman writes, "his sermons ... were not lectures but a search for truth, the continual confirmation of the durability of the covenant between God and the nation."[100]

At the heart of his national kerygma Woronicz placed a picture of God the loving Father, who had disciplined the wayward Poles for breaking the covenant he had forged with the nation. Such a ready explanation of the nation's tragedy was at odds with the outrage Polish

---

96. Ibid., 69.

97. Rejman writes that "among all priestly responsibilities, without a doubt the most important for Woronicz was preaching." Rejman, *Jan Paweł Woronicz*, 159.

98. Ibid., 185.

99. Rejman, *Jan Paweł Woronicz*, 161.

100. Ibid., 162–63.

patriots felt towards the foreign monarchs who had divided and now ruled Poland. In *Romanticism and History*, Janion and Żmigrodzka go so far as to argue that "the conviction regarding Poland's guilt undoubtedly favored moods amenable to accepting the decrees of Providence, but it was an agreement that (paradoxically) removed the entire pathos of revolt and doubting that preceded it, [which is] so evident within the sphere of national theodicy."[101] This statement suggests that Woronicz's providentialism promoted passive resignation to the divine decree. It also implies that Woronicz's theodicy, which understood Poland's suffering as a divine judgment for the nation's sins, led to denying the very "pathos of revolt and doubting" that led to its creation.

Woronicz's own writings show how intensely he suffered under the crushing blow of Poland's loss of sovereignty. Unless we take the struggle with doubt and despair captured in his works as a purely rhetorical device, his own faith in divine providence was shaken by the nation's catastrophe. Prior to the partitions Woronicz believed in the God of Abraham, Isaac, and Jacob, who had established an eternal covenant with the Polish people. After the partitions, Woronicz could either reject this faith, or revise it. He overcame despair and retained belief in God by adopting the viewpoint of the Old Testament prophets, who first foretold and later interpreted the exile of God's chosen people. The Hebrew prophets did not hide their "pathos of revolt and doubting." Their proclamation of God's word grew out of the passion with which they approached God, either to accuse him of abandoning the nation, or to demand answers to those tough questions that do not fit easily into a neat theological system. Scripture records their boldness in speaking, first to God and then to the nation. These prophets taught Woronicz to express his "revolt and doubting" before God's throne and to wait, patiently or no, for his answer.

Woronicz understood the events of history as God's self-revelation and the outworking of his plan. He reread the Bible and reworked his theology, in the process taking on the role of an apostle whose mission was to proclaim the gospel of the once and future Kingdom of Poland. For Woronicz, the pathos results not from God's righteous discipline but from its severity, and from the choice of the agents who carried it out. How could God allow his chosen people to be conquered by their more wicked neighbors? The vigor of Woronicz's providentialism lies in the bona fide possibility that his faith might founder on the rocks of

---

101. Janion and Żmigrodzka, *Romantyzm i historia*, 68.

Poland's historical shipwreck. Conscious of his own doubts, Woronicz knew that his hearers' faith in God's care was endangered by Poland's political demise. Belief in divine discipline does not remove the shock God's people feel when that discipline falls upon them and their children. Woronicz, their preacher, proclaimed that Poland's sufferings are proof that Poland still belongs to God, who loves the nation enough to chasten and purify it.

The Polish Patriot[102]

If the providentialism of Woronicz did not remove the Poles' pathos, did it favor "moods amenable to accepting the decrees of Providence"? Not if this means passive resignation to "fate," or the acceptance of Poland's partition as God's final plan for the nation. Woronicz fought to restore the Poles' faith in providence, not to counsel the gracious acceptance of defeat, but to restore hope for the ways things should and, by God's grace, one day will be. This hope in turn was to lead to action. Woronicz called the Poles to personal spiritual renewal and to active engagement in the nation's cause, which he modeled through his poetry, preaching, and political involvement.

Woronicz believed that when a nation falls from greatness through forgetting its past, the road to recovery is to recall the ancient paths trod by its noble ancestors. In his sermons, which described what Polish citizens should be and how they should live, he often communicated his vision of the consummate Polish patriot through idealizing the lives of great Poles.[103] Funerals thus provided Woronicz with unique opportunities to exhort the nation and to instruct its citizens as to their patriotic duty. Szczypa declares that "the funeral speeches of Woronicz ... sought to prepare the living to practice attitudes that were useful for the community."[104] As a well-known and popular preacher prior to the partitions, who held increasingly important church positions following 1795, Woronicz was chosen to deliver the funeral eulogies for many of the leaders of the pre-partition generation. He approached this task with a conscious agenda and a clear strategy. As Rejman notes, "The life

---

102. This section follows Rejman, *Jan Paweł Woronicz*, 163–67.
103. Ibid., 158.
104. Szczypa, *Jan Paweł Woronicz*, 100.

of each one of them was considered in three domains—as a person, as a citizen, and a Christian."

> The funeral speeches were constructed clearly and logically ... They consisted of three distinctive parts ... The poet in this way marked three stages in the life of a person—youth, maturity, and death. Youth was a time in "which there were formed those character traits that made them true and not defiled persons. In the age of maturity they were 'useful and not harmful citizens,' in the face of death they were shown to be 'living and not dead Christians.'"[105]

The character trait that Woronicz valued and promoted the most was a love for the fatherland that results in dedicating, and if need be sacrificing, one's life for its good. Yet all that the deceased had labored for crumbled with the fall of the Commonwealth. What came of their commitment to the nation? In answer Rejman supplies Woronicz's own words: "Let us love only that which is worthy of eternal love, let us strive for that which one can possess forever."[106] This is the paradox of patriotism as conceived of by Woronicz: Christians truly love their country when their love for God surpasses their patriotism. Rejman explains:

> In this way the original order of life: person—citizen—Christian undergoes a reversal. The perspective of eternity, i.e., being a Christian, [when set] next to everything else is shown to be cardinal and of greatest importance ... The defeat of earthly ideals is here transformed into the victory of the person—[as a] Christian. Woronicz's heroes fought with history but they did not surrender to it. For the command to be a Pole is secondary with respect to the demand of being a Christian, from which it originates.[107]

Considering a Christian's first allegiance to be towards God might lead some to conclude that love for one's country is of little value for spiritual pilgrims on their way to God's Kingdom. Woronicz drew the opposite conclusion. Setting God before nation by no means set loyalty to God against loyalty to the nation. To the contrary, argues Woronicz, a true patriot is first and foremost a true Christian. "Everything," he says, "begins with God and everything returns to him; therefore he who is

---

105. Rejman, *Jan Paweł Woronicz*, 164–65.

106. Woronicz, citied in: Rejman, *Jan Paweł Woronicz*, 164.

107. Szczypa, *Jan Paweł Woronicz, kerymat narodowy i patriotyczny*, 166.

not obedient to God cannot be faithful to the fatherland, his friends or the entire society."[108] For Woronicz, being a Christian is not the end of patriotism but its true beginning. Furthermore, Woronicz's Christian patriots are not nationalists, for when we follow this reversal (i.e., person—citizen—Christian) to the end of its path, Christian love for one's country leads on to a love for all humanity.[109]

The Polish National Catechism[110]

Drawing on his providentialism, and his philosophy of history that distinguished the nation from the state, Woronicz turned his word pictures of Polish citizens into a system of values to be inculcated, which he articulated as a national catechism for the religious and patriotic upbringing of the nation. Many of his practical conclusions followed from his belief in the covenant established between God and the Polish nation. It was the covenant that gave the "chosen nation" its own place and mission in salvation history, and which enabled, as Szczypa writes, "the linking together of two spheres of national life—patriotic and religious."[111] It was incumbent upon the nation to recognize and carry out its assigned task.

> Through getting to know its spirit every nation should seek to know its own purpose, in light of the ultimate cause which is God. For Woronicz this was one of the fundamental principles of philosophy and theology. It bore fruit in the literary ideal of Mickiewiczan messianism.[112]

Following Woronicz, the idea of covenant relationship as developed by the romantics would link the religious and patriotic aspects of Polish life for generations. The romantics developed this principle into a full-blown messianism that proclaimed Poland to be the "Christ of the Nations."

---

108. Woronicz, quoted in Rejman, *Jan Paweł Woronicz*, 166.

109. This order is not inviolate. As chapter 4 will show, it was through the love of his fellow humans that Jacek Kuroń learned to love the God he could not believe in without reservation.

110. The argument here follows Szczypa, *Jan Paweł Woronicz, kerymat narodowy i patriotyczny*.

111. Ibid., 61.

112. Ibid., 62.

> ... the idea of atonement for the sins of the world or the messianic motive of Poland's international role—that would be the contribution of the romantic thinkers, after the November Uprising, when the already mentioned messianic calling was read in the context of Divine Providence, and one was commanded to see in Poland the second "Christ of the nations"—suffering, dying, but also rising again.[113]

The providentialism expounded by Woronicz left no room for apathy or passivity. Though God was the final guarantee and ultimate cause of Poland's future freedom, his people were to fight to regain the "promised land" from which they had been figuratively driven by the partitions.[114] If the covenant marked the nation's birth, the renewal of the covenant was the essential requirement for its rebirth. "On what did Mieczysław[115] hang the first cradle of his state? On the covenant and friendship with God! From the same starting point there begins the second engrafting of our reborn seed."[116]

Woronicz discerned other elements from the past that he believed would contribute to the form taken by a renewed Polish state. These included the myth of "brotherhood" between the Polish, Russian, and Lithuanian peoples, who were destined to live in peace and equality as descendants of the ancient Sarmatians. Another element of Poland's past was the distinction between the gentry and the peasants, although for Woronicz this was not an ideal to maintain but a tradition to overcome. Reduced at times to virtual slavery, and excluded from the political life of the nation, peasants had neither a part in its ongoing development, nor anything to gain from its resurrection. Here we must recognize the "entirely new, original significance taken on by the initiatives of patriotic sermons addressed by Woronicz directly to the peasants."[117] Woronicz, who considered serfdom a "mortal illness of a political body,"[118] called for the peasants' economic liberation, to be accompanied by education and the recognition of their legal rights. He campaigned strongly for

---

113. Ibid., 70.

114. A compatibilist account of divine sovereignty and human free will.

115. The long form of Mieszko, the first historical ruler of Poland.

116. Woronicz, cited in Szczypa, *Jan Paweł Woronicz, kerymat narodowy i patriotyczny*, 64.

117. Szczypa, *Jan Paweł Woronicz, kerymat narodowy i patriotyczny*, 126.

118. Woronicz, cited in ibid., 126.

peasants' rights to be included in the constitution of the Principality of Warsaw, and sought as well to enlist the support of the gentry for this cause.

Woronicz considered the Church and the family responsible for instilling these values. He was aware of the role that the state and the educational system can play in moral and patriotic upbringing, but these were under the control of the partitioning countries, who used them more or less flagrantly to Germanize or Russify the Polish nation.

Although Woronicz considered patriotism secondary to faith and derived from it, he counted it superior to all other virtues, as the highest expression of selflessness and self-sacrifice. He could write, "Patriotism is a collection, or I might say the essence of all exalted virtues. Its source and guarantee of authenticity is religion, which alone is able to give it inspiration and motivation to this end, that one loves the common good more than their own."[119] If such exalted patriotism provokes a certain tension between love for one's nation and the respect of other nations, Woronicz tempered any incipient nationalism with the idea of the brotherhood between the Sarmatian peoples. At a deeper level, he considered freedom and international brotherhood to be the special contribution of Christianity to the Polish national character or spirit. As Szczypa writes, "The decisive factor in the role of religion in the patriotic upbringing of society is the fact, that Christianity brought in the Gospel the picture of true freedom and showed the road that led to it . . . These on the one hand are capable of making all people equal before the law, and on the other to protect them from the abuse of wrongly understood freedom and social egalitarianism."[120] If we refrain from second-guessing what is meant by "wrongly understood freedom and social egalitarianism,"[121] Szczypa's quote captures the heart of the message proclaimed by Woronicz and his romantic heirs, who believed just as fervently that the person or nation that would be free in this world must first become free spiritually. Like Woronicz, Mickiewicz and the romantics would make this message the heart of their program for national renewal and deliverance.

119. Ibid., 92.
120. Ibid., 94.
121. Szczypa understands freedom as "positive" freedom to do good, vis-à-vis "negative," libertine freedom. What he means by "social egalitarianism" is a thornier matter.

The Poet as a Politician

The Polish nation looked to its poets for direction in socio-political affairs. Writing of the role Polish romantic poets played in the political life of partitioned Poland, Przybylski stresses the part Woronicz played in establishing this model in a nation deprived of normal political expression:

> The social function of the poet was here equated with the function of a religious leader . . . Polish bards and druids rather quickly began to fulfill political functions, for the simple reason that every form of leadership by its very nature belongs to the political sphere.[122]

Woronicz himself followed this path from poetry to politics. His many positions in the Church hierarchy led to his appointment in 1815 as the bishop of Kraków. In 1828, towards the end of his life, he was installed as the archbishop of Warsaw and the Primate of Poland. Throughout his life he was involved in academic and charitable societies. He also held many government posts. During the Kościusko Uprising he served as the commissar of the Committee for Order of the Principality of Mazovia[123] (1794–1795). In the Principality of Warsaw[124] he was a member of the Department of War and Administration from 1806 until 1810, when he joined the Bureau of Internal Affairs and Religious Rites. In 1816 he became a senator of the Kingdom of Poland.[125] On May 24, 1829, in one of his last political acts as Primate, he crowned Czar Nicholas I as the King of Poland.

Studying this list, one observes that Woronicz served in the administration of several governments, including that of the last lawful king, an administration appointed by the leaders of a national uprising, and two more or less autonomous regimes established through the "benevolence" of France and Russia. Despite appearances, his political career has a more plausible explanation than mere opportunism. Believing that history is the revelation of God's providential plan, Woronicz was on constant lookout for signs that God was about to restore Poland's lost

---

122. Przybylski, *Klasycyzm, czyli prawdziwy koniec Królestwa Polskiego*, 210.
123. The central district of Poland, of which Warsaw is the capital.
124. A small rump state established by Napoleon.
125. A semi-autonomous region established by the Treaty of Vienna (1815). The Treaty gave the bulk of Poland to Russia and declared its czar as the Polish king.

glory, as well as for the divine agent who would accomplish the people's deliverance. His philosophy of history, his confidence in God's covenant faithfulness, and his passionate love for Poland led him to "recognize" its deliverer in such diverse figures as King Stanisław August Poniatowski, General Tadeusz Kosciuszko, Emperor Napoleon Bonaparte, Prince Józef Poniatowski, and Czar Nicholas I.

Although Woronicz was active in politics and government, perhaps his most significant impact on the political life of the nation came through his sermons and speeches. The dramatic events of his day imparted urgency and relevance to his public addresses and overtly political sermons. Called by the nature of his office to address current affairs, he knew the dangers inherent to interpreting salvation history or predicting the future.[126] To complicate matters his messages were often read by censors, or addressed to audiences that included both Poles and their conquerors. Yet Woronicz faced the challenge squarely. The address entitled, "A sermon at the funeral of the remains brought to Warsaw of Prince Józef Poniatowski" illustrates well the ethical dilemmas and historiosophical pitfalls that Woronicz faced. Prince Józef, the nephew of Poland's last King, led the Polish forces serving under Napoleon. He perished with his troops when he refused to surrender even though the battle's outcome was no longer in doubt. This act endeared him to his fellow countrymen, and earned him a place within the pantheon of romantic heroes. The striking thing, however, about Woronicz's sermon is that it praises both Prince Józef and the Russian czar Alexander against whose troops he was fighting. Such a seemingly contradictory attitude was typical of the entire funeral celebration. Alexander, who allowed the Prince's remains to be returned to the country and buried there, as an outlet for the Poles' patriotic feelings and to salve their wounded honor, reportedly said to an Austrian delegate in 1816: "For the purpose of quieting the Poles one must praise their national self-love. Treating them as I currently do, I make them Russians, while at the same time it will seem to them that they are still Poles."[127]

Regarding the funeral, Rejman agrees with the opinion of Kijowski, who suggests that "everything was orchestrated from beginning to end, the authors of poems, eulogies acted 'in accordance with the written or unwritten instructions' of the czar." Yet as Rejman goes on to show,

---

126. Rejman, *Jan Paweł Woronicz*, 167.
127. Alexander I, quoted in ibid., 169.

the actual situation was much more complicated. As she writes, "The Czar was not the sole author of the script of these ceremonies. There were actually two contradictory scripts."[128] To prove her point, Rejman quotes Woronicz's eulogy to Prince Józef. In words addressed to the "powerful and sensitive victor," the "new Titus" of the North, Woronicz proclaimed his expectation that Alexander, "by the inspiration of his renowned goodness, [by] his brotherly heart, and [by his] might, will lift up this land flooded with tears and return its natural-born form for the peace of the whole world." As Rejman makes clear, this expectation belongs to the "second" alternate script, for "the challenge to, or rather the oath sworn upon Alexander, makes him the one who would return Poland her fatherland in its old form. Against his own desire, or will."[129]

A long line of Polish preachers and patriotic priests have carried on the tradition that Woronicz passed on to his successors, including such twentieth-century examples as Cardinal Stefan Wyższyński and Pope John Paul II. Another is Father Jerzy Popiełuszko, who was abducted and murdered in 1984 by agents of the Peoples' Republic of Poland. Wojciech Maziarski sets the stage for understanding the significance and impact of Popiełuszko's sermons:

> Those were strange times—in spite of censorship and the flood of raucous propaganda, [there were] certain things about which One Knew, certain things that One Did Not Do, certain newspapers that One Did Not Read, certain people to whom One Did Not Extend one's hand, and certain organizations to which One Did Not Belong.[130]

But how did One Know? Where did this knowledge come from? And why did One Not Do certain things? Jesus said, "You shall know the truth and the truth shall set you free." To which the Apostle Paul adds, "But how will they believe unless they hear? And how will they hear unless somebody tells them?" Popiełuszko, like Woronicz before him, told them. He recalled the truths that were hidden deep within their hearts, and which had their source in the Polish pentateuch, in the myths gathered and passed along by Woronicz and the romantics,

---

128. Rejman, *Jan Paweł Woronicz*, 170.
129. Ibid., 172.
130. Madziarski, "One Remembers the Priest," 16.

in the stories generations of patriotic fathers and mothers told to their children.

> Father Popiełuszko did not reveal unknown facts, did not proclaim any revelations. He simply gave verbal expression to that with which his hearers sympathized and to what they believed. His public appearances created a space in which the individual "I know," "you know," and "he knows" were transformed into the common One Knows. Furthermore, from this One Knows there resulted practical consequences—for after all since One Knows, One also Acts accordingly.[131]

In a world of lies Father Popiełuszko said what everyone knew in their heart to be true. And that changed everything, for since One Knew the truth, One also Acted according to it. Maziarski continues,

> Individuals who do not remember those days find it hard to imagine how it was possible that under the conditions of dictatorship so many people behaved so decently and courageously. [. . .] The moral command to behave decently—behind which stood only the sanction of infamy and the ostracism of the community—turned out to be stronger than the pressures and threats of the rulers. [. . .] Father Popiełuszko was one of the most important people by whose efforts this unwritten ethical code of a proper citizen maintained its obligatory power. The norms formulated in the Warsaw church of St. Stanisław Kostek radiated throughout the entire country.[132]

When one knows the truth, one is obligated to live by it. When a nation knows the truth, its people have a common responsibility to live by it. For over 200 years Poland has not lacked for priests and prophets who would call the nation's citizens back to their God and remind them of their duty to their country. This is the lasting legacy of Jan Paweł Woronicz.

---

131. Ibid.
132. Ibid.

3

The Flowering of Polish Messianism
Adam Mickiewicz: Patriotic Pilgrim

THE IMPORTANCE OF MICKIEWICZ TO POLISH LITERATURE, CULTURE, national identity, and political aspirations over the last two centuries can hardly be overstated. His work, in particular his poetry, is therefore given a fuller treatment in this chapter than was the case for Woronicz. The discussion here focuses more on description and interpretation, in anticipation of the critique that will come in chapter 6.

The Pilgrim's Path: "Ode to Youth"; "The Sailor"; "Romanticity"

Adam Bernard Mickiewicz was a patriotic pilgrim. His life was a physical pilgrimage, from the family home in Belarus, to his college days in Vilnius, to forced service in czarist Russia, and finally to political exile in France. His life was also a spiritual pilgrimage, in search of truth, freedom, and liberation. Three early poems, "Ode to Youth," "The Sailor," and "Romanticity," capture the essence of Mickiewicz's life as a pilgrim, express the inner tensions he wrestled with throughout his life, and set the stage for the discussion of his major works that follows.

Legend[1] has it that Mickiewicz was born on Christmas Eve, 1798, three years after the final partition of Poland. He was raised a member of the minor gentry, in a multi-ethnic society where Poles mixed with Byelorussians, Lithuanians, Jews, and Tatars. His father died in 1812, the same year that Napoleon's Grand Army passed through Lithuania en route to Moscow. The Polish Legion's stay in Nowogrodek that spring provided young Mickiewicz with his only taste of freedom within the boundaries of the old Polish Commonwealth, a memorable event later

---

1. Accounts of the date, circumstances, and place of Mickiewicz's birth differ.

recorded in his national epic, *Master Thaddeus*. In 1815 he entered the University of Vilnius, then the leading intellectual center of the Polish Enlightenment, where he received broad exposure to European literature and thought.

In Vilnius Mickiewicz was co-founder of the Philomatic[2] Society. Its members' interests went beyond intellectual curiosity and comradeship. Living in a world of books and ideas, they sought to lay the foundation of a revived Poland by creating a republic of the spirit. As Siwicka writes, "the Philomats believed that the wise ideas and moral patterns that they worked out in a small community would in the near future take on strength sufficient to impart a new shape to social reality."[3] The Society was thus at heart, and soon became in fact, a conspiracy for Polish independence. In 1819 Mickiewicz left Vilnius for his assigned post as a teacher, but kept in touch with his Philomat colleagues through letters and visits. In 1820 he sent them a poem entitled "Ode to Youth," which reflects the influence of Frederick von Schiller and Lord Byron. This poem marks the "official" birth of Polish romanticism, and became the battle cry for Polish independence. In it Mickiewicz advocates an ethic of personal sacrifice for the common good that remained a cardinal principle of his thought throughout his life. The Poles understood his call to "throw off violence with violence" as a summons to armed uprising.

"Ode to Youth" reflects the "generation gap" typical of romanticism. Although the social transformations occurring throughout Europe contributed to a sense of youthful alienation across the continent, in Poland tensions between young and old were particularly strong. Mickiewicz, who like his peers blamed the "elders" for Poland's downfall, perceived them as a reactionary force unable to chart a forward course. They are described in "Ode to Youth," as being "without hearts, without spirit, mere skeletons of men." Blind to spiritual reality, their heads bowed with age, they could see only the world of "things," which like those who gaze upon it is dead. In contrast, "Youth" is personalized as a creative force that inspires and empowers. Those with eyes to see and hearts to feel rise above this dark world on the wings of Youth, to a paradise of the spirit where "enthusiasm" gives birth to hope and to miracles. There, in a poetic summary of romantic epistemology, they will "Reach, where

---

2. I.e., "lovers of learning."
3. Siwicka, *Romantyzm*, 11.

sight cannot reach, Break, what reason cannot break." However, theirs is not a solo flight. If faith grants them sight, it is unity that gives them strength. Life has purpose and joy only in the fellowship of kindred souls who strive for a common purpose. If they would unite in the fight for freedom, and together conquer their fears and weaknesses, then victory over oppression and darkness was sure!

> Behold, love is breathing fire,
> The world of the spirit emerges from the tumult:
> Youth conceives it in its womb,
> And friendship unites it with eternal bonds.
>
> The unfeeling ice is cracking
> And the superstitions that obscure the light;
> Greet the dawn of liberty,
> Salvation comes with the rising sun![4]

Significantly, love and not vengeance is the motivating force behind youth's creative power. The "world of the spirit" will usher in a new age in which love, the ethic of the Christian gospel, rules relationships between the nations. Here an apocalyptic eschatology takes center stage. As Mickiewicz announced a few lines earlier,

> One "Let there be!" by God's might,
> And the world of things shall fall in line.[5]

The winter snow, or "unfeeling ice," that covers Siberia is a metaphor both for imperialistic Russia, impervious to the cries of oppressed nations, and for the classicists, whose cold hearts were insensitive to the "dawn of liberty." Both must make way for the coming of the new world. Autocracy's freezing winter will crack and melt beneath the rising sun of liberty. By replacing the dead world with the world of the spirit, Mickiewicz imparts a universal significance to the vision. The salvation he proclaims is freedom not just for Poland but for the nations.

While the Philomatic Society provided Mickiewicz with a community of the spirit, his poem "The Sailor" reflects the individual nature of his spiritual pilgrimage. Not all the Philomats approved of the new directions that he was taking. Some, afraid he would founder in un-

---

4. Mickiewicz, *Wiersze*, 16.
5. Ibid.

charted waters, urged him to return to the safety of their known paths. His response minced no words:

> What I feel, others long in vain to feel!
> [The right] to judge us is given to no one except God.
> If you want to judge me, you must be not with me but within me,
> I shall sail on, you go back home.[6]

Mickiewicz prefers a small boat in a great storm to the safety and stability of the shore. Determined to discover truth, he will explore the spiritual world, and unravel the meaning of history—alone, if none will follow. In this poem, as Chlebowski writes, "he opposed his own closest environment, his circle of friends, the Philomats, to whom he announces, that they are neither able to share his feelings, nor to pronounce judgment upon him."[7] What then became of the Philomats' efforts to create a new society? Would salvation come from the people, from a band of dedicated comrades, or through a great leader? This tension is inherent in messianism, which oscillates between expectations of individual and corporate messiahs. Mickiewicz never resolved this question definitively. Throughout his life he sought comrades to share his journey, yet he was frustrated by the failure of their corporate endeavors. Both *Konrad Wallenrod* and *Forefathers' Eve*, Part III[8] reflect his increasing anticipation of an individual deliverer.

"Ode to Youth" and "The Sailor" share the conviction that truth cannot be gained through empirical research alone, for it concerns the spiritual world. This theme is further developed in "Romanticity" (1822), where Mickiewicz announced this revolutionary slogan:

> Feeling and faith speak more powerfully to me,
> Than the glass and eye of the wise.[9]

In the poem, a peasant girl meets the spirit of her dead lover. The village people, who see nothing, nevertheless believe that she sees and speaks with her beloved. The words above are addressed to an old man, who as Siwicka explains, "personifies in this ballad narrow-minded rationalism, which admits to be true only that which has been empiri-

---

6. Ibid., 102.

7. Chlebowski, *Literatura Polska Porozbiorowa jako Główny Wyraz Życia Narodu po Utracie Niepodległości*, 94.

8. Both works are discussed below.

9. Mickiewicz, *Wiersze*, 29.

cally tested and scientifically proven."[10] Mickiewicz addresses the old man:

> You know dead truths unknown to the people,
> You see the world within a grain of powder, in every spark of the stars,
> You know not living truths, you shall not see a miracle;
> Have a heart and look within the heart.[11]

In the poem's header, as Przybylski points out, Mickiewicz employs the phrase "the eyes of my soul" from Shakespeare's *Hamlet* to express a new idea.[12] Hamlet saw his father's spirit with his real eyes, a sight presumably visible to anyone present that night. The girl in "Romanticity" saw her lover with the spiritual eyes of her soul; he was visible to no one else. Mickiewicz's advice to the old man, "Have a heart, and look within your heart," became the battle cry of his generation. The enlightenment's faith in reason and science allows only what can be seen with "glass and eye," i.e., the telescope and microscope, the instruments of empirical science. Mickiewicz relied instead on "feeling and faith" in his search for truth. This romantic epistemology and view of inspiration will be critiqued in chapter 6.

The Pilgrim's Poetry

In the World But Not of the World: Forefathers' Eve, Parts II and IV (1822)

Forefathers' Eve, an example of romantic "open form" literature, purposefully breaks the set forms of Enlightenment classicism. Behind this genre lies the view of a world full of turmoil and conflict, though not devoid of purpose or hope. The world is in process—along with Gustaf-Konrad, the hero of *Forefathers' Eve*. Parts II and IV provide insight into Mickiewicz's personal pilgrimage essential to the understanding of Part III.[13]

   10. Siwicka, *Romantyzm*, 17.
   11. Mickiewicz, *Wiersze*, 29.
   12. Przybylski, *Klasycyzm, czyli prawdziwy koniec Królestwa Polskiego*, 415–20.
   13. Parts II and IV, written in Vilnius and Kowno, were published in 1823. Part III, which follows Part IV, was written in Dresden following the collapse of the November Uprising and published in Paris in 1832.

Part II is based on the observance of "Forefathers' Eve" and reflects the author's romantic fascination with folk-lore. Lithuanian and Byelorussian villagers would gather annually in a chapel or cemetery to call up the restless dead, who remained trapped between this world and the afterlife. The living offered food and drink to comfort those spirits who appeared. In Mickiewicz's literary rendition of such a séance, an apparition with a bleeding heart appears unbidden. Coming at his own initiative, he refuses to obey the medium or return to the spiritual world. Although he is described more fully in "Ustęp," which bridges Parts II and IV, it is still not clear if he is alive or dead. In Part IV, written two years later, we learn the man-spirit's name: Gustaf. Gustaf lives in two worlds, neither fully alive nor completely dead, and his appearance to the parish priest shatters his former teacher's orderly vision of the world. Gustaf's story reveals the cause of his bleeding heart. Though he and his lover Maryla were destined for each other in the spiritual world, in real life such happiness was not to be. Maryla marries another who offers her comfort and material possessions.

Part IV is largely autobiographical, relating Mickiewicz's romance with Maryla Wereszczakówna. Already engaged when they met, and under pressure from her family, she married Wawrzyniec Puttkammer, who knowing her affection for the young poet granted her the freedom to give her heart to Mickiewicz. Mickiewicz's adoration soon turned to passion. The resulting account of their ill-fated love, a masterful reflection of human psychology, betrays the poet's interest in mysticism, and his life-long belief that the visible and spiritual worlds intersect and influence each other. This experience of unfulfilled love destroyed Mickiewicz's youthful faith in happy endings, along with the idealism of the Philomats. Though he maintained his friendship with the Philomats, the themes of the Fatherland, learning, glory, and friendship ceased for a time to move his soul or motivate him to action, The Society, however, met an abrupt end on November 4, 1823. Mickiewicz, arrested along with other members of the Society, spent Christmas Eve with them in his cell, a night that he later described in *Forefathers' Eve*, Part III. He was released a few months later and deported to Russia, where he spent the next five years.

The Ethics of Resistance: Konrad Wallenrod [14] (1828)

Mickiewicz introduces the theme of *Konrad Wallenrod* with the words of Machiavelli: "But you must know this, that there are two ways of fighting . . . one must be a fox and a lion." The story line is revealed in Konrad's songs, and the tales and ballads of Halban, an old Lithuanian bard. The story begins during a raid into Lithuania, when the Teutonic Knights capture a small boy named Alf. Though adopted and given the name of Walter by the Knights' Grand Master, in his heart he remains Lithuanian. Among the warriors who killed his father, with his mother's death cry ringing in his ears, Walter cannot find a home. Halban's songs reawaken his longing for the country he barely remembers, and he longs for revenge. During another foray into Lithuania, Walter and Halban escape to rejoin the Lithuanians. There Aldona, daughter of the chieftain Kiejstut, teaches him the language and meaning of love. Halban sings:

> He heard from her lips the long forgotten words.
> With every revived word there awoke new emotions
> Like sparks from the ashes; they were sweet names
> Kinship, friendship, sweet friendship, and further
> The sweetest word of all, the word love, which
> Has no equal on earth, except the word—fatherland.[15]

Alf and Aldona soon marry, and spend years of happiness together. But there is a word greater than love—the "fatherland." Their idyllic world is threatened, for the Teutonic Knights renew their attacks, and Alf joins his father-in-law in the fight. Here Mickiewicz follows Woronicz, who declared that love for the fatherland is a Christian's highest duty, above romantic love and the meeting of kindred hearts.

> Walter loved his wife, but he had a noble soul;
> He found no joy at home, for there was no joy in the fatherland.[16]

Alf cannot escape his patriotic duty to enjoy marital bliss. He must defend Lithuania's freedom and avenge its enemies. But the Order is strong and it continues to recruit new forces. Although Lithuania may

---

14. Mickiewicz wrote of Lithuania and Prussia to describe Polish efforts to regain their independence from Russia. His story somehow passed the Czar's censors, but it's message was not lost on his Polish readers.

15. Mickiewicz, *Powieści poetyckie*, 107.

16. Ibid., 108.

win many battles, he knows it eventually must fall. The personal tragedy of his youth will be multiplied thousands of times over. Aldona suggests they move deep into the Lithuanian forests, yet Alf knows that their enemies will come there too.

> Wringing her hands she asks Walter, what is there to do?—
> One way, Aldona, one only is left to Lithuanians
> To break the power of the Order; I know that way,
> But do not ask, for God's sake! The hour is cursed a hundred times over
> In which I am forced by the enemy to seize that way![17]

Halban had revealed that cursed way to Walter when they were still captives of the Order.

> Free knights—he said—are free to choose their weapon
> And in the open field fight in fair battle;
> You are a slave, the only weapon of a slave—[is] treachery
> Stay yet and learn the arts of war from the Germans,
> Seek to win their trust, then I shall see what to do.[18]

The knightly code calls for a fair and open fight, but this privilege is denied to slaves, whose only resort is to trickery and deceit. Mickiewicz's generation accepted this as a plan of action. The November Uprising of 1830 began with young Polish officers in the Czar's army, who enacted this play in real life. Yet Halban's advice creates a moral dilemma for Alf. He is willing to die to defend his country, but he knows its cause is doomed. Perceiving that treachery alone gives hope for victory, he shrinks from that "cursed way," at once contrary to the chivalric code and foreign to Christianity, which teaches that noble ends do not justify ignoble means. Alf's battle for his nation becomes a battle for his honor, and ultimately for his soul. Can he be true to Lithuania by deceiving her enemies? Can he remain faithful to his wife while betraying his enemies? These questions do not trouble the pagan Halban, but haunt Alf's Christian soul. Ironically, this hero of a yet-pagan nation grasps the Gospel's essence more clearly than the "Christian" knights of the Order.

In the end, Alf chooses the cursed way. He rises early to leave his beloved Lithuania, and his beloved wife. But Aldona intercepts him on

17. Ibid., 111.
18. Ibid., 106.

the road. Sharing his terrible plan with her, he urges her to consider him dead and to return to her previous life. And so Alf leaves, sacrificing his personal happiness and knightly honor for his nation's good. Now all that remains is Walter and his dreadful mission. Leaving Lithuania to fight in the Crusades, he takes service under Konrad Wallenrod, a German count whom he then murders. Assuming the dead man's identity, "Konrad" wins fame as a brave, cruel warrior. He joins the Order and is chosen as its Grand Master. His plan is to lead the Knights to a crippling defeat through his purposefully inept leadership. His words to Aldona are prophetic: he will "betray, murder, and then die a shameful death." Knights who win great battles, or die trying, are honored for their bravery and sacrifice. But the knight who stoops to murder, lies, and treachery dies a traitor's death. A great but tragic man, he assumes the burden of saving his nation at the risk of losing his own soul. Aldona's only comfort is that Konrad will save Lithuania from destruction. He will perish, but his deeds will live on in song.

There is another hero in this story, or rather heroine. As a child Aldona dreamed of great deeds, of flying away into the sky. She taught Alf to love, and in return he gave her wings on which to soar. Theirs are two hearts joined in a higher, spiritual union. He told her tales of the wider world, taught her to read, and introduced her to the true God in heaven. She declares,

> For to where shall one fly, for what delights,
> Who has known the great God in heaven,
> And has loved a great man on earth?[19]

Aldona does not hold her husband back, for she too loves Lithuania more than Alf. This greater love rescues them from Gustaf's despair, and enables them to act decisively in this world, while remaining spiritually one with each other and their nation. Instead of returning home or retiring to a convent, Aldona secretly accompanies her beloved on his dreadful mission. Knowing that Alf will one day return to the Order's seat in Marienburg,[20] she is closed at her own request in the tower outside the castle that becomes her hermitage. Her new life of solitude becomes, like Konrad's, a life behind a mask. Though she would never embrace him again, she is content to pray for him and stand by him in

---

19. Ibid., 89.
20. In Polish, *Malbork*.

spirit, hoping someday to hear his name from a passing soldier's lips, to see his face, perhaps to speak to him when he passes beneath her tower. That chance arrives just when Konrad's opportunity comes to wreak his vengeance on the Order. Prepared to guarantee his people's safety by leading the Knights to destruction, he discovers Aldona hidden within the tower. Their reunion is joyous but painful. Konrad's tender feelings awake, and he is torn between his terrible duty and his longing for Aldona. Gone is the youthful idealism that enabled him to make superhuman sacrifices. The young man who was ready to sacrifice all for his country now falters in his maturity.

> Youth! How great are your sacrifices!
> In my youth, I could sacrifice
> Love, happiness, heaven, for the good of my country,
> With regret, yet with courage![21] But today I am old,
> Today duty, despair, God's will
> Drive me into the field! And I, gray-haired
> Do not dare to tear myself from the feet of these walls,
> That I might not lose—your conversation![22]

Not even Halban's songs can keep Konrad from forsaking his mission. Had Aldona also wavered, he might have turned aside to enjoy her presence once again. Instead, she reminds him of his commitment and calling. It is her strength and resolve that enable him to persevere. Aldona thus became the model for generations of Polish women, who watched and prayed while their husbands and lovers took part in conspiracies or fought in uprisings.

Konrad leads the Knights into battle, and their forces are shattered. Returning to Marienburg with a few survivors, he announces to Aldona that the deed is accomplished. Now they can take off their masks and share the remaining years of life. Konrad, renouncing further vengeance, confesses that "I too am a man," and declares that "Germans are also human."[23] Despite playing the role of a ruthless warrior, and destroying those whose trust he labored to win, Konrad still has human feelings. He also remains a Christian, for he recognizes that his enemies are also human beings, created like him in God's image.

---

21. This recalls the words of the Philomats.
22. Ibid., 93.
23. Ibid., 128.

But there is no happy ending for Alf and Aldona, for the Knights discover Konrad's betrayal. Condemned to death, he forestalls his executioners by drinking poison. But the story does not end there. Halban declines the cup, for he must return to Lithuania to sing of Konrad's dark victory and tragic fall. In a romantic variation on Virgil, the bard declares: "From our song the avengers of our bones will arise."[24] Such songs, by bringing their hearers into contact with the nation's past, enable them to discover the nation's spirit beating within their breast. Halban exclaims:

> If I were able to pour my own fire
> Into the breast of my listener, and revive the figures
> Of the dead past; if I could shoot
> With resounding words to my brothers' hearts,
> Perhaps in that single moment,
> When they are yet moved by the song of their fatherland,
> They would feel within themselves the beating of ancient hearts,
> Feel within themselves the ancient greatness of spirit,
> And in that single moment experience such exaltation,
> As their ancestors experienced throughout their entire lives.[25]

Thus Mickiewicz understood his mission. As Kozicki wrote, "Mickiewicz never departed from this conception of the task of the poet-seer. Everything that he wrote or said was shooting 'with resounding words to my brothers' hearts.'"[26] As intended, these songs inspired their readers to patriotic feelings and deeds. Generations of Poles read *Konrad Wallenrod* as a handbook for conspiracy and a call to armed uprising. Those who took up arms, particularly in the January Uprising (1861–1863), fought not only to regain Polish independence but to keep the national spirit alive. After years of foreign rule, the nation was falling inexorably into slumber. Even if their efforts failed, the partisans believed they could at least awaken the sleeping nation. Successive generations, decimated in failed conspiracies and suppressed uprisings, paid the ultimate price to keep freedom's hope alive.

Chlebowski's positivist agenda is visible in his comments on *Konrad Wallenrod*. Shying away from the moral dilemma faced by Konrad, he downplays the role of deceit and treachery, while praising

---

24. Echoes of Woronicz, in his call for the creation of a national pentateuch.
25. Ibid., 103.
26. Kozicki, *Dziedzictwo polityczne trzech wieszczów*, 74.

the work's contribution to awakening patriotism and encouraging dedication, sacrifice, and solidarity with the nation.[27] It is thus Chlebowski[28] who removed the "entire pathos of doubt and rebellion," by skirting the thorny questions the poet took on in hand-to-hand combat. As Siwicka explains, "the duality of the figure of Wallenrod has also a moral dimension . . . His actions are governed by two contradictory principles: faithfulness and treachery. In the name of faithfulness he must be unfaithful, he must betray. It is a tragic conflict."[29] The Poles, who valued freedom above everything, knew that freedom is not everything. In their fight for independence, they sensed that those who use terror to win freedom become terrorists, not free human beings. Those who live behind a mask find that it slowly but inexorably becomes part of their identity.

Mickiewicz, under Towianski's spiritualizing influence, later recanted the view that ends justify the means, and that patriots may risk their souls to save their nation. Nevertheless here, deep in the heart of Russia, that enormous and powerful country that threatened the existence of his beloved Poland, he stated it clearly: You must be a fox as well as a lion. Kozicki, commenting on *Konrad Wallenrod*, betrays his affiliation with the *endecja*[30] movement when he asks rhetorically, "Are the same moral directives binding in the battle between nations as in relationships between individuals? Can Christian morality be introduced into relationships between groups of people?"[31] The *endecja* taught that while personal life is governed by the Gospel, national existence is a matter of "kill or be killed." Such consistent social Darwinism allows no room for weakness and compassion, nor does it refrain from employing any and all means judged likely to be "effective" in furthering the national cause. Were Poles then forced to choose between Chlebowski's positivism and Kozicki's integral nationalism? Must they either renounce treachery, or relegate their Christian faith to the private domain? Is it to be reform or revolution, compromise or eternal conflict? Such vexing questions would continue to haunt the Poles, who waited for generations to

---

27. Chlebowski, *Literatura Polska Porozbiorowa jako Główny Wyraz Życia Narodu po Utracie Niepodległości*, 105.
28. Not Woronicz as Janion suggested.
29. Siwicka, *Romantyzm*, 38–39.
30. I.e., the National Democrats.
31. Kozicki, *Dziedzictwo polityczne trzech wieszczów*, 72.

discover a third option.³² For now we simply note with Cieśla-Korytowska that Mickiewicz erred by his later rejection of Konrad Wallenrod, for he forgot that he had created a hero of action and not only of deceit.³³

The Pedagogy of Resistance: "To a Polish Mother" (1830)

In 1829 Mickiewicz's Russian friends arranged a passport for him to leave the country. For the next year and a half he traveled through Europe, where the outbreak of the November Uprising found him in Rome. Torn between a feeling of obligation to fight, and his own political judgment that the Uprising was untimely and doomed to collapse, he failed in a belated attempt to cross into the Russian-controlled Kingdom of Poland. With some notable exceptions, his fellow Poles largely forgave his non-presence on the frontlines.³⁴ Perhaps he rightly sensed he was worth more to the nation as a poet than as a fighter. Yet his poetry called for congruence between word and deed, and there is no greater transgression for a romantic poet than to obey the mind rather than follow the heart. Mickiewicz's later efforts to organize Polish legions in Italy and Turkey may have been in part attempts to redeem this dereliction of the self-imposed romantic duty to fight with sword as well as with pen.

While still in Rome, Mickiewicz wrote "To a Polish Mother." Kozicki reports that the poet later told Michał Chodźka that he had sensed the outbreak of the Uprising while writing this moving poem.³⁵ Mickiewicz's friend and confidant Armand Levy, confirms that the poet foresaw both the Uprising and its disastrous outcome, and wrote "To a Polish Mother" to prepare the Poles for the "great days of suffering" that were approaching.³⁶ Kozicki sees this poem as "pessimistic," which certainly describes its author's attitude at the time. Mickiewicz instructs the mother that her son,

> Will not go out, like knights of old,
> To thrust a victorious cross in Jerusalem,

---

32. Cf. chapter 4, IIC, "Citizens' Society."

33. Cieśla-Korytowska, "O polskim bohaterze romantycznym po latach," 143–45.

34. Later critics more often condemned him for inspiring others to die in a futile cause.

35. Kozicki, *Dziedzictwo polityczne trzech wieszczów*, 77.

36. Levy, from a 1877 oration delivered at the unveiling of a memorial plaque to Mickiewicz in Rome, in Kridl, *Mickiewicz*, 239.

> Or like the soldiers of a new world[37]
> To fight for freedom, to soak the earth with blood.[38]

Rather than meet victory or death on the battlefield, her son will conspire in secret, stand before a traitor's court, hang on the gallows, wallow in the czar's prisons, or perish in the Siberian snow. No hero's welcome awaits, no honorable burial, not even the bard's song that immortalized the deeds of Konrad Wallenrod, only "the tears of women, and the long, nighttime conversations of his countrymen." The Polish mother must prepare her sons for a life of treachery, pain, suffering, and death, for only by refusing to surrender to defeat can the nation keep alive its hope for freedom. It is a chilling picture.

Ruszkowski, noting the relationship here between the Crusaders' Cross (a controversial symbol at best) and the American Revolution, explores the metaphorical significance of Jerusalem and the New World. In the end he agrees with Kleiner that this poem, by denying hopes of reaching the Promised Land or replaying the American and French Revolutions, plants the seeds of new directions that would soon appear in Mickiewicz's writings.[39] Kleiner writes:

> This double negation announces a new positive idea of unheard-of importance, [i.e.,] equating the battle for freedom with the battle for religion, confessing the matter of freedom to be a religious matter, the current fighting cause of Christianity. This makes the hopelessness of the verse "To a Polish Mother" the first step on the road towards the faith of *The Books of the Nation* and the "Vision of Father Peter."[40]

The Christ of the Nations: Forefathers' Eve, Part III (1832)

THE BIRTH OF A HERO

The aftermath of the November Uprising left Mickiewicz an exile. He expressed the insights gained through his identification with the sufferings of his beloved nation in *Forefathers' Eve*, Part III. Although *Forefathers'*

---

37. A reference to the American Revolution.
38. Mickiewicz, *Wiersze*, 281.
39. Cf. Ruszkowski, *Adam Mickiewicz i ostatnia krucjata: studium romantycznego millenaryzmu*, 67–69.
40. Kleiner, *Mickiewicz*, 240.

Eve is a complex and fragmentary work, its unifying thesis is that the spiritual and physical worlds intersect and impinge on each other. It was Mickiewicz's life-long conviction that we are all caught, like Gustaf, between the physical and spiritual realms. Unity is also achieved in the figure of Gustaf-Konrad, whose personal transformation in *Forefathers' Eve* mirrors that of Mickiewicz himself. The drama begins in Vilnius, with a prisoner alone in his prison cell on All Hallows' Eve. Grasping a piece of charcoal, he writes these words on the wall:

> Gustaf died, November 1, 1823. Here was born Konrad, November 1, 1823.[41]

Thus Gustaf, the jilted lover from *Forefathers' Eve*, Parts II and IV, adopts the name and character of the loving husband from *Konrad Wallenrod*, who sacrificed his idyllic life for his country. This transformation from lover to patriot became a sacred model for Poles. Chlebowski exclaims that, ". . . from Maryla's despairing lover, grown temporarily indifferent to all the slogans of the Philomats, [and] to the tasks enumerated in 'Ode to Youth,' there comes forth a man, capable like Konrad of committing everything for the fatherland, and above all of dedicating to its cause the entire power of his spirit, all the magnificence of his artistry."[42] Siwicka aptly summarizes this casting off of one's private life and personal happiness for the common good:

> Konrad begins to live for other people, for the nation. The "lover of women" becomes the "lover of the Fatherland." The biography of the hero is hereafter united with the history of the nation.[43]

Later that night Konrad's friends and fellow-prisoners are allowed to visit him.[44] A fellow prisoner, Jan Sobolewski, has just returned from being interrogated. A teacher in Żmudź until his arrest, he was co-founder with Cyprian Janczewski of the "The Black Brothers," an offshoot of the Philomats that operated among high school students. In the city Sobolewski saw young Polish prisoners being taken away to

---

41. Mickiewicz, *Utwory Dramatyczne*, 129.

42. Chlebowski, *Literatura Polska Porozbiorowa jako Główny Wyraz Życia Narodu po Utracie Niepodległości*, 133.

43. Siwicka, *Romantyzm*, 95.

44. The Philomats actually gathered on Christmas Eve. Shifting the meeting to All Hallows' Eve heightens the dramatic tension and introduces the spiritual battle about to take place.

Siberia. Mass was being held in a nearby church—yet the crowd rushes out to observe the scene. Sobolewski recognizes Janczewski, arrested together with his students. His friend has aged in prison. The happy, easy-going youth now bears the countenance of an Emperor,[45] his noble features carved by faithfulness and suffering. His courage comforts his fellow-prisoners. Gazing upon the crowd, he laughs and shakes his chains to show that his sufferings are light compared to those of the nation, and gladly borne for its sake. He does not regret his actions that led to imprisonment, torture, and exile. He remains a free man, for the chains that bind his body cannot enslave his spirit. As the wagon draws away, Janczewski stands to proclaim, "Poland has not yet perished . . ."[46] His head and his hand are held high, declaring him an innocent victim of injustice and oppression. Signs of his unbroken spirit, they are "a compass" to show "where virtue lies." Patriotism and sacrifice are thus endowed with a moral (spiritual) dimension. Sobolewski pledges to remember the martyrs, to endure suffering, and to remain free. The blessing conferred by Father Lwowic confirms this as the path of personal and national salvation. In liturgical fashion, Sobolewski's vow is vicariously taken up for all Poles by their representatives in the cell.

Sobolewski sees another group of prisoners being led out—the schoolboy members of the Black Brothers. One of them, beaten terribly, can barely walk. Climbing onto the wagon, he falls and lies dead. Picked up by a soldier and slung onto the cart, he has already gone stiff, his arms outstretched like one lowered from a cross. The crowd, gazing at his white eyes, wide open and terrible, utters one deep, common moan—as if the corpses in the nearby graveyard moaned with them. As the tortured body is lifted and the wagons begin to roll, a bell rings in the church to signal the changing of bread and wine into the body and blood of Christ. Seeing the priest lifting up the elements to God, Sobolewski utters a prayer that expresses the heart of Polish messianism: just as Christ died for the eternal salvation of the world, God means through the suffering of these innocent youths to accomplish temporal salvation for Poland and the nations.

> Lord! You, who by the judgment of Pilate
> Poured out innocent blood for the salvation of the world,
> Receive this childlike offering from the judgment of the czar,

45. I.e., Napoleon.
46. The opening words of "Marsz Dąbrowski."

Neither as holy nor as great, yet equally innocent.[47]

Chlebowski writes, "The unmatched beauty and gravity of Sobolewski's story about the deportation of the high school youth condemned to exile has its basis in the sublimity of religious feelings, which join together with patriotic agony to reveal in these youths, the underage prisoners condemned by Nowosilcow's[48] courts, the sacrifices who redeem before God a better future for the homeland."[49] This represents a significant modification of Woronicz's vision. Poles are no longer suffering as sinners, but as innocent victims of oppression and violence. Their affliction is not caused by their own guilt, but the guilt of the nations who sinned against them. In God's plan this seemingly arbitrary, senseless sacrifice of a generation, "neither as holy nor as great" as Christ but just as innocent, has significance in salvation history. The blood of these exiles and martyrs is the price of freedom, the guarantee of the nation's resurrection, and the source of blessing for the nations.

Konrad however reacts to Sobolewski's story with a song of vengeance. He sings of a common, mass grave holding the Polish martyrs who died in the struggle for freedom, and whose blood cries out for vengeance. The grave has cooled Konrad's fiery passion into a terrible, cold resolve, and he has become—like his oppressor—a vampire. He shuns the mask his namesake Wallenrod assumed, for he is not torn between love and hatred. There is no joy, no hope, and no love in his song, only hatred and vengeance. It is death, not life, which gives him strength. He seeks companions to join his cause, but his appeal is a far cry from *Ode to Youth*! Among his dead comrades in Hades, Konrad too has become a phantom. Rising from the grave to bite the living, he plants the venom of his vengeance in their hearts. They become a vast army of vampires who will not rest until the enemy is dead forever.

Konrad the vampire goes out (in song) to drink his enemies' blood. Sacrificing his own soul to avenge his fallen countrymen, he pursues his victims to hell, where he cuts their bodies in pieces, and "nails them fast." In Konrad's spiritual world, this is the inspired, prophetic song of poetry. Yet an ethic of revenge does not fit easily into the biblical

---

47. Mickiewicz, *Utwory Dramatyczne*, 143.

48. Head of the Czar's secret police, Nowosilcow led the investigation of the Philomatic Society.

49. Chlebowski, *Literatura Polska Porozbiorowa jako Główny Wyraz Życia Narodu po Utracie Niepodległości*, 187.

framework. What then is the source of this inspiration? The practice of driving a spike through the body of alleged vampires to prevent their return also hides an allusion to Christ's crucifixion, and points to the one who inspired this song—the Devil himself, who knows only one emotion—hatred, and has only one strategy—to kill. Lacking God's creativity, he falls back upon his previous mode of destruction. Though Konrad's cellmates join the cry for vengeance Father Lwowicki, the voice of orthodoxy, cries out, "Konrad, stop, for God's sake, that is a pagan song." Though Lwowicki offers no alternative, Mickiewicz concurs with his judgment. As Janion writes, "this entire work of Mickiewicz can be understood as an attempt to provide despairing patriots another way of acting than vengeance, vengeance on the enemy—to be sure completely justified, but remaining in conflict with the Christian canon of ethics."[50]

The Great Improvisation

Later that night, alone in his cell, Konrad feels powerful enough to single-handedly change his nation's fate. Whereas Wallenrod fought "like a lion and a fox" on the earthly plane, Gustaf-Konrad now carries the battle to the spiritual world. He will fight with God himself.

> Now my soul is incarnate in my fatherland;
> I have swallowed her soul with my body,
> The fatherland and I are one.
> My name is Million—because for millions
> I love and suffer torment.
> I look upon my poor fatherland,
> As a son upon his father tied to the torture wheel;
> I feel the suffering of the entire nation,
> As a mother feels the pain of her offspring in her womb.
> I suffer, I go mad—and you are always wise and happy
> You always rule,
> You always judge.
> And they say that you never err![51]

Konrad's cry of pain and exaltation, "The fatherland and I are one," asserts his right to exert spiritual authority over the millions for whom he loves and suffers torment. God, in contrast, appears to sit smugly in heaven, safe and aloof from the world below. This divine watchmaker,

---

50. Janion, *Reduta*, 483.
51. Mickiewicz, *Utwory Dramatyczne*, 162.

this deistic God of the Enlightenment, is the God of that simple providentialism attacked by Voltaire that considers all questions and doubts resolved by philosophical proofs that "this is the best of all possible worlds." The following lines confirm that the very character of God is at stake. Konrad challenges God to prove that he is the loving Father, that the millions who cry out for deliverance mean more to him than numbers in a mathematical equation. But God is silent.

Since God will not save Poland, Konrad asks for the power to bring happiness to his suffering nation. Contrasting his love with the avarice of Czars and tyrants, Konrad asks for a fraction of the power such rulers gained in their pride. In "Ode to Youth" Mickiewicz had urged his fellows to join him in flight, now as Konrad he asks for power to rule over their spirits. To make them happy, he would deny them their freedom, not realizing that he is becoming like the czar. In Konrad's brand of providentialism, human freedom is incompatible with the realization of God's divine decree or, as in this case, Konrad's superhuman plan. Though full of love, Konrad's heart is also infected with pride. God remains silent.

Konrad next appeals to reason. It will pay off, he says, for God to use him as his agent; he will do the hard work, and God will receive the praise. For a romantic like Konrad, such an argument makes God a calculating rationalist, no better than the spiritually blind representatives of the Enlightenment. Konrad claims to be the first to see God as he truly is, i.e., a calculating businessman or entrepreneur who thinks and acts selfishly in order to further his own power and glory. Konrad challenges God to prove him wrong, by speaking and by acting on behalf of his people. But God remains silent.

Though God may feel secure from all attacks, Konrad warns him that *feelings* will burn what reason cannot break. He vows to attack God's very throne, to overthrow this unmasked merchant masquerading as the loving, Heavenly Father. Reaching the height of his heavenly flight, he fires his heaviest cannons.

> You see my fire: feelings!
> I gather them up, clasp them tight, that they would burn the brighter,
> I press them into the iron bonds of my will,
> As a shell into a blazing cannon. [...]

Answer—or I will fire against your nature;
If I do not reduce it to rubble,
I will shake the entire expanse of your countries;
For I fire my voice into the whole creation:
That voice, which passes from generation to generation:
I cry, that you are not the father of the world, but ...
THE VOICE OF THE DEVIL
A Czar[52]

The spiritual battle has reached its climax. To call God a Czar is to identify him as an evil tyrant, not a loving father. Driven by demons, who exploit the fact that Konrad's great heart is matched only by his pride, Konrad comes to the brink of blasphemy and thus of losing his soul. But it is the devil, over-anxious to claim his prey, who shouts the actual word of blasphemy, thus inadvertently saving his victim. Konrad falls to the ground, unconscious. Father Peter arrives, exorcises the demons, and releases Konrad from his spiritual bondage.

The conflict between God and Konrad, Konrad and the nation, and within Konrad himself, takes place on several levels. Theologically, Konrad's chosen weapon is *feelings*, i.e., prophetic inspiration, the divine gift that puts the poet in touch with spiritual truth, hence with God Himself. Konrad has determined to fight God with God! Furthermore, he believes that God is love, for his appeal would mean nothing to one who is unfeeling. Konrad pits his faith in the God of love and inspiration, against the gods of reason, might, and good business practices. Rather than rebelling against God, he is overthrowing an idol, a usurper who puts reason above feelings and sits unmoved by his people's suffering. To unmask this false god, this czar, is to defend the goodness of the Heavenly Father. Furthermore God, who inspires the poetic word, joins Konrad in debunking this impostor.

As autobiography, the Great Improvisation describes Mickiewicz's own spiritual struggle that occurred in Dresden following the failed Uprising. He emerged from that fight a changed man. The poetical result is not a theoretical dissertation on theodicy,[53] but an existential expression of protest theism. As Chlebowski writes, "In the Improvisation of Konrad Mickiewicz preserved for the furthest generations of humanity

---

52. Ibid., 163.

53. Despite Konrad's passion and poetic elegance, his claim to have been the first to have discovered the theodicy problem reveals both his pride and naivety.

Poland's pain, proclaiming by its intensity the greatness of the wrong experienced and the level of feeling that justifies the shocking force of the protest."[54]

The November Uprising was for Mickiewicz what Poland's final partition was for Woronicz. In *Forefathers' Eve,* Part III he interpreted the Uprising, just as Woronicz had interpreted the partitions in *Hymn to God.* Their versions of these events, intensely personal and yet so in touch with the spirit of their suffering nation, produced a distinctly Polish form of romantic messianism. As actor Gustaw Holoubek said recently in an interview:

> ... this same period as recorded at the same time by Europe meant something entirely different. In no way did it resemble Polish romanticism. How can you compare Gustaf-Konrad with Werther, Oniegin? They were people of flesh and blood. Whereas our Kordians,[55] our Gustafs, our Konrads were the equivalents of ideas, of some sort of road signs.[56]

Mickiewicz's "road signs" long retained their power to move the Polish people. Holoubek's own performance of Konrad sparked the street demonstrations of March, 1968 that led to government crackdowns on students and dissidents, and to the last organized pogrom in Poland.[57] Holoubek notes how Konrad, arguing for the inadequacy of words to express one's true feelings, began the Great Improvisation with typical romantic skepticism regarding epistemology.[58] Yet almost immediately he "forgets" what he just said to assert that the inspired poetic word is a creative force that can effect change in the real world. In the telling, the word becomes "something concrete" to the listener:

---

54. Chlebowski, *Literatura Polska Porozbiorowa jako Główny Wyraz Życia Narodu po Utracie Niepodległości,* 190.

55. Kordian is the hero of Słowacki's poetic drama of the same name, written to press his battle with Mickiewicz for the "rule of souls."

56. Holoubek, "Byłem Konrad," 10–11.

57. To discredit the opposition, the communist authorities cynically played the anti–Semitism card. Most of the 60,000 Jews that remained in Poland jn 1968 were forced to leave, stripped of their belongings and their Polish citizenship.

58. Cieśla-Korytowska argues that Mickiewicz was less skeptical than most romanticists in this regard. Admitting that no epistemological method, including romantic intuition, gives 100% certainty, he remained convinced that we can know, thus the effort to perceive and understand reality is worthwhile. Cf. *O Mickiewiczu i Słowackim,* 173–84.

an explanation why Poland is suffering and why it lost the power of national self-determination. As Holoubek explains, "the first transgressor in this situation could be none other than the Lord God. And only human impotence could lead to such an eruption of anger, hatred, rebellion, and accusation. Precisely impotence, not strength."[59] Holoubek touches here on a crucial point; Konrad is not attacking God from a position of strength, but of weakness. It is impotence that drives him to accuse others, and ultimately God himself, of causing the suffering of his people.

Holoubek proceeds to describe the audience's reaction to *Forefathers' Eve*: "There is no other answer to the astonishing event of *Forefathers' Eve* than this: it awakened patriotic feelings in the viewers, i.e., a terrible anger and terrible, despairing tears. The audience cried, the entire time they cried."[60] When the interviewer suggests that "such euphoria has the characteristics of tragedy," the actor replies that, "to me it seems just the opposite—that the ability to evoke these kinds of feelings in a human gathering is a joyful phenomenon." Leaving the theatre, the audience neither blamed God nor fell into hopeless despair. The spontaneous demonstrations that followed the performances of *Forefathers' Eve*, Holoubek explains, "was the breaking of powerlessness, an act of joy and not hatred, not even of rebellion. Joy that is caused by the feeling of freedom, of deliverance from lies, [of release] from the camouflaging of true feelings."[61] As Holoubek concludes, tyranny can never understand the nature of freedom, nor tyrants the hearts of free people.

> Above all, the clubs of the militia, which later fell on the youth, killed joy. The folly of the militia and secret police depended precisely on this, that they knew nothing about this.

---

59. Holoubek, "Byłem Konrad," 10. Cieśla-Korytowska comes to the same conclusion through rhetorical analysis of Konrad's arguments. Sensing his own weakness, Konrad employs various gimmicks, mostly variations on *ad homines* arguments, in an attempt to manipulate God into fulfilling his demands. Cieśla-Korytowska, "Spór jako element kreacji świata wprzedstawionego w Dziadach", in *O Mickiewiczu i Słowackim*, 156–72.

60. Ibid., 10–11.

61. Ibid., 10–11. The allusion is to Vaclav Havel's essay, "Power of the Powerless."

And that which took place 20 years later[62]—that was the awakening of suppressed joy, and not of suppressed hatred.[63]

Such a reaction reveals the degree to which the romantic poets impacted the lives of their fellow Poles. Their expression of what others were experiencing and feeling both reflected and became part of the nation's "spirit." As the interviewer comments to Holoubek, Professor Bohdan Korzeniowski said concerning your role: "The prayer of Konrad, *Give me the rule of souls,* was answered, and God gave it to him."[64]

Father Peter's Vision

After the fireworks cease, God breaks his silence at last, speaking not to proud Konrad but to the humble priest Father Peter. In a vision, God reveals the meaning of Poland's suffering and foretells her future deliverance. As the scene opens, Father Peter lies praying in his cell. He cries,

> Lord! Who am I to come before You?—
> Dust and nothingness;
> But having confessed to You my nothingness,
> I, dust, will talk with the Lord.[65]

In an account full of prophetic symbolism and metaphor, Father Peter witnesses Poland delivered to Herod's custody and judgment. The priest sees many "stations of the cross"[66]—long, snow-covered roads running into the north, filled with wagons carrying Polish prisoners into Siberian exile, and he asks whether the entire generation of Polish children must perish. Suddenly he exclaims:

> Look!—Ha!—one child escapes unscathed—he grows—the defender!
> The restorer of the nation,—
> From a foreign mother; his blood that of ancient heroes,
> And his name will be forty and four.[67]

---

62. I.e., the Solidarity movement.
63. Ibid., 10–11.
64. Ibid., 11.
65. Mickiewicz, *Utwory Dramatyczne*, 185.
66. In Polish, "the road of the cross." Poles' sufferings are thus likened to the sufferings of Christ.
67. Ibid., 185–86.

Who is this defender, the nation, or a great leader who will restore Poland's freedom? In the prophetic genre Mickiewicz here employs, "forty and four" is both inspired and ambiguous. His friends reported that Mickiewicz, emotionally distressed following the Uprising's failure, experienced some sort of vision in Dresden. If the Great Improvisation conveys this vision in poetic form, its images and details may be spontaneous, neither intentionally invested with meaning nor intended to be interpreted literally. If Mickiewicz did have an individual in mind, it was most likely himself. Released from prison and ultimately allowed to emigrate from Russia, he did escape Siberia. Those who believe that Mickiewicz's mother was of Jewish (Frankist) background argue that his reference to a "foreign mother" confirms their hypothesis. The blood of ancient heroes could refer to his Polish descent, or even to Poland's mythical Sarmatian origins. Forty and four may be intended to denote the numerical value of "Adam" in Hebrew, though the numbers do not strictly match up.[68]

The vision proceeds, styled closely on the Gospel account of Christ's passion. The tyrants capture and bind the nation, personified as a man. In the succeeding lines the image of "Poland the Christ of the Nations" is clear. The tyrants drag the man before a judge named "Gaul," i.e., France. Like Pilate at Christ's trial, Gaul declares him innocent, then washes its hands of him, an allusion to France's failure to come to Poland's aid during the November Uprising. The kings call for the man's blood to be upon them. "Crucify the Son of Mary,[69] give us Barabbas," they cry, continuing the figurative identification of Poland with Jesus Christ. Placing a bloody crown of thorns upon his head, they present him to the nations. Gaul cries out, "Behold a free and independent nation!," thus alluding to the sign Pilate placed on Jesus' cross that read, "Behold, the King of the Jews."

Father Peter sees an enormous cross, its arms stretched out over all Europe. It is made from the three withered nations of the old Commonwealth, i.e., Poland, Lithuania, and the Ukraine. He asks God to strengthen the man, lest he fall and die along the path. Nailed to the cross ("the martyr's throne"), the man calls out "I am thirsty." Austria gives him vinegar to drink, Prussia gall, while Mother Freedom[70] stands

---

68. "Adam" in Hebrew actually has the numerical value of 45.
69. Here Mary's "child" is Poland the "Christ of the nations."
70. A mixed metaphor; here the nation's mother is Freedom.

crying at his feet. Russia pierces his side, and the nation's innocent blood flows, yet Russia alone will repent and be forgiven for its sins.[71] The man cries, "Lord, Lord, why have you forsaken me?" And he dies. The choir bursts into an Easter hymn, finishing with "Hallelujah!" The man rises, and trailing a long white robe that covers the whole world ascends into heaven, where all can behold his raised hands, pierced for them. The significance of this seminal account of Poland's "Passion" is captured by Chlebowski, who writes,

> The comparison [of Poland to Christ] developed in Father Peter's vision by the artistic image of Poland's crucifixion, already contains the entirety of Polish messianism within itself, distilled from the conceptual image of the Polish—Christ as formulated above all by the leader and seer himself, in the *Books of the Nation and the Polish Pilgrimage* (published in 1832 in Paris), and expanded by Polish poets, thinkers, and politicians in many works and books in the 30 year period until the reaction brought on by the defeat of 1863.[72]

Father Peter asks, "Who is this man?"[73] this child grown strong in body and soul,[74] who will build the hosts of his church "on glory."[75] Exalted above the nations and their kings, with three faces and three foreheads,[76] he stands on three capitols and three ends of the earth quiver when he speaks. Although these capitols represent the partitioning powers, i.e., Russia, Prussia, and Austria, they symbolize the forces of tyranny and injustice everywhere. The man's feet rest on three crowns but he himself wears no crown, for his victory is not won over the people of Russia, Prussia, and Austria but their autocratic rulers.

> His life—hardship of hardship,[77]
> His title—people of peoples;[78]

---

71. This is the Sarmatian myth of pan-Slavic brotherhood.

72. Chlebowski, *Literatura Polska Porozbiorowa jako Główny Wyraz Życia Narodu po Utracie Niepodległości*, 138.

73. Cf. Matt 8:27.

74. Cf. Luke 2:52.

75. "Sława" = glory, fame. Held by Mickiewicz to be derived from "słowo," i.e., the poetic, inspired word.

76. Once again, a likely reference to Poland, Lithuania, and the Ukraine.

77. That is, incomparable suffering.

78. The nation's exalted status, commensurate with its unequaled sufferings.

From a foreign mother; his blood that of ancient heroes,
And his name will be forty and four.
Glory! Glory! Glory![79]

Just when the nation's unequaled sufferings and subsequent exaltation suggests Poland as a corporate messiah, Mickiewicz reintroduces the hero whose name is forty and four. The tension between the Messiah as a group or nation and as an individual, already visible in "Ode to Youth" vis-à-vis "The Sailor," reappears with redoubled force. Mickiewicz does not confirm either reading, and neither should we resolve this question hastily. Indeed, debate over the man's identity may cause us to miss the point of the priest's vision, which is to restore the nation's hope, give the people strength to endure, and motivate them to persevere in the struggle for freedom. That said, there have been many who tried to guess the man's identity. Mickiewicz, conscious of his own genius, saw himself at times as this man. Later, discouraged by ensuing events and aware of his own failings, he fell for a while under Towiański's spell, and accepted the mystic's claim to be "the defender." The burden the poet tried to carry ("for millions I love and suffer torment") proved too great for one individual to bear. Grasping at straws, he put his hope for a time in a man whom he believed God had appointed to bring the promised new age.[80]

The Personal and Spiritual Journey of Gustaf-Konrad

A major interpretive issue in *Forefathers' Eve*, Part III is the relationship between Konrad and Father Peter. The literary unity of the "Great Improvisation" and the "Vision" is clear. So is the author's own moral judgment condemning Konrad's pride and commending the priest's humility. Though we will revise this judgment below, for now Father Peter appears to have the last word. In his humility he becomes the spokesman for the Polish people. His message is one of hope and future deliverance. Writes Chlebowski, "The prophetic vision reveals to the humble and trusting the moral significance of the sufferings and wrongs [inflicted] on Poland, the victim of contemporary politics, stretched out on the cross and embracing all of Europe in its arms, and at the same time

---

79. Mickiewicz, *Utwory Dramatyczne*, 187–88.
80. The reasons behind Mickiewicz's allegiance to Towiański are complex.

points to and foretells its future savior."[81] Chlebowski concludes that Mickiewicz's own "moral triumph,"[82] won in *Forefathers' Eve*, confirmed his belief in the messianic idea, which not only "refreshed hearts following the defeat" but became "the basis for the national program."[83]

The issue is the identity of the two individuals. Does Father Peter represent a further transformation of Gustaf-Konrad?[84] If Konrad had died and been reborn[85] as the priest, the personal link uniting the two would be clear. Yet unlike most romantic heroes, Konrad survives the end of the story. Deported, like Mickiewicz, to St. Petersburg, he meets Russians; they are good, bad, and indifferent. He sees Peter the Great's statue, which presents the Czar astride his horse atop the trampled corpses of conquered nations. Before leaving Russia, he talks with Father Peter, and meets a holy man, who prays for him and instructs him. We must therefore consider the possibility that Father Peter is Konrad's mentor, not his replacement. Two questions help to guide our investigation. If Gustaf-Konrad is, as Holoubek suggested, a road sign, what path does he point to? Alternatively, if we take Konrad to be a flesh-and-blood person, who is he, where does he go from here, and what will he become?

A 1983 article by Cieśla-Korytowska[86] explored Konrad's identity as a national idea and patriotic hero, hence as a road sign for ethical and patriotic behavior amidst the moral ambiguity and political wasteland of the People's Republic of Poland. Gustaf the jilted lover was a thoroughly Byronic hero. Now as Konrad he has adopted two supreme values, poetry and love for his nation. But why did Konrad fail to breach the gates of heaven? His real problem, argues Cieśla-Korytowska, was not personal weakness but a case of mistaken identity, particularly evident in his interpersonal relationships. As a poet, he thought he could impact the world directly, instead of indirectly through the reception

---

81. Chlebowski, *Literatura Polska Porozbiorowa jako Główny Wyraz Życia Narodu po Utracie Niepodległości*, 136.

82. I.e., over his pride.

83. Chlebowski, *Literatura Polska Porozbiorowa jako Główny Wyraz Życia Narodu po Utracie Niepodległości*, 138.

84. Thus Kozicki, *Dziedzictwo polityczne trzech wieszczów*, 80.

85. Or vanished and reappeared as Jacek Soplica/Father Robak did in *Master Thaddeus*. Cf. discussion below.

86. Cieśla-Korytowska, "Polski romantyk w poszukiwaniu tożsamości," *O Mickiewiczu i Słowackim*, 120–42.

of his work. As a human being, he dared to compare himself with God. As a lover, he loved first a woman and then Poland, but as abstract entities, not flesh and blood human beings. He also mistook his destiny. As Gustaf, he thought (platonic) love was the ultimate good. As Konrad, he overestimated his own role in realizing a great idea. He failed to achieve either goal. But, as Cieśla-Korytowska argues, these mistakes taught Konrad a lesson all romantics need to learn; he must choose to live and act in the real world, rather than to dream of an ideal, spiritual world.

Gustaf the specter elects to re-enter history (a good choice), but makes wrong choices within it. He chooses love (another good choice), but seeks to realize it in the wrong way. Later, as Konrad, he wants to create a paradise of freedom single-handedly, by working without others rather than with them. He wants to remove all suffering from God's plan, though thanks to Father Peter he learns that he cannot "save" history by making it pain-free. He can, however, save himself, by choosing to live within history, by accepting life's joy and pain, and by not demanding a blueprint of God's plans and purposes. Konrad learns that life is full of choices, choices that he is responsible to make, and which have genuine this-worldly consequences.

As has been shown, Poles looked to Mickiewicz to learn how to live under communist rule. Poland's changing historical circumstances, however, suggested the need to rethink its national myths and the ongoing usefulness of traditional role models. Now that Poland has regained the right of self-determination, can one at last appreciate Polish poetry as poetry, rather than for its prophetic, political or propaganda value? In 1993 Cieśla-Korytowska revisited *Forefathers' Eve* to ask what Konrad has to offer post-communist Poland. What is more, if we approach him as a human being rather than the quintessential Polish patriot, might we discover he has something to say even beyond Polish borders? To begin with, she reminds us that *Forefathers' Eve* relates the history of one autobiographical hero. Mickiewicz is fascinated by young Gustaf's unending growth process. Since growth is endemic to life, she argues, our commitment to participate in the process is fundamental, and more important than who we are at any given stage along the way. By tracing the life of a memorable individual, *Forefathers' Eve* provides a role model for others. His battle for personal salvation and maturity can become anyone's battle.[87]

Gustaf-Konrad fails a series of tests, which nevertheless teach him valuable lessons. Failing at love, he attempts to escape the world by committing suicide.[88] His appearance at the priest's door is the first, hesitant step back from his self-imposed exile and towards the world of living people. The debate with his former teacher has the potential of becoming a dialogue, where he listens to others' viewpoints and considers how to integrate them with his own.[89]

Cieśla-Korytowska next notes that Konrad, in his prison cell, fails the test of loneliness, although this time solitude is imposed upon him and not something he chose himself. Gustaf's personal suffering led him to attempted suicide; now Konrad's identification with the suffering of others leads him to blasphemy. In both cases the root problem is that he is living *for* others in an abstract world, rather than *with* others in the real world. More specifically, he lives first for the idea of a romantic star-crossed lover, and later for the quite impersonal idea of the nation. As Cieśla-Korytowska explains, in Konrad's case 'living for others' means to think and decide for them, "for they are like children, they don't know what is good . . . This is a terrible error and no less terrible sin. A sin against one's neighbor, for the nation is made up of these individuals, these neighbors."[90] But once again this failure is not the end but a new beginning. Konrad's battle with God, like Father Peter's vision, is only a stop (though a memorable one) along the highway. Gustaf-Konrad failed because he was immature. Yet he still has a chance for growth, for salvation, and reconciliation. Father Peter's vision is not a prophecy, but a possibility. What has Konrad learned? That on a human level, what counts most is relationships. Now he must choose, either to live and labor with others, or to continue his lone struggle "for" them in a paternalism that reduces to contempt and comes dangerously close to the tyranny it started out to oppose. Ironically, a romantic genius,

---

87. Cieśla-Korytowska, "O polskim bohaterze romantycznym po latach," *O Mickiewiczu i Słowackim*, 143–5.

88. *Nota bene*, he also fails at this, perhaps because unconsciously he still desires to live?

89. Cieśla-Korytowska, *O Mickiewiczu i Słowackim*, 146–47.

90. Ibid., 147.

though perhaps willing to create such a world, would never agree to live in one.

It appears at first glance that Mickiewicz is proposing Father Peter as the ideal model of a citizen and patriot. Yet Mickiewicz himself continued to grow, and to the extent that *Forefathers' Eve* is autobiographical, its hero must remain a man in process. Konrad, and not Peter fits this criterion. Although Mickiewicz never published the further tale of Konrad's journey, the fact that he remains Konrad already signifies that has learned humility. Rather than undergoing another romantic transformation, he has begun to face the responsibility to live in the real world. Released from his self-imposed messiah-complex, Konrad can at last learn to be himself. He remains Konrad, humbler but wiser, still growing, and still trying. He now knows he must live in this world, where ethical choices are often grey rather than black and white. He has learned that in spite of ambiguity and doubt one still must choose. To the extent that Father Peter's humility is inborn, his is a hard act to follow, unless one is naturally endowed like the priest.[91] Konrad, like most of us, has to learn the hard way, and thus provides a model ordinary mortals are able to follow. For all the significance of Father Peter to the story, not to mention the "terrible man" whose number is forty and four, Konrad remains the hero of *Forefathers' Eve*, prepared to take the next step towards becoming a more mature, responsible human being.

A 1994 article by Cieśla-Korytowska,[92] applying rhetorical analysis to Gustaf's debate with the priest and Konrad's confrontation with God, highlights the utter frankness with which Mickiewicz describes himself and his journey. Mickiewicz's schoolboy friends were horrified at the candor with which he wrote of his youthful, ill-fated, and somewhat scandalous love-affairs. Once again with Konrad, Mickiewicz bared his own soul, revealing his frailty and fallibility. And as a result we have lost nothing, and gained a great deal. For when we consider Konrad as a real person and not only as a road sign, we are moved not so much by his genius as by his humanity. He has taken off his mask, he has said what we all feel in our heads and know in our hearts to be true. He has freed us from lies and from the need to lie. We find ourselves like Konrad, at the pause in the story that ends *Forefathers' Eve*, Part

---

91. Father Robak in *Master Thaddeus* is a much more complex character.

92. Cieśla-Korytowska, "Spór jako element kreacji świata przedstawionego w Dziadach," in *O Mickiewiczu i Słowackim*, 156–72.

III. We have received a lesson in humility, not only from Father Peter, but even more convincingly from his alter-ego, the proud Konrad. For Father Peter was humble by nature, but Konrad had to learn humility. Now we too must choose to live in the real world, where our decisions have consequences and our relationships are paramount, to live freely, humbly, and responsibly, in community and partnership with others. And we must accept, for reasons we don't have to like and cannot fully explain, that a good and loving God does not always intervene to spare his children their suffering.

For Your Freedom and Ours: To Muscovite Friends (1832)[93]

Mickiewicz wrote 'To Muscovite Friends' shortly after completing *Forefathers' Eve*, Part III. At his explicit instructions it was appended to the longer work. The poem is addressed to Russian intellectuals and dissidents whom Mickiewicz befriended during his years in St. Petersburg and Moscow (1824-1829). Among them was Alexander Pushkin, as well as the Decembrists, who on December 26, 1825 led an abortive uprising against the czar that led to their arrest, torture, exile, and execution.[94] Mickiewicz regards his Russian friends, many of whom lost their lives and freedom for opposing the czar, as fellow citizens of that spiritual country where free people dwell. But not all Russians were (or remained) his spiritual companions. Some, enamored by the splendor of the Czar's court or enticed by his favors, accepted imperial posts, others killed their Slavic (Polish) brothers while serving in the imperial armies.[95] Mickiewicz declares that those who receive honors from the Czar's hand only disgrace themselves. By selling their political souls to the Czar-devil, and serving his imperialistic system, they commit treason against the cause of freedom.

In a lightly veiled allusion to Pushkin, Mickiewicz attacks those who write poems praising the Czar's military victories. This barb cut deep. Pushkin knew the Decembrists, felt sympathy for their cause, and was shattered by their defeat. However, following the uprising's failure the Czar convinced him that reforms could only take place from above.

93. The term *moskal* (lit. Muscovite) often signified *Russian*. That is its sense here.

94. Prior to the 1825 uprising, the Decembrists and Polish underground groups discussed mounting a joint Polish-Russian uprising against the Czar (the November Uprising took place five years later in 1830).

95. A transgression against the myth of Sarmatian (Pan-Slavic) brotherhood.

Wounded by Mickiewicz's bitter words, and offended by his caustic description of Peter the Great's statue included in *Forefathers' Eve*, Part III, Pushkin wrote his famous 1833 poem 'The Bronze Horseman', praising the Czar whose efforts to modernize the Russian nation Pushkin thereby urged the current Czar Nicholas I to follow.

Mickiewicz refers to his forced exile in Russia, during which period he wrote *Grażyna* and especially *Konrad Wallenrod*, where stories of Lithuania's fight against the Teutonic Knights hide veiled allusions to Poland's resistance to Russia. Thus Mickiewicz the "serpent" deceived the despot's censors. Yet he spoke to his Russian friends with the "simplicity of a dove," i.e., the straightforwardness and sincerity enjoyed by true friends, who share on the personal, intimate level of feelings. Beyond the obvious dependence here on the Gospel command to be "as wise as serpents and as gentle as doves," mention of "the secrets hidden in feelings" hints at the poet's romantic epistemology.

Mickiewicz shares his people's pain and suffering, yet he does not curse the Russian people. Instead he directs his anger against the bonds that hold both Russians and Poles captive to the Czar. Instead of seeking vengeance on the Russians for the enslavement of his people, he desires their deliverance as well. His words are harbingers of freedom to his foreign friends (and enemies) as well as to his own countrymen.

> Now upon the world I pour out this cup of poison,
> The bitterness of my speech is caustic and burning,
> Bitterness sucked from the blood and tears of my fatherland,
> May it corrode and burn—not you, but your chains.[96]

This is a quantitative, not qualitative development for Mickiewicz. Even Konrad Wallenrod, after wreaking his terrible vengeance against the Teutonic Order, cried out "enough," and proclaimed that "Germans are also humans." The recognition that your enemy possesses a soul, that a foreigner is also a human being, implies the possibility of dialogue and reconciliation. Patriots, says Mickiewicz, will fight if they must to defend their freedom and their homeland against tyranny and aggression. But their true desire is to overcome old antagonisms and greet their former enemies as brothers.

---

96. Mickiewicz, *Utwory Dramatyczne*, 300.

But Seek Ye First the Kingdom: Sentences and Comments from the Works of Jacob Boehme, Angelus Silesius, and Saint-Martin (1833–34)

What can a collection of proverbs borrowed from the mystics tell us about their translator? Quite a lot, as Anna Grzywna-Wileczek argues. Agreeing with Pigon that *Sentences and Comments* is highly original in form and content, she contends that the work's real inspiration is the Bible, and suggests that the self-depreciating title, rather than implying dependence on others, indicates the poet's desire to express his own reflections in the form of gnomic, universal truths.[97]

Sentences reveals the lifelong importance Mickiewicz placed on spiritual exploration and growth, and its implicit worldview helps justify the use of the word "Christian" with respect to the poet. The poet displays his antipathy towards rationalism by numerous sayings criticizing secular wisdom and sophistry. Characteristically, Mickiewicz focuses here on spirituality at the existential level, achieved through conscious decision and personal effort.[98] This fundamental premise of *Sentences and Comments* is revealed by its first maxim, entitled "The Neglected Question":

> There's one question on earth worthy of human reflection;
> People think about everything, except this one question.[99]

Mickiewicz forces the reader to think about what really matters "on earth," i.e., in one's existential experience, where the profane often hides the sacred from view. As Grzywna-Wileczek writes, ". . . the tragic tearing asunder of the *sacrum* and *profanum* is documented by observation and existential experience, the eye-witness statement that "people think about everything 'except this one question.'"[100] How then can one experience God and the supernatural in the midst of everyday, mundane

---

97. Grzywna-Wileczek, *And There are More Truths in Scripture*, 12. Weintraub agrees: "it is obvious that the collection is a highly personal choice, and bears the clear imprint of Mickiewicz's specific religiosity." Weintraub, *The Poetry of Adam Mickiewicz*, 270.

98. Weintraub writes, "He is mostly preoccupied with man's relation to God." Ibid., 268.

99. Mickiewicz, *Wiersze*, 337.

100. Grzywna-Wileczek, *And There are More Truths in Scripture*, 17.

life? In the following proverb, "Distance," Mickiewicz invites his readers to recognize that they live in two worlds, the spiritual and the material.

> That it is far to heaven, not a few complain;
> The earth is farther from man than heaven.[101]

The point, says Mickiewicz, is not to escape the physical world for the spiritual world, but to recognize the presence of the sacred in the secular world. For these worlds intersect, and those who open their eyes to see and their hearts to believe will find God has made his home within them. Grzywna-Wileczek is on solid ground when she states that, "The maxims and sentences of Mickiewicz can be treated as an answer to the question of the meaning and essence of human existence, an answer given in the spirit of the Christian tradition."[102] This "spirit" is evident throughout *Sentences*, where Mickiewicz speaks of creation, the dignity and depravity of man, the incarnation and the crucifixion of Christ, and the childlike faith required to enter the Kingdom of God. Yet, as Weintraub notes, the poet's focus is on "the inwardness of religious feelings," not the "dogmatic structure of a religious system."[103] In other proverbs, Mickiewicz declares that the God who makes the things of the spirit available to all also calls everyone to faith.[104]

The basic decision to set one's will towards God was for Mickiewicz the foundation and source of ethics, and hence of patriotism. Smaszcz writes that "Mickiewicz unceasingly returned to the thought of the Apostle to the Nations, that we were 'created in Christ Jesus for good works.'"[105] The maxim below entitled "Word and Deed" expresses romanticism's insistence on the congruence of word and deed, as well as reflecting the biblical command to be a doer of the word.

> In words I see only desire, in action power;
> It is harder to live one day well than to write a book.

Mickiewicz believed that though we constantly fall short of the ideal we must keep on trying, not from the fear of God's wrath but an

---

101. Mickiewicz, *Wiersze*, 346.
102. Ibid., 127–28.
103. Weintraub, *Poetry of Adam Mickiewicz*, 270.
104. Grzywna-Wileczek explains Mickiewicz's view of God's plan of salvation, "One can accept it (an attitude of faith) or reject it (an attitude of trusting evil)." Mickiewicz, *Wiersze*, 127.
105. Smaszcz, *Rozum i wiara*, 118–21.

awareness of God's love. A deeply religious man, his works were not an intellectual game but a search for direct, experiential knowledge of truth. As he reportedly said to his friend Stefan Garczyński, who was enamored by Hegel, "the sun enlightens and enlivens nature, a mirror reflecting the light of the sun can only weave theories. Only true wisdom and holiness (for these are one and the same) can be this sun for people, philosophy, as a lesson will be only a mirror."[106]

The Once and Future Kingdom: Master Thaddeus (1834)

Mickiewicz was raised by the last generation to live in a free Poland, and belonged to the first generation to live in occupied Poland. He studied the Greek and Roman classics, the neo-classical literature of the Enlightenment, and the classics of Polish literature, yet he initiated and shaped the romantic period in Poland. Konrad Górski recalls the poet's own claim to be "the ark of the covenant between the older and younger years."[107] *Master Thaddeus* is a verbal incarnation of what Mickiewicz was to pre- and post-partition Poland. The work forms a bridge between the old Polish Commonwealth of the gentry, and the future Poland where all would be equal citizens. *Master Thaddeus* describes in a beautiful, nostalgic tone the now vanished life of the minor Polish gentry in the provinces of Lithuania that Mickiewicz remembered so fondly from his childhood.

But *Master Thaddeus* is more than an idyll. *Master Thaddeus* debunked the claim, sown by the partitioning powers to legitimize their political crimes, that Poland's moral decline was the cause of its downfall. It also made a powerful statement regarding the nature and imperative of Polish patriotism that is consistent with Mickiewicz's other works of the period. Kozicki goes so far as to say that "this poem contains all the elements of Mickiewiczan ideology; it is the perfect expression of the desires and goals of the seer, only contained in a different form that in his earlier works."[108] The poem reflects the poet's opinion regarding the source and propagation of the "national spirit," which he believed was preserved in the homes and hearts of the Polish

---

106. Adam Mickiewicz, to his friend Stefan Garczyński, related by Odyńca. Cited in: Ibid., 142.

107. Górski, cited in: Smaszcz, *Rozum i wiara*, 119.

108. Kozicki, *Dziedzictwo polityczne trzech wieszczów*, 99–100. Miłosz and Koropeckyj agree.

people, from where it must be re-exported to the nation at large.[109] As Chlebowski exclaims, "It was the most powerful and most effective overcoming of the patriotic pain of the Polish soul, demonstrating that it could achieve its deliverance, not in escaping from life, but in achieving the full spiritual strength that makes possible the transformation of the hard reality of life."[110]

In *Master Thaddeus* Mickiewicz recapitulates both the idyllic and Sarmatian myths, describing peace-loving and hospitable Poles who rise up to defend the nation when its freedom is threatened. Their country life is first disturbed by the renewal of an ancient land dispute among rival families. Yet news that Napoleon plans to attack Russia raises hopes for the restoration of Polish sovereignty. To prove that the former Polish territories in Lithuania should be included in a revived Polish State, the mysterious priest Father Robak seeks to organize an uprising. When the Russian garrison arrives to quell the gentry's internal disputes, the nobles quit fighting among themselves and band together against their common enemy. The story ends with Napoleon's arrival en route to Moscow with his Grand Army. At his side are the Polish divisions, including Master Thaddeus, bearing their own standards and fighting under their own generals. History pauses at a moment when the possibility of regaining freedom seemed quite real.

Another major theme in *Master Thaddeus* is the coming transition to the new Poland. Mickiewicz's sensitive treatment of Jankiel, the Jewish innkeeper and musician, demonstrates his belief in the feasibility and richness of a multi-ethnic, religiously pluralistic society. The epic ends by foretelling the elimination of class distinctions. Thaddeus and his new bride Zosia free their serfs and grant them the land on which they live and farm. Equality is achieved by turning peasants into nobles,[111] not by making nobles and merchants into peasants. Such voluntary social reformation at the initiative of the privileged class actually took place on a limited scale, and formed an essential element of the social and political programs proposed by various patriotic factions.

---

109. Cf. Mickiewicz, from a speech delivered in November, 1832 in the "Lithuanian and Belarusian Lands Society," cited in Kozicki, *Dziedzictwo polityczne trzech wieszczów*, 100.

110. Chlebowski, *Literatura Polska Porozbiorowa jako Główny Wyraz Życia Narodu po Utracie Niepodległości*, 192.

111. I.e., by granting them the nobleman's name.

As Chlebowski writes, "there is formed in *Master Thaddeus* the outline of the arising new Poland, being democratized via the participation in public life of the merchant class, Jews, and the peasantry, who are only beginning to awaken to national life."[112]

In *Master Thaddeus*, patriotism includes participation in an armed uprising, but also the nobles' reception of new social ideals, demonstrated by the freeing and enfranchisement of the peasants in the spirit of the May 3rd Constitution and the Kosciusko Uprising. What armed resistance and voluntary social reform have in common is sacrifice, as exemplified not only by Thaddeus but also the romantic figure of Count Horeszków, last representative of his house and enemy of the Soplice clan to which Thaddeus is heir. Given the opportunity to regain his property and take revenge upon his enemies, he spares their lives and joins the premature uprising. Forced to flee with the other "rebels," he personally funds a mounted division of Polish troops and, having distinguished himself in battle, returns at their head along with Napoleon's army.

However, the most important figure in the poem is Thaddeus's long-lost father, Jacek Soplice. Years before, the patriarch of the Horeszków clan had spurned Jacek's request for his daughter's hand. Soon afterwards, while suppressing the gentry's resistance to the partition of Poland, Russian troops attack the Horeszków castle. In his youthful rashness Soplica, an excellent marksman, fires a random shot in the general direction of Count Horeszków that kills his foe. To atone for his sins, Soplica becomes a priest and takes the name of Robak (insect), which signifies his humility and repentance. Having long served the cause of Polish independence, in *Master Thaddeus* he is fatally wounded while saving the life of the young Count Horeszków. His dying confession is the centerpoint of the entire epic.

> More than from love, perhaps from foolish pride
> I killed: therefore, humility ... I joined the monks.
> I, who was once proud of my family, I who was once a rogue,
> Bowed my head, a priest, I called myself an insect ...[113]

---

112. Chlebowski Chlebowski, *Literatura Polska Porozbiorowa jako Główny Wyraz Życia Narodu po Utracie Niepodległości*, 156.

113. Mickiewicz, *Pan Tadeusz*, 297.

The rays of the setting sun falling through the window crown the dying sinner become saint, showing that his humility and service for his nation are accepted as expiation for his sins. It is thus in Jacek Soplice that patriotism and personal sacrifice are joined with the process of repentance and transformation that is central to Mickiewicz's religious and romantic worldview.[114] As Smaszcz writes of Mickiewicz, "He was a writer of evangelical truths, and it is above all in this context that one should speak of his accomplishments. His heroes, from the ballad *Father's Return* to *Forefathers's Eve* and *Master Thaddeus*, undergo such great transformation, that they become entirely different people."[115] Chlebowski comments that, through the character of Jacek Soplica, Mickiewicz "proclaims the teaching-truth, founded in the development of his own soul, which in 'the improving and expansion of souls' points to the only means of achieving the right to exist for the fatherland, whose borders are marked by the moral values of Polish hearts."[116] Chlebowski's positivism peeks through in his further comments, which constitute a somewhat lame attempt to salvage a social work ethic from this tale that "appears" to glorify armed resistance and insurrection. But he clearly understood (and shared) Mickiewicz's belief that the spiritual heart of the nation lies hidden behind the characters and customs described in *Master Thaddeus*. The poet's effectiveness in capturing the "national spirit" is seen in the comments of many Poles following the 1999 debut of Andrzej Wajda's screen version: "We are still the same today." The message of this epic, considered by many to be Mickiewicz's greatest work, is that the nation is still alive, that it possesses the will and ability to renew itself, that it is worthy of a place among the nations.[117]

---

114. As Wacław Borowy writes, "All of Mickiewicz's major works deal with people who become transformed." Borowy, "Poet of Transformation" in Kridl, *Mickiewicz*, 35.

115. Smaszcz, *Rozum i wiara*, 120.

116. Chlebowski, *Literatura Polska Porozbiorowa jako Główny Wyraz Życia Narodu po Utracie Niepodległości*, 163.

117. Ibid., 153.

The Pilgrim's Politics

The Gospel of the Kingdom: The Books of the Polish Nation and the Polish Pilgrimage (1832)[118]

Mickiewicz arrived in Paris in 1832, six months after the main body of Polish exiles.[119] The fledgling Polish community, shattered by the downfall of the November Uprising, and living as refugees in a foreign country, was still in the early stages of organizing itself, but clear divisions had already formed between various camps. Mickiewicz wrote *The Books of the Nation and the Polish Pilgrimage* to unite the exiles in the common battle for Poland's freedom. The *Books*' message to the exiles was clear: you have an identity and a purpose. You are leaders, not losers; you are Europe's vanguard, not its also-rans.[120]

The *Books*' mood was established by the manuscript of *Forefathers' Eve*, Part III that Mickiewicz had brought to Paris. Konrad's "Great Improvisation" reprised the suffering of the Polish nation, while Father Peter's vision provided comfort and hope. Chlebowski exclaims, "The messianic vision acts like a wonderful narcotic, anesthetizing the pain and awakening in souls an exalted mood, the pride, if not joy, of martyrs, who by their suffering are preparing the deliverance of humanity ... This new tone of patriotic feeling gave *The Books of the Nation and the Polish Pilgrimage* the sublimity and warmth of a national gospel."[121] The *Books* exhibit a unique blending of biblical concepts and literary genre with national ideology, which Stefanowska describes as "religious writing about politics."[122] The *Books* pronounce a few simple rules, defining the emigrants' patriotic duty, and urging unity in the battle for their country's freedom, which the poet believed was imminent. By styling his work on biblical revelation, he sought to ground these rules on a religious, hence universal and ultimate base.

118. This two-part work is made up of the *Books of the Polish Nation* and the *Books of the Polish Pilgrimage*.

119. The so-called "Great Emigration" included 13,000 political leaders, activists and military personnel. Kozicki calls them "the flower of the Polish intelligentsia." Kozicki, *Dziedzictwo polityczne trzech wieszczów*, 85.

120. As Siwicka writes, "the wanderers were changed into pilgrims traveling to the land of freedom—to a Poland and Europe of free peoples." Siwicka, *Romantyzm*, 104.

121. Chlebowski, *Literatura Polska Porozbiorowa jako Główny Wyraz Życia Narodu po Utracie Niepodległości*, 191.

122. Stefanowska, *Historia i profecja*, 233.

The Books of the Polish Nation, which define Polish identity, are patterned on Old Testament creation stories and sacred-history narratives, while the longer *Books of the Polish Pilgrimage* proclaim Poland's mission in the genre of gospel. Completing the *Books*' outline are "A Pilgrim's Prayer" and "A Pilgrim's Litany." Although the forms are biblical, their historical context is 1832, and their content is political theory and policies. Kozicki judged correctly that 'the assumptions formulated in the Books' were foundational to the poet's later political thought and activity.[123] To achieve the literary sense of universal truth, Mickiewicz speaks here as the anonymous voice of the Polish nation, drawing upon tradition strengthened by divine inspiration. *Books of the Polish Nation* begins with these words:

> BOOKS OF THE POLISH NATION
> FROM THE BEGINNING OF THE WORLD
> UP TO THE SUFFERING OF THE POLISH NATION
>
> 1. In the beginning there was faith in one GOD, and there was freedom in the world. And there were no laws, only the will of GOD, and there were no masters and slaves, only the patriarchs and their children.
>
> 2. But then people denied the only GOD, and made idols for themselves, and bowed down to them, and sacrificed bloody offerings to their glory, and fought for the glory of their idols.
>
> 3. Therefore GOD sent on the idolaters the greatest punishment, which is slavery.[124]

The interpretive key to the *Books of the Polish Nation* lies in the seemingly arbitrary choice of two events: the prehistoric creation of the world, and Poland's recent, historical suffering. For Mickiewicz's polemical purposes, the most important event since creation is not, as Christianity argues, the crucifixion and resurrection of Christ, but the partition (i.e., "crucifixion") and future "resurrection" of Poland. Poland's story becomes a national gospel relating the nation's historical struggle for freedom. "The beginning" refers to the ideal social conditions that prevailed in the primeval community, not creation *ex nihilo*. Humanity's fall is seen here as corporate, not individual, thus history's

---

123. Kozicki, *Dziedzictwo polityczne trzech wieszczów*, 87.
124. Mickiewicz, *Księgi narodu polskiego*, lines 1–3, 211.

goal is not personal salvation but the renewal of human society.[125] As Stefanowska explains, "Mickiewicz reversed the order: he did not ask what mission Poland is to fulfill in God's plan of salvation, but how the divine plan serves the cause of Polish freedom. Sacred history in the Books is not theocentric, and because of this it is no longer sacred history but the history of the nation."[126]

Mickiewicz employed typological interpretation throughout the *Books*. A philosophy of history where all things work toward their appointed end allowed him to maintain a biblical style while reshaping history to fit the nation's needs. Poland was idealized and every other nation demonized. These characteristics of the *Books* are facilitated by two organizing structural elements: the interplay between international history and Polish history, and the decision to focus on Christ rather than on Israel or the early Church as a type of Poland.[127] International history begins with primeval society where all people lived in equality and brotherhood. Humanity's idyll was destroyed by its spiritual and socio-political fall, which culminated in the Roman Empire's subjugation and oppression of the nations. Then Jesus Christ appeared, preaching freedom and proclaiming that "nothing is worthy of honor on earth, neither human wisdom, nor office, nor riches, nor crowns; but only one thing is worthy of honor, to sacrifice one's self for the good of others." Kozicki calls this principle, "Mickiewicz's deepest conviction, this is the rock, on which he built his entire view of human history."[128] Christ is portrayed here as the liberator and champion of social justice, not the savior and redeemer. The judges in Caesar's service thought that by killing Christ they could ban freedom and justice from the world forever. They were mistaken.

---

125. Here Mickiewicz is speaking eschatologically, not soteriologically, nevertheless it is easy to see why conservative Catholics such as the Resurrectionists criticized the poet's writings so severely. Far from denying personal salvation or the centrality of Christ's cross and resurrection, his focus is rather on the socio-political renewal of society, seen eschatologically as the culmination of human history. Poland's freedom, to be achieved by the "universal war for the Freedom of the Nations" (see discussion below), would inaugurate a new era of Christendom. This approach will be critiqued in chapter 6.

126. Stefanowska, *Historia i profecja*, 172.

127. Stefanowska's literary analysis of the *Books* in *Historia i profesja*.

128. Kozicki, *Dziedzictwo polityczne trzech wieszczów*, 86. Kozicki's National Democratic ideology limits this sacrifice to the good of one's own nation, whereas Mickiewicz extends it to the good of humanity.

22. But Christ arose, and driving out the Emperors, planted his cross upon their capitol; and then the masters freed their slaves, and recognized them as brothers, and the kings anointed in the name of GOD acknowledged God's law to be over them, and justice returned to the earth.

23. And all the nations that believed, be it the Germans, or the Italians, or the French, or the Polish, all considered themselves to be one nation, and they called that nation Christendom.[129]

And freedom spread, voluntarily, from the kings to the nobles to the merchant class. Had it reached the masses, all would have been free. But "the kings spoiled everything" by establishing national states. They rejected God's authority over them, and like Caesar became a law unto themselves. Unjust wars were fought in their name, wise men (i.e., philosophers) arose who justified the king's reign, and the people built idols and bowed down to worship them. The French worshipped the golden calf called *honor*, the Spanish Baal or *political preponderance*,[130] the English Mammon or *rule on the land and the sea*, and the Germans Moloch or *well-being*. Wars were fought in the names of these idols. Later they fashioned new gods that were called *political parity*, and finally *business*. But the ultimate and final fall of Christendom was the partition of Poland. This is the history of the nations.

The second, contrasting scheme of history concerns the Polish nation. Unlike other nations, Poland remained true to God. It did not worship the nations' idols, nor fight unjust wars for its own gain, but continued on an upward trajectory of increasing freedom that led to the May 3rd constitution of 1791. Here the two schemes of history intersect, for in 1795 the faithless nations killed their only faithful brother, Poland. This climactic fall of the idolatrous nations and devout Poland could only be overcome by the liberation of humanity. Thus Poland's freedom is tied directly, not to the defeat of other nations, but to their liberation and renewal. Poland's national "resurrection" would inaugurate a new European order, where the nations join together to free themselves from the rule of kings both domestic and foreign, and live together in peace and brotherhood. To fit this scenario, Mickiewicz chose Christ and not Israel as the type of Poland. Biblical Israel had often been unfaithful, but Christ was the innocent victim of injustice. Furthermore, while Israel

---

129. Mickiewicz, *Books of the Polish Nation*, lines 22–23, 213.
130. I.e., domination.

had returned for a time to the land, the Jews were once again wanderers and exiles. The risen Christ, however, was "never to die again."

Although Mickiewicz may offend our sensibilities here by praising the Crusades, he is writing about mythical and not real history. He is not advocating religious warfare, but urging the fight against unbelief, injustice and oppression. More shocking is his use in the *Books of the Polish Pilgrimage* of a politically incorrect allegory concerning Pagans, Jews, and Christians to express his historical judgment of the French Revolution. Though some consider this work anti-Semitic, all other nations (except Poland) come out far worse than the Jews. Is Mickiewicz then a latent xenophobic nationalist? No, for as we shall see below, he is not ultimately talking about Pagans, Jews, and Christians. Indeed, the *Books* proved immensely popular throughout Europe among members of those nations striving to realize their own national aspirations. Damiani attributes the warmth Italians feel towards the popular Polish poet to "the personal charm of the man who, by his works, his activities, his words, his example, felt in his heart the union of Italy and Poland in a common cause, through identification of their destinies, their sufferings, their struggles, their sacrifices, their heroism in the service of a supreme common ideal."[131]

Mickiewicz was ambivalent towards the French Revolution. He admired its ideals but rejected its reign of terror and its anti-religious stance. Furthermore, it problematically undermined Poland's status as the only faithful nation. As Stefanowska argues, to include the Revolution in the starkly dualistic *Books of the Polish Nation* would have reduced Poland, the "Christ of the Nations," to another historical example of the struggle for freedom. Unable however to ignore such an important event, Mickiewicz placed his analysis of the French Revolution among the parables in the *Books of the Polish Pilgrimage*. In book XVIII he addresses the Polish pilgrims:

> 1. You are among foreigners like Apostles among idolaters.
>
> 2. Do not be too offended by the idolaters, strike them with words, and others will strike them with swords, and those who strike them are the Jews, that is the people of the Old Covenant, who worship the Sovereignty of the People, and Equality, and Freedom. They hate the idolaters, and do not have love for

---

131. Damiani, "Mickiewicz's Position in Italy," in Kridl, ed., *Mickiewicz: Poet of Poland*, 225.

their neighbors, and they are sent to destroy the idolatrous Canaanites.

3. And they will smash their idols, and they will judge the idolaters by the law of Moses, and Joshua, and Robespierre, and Saint-Just,[132] destroying them [all] from the elderly to the sucking child, from the cattle to the dogs. For their GOD, who is called the Sovereignty of the People, is righteous, an angry, and consuming fire.

4. And just as Christ and his law arose among the Jews in their capitol, so in the capitol of the European liberals there will arise Your law, the new law of self-sacrifice and LOVE.[133]

In this allegory, the Pagans are the kings and ruling classes of Europe, the Jews are the people and leaders of the French Revolution, and the Christians are the Polish "pilgrims" in exile in France, the land of Robespierre. In Mickiewicz's judgment, Christianity fulfilled and surpassed Judaism, so Poland's task was to surpass the French Revolution, fulfilling its aspirations without compromising its ideals. On a personal and national level, the "new law" that Poland's "apostles" are to announce includes patriotism instead of materialism, dedication and self-sacrifice in place of "egoism," and spirituality rather than unbelief. Internationally, it proclaims the *liberté, egalité, fraternité* of the French Revolution, accompanied by a new spirit of love for brother nations. Eschatologically, it represents Poland as the lover of freedom unjustly murdered by the tyrants, whose resurrection will usher in a new age of international brotherhood and peace.

Paraphrased, the *Books* message to the Polish pilgrims was this: "Soon the oppressed peoples of Europe will rise up against the tyrants. Get ready for the Spring of Nations that you are destined to lead." The Books end with "A Pilgrim's Prayer." As Stefanowska writes, "Do not let the prayerful form of the ending fool you. It is above all a call to battle."[134]

> For a universal war for the Freedom of the Nations!
> We beseech thee, O Lord.

---

132. One of the Jacobin leaders of the French Revolution, known for his cruelty, He was beheaded together with Robespierre on July 28, 1794.

133. Mickiewicz, *The Books of the Polish Pilgrimage*, book XVIII, verses 1–4, 250–51.

134. Stefanowska, *Historia i profecja*, 228.

> For weapons and the national banners.
> We beseech Thee, O Lord.
> For a blessed death on the field of battle.
> We beseech Thee O Lord.
> For a grave for our bones in our land.
> We beseech Thee, O Lord.
> For the independence, unity, and freedom of our Fatherland.
> We beseech Thee, O Lord.
> In the Name of the Father, and the Son, and the Holy Spirit.
> Amem.[135]

Mickiewicz's belief that a revolutionary upheaval was imminent proved premature, and he confessed in 1833 that the time was not yet ripe for an armed uprising. Yet his prediction of "a universal war for the Freedom of the Nations" was nearly realized in 1848. Although many European nations had to wait until the twentieth century to receive their freedom, his call to replace the obsolete "balance of power" with a federation of independent states sounds almost prophetic today. Furthermore, Mickiewicz boldly addressed the issue of when to move from passive to active resistance. The tension sensed here between the condemnation of unjust wars of aggression and the call for an armed revolution to free the enslaved peoples reappears whenever structural evil surpasses certain limits.

Mickiewicz failed to unite the "pilgrims." Conservatives rejected his call for a social revolution; apart from Poland's absence, they thought Europe was largely the way it should be. Others considered his political Gospel at odds with the official stance of the Roman Church. Conversely, members of the democratic camp considered Mickiewicz's appeal to religion reactionary. Nevertheless, the *Books*' influence in Poland was great. It also became widely popular throughout Europe, for it captured the aspirations of other nations that were seeking their freedom. Stefanowska writes,

> The national feelings of Poles, Italians, Germans, Irish, Ukrainians, Romanians expressed itself in similar terms. The glorification by Mickiewicz of his own nation was for these readers something understandable and in light of their experience natural. Therefore in European culture the *Books* occupy an hon-

---

135. Mickiewicz, the closing lines of the "Pilgrim's Litany." Mickiewicz, *Powieści poetyckie*, 262.

ored place among the manifestation of those ideas that became incarnate in the revolutionary act of the Spring of Nations.[136]

Mickiewicz believed that faith is on the side of freedom and social justice, thus Christ's followers cannot serve the interests of the ruling class who oppress the weak and powerless. The *Books* reaffirm his commitment to spiritual labor and growth, and his belief that the spiritual and visible worlds influence each other. As Stefanowska argues, the biblical style proved conducive to Mickiewicz's purposes, for "a human being here is understood holistically, as a being whose drama is entwined with everyday situations, and between the expression of biological life and spiritual experiences there is a close connection, a mutual interpenetration."[137] Today, following modernism's depreciation of spiritual reality, we are witnessing a resurgence of belief in the spiritual and a more holistic approach to life, health, and relationships.[138]

Mickiewicz's condemnation of "political parity" brings to mind the "nuclear parity" of the Cold War era. The European and international communities are struggling today to replace this fragile "balance of power" system with new formulas that promise greater peace and stability. In June of 2000, Germany's Foreign Minister Joschka Fischer spoke in words reminiscent of the *Books of the Nation and the Polish Pilgrimage*. Fischer describes how the "European system of states," based on a balance of power enforced by treaties, or if need be by wars, was made untenable by industrialization and the rise of nationalism. The end of World War II saw Europe divided and dominated by outside powers—the USA and USSR. In this context the idea of European integration was born.[139] What Fischer goes on to call an "almost revolutionary idea," i.e., replacing military parity with a federation of equal, free nations, was proposed 125 years earlier by Adam Mickiewicz.

What about Poland's unique role in the cause of freedom? As a political program, Mickiewicz's declaration that Poland is the "Christ of the Nations" is best understood as arguing for the elimination of unjust and oppressive political and social structures. Today Poland's geo-political

---

136. Stefanowska, *Historia i profecja,* 234–35.

137. Ibid., 128.

138. Openness to spiritual experience alone does not imply agreement with the Biblical view of spiritual reality.

139. Joschka Fisher, in an interview with Adam Michnik, *Gazeta Wyborcza*, 3–4 June, 22–24.

position between East and West continue to make it a critical player in Europe. What Mickiewicz wrote long ago, when stripped of its romantic rhetoric, sounds remarkably like the following quote by Fischer:

> Poland was the thermometer, which showed the level of freedom or oppression in Europe. When Poland was free, that was a clear signal that the temperature of freedom in Europe was good. If it was oppressed, the whole continent was oppressed. Just as the last partition of Poland by Hitler and Stalin, and the war that Hitler waged against Poland, made visible that link between Poland and Europe, for the entire continent suffered and was divided. If we treat Poland as a measure of European freedom, then we are now heading for good times...[140]

The Politics of the Kingdom: The Polish Pilgrimage (1833)

Forefathers' Eve, Part III and *The Books of the Nation and the Polish Pilgrimage* were published in 1832. *Sentences and Comments* and *Master Thaddeus* appeared in 1834. In between, Mickiewicz undertook a short-lived career as a political journalist.[141] Predictably, his political articles reflected views characteristic of his major works of the period, such as an insistence on morality in politics, an appeal to traditional and family values, and support for a pan-European democratic movement of liberation leading to a federated Europe.[142] As Kridl notes, they display "an aversion to rationalist 'program discussions' while ... propagating concrete activity, *action* based on faith and intuition."[143]

Mickiewicz shared the premonition, common to revolutionary movements throughout Europe, that a great socio-political transformation was imminent. Polish democrats believed that the nations, with Poland at their head, would rise up together against the monarchs, and Mickiewicz wrote "to prepare the emigrants to take active part in

---

140. Ibid., 24.

141. Mickiewicz's journalistic career begins in 1832 with several letters, articles and speeches, including his programmatic November address entitled "On the National Spirit." Most of his political columns appeared in the *Polish Pilgrimage*, a periodical addressed to Paris exiles that Mickiewicz edited from April to June 1833. This period ended late in 1833 with the unpublished "Letter to Galician Friends."

142. Przychodniak, "Walka o rząd dusz," 138.

143. Kridl, *Mickiewicz*, 94.

the great upheaval."[144] Przychodniak argues that Mickiewicz timed his move carefully, believing that "as the editor of an important magazine he would truly find himself in the *avant-garde* of the revolutionary movement, that he would have influence on the development of events prophetically foretold in the *Books of the Polish Nation*."[145]

Mickiewicz the publicist sought to synthesize the romantic ideal of fighting "with pen and sword." As he wrote, "We call politics, acting only those deeds—or words and thoughts—that give birth to [further] deeds. Such deeds are battle, victory or martyrdom . . ."[146] His journalism was thus an attempt to produce "words and thoughts that give birth to deeds." The *political word* is thereby defined as an *action* that causes an action. In this way, Przychodniak explains, "remaining a writer—[Mickiewicz] became an activist, a man of action."[147] Ironically, according to his own definition, his truly "political" words, i.e., those that gave birth to deeds, were contained in his poetry and not his overtly political writings.

Mickiewicz chose to become politically active without becoming a politician. Advocating unity in the fight to liberate Poland, he stayed apart from the exiles' political infighting, preferring to take up Woronicz's mantle as the nation's teacher, preacher, and catechist. Commentators have hailed him as "the Great Translator," i.e., one who reads the signs of the times and explains them to his people,[148] and the "organizer of the national imagination."[149] Commenting on his 1832 lecture, "On the National Spirit," Trojanowiczowa writes:

> Mickiewicz raised the need to work out a new model of Polish patriotism; such a model whose realization—[by] liquidating the quarrels and divisions—would integrate the entire nation and in this way effectively defend it against death. [. . .] Thus he was after a home-grown consensus in the matter of this desired model of patriotism; a patriotism that would be a successful in-

---

144. Kozicki, *Dziedzictwo polityczne trzech wieszczów*, 96.

145. Przychodniak, "Walka o rząd dusz," 146.

146. Mickiewicz, "On the Unpolitical," cited in Przychodniak, "Walka o rząd dusz," 152–53.

147. Przychodniak "Walka o rząd dusz," 152.

148. Ibid., 159.

149. Trojanowiczowa, "Organizator narodowej wyobraźni" 13.

strument in the battle for freedom, and as such would be subject to an almost organized propaganda.[150]

As in *Master Thaddeus*, Mickiewicz based this new patriotic model on Polish traditions maintained by gentry and peasants alike. Yet this return to the nation's roots did not promote a program of isolation and xenophobia, for Mickiewicz held the 'European Spirit' to be intrinsic to Polish patriotism. As Trojanowiczowa explains, the poet expected his model of patriotism to contribute to the European spirit, for "just as of old Christianization united Poland with the 'European system,' and [just as] Poland had much to thank the West for, so now the Polish nation had a chance to enrich that system and to actively co-create it."[151]

Mickiewicz's lecture "On the National Spirit" preceded the publication of the *Books of the Polish Nation and the Polish Pilgrimage* by two weeks. It appears that this lecture was intended to set the stage for the reception of the *Books,* and to insist on the need to put their "messianic philosophy of history" into practice. Trojanowiczowa writes, that "one gets the feeling that the lecture to the Lithuanian and Belarusian Lands' Society, consistently conducted in the language of journalistic discourse, aimed to impose political pragmatism on the ideology of the *Books*: it closely linked the postulated model of patriotism with the recovery of independence, it argued for the inseparability of Poland and the future rebirth of Europe."[152]

Mickiewicz was criticized for an article in the *Polish Pilgrimage*, "Concerning Reasonable and Crazy People," which supported two ill-fated efforts to take action. One was the effort to join a rumored revolt in Germany, the other an attempt to initiate an uprising in Poland. He justified such deeds by arguing that while they were indeed foolhardy on an individual basis, they kept the nation's hopes for freedom alive, and nurtured the commitment to fight until this goal is achieved. Yet late in 1833, in his last significant political statement of this period, Mickiewicz wrote these words in a letter "To Galician Friends": "An armed uprising would be a declaration of war against three countries: Russia, Austria, and Prussia, whose policies are now completely in agreement and who

---

150. Ibid.
151. Ibid., 13.
152. Ibid., 14.

would support one another. I see no means at this time of conducting such a great war."¹⁵³ Kozicki's analysis of this letter is revealing:

> Mickiewicz remained faithful to his basic presuppositions: the belief in the coming upheaval in Europe, and the conviction that Poland could only be rebuilt with a weapon in hand and in cooperation with the peoples against the governments. But he came to the conclusion that the uprising was not close, that there could be no question of calling it forth immediately, [and] that it must be preceded by a long preparation period.¹⁵⁴

The "spirit of the times" had changed and the political wind was not blowing Poland's way. What then should a patriot do? Kozicki, to his credit rising above the darker side of National Democratic ideology, quotes and comments on Mickiewicz's simple answer:

> In light of this there remained only internal work, which "should have as its purpose the preparation and gathering of strength and means for the future uprising." One should spread the national spirit and awaken political consciousness among as wide a sphere as possible. Not awaken dislike between the specific levels, but on the contrary, to point out [their] common interests: "one should admit and encourage all classes of inhabitants to this work. Princes, nobles, peasants, and Jews are all necessary for us."¹⁵⁵

As this letter shows, Mickiewicz was not a "hopeless romantic." He could urge Poles to undertake the "organic work" promoted by positivism, or display a grasp of *Realpolitik* to be envied by National Democrats.

The Constitution of the Kingdom: "The List of Rules" (1848)

In 1834 Mickiewicz was at the peak of his creative power. It appeared he had a bright future ahead, yet the remaining years of his life were difficult and disappointing. The emigrant community was divided and quarreling, and the "universal war for the freedom of the nations" was nowhere visible on the horizon. Lonely and restless, he entered into an unhappy marriage, and was soon burdened with a family of five to sup-

---

153. Mickiewicz, cited in Kozicki, *Dziedzictwo polityczne trzech wieszczów*, 97.

154. Kozicki, *Dziedzictwo polityczne trzech wieszczów*, 97.

155. Ibid., 98. Material in quotation marks are citations from Mickiewicz's letter "To Galician Friends."

port and a wife who became mentally ill. Finances were always short. His endeavors to "earn his bread" by writing plays for the French stage ended in failure. He wanted to write a sequel to *Master Thaddeus* and dreamed of his "life work," a further installment of *Forefathers' Eve*, but these attempts either did not get far or failed to satisfy him. Apart from a few minor efforts, his only significant poetic output came during his brief, one-year tenure as a Classics (Latin) teacher at the University of Lausanne, where he wrote a series of beautiful, haunting lyrical poems, characterized by their serenity, simplicity, and intimacy.

Yet there were several episodes when the old fire, if not the poetic gift, returned, and Mickiewicz became a man of action. The first of these came in 1840, when Mickiewicz was called to Paris to accept the newly formed chair of Slavic Studies at the prestigious Collège de France. With renewed passion, he used his lectures to proclaim Poland's cause and his own messianic vision. The direction of this course changed in 1841, following his encounter with Andrzej Towiański, a minor Lithuanian mystic who came to Paris and proclaimed himself the "redeemer" from Father Peter's vision. Mickiewicz accepted his claim, partly because their messianic beliefs were similar, and partly because the mystic "healed" the poet's wife through his charismatic, authoritative presence.[156] Not only was his involvement in Towiański's "Circle of God's Cause" time-consuming and inimical to the creative process, the mystic explicitly discouraged him from writing. Mickiewicz's lectures at the College took on the role of propaganda for the Circle, which led finally to his dismissal in 1844. The "Paris Lectures" were edited and published. They are interesting and complex, yet add little that is new to the messianic vision and political views expressed during his great creative period that lasted from 1820 to 1834. In the end, Mickiewicz broke with Towiański in 1846 over the mystic's refusal to engage in the real world of politics and history. Towiański limited action to the spiritual realm, believing that when the Circle reached a sort of spiritual "critical mass," this would trigger the coming of the new era. In contrast, Mickiewicz from the very beginning treated the Circle's "spiritual labor" as preparation for action in the real world, where one must employ means that are concrete, if less than perfect. As Pigoń writes, "Mickiewicz did not consent to the

---

156. Although the healing, apparently a case of imposing an outward authority structure on a confused mind, proved temporary, Mickiewicz took it as proof of Towiański's spiritual power and calling.

Master's[157] principle, that in an ideal cause one may only employ ideal means, and until they are at hand—wait. He contented himself with relatively ideal means, the best of those available."[158]

A second period of journalistic activity came in 1849, when Mickiewicz became the founding editor of a French language journal, *La Tribune des Peuples,* which featured an international cast of writers, and proclaimed "republican, revolutionary, and socialist ideas."[159] As Kridl explains, the journal represented the "strong democratic and revolutionary tendencies" of the Europe of that day, which were directed against the rulers and which espoused socialism "as a general tendency rather than a program."[160] *La Tribune* was suspended in November of 1849 by the French authorities.

Mickiewicz also tried twice to organize a Polish Legion, in 1848 and 1855. These efforts did not come to much, and he himself died in Constantinople during the second of these attempts. But their idea and timing were not as foolhardy as seems. In both cases, local struggles against the partitioning powers had the potential of turning into wider conflicts, perhaps even the "universal war for the freedom of the nations" of the "Pilgrim's Prayer." More important than their accomplishments was their intent: the Legion was to be the model of renewed a Polish society, state, and government, or in the words of Pigoń, "a microcosmos of the New Poland."[161] The legacy of the 1848 Polish Legion remains the "List of Rules," otherwise known as the "Political Symbol for Poland," written by Mickiewicz to express the religious, social, and political goals of the Legion. Speaking of the "List of Rules," Mazzini declared, "If the Polish Legion of '48 had been nothing more than a political symbol, that alone would have assured its renown."[162] These rules have special significance, for they were meant to express the ideological basis for the constitution of a revived Polish State.[163] Far from spontaneous, the "List

---

157. I.e., Towianski.
158. Pigoń, "Fundamenty ideowe Legionu," 240.
159. Kridl, *Mickiewicz*, 94.
160. Ibid., 96.
161. Pigoń "Fundamenty ideowe legionu," 226.
162. Mazzini, cited by Maver in "Adam Mickiewicz in Rome in 1848," in Kridl, *Mickiewicz*, 235.
163. Maver writes that "in fifteen short articles [the 'Political Symbol of Poland'] included an organic plan for a radically reformed constitution for the Poland of the fu-

of Rules" resulted from Mickiewicz's labors and reflections in the reorganized "Circle of God's Cause" that he led during 1847 following the break with Towianski. Pigoń explains that "The Circle thus became sort of a testing grounds, a laboratory of future forms of social existence."[164] What was worked out in practice, first in the Circle, then in the Legion, was to finally be realized in the nation.

The "List of Rules" develop the three guiding principles of Mickiewicz's reformed "Circle": "1. the religious relationship with the nation, 2. the political issue: what should the future Poland be like, 3. the family issue." Concerning religion and the nation, Mickiewicz gives pride of place to the Roman Catholic faith, under the condition that it manifests its true spirit in acts of freedom. However, the List proclaims religious freedom, and grants all religious communities a free and equal place in the nation. Protestants and Jews are particularly singled out, but this presumably includes Orthodox, Uniates, and Moslems as well. The List adds ethnic pluralism to religious pluralism, and grants citizenship and equal rights to all regardless of race, ethnic background, religion or gender. Agrarian reform is promised that would grant peasants their own land. Free speech, democracy, and a declaration of the universal "brotherhood of nations" rounds out the main points contained in the "List." As Pigoń exclaims, "No Polish Uprising ever had such a clearly and boldly codified leading program."[165] This is the program, we recall, of Jagiellonian Poland, and as we shall see in chapter 4, its main points continued to serve as the common values and goals of the democratic opposition movement in the second half of the twentieth century.

Before closing this chapter, a word is in order on why Mickiewicz stopped writing poetry. Wacław Borowy claimed that the "poet of transformation" transformed himself into a non-poet, and that Mickiewicz stopped writing because he chose to stop. It seems more likely that the poetic gift had dried up and deserted him. Weintraub takes this position, and there is ample evidence to support his claim that the poet tried at various intervals to write more poetry, to little effect. Weintraub concludes, "The poet had lost his old poetic gifts, and inspiration, invoked

---

ture, or better, a suggestive vision of the future ideal state." Maver, in Kridl, *Mickiewicz*, 233.

164. Pigoń "Fundamenty ideowe legionu," 233.

165. Ibid., 243.

again and again, did not come back."¹⁶⁶ That said, the non-poetical endeavors that filled the last years of his life form an integral part of his personal and political pilgrimage. The Paris Lectures, the return in 1849 to the world of political journalism, and the two attempts to create a Polish legion represent Mickiewicz's lifelong commitment to matching words with deeds, and his ongoing desire to impact and change the world. Kridl summarizes, "Since, according to him, poetry is only one of the releases for inspiration, which may also be manifested in practical activity and everyday life, he did not restrict himself to cultivating his art."¹⁶⁷ As Mickiewicz declared in the Paris Lectures:

> "If your Crusade and your French Revolution have not yet taken place, hurry up, otherwise you will not be able to keep in step with today's generation. To build your temple and to live out your Crusade means something more than to read a description of a temple and the history of the Crusades." (lecture from 30 IV 1844)¹⁶⁸

---

166. Weintraub, *Poetry of Adam Mickiewicz*, 281.
167. Kridl, *Mickiewicz*, 97.
168. Cited by Janion and Żmigrodzka, *Romantyzm i historia*, 23.

4

The Polish Reception of Bonhoeffer

THE PRIMARY FOCUS OF THIS BOOK IS POLISH MESSIANISM. BONHOEFFER was chosen as a dialogue partner because of the potential his work offers for a theological critique of key messianic presuppositions and values. Before confronting messianism directly with Bonhoeffer, the decision was made to consider what use Poles have already made of his work. As this chapter will show, the Polish reception of Bonhoeffer took place mainly among members of the opposition movement that arose after 1968. Their program of "citizens' society," which shows the influence of Bonhoeffer, was itself a critical adaptation of the legacy of Polish messianism.[1] Therefore, while chapter 4 specifically examines the Polish reception of Bonhoeffer, and does not pause to identify every connection or distinction between citizens' society and Polish messianism, it also serves as a helpful bridge from messianism to the discussion of Bonhoeffer's thought in chapter 5 and the use of Bonhoeffer in chapter 6 to critique messianism.[2] Since a comparison of the opposition's thought and praxis with Bonhoeffer was required in order to demonstrate the influence he exerted on their program, the survey in this chapter of Bonhoeffer's reception in Poland crosses over at times into an initial critique of the Polish opposition movement.

Bonhoeffer and the "Polish Dialogue": 1968–1989

The climactic stage in Poland's 200-year struggle to regain national independence took place from 1968 to 1989. Drawing on the ideals of Polish

---

1. To over-simplify, in many respects the Polish reception of Bonhoeffer thus already constitutes an initial Bonhoefferian critique of messianism.

2. Chapter 6 also critiques certain aspects of citizens' society that are deemed to adapt or advance Polish messianism in a helpful way.

messianism, and applying the lessons learned from failed uprisings, the essential but unsatisfying stress on organic work, a brief period of independence between two world wars, and life in Soviet-backed People's Poland, activists created an independent civil society between the cracks in the socialist system. Crucial to this process was the dialogue between mutually estranged Catholic intellectuals and secular dissidents that coalesced into the Polish opposition movement. As Tadeusz Mazowiecki recently testified, "I saw, and Jacek [Kuroń] with Adam Michnik also saw, the need to cross the ditches, reaching back into the nineteenth century, between the secular intelligentsia and the Church."[3] This chapter sketches the formation of those "ditches" separating secular and Catholic intellectuals in Poland, before tracing the impact of Dietrich Bonhoeffer's life and writings on their rapprochement.

While De Gruchy's warning against overestimating Bonhoeffer's "direct or overt influence"[4] is as apt in Poland as in South Africa, his legacy became a crucial reference point for Polish activists, who joined together to affirm human rights and oppose the totalitarian communist regime. Although their engagement with Bonhoeffer did not create the Polish dialogue, it markedly influenced its course and content. The Polish reception of Bonhoeffer reflects his Polish readers' personal and national history, cultural legacy, and geo-political context. Understanding how Bonhoeffer influenced the Poles' appropriation of their own messianic tradition sets the stage for chapter 6, which draws on Bonhoeffer for a more direct critique of Polish messianism.

Historical Background: 1945–1968

Following World War II, in a course of events largely determined by the Yalta agreements, a Soviet backed communist government came to power in Poland. When the Stalinist period ended in Poland in 1956, the weakened communist party granted limited privileges to various segments of society. Some hoped this would lead to more deep-seated, sweeping reforms, and loose groupings of progressive Catholic and secular intellectuals (primarily those from leftist traditions) fought to deepen the reforms and promote democratization. However, as the new

---

3. Mazowiecki, "Żywioł i człowiek," 92. Mazowiecki, Kuroń and Michnik are introduced later in this chapter.

4. de Gruchy, "Bonhoeffer, Apartheid, and Beyond," 354–55. Neither should one underestimate his indirect and covert influence.

party leaders consolidated their position it soon became clear that these were only temporary concessions. Those who wished to wrench Poland from the Soviet orbit, or more modestly to promote greater democracy and social justice within the limits imposed on society from without, still faced the dilemma of "reform or revolution."

Adam Michnik's landmark essay "New Evolutionism"[5] discusses two disparate attempts to encourage the evolution of the Polish communist party; "revisionism" and "neopositivism." The *revisionists* were socialist intellectuals who accepted Marxist ideology but rejected its Soviet and derivative Polish incarnations. Anna Chmielewska describes her generation, the first to be raised in People's Poland. "We were taught a false history," she says, "but we were also taught to see social injustice as the most important matter." Furthermore, "we were taught that all are equal regardless of race and nationality . . . and we were taught vulgar atheism." Finally, she declares, we were taught "that one is either on the side of the oppressed or the oppressors."[6] Faced with what seemed a clear choice, Chmielewska and her peers took their stand "on the left," choosing, as she puts it, "activity against apathy." But reality refused to fit neatly into Marxist doctrine, and the future that Marxism's laws "objectively" predicted did not come to pass. Thus was born "revisionism," the belief of many socialists that the system was right, only its implementation had gone awry.[7] In contrast, the *neopositivists*, who identified with the Catholic Church, rejected Marxist doctrine while accepting Soviet control over Poland as a geo-political reality. Led by the leader of the Znak parliamentary group, Stanisław Stomma, they ". . . aimed at creating a political movement that, at the right moment, could lead the Polish nation."[8] Both revisionists and neopositivists believed that there existed or would emerge within the party a progressive reform wing that shared their values and goals, i.e., democracy, equality, social justice, and individual autonomy. Michnik explains the presupposition common to revisionists and neopositivists: "The two concepts shared the conviction that change would come from above."[9]

---

5. "Old" evolutionism, the hope of revisionists and neopositivists, referred to the gradual democratization of communist party structures.

6. Chmielewska, "List do Przyjaciół," 84.

7. Ibid., 85.

8. Michnik, "The New Evolutionism," 136.

9. Ibid.

Michnik, who acknowledges the contributions that revisionists and neopositivists made to Polish society, argues that both approaches were doomed to failure. Revisionist hopes' ended in 1968, when the party suppressed Polish students and intellectuals in a vicious campaign that appealed to national-chauvinism and anti-Semitism. Chmielewska adds that the communist authorities themselves gave up all but the pretence of allegiance to Marxist doctrine, making further dialogue with or within Marxism impossible, for the simple reason that there were no longer any genuine Marxists to talk to.[10] The suppression of the 1968 "Prague Spring" by Warsaw Pact forces, and the 1970 shooting by Polish security forces of striking workers, removed any remaining illusions that the communist party would willingly loosen or renounce its control over society. The final blow for the neopositivists came in 1976, when Stomma sacrificed his parliamentary seat but retained his honor by refusing to vote for the constitutional amendments to the Polish constitution[11] that affirmed the "leading role" of the party and Poland's eternal friendship with the USSR.

Bonhoeffer and the Heirs of Messianism: 1968–1989

In 1968 the fledgling anti-totalitarian opposition in Poland was divided into diverse camps. The farmers and workers were capable of some resistance, e.g., to collectivization and price rises, via strikes and demonstrations. The Catholic Church had resisted with considerable success the attempts of the party to marginalize its influence, impact its decisions, and limit its ministry. However, the Catholic hierarchy and intelligentsia remained suspicious of the secular, post-revisionist intellectuals who formed the core of the newly emerging opposition, while secular intellectuals continued to view the Church as reactionary and obscurantist. Michnik, with perhaps only slight exaggeration, describes the arctic chill that marked the initial meetings between these groups:

> They treated us as if we were Beria and Stalin's agents, and we saw them as agents of Torquemada's Inquisition. But after a while the ice began to melt . . . and we realized that we had more in common than not.[12]

---

10. Chmielewska "List do Przyjaciół," 86.
11. Out of all the deputies in Parliament, Stomma alone abstained.
12. Michnik, "Anti-authoritarian Revolt," 52.

Catholic and secular intellectuals held "in common" many values that Polish messianism had passed on to the post-WWII intelligentsia, including a commitment to freedom, human dignity, and social justice, a respect for cultural, religious, and ethnic diversity, and a readiness to act sacrificially for the nation's good matched with the vision of international brotherhood. Messianism, however, did not come to them directly from the poets' pens, for its ideals and program had been tested in the crucible of history. The failed uprisings of the 19th century, together with the positivist tradition, confirmed the need for organic work. The indomitables reasserted the need to take action and to strive for independence, the socialists deepened the commitment to social justice, while the National Democrats displayed a savvy for political organization matched with an astute analysis of geo-political realities. The failed attempts to reform the communist party, and the futility of an armed uprising against a government backed by Soviet tanks, led many to seek a more promising alternative to the options of "reform or revolution." It was in this political climate that the Polish dialogue began.

The initiative for dialogue between the secular leftist and progressive Catholic wings of the Polish intelligentsia came largely from Catholic intellectuals associated with the publications *Znak*, *Tygodnik Powszechny*, and *Więź*, as well as the Catholic Intellectuals' Clubs (KIK).[13] Michnik paid a special tribute to the journal *Więź*:

> The *Więź* group of the Polish Catholic Left [combined] revisionist hopes with the political strategy of Znak's neo-positivists. The innovative ideas of Tadeusz Mazowiecki,[14] Anna Morawska, and other essayists published in *Więź*... made possible an ideological dialogue with the lay intelligentsia. As paradoxical as this may sound, it was the *Więź* group that enabled the leftist intelligentsia to revise traditional stereotypes of Christianity and the Church.[15]

Więź's "innovative ideas" reflected the journal's programmatic orientation to remain true to Christianity while entering into conversation

---

13. Five such clubs were registered during the brief thaw following Stalin's death.

14. Tadeusz Mazowiecki, one of five *Znak* deputies to the Polish Parliament (1961–1971), founded *Więź* in 1958. He left the journal in 1980 to serve as an advisor to Solidarity. In 1989 he became Poland's first non–communist prime minister since WWII.

15. Michnik, "Dispute over Organic Work," 140.

with the socialist revisionists. *Więź* promoted Catholic personalism and the thought of Pope John XXIII, while stressing humanist ideals of justice, equality, and the value of the individual. It called for the "development of democratic forms of public life," and for treating "society as a subject."[16] Mazowiecki supplied the following definition of dialogue, an explicit element in the program of *Więź*:[17]

> A dialogue is made up of three components: people, a common platform, and values...A dialogue depends on the communication and transfer of values. A dialogue thus occurs whenever there is a readiness to understand the validity of someone else's position and to enter into a different way of thinking: that is, whenever there is an openness to the values embedded in other points of view...A dialogue is not a compromise; the tension of contradiction still exists...Dialogue is a method by which an ideologically diverse society can learn to live together.[18]

Secular intellectuals accepted this definition as a basis for dialogue between opposition members. Barbara Falk writes, "Diametrical opposition between the Left and the Church in the Polish context evolved to a point where intellectual strata in both sides came to have a set of similar goals, learned to speak a similar language, and could thus engage in a dialogue."[19] Soon secular intellectuals were meeting with their Catholic counterparts, and publishing in their periodicals.[20] Representatives of both groups signed the same protest letters and cooperated in many ways in building an independent civil society. And they read Bonhoeffer.

Anna Morawska, a scholar and writer associated with Więź, introduced Bonhoeffer to Polish intellectual life. Her 1968 article, "Dietrich

---

16. "Historia miesięcznika Więź,." Online: http://www.wiez.com.pl/?s__historia_pisma.

17. In 1963 Julian Eski, assistant editor of *Więź*, published *The Open Church*. *Więź* comments: 'For [Eski], openness was a moral postulate, an evangelical requirement of openness to all people, regardless of their convictions. From this attitude there flowed the readiness for dialogue with Christians of other confessions, Jews, unbelievers, neighboring nations, that is characteristic of *Więź*. "Historia miesięcznika Więź." Online: http://www.wiez.com.pl/?s__historia_pisma.

18. Mazowiecki, cited by Adam Michnik, *Church and the Left*, 183.

19. Falk, *Dilemmas of Dissidence*, 170.

20. Michnik writes, "The only newspapers that published my articles in those days were Catholic newspapers: Tadeusz Mazowiecki published them under a pseudonym in *Więź*. And Bohdan Cywiński published Kuron's texts in the journal *Znak*." Michnik, "Dispute over Organic Work," 52.

Bonhoeffer,"[21] was followed in 1970 by Selected Writings[22] and a book-length biography,[23] which helped both Catholic and secular readers understand the German Lutheran pastor and theologian. While exhibiting a clear understanding of Bonhoeffer's thought and his historical, theological, and cultural context, she highlights issues relevant to Poland's own situation, and ways in which his legacy continues to inform and challenge us today. Her portrait of Bonhoeffer, decisive in her generation, retains its influence today in post-1989 Poland.

Among secular intellectuals, Adam Michnik[24] most frequently refers to Bonhoeffer. His first references to Bonhoeffer appear in The Church and the Left,[25] written in 1977 in response to Bohdan Cywiński's, The Geneologies of the Indomitables.[26] Cywiński's work, which showed how Poles from socialist and Christian traditions had often worked together for freedom, social justice, and human dignity, helped Catholics rediscover their heritage of social activism, and enabled their secular counterparts to recognize the Church as a potential ally. As Lipski notes, Cywiński's book helped establish a "common ideological language" in which Catholic and secular opposition members could express the values that united them in their resistance to the Communist regime.

> Bohdan Cywiński . . . gave a historical-ideological formula to this new unity. This book gained enormous popularity and exercised great influence on the circles that formed KOR,[27] not least on their ethical consciousness, by showing the harmony between the tradition of ethical-social Catholics and "secular

21. Morawska, "Dietrich Bonhoeffer," 1340–64.

22. Morawska, *Wybór Pism*.

23. Morawska, *Chrześcijanin w Trzeciej Rzeszy*.

24. Adam Michnik (1947–), historian, essayist, political activist, a member of the "commandos" (a term coined to describe students involved in the 1968 demonstrations), co-founder of the Committee for the Defense of Workers (KOR), advisor to Solidarity, participant in the "Round Table" discussions of 1989, member of Parliament (1989–1991), since 1989 the editor of *Gazeta Wyborcza*, the largest daily newspaper in Poland.

25. Michnik, *Church and the Left*, 1993.

26. Cywiński, *Rodowody niepokornych*. Bohdan Cywiński, writer and editor of *Znak*, eventually resigned as *Znak's* editor so that his "political" activities with KOR would not bring unnecessary attack on the journal.

27. The "Committee for the Defense of Workers" (KOR) was formed in 1976 to provide legal and material aid to workers (and their families) who were fired, arrested, or imprisoned for their protests against the government.

laypersons" in their respective, related streams of social work for the good of one's neighbor and the nation in a spirit that exceeds tolerance.[28]

Michnik argued that since WWII the Catholic Church in Poland had consistently stood for freedom and against totalitarian rule.[29] Declaring the dividing lines of right and left, as well as of Christian and secular outdated, Michnik argued that from now on, "those who believe in the ideals of liberty, equality, and the freedom of labor can only be found in the ranks of the antitotalitarian opposition."[30] Bonhoeffer played a crucial role in this new approach. As Michnik confessed in 1987, ". . . reading Bonhoeffer was essential for me because he explained how to be an anti-totalitarian Christian."[31] Michnik's new attitude betrays the influence of his mentor and friend, Jacek Kuroń.[32] In 1971 Cywiński invited Kuroń to a meeting of the Catholic Intellectuals' Club of Warsaw, where Kryzstof Śliwiński gave him a copy of Bonhoeffer's writings.[33] Kuroń was deeply impressed by Bonhoeffer's vision of non-religious Christianity. In his 1975 article in *Znak*, "Christians Without God," he quoted Bonhoeffer's reflections on the endangered, homeless values of Western culture that sought refuge from the Nazi threat in the "shadow of the Christian Church," and which as estranged "children of the Church . . . returned to their mother."[34] Kuroń declared himself to have accepted Christianity "as a system of values and not a religion."

> I am one of those, who in recent years have come to Christianity, have accepted it, or rather—want to accept it, but as a system of values and not a religion. I feel myself to be one of many, who think alike in many respects . . . Therefore that which is common

---

28. Lipski, "Etos Komitetu Obrony Robotników," 44.

29. As Falk comments, "Michnik's own reassessment of the Church as a potentially progressive source of democratic values was instrumental in redefining the relationship between Catholic intellectuals and the secular Left." Falk, *Dilemmas of Dissidence*, 167.

30. Michnik, "The Prague Spring Ten Years Later," 158.

31. Michnik, "Anti-authoritarian Revolt," 52.

32. Jacek Kuroń (1934–2004), mentor to Michnik and his generation, began as a Marxist revisionist. Increasingly disenchanted with the communist party, from which he was expelled in 1964, he became a leader of the opposition movement, and was co-founder in the 1970's of KOR.

33. Lipski, "Etos Komitetu Obrony Robotników," 342–43.

34. Bonhoeffer, "Church and the World," 55–56.

to the formation to which I feel attached is a direction of this attitude and reflections. A direction towards Christianity.[35]

Lipski has called Kuron's essay "the most Christianizing influence"[36] among Poland's secular intellectuals. Henceforth Polish intellectuals, both secular and Christian, called on Bonhoeffer to affirm the ideals of Polish messianism, including its vision of Jagiellonian Poland as an ethnically, linguistically, socially, and religiously diverse society. As architects and builders of Polish citizens' society, they drew upon his legacy to promote an ethos of freedom and social responsibility, the practice of non-violence, the development of a political culture that practices dialogue with one's adversaries.[37] In short, they found Bonhoeffer a helpful guide and support in crafting their proposal for an independent citizens' society as an alternative to the Polish dilemma of "reform or revolution." In the following discussion these selected themes, introduced by Morawska and addressed by Michnik, Kuroń, Mazowiecki, and others, serve as an organizing structure for analyzing the Polish reception of Bonhoeffer.

The Polish Reception of Bonhoeffer: Selected Themes

Bonhoeffer was perceived by members of the Polish opposition movement as a Christian humanist, who shared with them the core values of European civilization that they had inherited, among other sources, from Polish messianism. Bonhoeffer's Polish readers returned often to several key themes. They found his work relating to responsibility, resistance, reconciliation, and religion particularly helpful in their efforts to create an independent civil society. Since these themes were also important to Bonhoeffer and Polish messianism, their treatment here sets the stage for the discussion of Bonhoeffer's theology in chapter 5 and its use to critique messianism in chapter 6.

Christian Humanism

From the beginning, Bonhoeffer has been portrayed in Poland as a Christian humanist. Morawska suggested that Polish intellectuals who

---

35. Kuroń, "Chrześcijanie bez Boga," 17–18.
36. Lipski, "Etos Komitetu Obrony Robotników," 43.
37. As opposed to conflict with one's enemies.

survived WWII were "people at the crossroads," who formed a living bridge between successive cultures.[38] Living like Bonhoeffer in times of war and radical social change, they faced the challenge of passing their humanist heritage, inherited in their case from messianism, on to the next generation. By contending that under Nazi or Soviet-style regimes the defense of humanist values and freedoms constitutes a political as well as cultural stance, Morawska hints at what Vaclav Havel made explicit: when a totalitarian government claims authority over all spheres of life, every action has political overtones.

To this cultural-political mandate Morawska adds a commitment to social justice, noting that when Bonhoeffer returned to the "secular" sphere, "His Christianity . . . no longer fit within the narrow bourgeois, nationalistic categories of the national-interest," arguing further that his final letters "truly go beyond the world of the 'post-feudal intelligentsia' and its ideals."[39] Christianity as "being for others" requires, "that one in solidarity takes on all their guilt and uncertainty, and that of the world in a common, humanist effort."[40] In 1968 Morawska held that Bonhoeffer's theology of the cross from *Nachfolge* reflects, besides the passion of Christ, the "tragic situation of the Dahlemites," who were ostracized from the temple fellowship to suffer "outside the gate." Accordingly, following Christ entails the recognition that Christ is truly present "where there is weakness, wrong, powerlessness."[41] To stand with those who are wronged is to embark on the road of true discipleship. Such solidarity with the weak and oppressed became a hallmark of the Polish opposition movement. Morawska draws out other programmatic themes from *Więź*. She appeals to humanist values, calls upon Christians to take a stand on ethical issues, and promotes a Christian social vision that rises above "bourgeois national-interest" and transcends "post-feudal" society. She urges responsible engagement with the world in solidarity with others, even when that entails "soiling" one's own hands. Though Morawska may overstate the degree to which Bonhoeffer exhibits social sensitivity in his later works, she cogently interprets the trajectory of his maturing thought.

38. Morawska, *Chrześcijanin w Trzeciej Rzeszy*, 3–4.
39. Ibid., 16–17.
40. Ibid., 17.
41. Morawska, "Dietrich Bonhoeffer," 1352.

Two Polish dissertations also treat Bonhoeffer's ethics as a form of Christian humanism. A 1972 article[42] by Kosian argues that Bonhoeffer's ethical agenda entailed a systematic redefinition of traditional theological concepts such as "God" and "Christ" in purely sociological terms. This process reached its apogee in the prison letters, where "nonreligious Christianity" is reduced to a social program, the "assured hope" of Christ becomes a necessary "illusion," and transcendence is lost in the immanence of the earthly struggle for justice.[43] Kosian's article[44] parallels early radical readings in the West,[45] even hinting at the Marxist interpretation Müller developed more fully in the GDR.[46] However, Müller's Marxist interpretation of Bonhoeffer was thoroughgoing and programmatic, whereas Kosian only suggests that Bonhoeffer's thought is "worthy of detailed Marxist analysis."[47] Kosian himself soon realized that by highlighting the importance of humanistic ethics in "non-religious Christianity," Bonhoeffer's own experience of Christ was lost. In his 1997 contribution,[48] there is no longer any mention of materialism, Marxist analysis or the class struggle. Kosian's new reading, while still focused on Bonhoeffer's ethical stance, grants an equally central role to his incarnational Christology. The fundamental reality driving his ethic of responsibility is now explicitly recognized to be "the reconciliation of the world with Christ." While the message of the cross still calls us to social justice and ethical responsibility, the power of its call is now drawn from the reality of the God-Man's own humiliation on the cross.[49]

Bonhoeffer's conservative family background and worldview raises reservations over attempts to transform his growing sensitivity to social issues into even incipient forms of socialism. A world full of Nazis left Bonhoeffer little time to develop the social insights evident in the liter-

42. Kosian, "Miejsce etyki w Bonhoefferowskim modelu Chrześcijaństwa bez religii." This article is based on Kosian's PhD thesis.

43. Kosian's radical reading highlights the reductionist tendencies of the secular reception of Bonhoeffer.

44. Józef Kosian is professor of Philosophy at the University of Wrocław.

45. For another radical reading of Bonhoeffer, cf. Lisicki, "Nie-ludzki Bóg," 101–16.

46. Müller, *Von der Kirche zur Welt*.

47. Kosian, "Miejsce etyki w Bonhoefferowskim modelu Chrześcijaństwa bez religii," 160.

48. Kosian, "Dietrich Bonhoeffer—w poszukiwaniu modelu Chrześcijańskiego przyszłości."

49. Ibid., 106.

ary fragments from Tegel prison. It is fascinating to speculate over the direction his thought might have taken had he survived the war, so long as we remember that one soon leaves behind terrain that Bonhoeffer personally traversed. Yet it was his call for responsible action in the defense of freedom, justice, and human dignity that appealed to secular activists in Poland, and that helped Catholics take a more active stance towards social injustice and totalitarian rule. To the extent that Kosian's call for Christian-Marxist dialogue was based on the social reality of economic disparity, unequal opportunity, and exploitive socio-political structures, his appeal may be redirected to address modern Poland's pressing economic and social issues.

Jolanta Wędzel[50] argues in her doctoral dissertation[51] that Bonhoeffer's prison letters impacted contemporary theology by stressing "the value of authentic and responsible human existence in the world and the meaning of personal faithfulness to the Gospel Truth."[52] The author traces the development of Bonhoeffer's thought from his early academic period up to the concept of "religionless Christianity," which was grounded theologically in "the idea of God [who is] immanent, who thus affirms the earthly existence of humanity together with all created reality." This world-affirming theology of incarnation "bore the fruit of a universalistic vision of Christian humanism,"[53] which was all the more striking for having been forged in the crucible of Nazi totalitarianism. Bonhoeffer's ethics, she claims, were an attempt to "cast spiritual values on the level of temporal life . . . to create a sort of Kingdom of God in time, on earth," not as an ideology to be programmatically implemented, but as a "parable" that envisions and works towards a civilization inspired by "evangelical ethical-moral values."[54] Bonhoeffer's Christian humanism provides no stock answers, but opens up real, creative possibilities for responsible action in life's concrete situations. By drawing on the "universalistic ethical-moral principles of the Gospel," enriched

---

50. Jolanta Wędzel is an adjunct professor at the University of Silesia, Institute of Philosophy, Department of Ethics.

51. Wędzel, *Egzystencjalna orientacja teologiczno-etycznej myśli Marcina Lutra i Dietricha Bonhoeffera*, 35:189–245, 38:127–98.

52. Ibid., 128.

53. Ibid., 188.

54. Ibid. By "evangelical" she means Christian, i.e., flowing from the Gospel witness.

by the "metaphysical[55] element," it provides a framework for "working out solutions of a rational nature" that can be endorsed by "people of good will."[56] This aptly describes the "Polish dialogue" that took place within the opposition movement, and remains a promising approach to new challenges presented by the twenty-first century.

Jacek Kuroń represents another approach to Bonhoeffer's Christian humanism. The following testimony from 1989 shows the profound effect that Bonhoeffer's *Letters and Papers from Prison* had on Kuroń.

> ... his religious writings were the most important—incredibly open to all the human problems that were important for us. In one letter, already from death row, out of concern that one would not believe in God out of fear, he says: "One must live as if there were no God." This statement became another great discovery for me. Up until now, perhaps in a not entirely conscious manner, I suspected that Christian morality was based on the principle of the fear of punishment and the desire for reward. For I did not know how to imagine love for God, and only now did I learn that it might grow out of love for humanity. In Bonhoeffer's declaration I was captivated and convinced by the entirely heroic effort to oppose the religion of reward and punishment. Above all I found in this declaration a chance for myself. For after all it means this: to live in a world without God according to His law, and thus I am to live as if there were a God.[57]

In "Christians without God," Kuroń acknowledges Christianity as "the air of European culture," and the source of the humanistic values that his formation prized most highly, i.e., autonomy (free will) and love. He writes, "In Christian values—in the Decalogue, the Gospel, and perhaps above all in the commandments of love and this fundamental commandment, that in creating mankind God gave him free will—there are rooted all the achievements, great and small of our cultural sphere."[58] However, Kuroń argues, love and freedom must be held in tension. Separated, they foster indifference to the plight of others, or

---

55. Truer to Bonhoeffer would be to write "ontological element" or perhaps "transcendence."

56. Ibid., 188.

57. Kuroń, "Lewica—prawica. Bóg," 340.

58. Kuroń, "Chrześcijanie bez Boga," 20.

else a well-intentioned but abusive and ultimately self-defeating attempt to make others happy against their will.

Kuroń recognizes moral transcendence in the encounter with another human being. As he writes, "If therefore all human life is a never-ending attempt to love and create . . . then the Other Person, that one and only, and at once every [person] in all their full distinctiveness is at once the highest value, the purpose of our life, and its essential condition." In the passage below, Kuroń explicitly draws on Bonhoeffer to argue that every interpersonal encounter is an ethical encounter, leading to the recognition of transcendental values that are external to our own existence and actions.[59]

> I do not believe in moral relativism . . . I do believe however in conflicting values [. . .] In this conception interpersonal conflicts and the related conflict of values deny [those values], but also confirm them. For every human deed is directed towards values—motivated by their realization . . . Therefore, if every one of our deeds is directed towards values, then in every situation they are transcendent, that is they supersede me, they are external in relation to our actions—*etsi Deus non daretur*.[60]

In 1975 Kuroń asked if Christianity without God is possible. Though answering in the affirmative, he acknowledged that such Christianity is not easy to maintain. "I realized and became conscious that only transcendental moral law, which is difficult to obtain without God, can protect one from becoming entangled in moral error."[61] Kuroń's denial of moral relativism together with his affirmation of transcendental values appears problematic, coming from one who fell short of confessing faith[62] in a personal God. Yet Bonhoeffer also reintroduced lost transcendence into this-worldly life by locating it in I-You encounters with other human beings. While I define objects outside of me, argues Bonhoeffer, subjectively at least I am the one creating and controlling the world around me. However, when I perceive an "object" *speaking to me*, I am

---

59. Barańczak also locates transcendence in "the other person." Cf. Barańczak (pseud. Niedolski), "Dlaczego nie całkiem jestem Chrześcijaninem," 127.

60. Kuroń, "Chrześcijanie bez Boga," 27–28.

61. Kuroń, "Lewica—prawica. Bóg," 377.

62. Following his disenchantment with socialism as an oppressive, ideological political system that betrayed its own ideals, the issue here for Kuroń was not faith as belief or trust in an absolute being, but as allegiance to a system (i.e., "Christianity") that requires (as he understood it) an advance commitment to obedience.

forced to acknowledge this "other" is a person (you), not a thing (it). I am now being defined by this ethical encounter with another person, to whom I must respond. While this not yet an encounter with God, God speaks to me through the other person, for in admitting the existence of personal reality outside of myself, which I neither created nor control, I admit that I am not God.[63]

Michnik also stresses Bonhoeffer's Christian humanism. He draws on the teaching of Cardinal Wyższyński, Pope John XXIII, and the Polish bishops, to argue that the Church and the left share "an antitotalitarian view of the unity of human rights and human duties … these ideas and values are deeply rooted in Christian and secular traditions alike."[64] To validate this claim, he cites the passage from Bonhoeffer's *Ethics* about "the children of the Church … returning to their mother." Michnik proceeds to comment on Bonhoeffer's declaration that both Mother and child discovered their common "source" in Jesus Christ. Arguing that Christ's commandments are the "canonical foundations of European culture," Michnik expresses his discovery that truth, freedom, dignity, tolerance, social justice, and human solidarity have their origin in Christ and his teaching.

> Bonhoeffer's reference to Jesus Christ as the "source" also has a profound meaning for nonbelievers: it means that one cannot reject the Christian tradition with impunity. For by rejecting Christ's teachings of love for one's neighbor, one rejects the canonical foundation of European culture. By rejecting these teachings, we lose the foundation of our belief in the autonomous value of truth and human solidarity. Belief in the divinity of Christ is a matter of grace, and in this sense is given only to a few. But belief in the hallowed nature of Christ's commandments is the duty of all, because it is the light that protects

---

63. Bonhoeffer's view of ethical transcendence is presented in chapter 5, while the view of transcendence held by secular opposition activists is critiqued in chapter 6.

64. Michnik, *Church and the Left*, 121–22. Thirty years later, Michnik wrote, "We will never forget the wise heroism of the 'Primate of the Millennium,' Cardinal Stefan Wyszyński, who was able to unite Christian testimony with the sense for compromise for the common good. … The election of Karol Wojtyła to the papal throne confirmed us in the conviction that the Catholic Church, which had always been a sign of resistance, would never again be a sign of coercion. The martyr's death of Father Jerzy Popiełuszko confirmed us in the feeling that the Church represents everything that is best in Polish spirituality." Michnik, "Polska na zakręcie, Gazeta na zakręcie."

human freedom and dignity against violence and debasement, against nihilism and the hell of solitude.[65]

Anna Chmielewska, a young socialist who later came to the Christian faith, agrees that the battle is now between enslaved humanity and various concepts of human freedom, not between socialism and the Church. In "A Letter to Friends," Chmielewska argues that Christianity affirms the intrinsic value of the individual.

> These two elements: the inalienable value of every individual and its freedom in the decisions that determine the meaning of its human existence, were brought into our culture by Christianity [. . .] Perhaps the fact that this value was built into the source of Christianity, into its very foundation, enabled it to find the strength to proceed from totalitarian to pluralistic universalism.[66]

Chmielewska closes with Bonhoeffer's canonical passage regarding the return of the West's endangered values to "Mother" Church, arguing that Christianity was thus revealed as the source and the defender of the humanistic values that she and her revisionist friends shared. She writes, "This letter . . . speaks about a paradox, which is this, that the values unsuccessfully sought on the left are found on its antipodes; and [it speaks] also about this, that if in your view of the world you have restored sovereignty to the individual over against the objective laws of history, then you need to try to look differently at the place where that sovereignty was always defended."[67] But why were secular Poles so prone to look to Christianity, or at least for some sort of transcendence? Negatively, they concluded that socialist ideology is inadequate as a philosophical support for humanism. Observing his peers joining the crude, government inspired anti-Semitism that swept Poland in 1968, Stanisław Barańczak wrote:

> I understood that the worldview [i.e., Marxist-Leninism], that we had until now held in common, the worldview gained in school and read in the newspapers, was not enough to retain moral integrity and to resist the wave of animal hatred. It lacked any kind of transcendence, which could become a support

---

65. Michnik, *Church and the Left*, 123. This text echoes Bonhoeffer's reflections in "Inheritance and Decay" from *Ethics*.

66. Chmielewska, "List do Przyjaciół," 97.

67. Ibid., 107.

for the mind in the form of a system of constant, humanistic values, regardless of the situation, state of affairs, and external pressures.[68]

Positively, ethical transcendence met an existential need for a belief or philosophy strong enough to resist totalitarianism. Jacek Kuroń recalled how he and his wife Grażyna, convinced that the purpose of their life was to "fight for the fulfillment of the 'kingdom of freedom'—of humanity's great cause," reached the conclusion that "persons who set themselves such a goal need a philosophy that would give hope and define goals, as well as a group to belong to, for this is not a task for two."[69] They found such a philosophy and group through their interaction with Catholic intellectuals. "From the dialog with Catholics," as Kuroń would later write, "we came away enriched by transcendental Moral Law."[70] Nor were they alone. Lipski notes the common feeling among secular intellectuals that resistance to the inroads, moral traps, and outright terror employed against them required a transcendental foundation for their ethical, humanistic beliefs, and led to their widespread acceptance of the "ethos of Christianity."

> Various sources and traditions contributed to the ethos of KOR. It must be said that most important [among these] was the ethos of Christianity, to which the clear majority of the nonbelieving members of KOR also confessed. Earlier . . . Jacek Kuroń expounded this attitude in *Znak* in the essay entitled "Christians without God." The far-reaching acceptance on one hand of the ethical principles of Christians ethics, the rejection of ethical relativism, the treating of ethical values as if they had a transcendental character, [the refusal] from the viewpoint of ethics to differentiate two different spheres[71] of public life and the ethics of private life—[all these] made him, among those who did not accept the Christian faith (or another theism), one of the most Christianizing and at once representative spokesmen of his ideological circle.[72]

---

68. Barańczak, "Dlaczego nie całkiem jestem Chrześcijaninem," 127.

69. Kuroń, "Lewica—prawica. Bóg," 343.

70. Ibid., 358.

71. Note the rejection of "two-spheres" thinking—terminology clearly adopted from Bonhoeffer.

72. Lipski, "Etos Komitetu Obrony Robotników," 43.

This discovery of allies in unexpected places was mutual. Kuroń recalls his first audience with Cardinal Stefan Wyszyński. "He said that up until now the Church was here alone and he was alone . . . He said that in this battle we are fighting for supreme moral, national, human values. And one felt in this, in what he said, at least this is how I took it, relief that yet other forces had appeared."[73] If Bonhoeffer introduced secular leftists to "non-religious Christianity," he also helped Catholics accept the positive contributions these "people of good will" made to their joint Judeo-Christian heritage. Lipski summarizes the "ethos of KOR"; "throughout the centuries various ideas from our cultural sphere enriched the ethos of Christianity, joined with it, forming a richer whole. Only those enrichments proved essential, which were not contrary to the fundamentals of Christian ethics."[74]

While, as mentioned above, not all connections between citizens' society and Polish messianism will be noted here, in this section alone those familiar with Woronicz and Mickiewicz will have little trouble recognizing such familiar messianic values as freedom, social justice, responsibility, and respect for other individuals. It appears that Poles found in Bonhoeffer a way to jointly recognize and reaffirm their own values and beliefs.

Responsibility

Poles most widely respected Bonhoeffer the "Christian humanist" for his emphasis on living responsibly. For Catholic readers, Morawska declares that Bonhoeffer shows not so much *what* but *how* someone from a different [i.e., Reformation] tradition believes,[75] arguing that a meeting that stresses spiritual experience and praxis over doctrine, "is an experience more deeply ecumenical and more inspiring than even great facility in comparing pure theories."[76] Her portrait of Bonhoeffer aims to inspire a faith that expresses itself in responsible action. This quintessential Bonhoefferian theme became the chief motif uniting the various strands of Bonhoeffer's reception in Poland. Morawska entitles her discussion of Bonhoeffer's role in the conspiracy "*Natus est*

---

73. Kuroń, "Lewica—prawica. Bóg," 351.
74. Lipski, "Etos Komitetu Obrony Robotników," 44.
75. Morawska, *Chrześcijanin w Trzeciej Rzeszy*, 4–5.
76. Ibid., 5.

Konradus," suggesting parallels with Gustaf-Konrad from Mickiewicz's *Forefathers' Eve*[77] that include love and sacrifice for one's country, and specifically the shift in focus from life in the private (i.e., Church) to the public (i.e., political) sphere. Declaring Bonhoeffer's "worldly" experiences inseparable from his literary works, she writes, "One needs to keep in mind this existential context in order to understand why during this period Bonhoeffer began to ask once again, and why later in the *Letters* [he] would ask so radically, "what is Christianity for us today?"[78] Many Poles were moved by her vision of Bonhoeffer to a life of "social, earthly responsibility."

> His lot was of necessity one of unending losses ... but also the lot of harsh, manly achievements: maturity, the ability to undertake responsible action in full knowledge that there were no guarantees for it, human solidarity, which does not shrink from evil and guilt, and finally the affirmation of life, just life, and not some defensive theory about it.[79]

Jan Kłoczowski[80] agrees that Bonhoeffer's sense of responsibility moved him inexorably towards involvement in the secular, political sphere.[81] Interestingly, Kłoczowski approaches this topic by highlighting Bonhoeffer's re-discovery of natural values, whose loss had left the church with little or nothing to say regarding the ethical issues of the day. He also notes Bonhoeffer's rejection of casuistry, and its tiresome search for evil in even the strongest and most beautiful of human endeavors. Bonhoeffer thus gained room for a realistic appraisal of the human situation that recognizes relative distinctions in the natural realm, and hence allows for ethical judgments between shades of good and evil. The "natural" did not degenerate into naturalism, thanks to Bonhoeffer's distinction between the ultimate and the penultimate. The radical negation of things penultimate is rejected, as is the temptation to compromise with the penultimate that leads to a separation of nature and grace. Through the unity of his person as the incarnate, crucified, and risen One, Christ has both affirmed the penultimate and redeemed

77. Cf. Chapter 3 of this book.
78. Morawska, *Chrześcijanin w Trzeciej Rzeszy*, 176.
79. Ibid., 189.
80. Fr. Jan Kłoczowski, a Dominican priest and philosopher, lectures in Kraków at the Catholic Seminary and Jagiellonian University.
81. Kłoczowski, "Lekcja Bonhoeffera."

it for the ultimate. Kłoczowski concludes that Bonhoeffer considered his move to "worldly" political involvement as the fulfillment of the Christian gospel, not its rejection.

> In Christ the world and humanity have been called into existence and in him they have been once again reconciled with God. Only in Him does nature regain its naturalness, beauty, and spontaneity. It is faith that causes us with all our strength to engage in the worldly sphere, in the world, not on its borders in the intimacy of a pietistic heart, but in its full glory; [it is faith that] causes us to enter into the whirlwind of life.[82]

The choice in 1971 to focus on Bonhoeffer's struggle to engage in "worldly political involvement" is significant. At the time Kłoczowski's own circles, in particular Catholic intellectuals associated with *Tygodnik Powszechny* and *Znak*, were seeking to critically influence their own political realities. Bonhoeffer at once inspired them to creatively resist Poland's totalitarian regimes, and encouraged to join in that struggle with secular "people-of-good-will."[83]

Responsibility is just as prominent a theme among these Catholic intellectuals' secular counterparts. Michnik closed *The Church and the Left* by juxtaposing a 1968 essay by Tomasz Burek, "On the Razor's Edge," with Bonhoeffer's probing question, "Are we still any use?," and his description of living *as if there were no God*: "God is teaching us that we live as people who can get along very well without him ... the God who makes us live in this world is the God before whom we are ever standing. Before God and with God we live without God."[84] Michnik draws a common theme from Burek's and Bonhoeffer's seemingly disparate texts, that of living responsibly in this world.

> The Christian theologian seems to be saying here that the Christian duty is to live in the world "as it there was no God," as if humans bore total responsibility for the shape of the human world. At the same time, the leftist critic associated with Marxism asserts that one's moral obligation is to live in the godless world as if God did exist and was judging us daily.

---

82. Kłoczowski, "Lekcja Bonhoeffera," 517.
83. Kłoczowski, "Droga Krzyżowa—labirynt życia."
84. Quoted in Michnik, *Church and the Left*, 207. The citation is from Bonhoeffer's July 16, 1944, letter to Bethge.

> [...] The relevance of this contrast, I believe, can be seen in the Polish intellectual context of recent years. The journals of Bonhoeffer, published here a few years ago, provided a critical new dimension to "open Catholicism" in Poland. The literary essays of Burek played a very important role in shaping the moral consciousness of literature of the young generation. In juxtaposing these texts, the point of contact becomes clear: we see two concepts of responsibility that differ in their origins yet are still somehow alike.[85]

"It is this concept of responsibility," says Michnik, "that is the basis of the dialogue between Christianity and the secular Left."[86] Ending his reflections on the Polish dialogue, Michnik cites "After Ten Years" concerning the loss of "solid ground" beneath one's feet.

> Who stands his ground? Only the man whose ultimate criterion is not in his reason, his principles, his conscience, his freedom or his virtue, but the one who is ready to sacrifice all these things when he is called to obedient and responsible action in faith and exclusive allegiance to God. The responsible man makes his whole life a response to the question and call of God.[87]

For Bonhoeffer, living responsibly simply means to answer, unequivocally, the call of God. Michnik testifies that his life is also an answer to a "question and call," an answer to what he calls "the basic canon of values of European culture in its specific Polish form," the eradication of which "would mean the annihilation of all the principles of human existence for which it is worth living and suffering."[88]

> No one can absolve me from my responsibility. The road that I choose and seek to follow, while fearing the police, malicious gossip, and my own conscience, is a road on which, my teacher Słonimski taught me, "there are no final victories, yet also no final defeats." I have found this road thanks to the determination, and the writings, of many different people who shared a stubborn insistence on living in truth. On this road we of the secular left can meet with Christians...[89]

---

85. Bonhoeffer, as quoted in Michnik, *Church and the Left*, 207–8.
86. Ibid., 208.
87. Ibid., 214.
88. Ibid.
89. Ibid.

In a 1995 discussion[90] with Józef Tischner,[91] Michnik reaffirmed the crucial role Bonhoeffer's writings played in the Polish dialogue,[92] and the lesson in responsibility that he received from Bonhoeffer. He declares that, "Even then, when I described myself as a complete atheist, there was in my thinking ... an intuition of ethical responsibility, specifically responsibility for the other person. This seems to me today to be a kind of religious or metaphysical experience. The literature that then moved me the most were the writings of Bonhoeffer."[93] Kuroń also wrote extensively on responsibility, and the theme had wide appeal among opposition members. Chmielewska, for instance, contrasts Bonhoeffer's vision of Christian "pluralistic universalism" with other-worldly, individualistic forms of Christianity, whose focus on individual salvation may be mitigated locally by the command to love one's neighbor, but which does not accept or address sin on a social or structural level.[94] She balances Bonhoeffer's critique of religion, including "metaphysics," "other-worldliness," and a personal righteousness that washes one's hands of society's sins with his affirmation of earthly life from Tegel prison.

> Is not righteousness and the kingdom of God on earth the focus of everything? ... It is not with the next world that we are concerned, but with this world as created and preserved and set subject to laws and atoned for and made new.[95]

Chmielewska, arguing for a "pluralistic" Christianity that acknowledges evil as a matter of unjust social structures as well as individual sin, points out the difficulty many Christians face in reconciling social responsibility with "individualistic ethics." Acknowledging that social responsibility may require the use of violent means, she nevertheless declares radical forms of liberation theology that justify such violence by the sacredness of the "cause" to be inadequate.[96] In a running com-

---

90. Michnik, *Między Panem a Plebanem*.

91. Fr. Józef Tischner (1931–2000), Roman Catholic priest, philosopher, author and essayist, conducted a dialog with Marxism (c.f. *Polski kształt dialogu, 1981*), served as the *de facto* pastor of Solidarity (cf. *Etos Solidarności, 1981*), and the author of the "philosophy of encounter" (cf. *Filozofia dramatu, 1998*).

92. Michnik, *Między Panem a Plebanem*, 185, 229, and 235.

93. Ibid., 185.

94. Chmielewska, "List do Przyjaciół," 98.

95. Ibid., 99.

96. Ibid., 102.

mentary on Bonhoeffer,[97] she insists that evil must always be called by name, lest breaking the law becomes the norm.

> Every person in a certain situation has the right—and at times the responsibility—to take up the fight and thus to kill. But this fight remains just only as long as the question: "Does the death it brings cease to be a moral evil?" is given the answer: "No." For if one has to choose evil, then let it still be called such, let this choice always be considered anew, or else evil will become a routine and a principle, and so that victory—if it comes—would not be twisted in one's hand.[98]

Chmielewska argues that choosing a course of action may well require the willingness to get one's hands dirty. While Chmielewska quotes Kołakowski, who writes, "The lesser of two evils should not be called good simply because it is lesser, and because we are morally obligated to carry it out,"[99] her reference to "clean hands" also confirms her dependence here on Bonhoeffer.

In a world longing for freedom from responsibility, an overly-narrow definition of responsibility is often employed to escape from freedom.[100] Chmielewska calls instead for freedom that leads to responsible action, and argues that responsibility properly conceived requires that one be free. Here again she quotes Bonhoeffer at length, first a text from *Ethics* ("The man who acts ideologically sees himself justified in his idea; the responsible man commits his action into the hands of God and lives by God's grace and favor."[101]), and then the prison letters: "... our coming of age forces us to a true recognition of our situation *vis-à-vis* God. God is teaching us that we must live as people who can get along very well without him."[102] Chmielewska describes such a life as "giving testimony," by which she means "an active faithfulness to moral values, which is an indirect proof of their power and worth." She continues:

---

97. Bonhoeffer, "Immanent Righteousness," 240–41.

98. Chmielewska, "List do Przyjaciół," 102.

99. Kołakowski, *Etyka bez kodeksu, cited by* Chmielewska, "List do Przyjaciół," 103. Kuroń's essay, "Zło, który czynię, *Polityka i odpowiedzialność*, 5–16.

100. Freedom here is understood, as in Bonhoeffer, as "freedom-for-others."

101. Bonhoeffer, *Ethics*, 233–34.

102. Bonhoeffer, cited in Chmielewska, "List do Przyjaciół," 103. The passage comes from the letter of July, 1944 to Bethge.

> [Living *etsi deus non daretur*] means openly applying [moral values], regardless of the situation. It does not impose the truths it confesses; rather it plants them in human minds. It requires, that one be a just person amidst injustice, free amidst enslavement, courageous amidst fear, and in extreme situations [it requires] one to take up a lost cause.[103]

Barańczak[104] in turn respects those who find a basis for moral integrity in Christianity, but suspects that all religion has at least a bit of an authoritarian character. Fooled once by Marxism, he now fears all submission to external supra-rational authorities, even when they command love for one's neighbor. If I submit to authority today, he reasons, tomorrow someone may convince me in the name of that authority to burn my neighbor at the stake. Echoing Bonhoeffer and Kuroń, who situated transcendence in the ethical encounter with another human being, Barańczak notes that a few, though lacking any external authority stemming from ideology, faith or human institutions, were yet able to "create such transcendence for themselves" in the "other person." Thus when he asks, "Is non-religious Christianity possible?," the answer he gives is in the affirmative. "Bonhoeffer, who is an authority for me, albeit a rational one, wrote about it in his *Ethics*: what's more he confirmed his ethical theses (just as Christ did as well) by the fate he consciously chose." Why is Barańczak convinced of the need for "Christianity without God"? "Because," he writes, "that way it's harder. That way it's more responsible."[105]

Chmielewska, Barańczak, and Michnik belonged to a generation of leftist, post-revisionist secular humanists searching for a sense of transcendence that would sustain their commitment to work for social justice and defend human dignity and freedom. In Chmielewska's words, they believed that "it is a requirement to feel responsibility for every evil and injustice, and that it is blameworthy to defer from this responsibility."[106] Some found a basis for this responsibility in Christ, others in the human person made in Christ's image. For their formation as a whole, Bonhoeffer helped to point the way.

103. Chmielewska, "List do Przyjaciół," 104–5.
104. Pseudonym "Feliks Niedolski."
105. Barańczak, "Dlaczego nie całkiem jestem Chrześcijaninem." 132.
106. Chmielewska, "List do Przyjaciół," 95.

Citizens' Society

Michnik's article "New Evolutionism" defined what came to be known as "citizens' society." Before we can address the extent to which citizens' society reflects the influence of Bonhoeffer, a brief description of its program is required. Michnik began by drawing several lessons from history. First, "the lesson of Czechoslovakia is that evolution has its limits and that it is possible."[107] Secondly, "the dilemma of nineteenth-century leftist movements—'reform or revolution'—is not the dilemma of the Polish opposition."[108] There was no hope for overthrowing a communist regime backed by Soviet tanks, nor for reforming it by implementing change from within (revisionism) or pleading for concessions from without (neo-positivism). However, although the USSR could crush Poland if war broke out, this would nevertheless be a "political catastrophe" for the Soviet Union. There was room, therefore, for gradual, evolutionary change. As Michnik argued, "An unceasing struggle for reform and evolution that seeks an expansion of civil liberties and human rights is the only course that Eastern European dissidents can take."[109] In adopting "New Evolutionism" as their program, Polish dissidents turned their attention from the party to the people. The "program for evolution," wrote Michnik, ". . . should give directives to the people on how to behave, not to the powers on how to reform themselves."[110] Or, as Kuroń often repeated, "Instead of burning [party] committees, establish your own!" The opposition's efforts were now directed towards developing an independent civil society that could, from a *de facto* position of strength, force concessions from the party.

The program of New Evolutionism appeared in the writings of numerous secular activists.[111] Their Catholic counterparts also came to share the vision of citizens' society. In 1977 Mazowiecki called for "reclaiming human and civil rights," via protest, i.e., "unmasking the abuse and trampling on of rights, insisting on their reinstatement." But protest must be matched by the creation of a "social infrastructure of human rights," which, in addition to the activities of the Church, publications

---

107. Michnik, *Letters from Prison and Other Essays*, 80.
108. Ibid., 83.
109. Ibid.
110. Ibid., 144.
111. Cf. Kuroń, "Myśli o programie działania," 1984.

of the Catholic press, and meetings of Catholic Intellectuals' Clubs, Mazowiecki held to include any and all "authentic actions in academic and cultural fields," whether of individuals or groups, that are born from "inner freedom."[112] His further comments demonstrate a broad agreement with his secular counterparts concerning the activities that lead towards the goal of citizens' society. In respect to what he terms "the new forms of fighting for human rights," he declines to give a recipe that applies to all, but declares that "all must answer for themselves what we should do in the struggle for human's rights." Mazowiecki even includes the raising of children in the battle for human rights, under the condition that it does not lead to the "privatization of life."[113] Further on, he addresses the question of "heroic" resistance, not to demand of everyone the ultimate sacrifice, but to urge an ethic of responsibility that applies to normal people in their everyday lives.

> It was said during our discussion that is not good in human activity, particularly in the area of culture, when there remains only the choice between conformism and heroism. This certainly is not good. Certainly at times this choice cannot be avoided. The brunt of the matter, however, depends on this, that in the course of the battle of reclaiming [civil rights] the level of requirements set before a person living a normal, every-day life, would be set correctly. Not too high and not too low.[114]

Mazowiecki's words echo Bonhoeffer's argument that the decision to step beyond the normal limits of one's "vocation," i.e., the responsibilities that result from one's familial, social, vocational, and professional roles, is dependent solely on the "concrete call of Jesus."[115] The sense that Mazowiecki employs a working knowledge of Bonhoeffer's thoughts on vocation and the "normal life" is strengthened by another essay from this period that refers to Bonhoeffer's discussion of the penultimate. As Mazowiecki explains,

> Bonhoeffer wrote, that we live, taking things normally, in the penultimate zone. However, there can be many ways of living in that zone: not only in a Christian sense, but also in the sense that

---

112. Mazowiecki, "Czuj się wolny," 94–95.

113. Bonhoeffer also described the responsibilities of parents to explain the concept of "deputyship."

114. Ibid., 96–97.

115. Cf. Bonhoeffer, *Ethics*, 257–58.

is simply human. And normality differs. Our normality today is somehow mixed continually with the border.[116]

Mazowiecki confesses with Michnik the inadequacy of neo-positivism and revisionism to bring significant and lasting reform within the communist party.[117] He declines to categorically reject either "conformism" (the doctrine of Polish positivism) or "heroism" (romanticism's "revolutionary deed"), for "at times this choice cannot be avoided." Yet he argues that there are many ways of living in the penultimate reality of People's Poland, where normality and the border are mixed. In 1977 Poland, the border he refers to is not conspiracy, assassination or violent revolution, but "new forms of fighting for human rights," e.g., publishing in the underground press, or belonging to KOR. In Bonhoeffer's day not all could conspire against Hitler, neither could all Poles join the ranks of KOR. Fortunately, for individuals living "a normal, every-day life," there were many ways to "give testimony" and to "live in the truth."

The choice of "conformism or heroism" in the Polish border situation is not to be confused with Bonhoeffer's rejection of "radicalism and compromise." Whereas radicalism seeks to impose the ultimate, i.e., the Kingdom of God, on this penultimate life, compromise surrenders the moral, transcendental values of the ultimate, and capitulates to the penultimate. In contrast, Mazowiecki and Michnik retained messianism's ideals while rejecting its eschatological vision of the establishment of the Kingdom of God on earth. As they learned from Poland's tragic history, attempts of the part of human beings to bring about the Kingdom regularly end in terror and bloodshed. What then is left, when we rule out radical visions of utopia and servile conformism? Just this: "giving testimony" in the border situation, while clearing out a space in the penultimate zone to live a normal life, with freedom and integrity, in the sense that is Christian or "simply human."

---

116. Mazowiecki, "Powrót do najprostszych pytań," 53.

117. Mazowiecki writes, "The sixties ended with a crisis of faith in the evolution of structures." The reference is to "'old' evolutionism," and "structures" denotes the communist party apparatus and regime. Mazowiecki, "Powrót do najprostszych pytań," 53–54. Mazowiecki's comments also reflect disappointment over the failure of the Polish Church to vigorously implement the teaching of the Vatican II Council. As he writes, "He For many of us [this crisis] is double, because it also touched on post-Vatican II council Christianity, when what was a great breath of prophetic spirit entered into the mode of organizing mechanisms."

Although New Evolutionism had many sources, there are many points of comparison with Bonhoeffer. Bonhoeffer's labors in the Confessing Church, his ecumenical activities, and his circular letters to the Finkenwalde brethren were attempts to create a community that would remain true to Christ and the Sermon on the Mount in the face of National Socialism. Bonhoeffer believed that the witness of such a community was of primary importance in the battle for truth and justice, and he wasted no effort attempting to reform the Nazi party or pleading for concessions from the regime.

Another parallel may exist between the Polish opposition's program of gradual evolutionary change, and Bonhoeffer's discussion of "The Structure of Responsible Life." Bonhoeffer argues that our decisions are limited by our circumstances, our "creatureliness," our knowledge, and our motives. We must also consider the potential outcomes of a given course of action,[118] and the measure of responsibilities that we can carry "without breaking down under their weight."[119] As Bonhoeffer declares, "one must ask what are the actual possibilities; it is not always feasible to take the final step at once. Responsible action must not try to be blind."[120] Similarly, New Evolutionism was based on a shrewd analysis of Poland's geopolitical realities. Following Yalta, Michnik and his friends understood that Poland lay within the Soviet sphere of power, "not on the moon." As Mazowiecki wrote in 1977,

> there is a nation, the nation of Poland, which for 30 years has proven in difficult and dramatic times that it knows where the borders of the possible and the impossible lie . . . A nation, in which there exists the idea and will to act for a better tomorrow. Not one idea, but many competent ideas, zealous and full of compassion, which through their exchange can thrust the nation forward. A will to act . . . that comes from hope and the feeling of responsibility.

He continues, in words that "prophesy" the birth of the Solidarity trade union in 1980, or the 1989 "Round Table" discussions between Solidarity leaders and the Communist authorities.

> In a word . . . compromise between the rulers and the ruled is not beyond the boundaries of our discussion concerning hu-

118. Bonhoeffer, *Ethics*, 233.
119. Ibid., 246.
120. Ibid., 233.

> man and civil rights, nor of the process of reclaiming those rights. But we are speaking of compromise, not servility of human thought and attitudes. We know, however, that such a compromise, which is not servility, must be won.[121]

Avoiding rash claims that the Poles discovered the program of citizens' society in Bonhoeffer, there are yet clear grounds to argue that Poles studied Bonhoeffer's thought and actions as an example to adapt and follow in their own historical context. We remember that Bonhoeffer urged the Church to be the Church by defending the rights and dignity of the oppressed. While one can only speculate what impact Christians in the Third Reich could have made by answering his call to follow Jesus Christ, the "man-for-others," Bonhoeffer's Polish readers understood the failure of German Christianity as a warning of what happens when good people deny their responsibility for their fellow-humans. As Mazowiecki wrote in 1971:

> ... the failure of that period demonstrates how far the Church can be defeated morally if it makes itself the supreme value, and if it does not fulfill the requirements of human solidarity, always expected from Christianity by those who suffer and who are humiliated. The German churches failed to rise to the occasion, not because they were institutionally weak, but because in too many extreme situations they placed the defense of their own ability to act above the defense of principles; they did not fail because they were rooted in the life and tradition of their nation, but because they forgot that Christianity does not allow following national tradition uncritically, but demands standing against it, when what is dark within it raises its voice.[122]

The question to Christians then and now is implicit: "Will we as a community live today in solidarity with our fellow human beings? Will we stand against what is dark in our own national tradition?"

Politics, Patriotism, and Resistance

From the opening pages of *A Christian in the Third Reich*, Morawska starts to develop the concept of responsible action in People's Poland. Arguing that studying Bonhoeffer's legacy will further German-Polish reconciliation, at a deeper level she declares that he can assist the

---

121. Mazowiecki, "Czuj się wolny," 98.
122. Mazowiecki, "Naucżył się wierzyć wśród tęgich razów," 18–19.

Poles in their "uncompromising battle with that with which one must fight."[123] Like Lutherans in the GDR, Morawska saw parallels between Bonhoeffer's resistance to National Socialism and the Poles' resistance to communism, which itself constituted an extension of their long patriotic struggle with Germany and Imperial Russia to regain their lost independence. Writing under the censor's watchful eye, she refers here to Poland's communist regime as "that with which one must fight."[124] In a conversation with Eberhard and Renata Bethge, Morawska explained Bonhoeffer's importance to Polish believers.

> Bonhoeffer is so exciting because he has dared to anticipate in thought our problem of how to meet Christ in a religionless world. Who are we, who, in the midst of atheism, do not wish to understand ourselves as agnostics, but feel veneration for Christ; how are we to interpret our relation to Jesus? In Bonhoeffer we see somebody who might be able to help us when we feel that it is simply wrong to see the barriers dividing the so-called believers from the so-called unbelievers. Do not the barriers run right through the group of believers and that of unbelievers: namely, separating those who live for others from those who do not, whatever group they may belong to?[125]

This text requires some unpacking. Morawska's "religionless world" alludes to the official atheism of the Polish communist party,[126] while her reference to "so-called" believers and unbelievers refers to the dialogue between Catholic and secular intellectuals that was already under way. Morawska chose to stand with "so-called unbelievers" (such as Kuroń and Michnik) who lived for others, rather than with "so-called believers" who did not. Did her decision to "cross the ditches" with Mazowiecki, and to "be found in the ranks of the antitotalitarian opposition" with Michnik result from reading Bonhoeffer? Given the long-established program of *Więź* and *Znak*, it seems rather that her words reflect the

---

123. Morawska, *Chrześcijanin*, 6. Cf. also Ludwig Melhorn's article, "Na marginesie recepcji Bonhoeffera w Polsce."

124. Cf. Melhorn: "Anna Morawska desired to address the problem of responsibility for *res publika*, for matters common to all ... in the context of dictatorship ruling in the PRL." Melhorn, "Na marginesie recepcji Bonhoeffera w Polsce," 246–47.

125. Anna Morawska, quoted by Eberhard Bethge in *Bonhoeffer, Exile and Martyr*, 14.

126. Though Polish society remained quite "religious," the Catholic Church was systematically attacked by a hostile regime. Bonhoeffer understood both Nazism and communism as specific expressions of the "religionless" world.

appreciation of Catholic intellectuals, who had already sensed the need for rapprochement with secular "people of good will," for the guidance and moral justification they received from Bonhoeffer regarding how to do that as an expression of their faith in Christ.

Mazowiecki, in his 1971 review of *A Christian in the Third Reich*, picks up and develops Morawska's description of Bonhoeffer as a "nonpolitical politician," who exerted influence through *metapolitics*, that is through representing "the moral presuppositions that . . . lie beneath and determine every political program." As a non-political politician, wrote Morawska, Bonhoeffer insisted that the Church remains the Church, not by defending its own rights, but by speaking and acting in defense of others. Later, in the conspiracy, his unwavering commitment to his metapolitical worldview made him act to stop the Nazi madness. As Mazowiecki comments:

> "Nonpolitical politics" . . . is that kind of involvement in a given situation that defends the imponderables, and avoids accepting certain rules of the game, trying [instead] to mark them out in another dimension and on a different level. It is therefore a policy that must find a way out of the imposed situation, [that] must find its own way, [that] must be born from one's own brand of faithfulness to basic moral principles and from one's own manner of serving. And it must maintain the ability to act, accepting that events of the moment will not be gracious to it.[127]

Seeking "a way out of the imposed situation" that was consistent with their moral convictions, opposition leaders drew inspiration from Bonhoeffer's example. For them, "finding a way," or "maintaining the ability to act" was in the first place dependent on the decision to live responsibly. At a 1977 seminar on human rights, Mazowiecki warned his fellow KIK members against "smoke-screen thinking," a variation of "the gesture of Pilate" that excuses oneself from the responsibility to act by hiding behind the moral testimony of the church.[128] Mazowiecki gives only guarded approval of a friend's statement that the Church follows Christ primarily by being "a moral sign of opposition," meaning that "our entire being is communion with those who suffer." The problem, Mazowiecki contends, is what this leaves unspoken, for authentic communion with those who suffer requires "diving into the reality of

---

127. Mazowiecki, "Naucyzł się wierzyć wśród tęgich razów," 15.
128. Mazowiecki, "Czuj się wolny," 91.

the world." This in turn results in actions that are "in the moral sense ... also a political testimony and involvement."[129]

In another essay Mazowiecki argues that Poland's long battle for independence is best understood as a "battle for human rights,"[130] adding that the Church's fundamental role in the nation's struggle was "the defense of human rights."[131] As in Bonhoeffer's day, this defense took place under conditions where both individuals and society had lost the "solid ground under their feet."[132] Mazowiecki then alludes to Bonhoeffer's description of the Church's reunion with her estranged "children." Like Kuroń and Michnik, he applies his passage to the dialogue between members of the Polish opposition, describing it as the "uniting of Christian and human values, the overcoming of that old division that was the defeat of Christianity, its foreignness towards contemporary culture."[133] The "truth" gained in this experience, stresses Mazowiecki, is not something that can be found on the "official roads" of calculated political maneuvering, dispassionate academic discussion, or formal ecumenical dialogue. Rather, it is gained when flesh-and-blood individuals meet, in "an encounter of people of thought, culture, and social sensitivity."[134]

Mazowiecki's own prison journal describes a lecture on Bonhoeffer that he delivered in 1982 to other interned Solidarity activists and sympathizers.[135] We also know that he passed copies of Bonhoeffer's writings on to other prisoners. As Andrzej Drawicz wrote, "I got to know [Bonhoeffer] better in a state of imposed isolation, which as everyone knows fosters more in-depth reading.[136] I have Tadeusz Mazowiecki to thank for slipping me the basic source, the Bonhoefferian *Selected*

---

129. Ibid., 92–93. Albrecht Schönherr, Bonhoeffer's former student, wrote from the GDR, "Too late we have learnt that the origin of the deed is not thought, but the readiness to assume responsibility ... You will only think what you choose responsibly to do." Schönherr, cited in Baum, *Church for Others*, 88–89.

130. Mazowiecki, "Druga twarz Europy," 103.

131. Ibid., 104.

132. Ibid., 105

133. Ibid.

134. Ibid.

135. Mazowiecki, "Zapiski," 135. Following the lecture, a lively discussion took place comparing Bonhoeffer's martyrdom with that of Father Maximilian Kolbe.

136. Delicious irony.

Works, translated in Biblioteka 'Więzi' by Anna Morawska."[137] Surely Mazowiecki's own words, written ten years earlier in 1971, brought him comfort and a measure of hope during the dark days of internment.

> We do not know how to rid ourselves of the questions that the "world come of age" presents to our belief. Bonhoeffer leaves his mark on all of Christianity because he did not rid himself of questions and because he believed ... there is no way to avoid the question, can we rise to this measure of solidarity with human fate and to this measure of sensing God? Do you hear, lonely Christian full of questions and doubts? God has some plans for you, just for you. Be ready and alert. Don't forget, even when your weakness almost breaks you, that He has enormous, unheard of plans for you. He will be with you.[138]

These are suggestive thoughts, coming from one who later made his own mark as a "non-political politician."

Secular intellectuals also looked to Bonhoeffer's model of citizenship and patriotism. Michnik cites a letter by the Polish Bishops to support his contention that an independent Poland, united yet pluralistic, and living in peaceful fellowship and creative partnership with other nations, is more than a dream. The Bishops declared, "Through love for our own country, we move toward love for the entire human family; and through the development of our national virtues, we enrich the entire human family ... True love for one's country entails profound respect for the values of all other nations ... But it eschews hatred, for hatred is a disease that leads to a diseased and degenerated version of patriotism."[139] This view of patriotism, notes Michnik, which loves one's country in a way that enriches other nations instead of seeking to conquer and enslave them, is quite close to that held by leftists. In Michnik's view, it was through participation in the resistance movement against Hitler that Bonhoeffer discovered that patriotism so understood and lived could result from nonbelievers' secular ethics as well as from his own Christian faith. He writes,

> ... the "other Germans"—such as Dietrich Bonhoeffer, Willy Brandt, or Thomas Mann, who spoke out against their country—

---

137. Drawicz, "Bonhoeffer w zasięgu ręki," 25.

138. Mazowiecki, "Naucyzł się wierzyć wśród tęgich razów," 20.

139. Pastoral Letter of the Polish Bishops, from September 5, 1972. Cited in Michnik, *Church and the Left*, 149.

showed by their actions what true patriotism is and true love of country is all about. Among them were Christians, but also nonbelievers whose secular ethics guided them to the proper decision. Thus leftists cannot agree that a Christian worldview is a necessary condition for honest patriotism. Too many Christians fought in the *Wehrmacht*, and too many non-Christians participated in the anti-Hitler resistance. It was the same in Poland.[140]

Barańczak, another opposition writer who looked to Bonhoeffer as a model citizen and patriot, considers three kinds of heroism displayed by the German theologian. The first is that of a "rebel, risking life and rejecting personal happiness for higher goals, a conspirator raising his hand against a bloody autocrat." Such resistance stands in a long tradition of resistance to tyranny. While difficult and costly, it enjoys the support of a community that shares the dangers of resistance. As Barańczak writes, "In later years Bonhoeffer the conspirator possessed support in the community of opinions and the military discipline of the group of oppositionists, in the clearly delineated political goal of the coup, finally, most importantly—in the growing social discontent following the defeat at Stalingrad."[141]

According to Barańczak, Bonhoeffer demonstrated a second form of heroism during Hitler's rise to power, in such timely and powerful messages as his radio lecture on the *Führer* principle, or in his sermon on Gideon that denied a place in the church for any "side altars for the worship of people." This heroism was more difficult, for it required standing alone against tyranny.

> Bonhoeffer the preacher from the years 1932–1933, engaging in the fight with phenomena that appeared to virtually the entire nation and to virtually the entire Church to be natural, socially beneficial, rationally explainable or at least allowable—did not yet possess any support outside a few elementarily simple principles of humanism and tolerance, drawn from the spirit of the culture in which he grew up.[142]

Barańczak's claim that humanism was the only support Bonhoeffer could draw upon for his early resistance to Hitler hints of reductionism,[143]

---

140. Ibid., 150.

141. Barańczak, "Notatki na marginesach Bonhoeffera," 21.

142. Ibid.

143. As does any attempt to interpret the German theologian's work apart from its Christological center.

a charge only partially mitigated by Barańczak's caveat that during this period Bonhoeffer's ethics still drew upon divine, transcendental authority. He goes even further with a radical reading of the prison letters, arguing that in creating the concept of non-religious Christianity Bonhoeffer rejected even the remnant of divine authority.

> To live, *etsi Deus non daretur*, "as if there were no God," and at the same time to live honestly and responsibly: only then, says Bonhoeffer, will this be possible, if instead of God the foundation of ethics becomes "the other person," responsibility towards him, respect for his sovereignty and human dignity, willingness to bring him aid … It turned out, that after "the death of God" the Decalogue need not die. Precisely for this reason, I judge, the life of Bonhoeffer also compels reflection from nonbelievers, of which I myself am one.[144]

Here the Polish literary critic and activist asks which defeat is greater: public martyrdom, or setting oneself up to be silently ignored or even condemned by those one is trying to serve. This question reflects the modern dilemma of moral individuals, who face not only an evil system, but a "social *consensus omnium*, a silent agreement of evil." To explain this phenomenon Barańczak points to the sermon "The Truth Will Set You Free," in which Bonhoeffer shows that the "seekers of truth are at times rejected by the society in whose objective interest they act, because along with the truth they offer it freedom; and freedom upsets the peace and forces the taking of responsibility upon oneself."[145] Barańczak's incisive comments on the heroism of "clean hands," set in the context of his observations concerning the nature of totalitarianism, are worth quoting at length.

> This heroism of Bonhoeffer depends … on the demarcation of this line: in a situation, in which for safety one pays only the not-so-high cost of remaining silent, in which the boundary of unambiguous evil might yet seem to be enormously distant and a compromise with the conscience could easily be defended by various higher ends, which justify the means—he, one of the first, decided: not a step further. Not a step past that boundary, beyond which there begins—albeit motivated most reasonably—the undermining of the autonomy and freedom of the "other person," my neighbor.

144. Ibid., 22.
145. Ibid., 23.

> Only this principle allows one to save their own humanity in a world of total enslavement and lawlessness. Whoever hid at this stage in the shadow of the authority of an ideology, an institution, the collective—had to agree to further compromises for the "good of the nation," "the good of the Church," etc. But a totalitarian system does not acknowledge partial concessions, it requires everything, you must totally submit to it: who is not entirely for it is against it. And so those, who started with innocent compromises, ended in shameful compromises (like the German Church in the Jewish question). Bonhoeffer was one of a handful, who in the rising sea of moral filth kept his hands clean.[146]

Barańczak next describes the third form of heroism, demonstrated by Bonhoeffer the *Abwehr* agent and conspirator, i.e., the heroism of "dirty hands." Barańczak highlights the ethical dilemmas that Bonhoeffer described in "After Ten Years," and which Poles found portrayed their own existence under communism. The heroism of dirty hands requires compromise, which is the price that must be paid "in order that ethical norms did not remain a distraction." Barańczak explains:

> Participating in the fate of "the other person," "being for others" reached in this way, as Anna Morawska correctly notes, its highest level: it became the "taking on in solidarity of the entire guilt and uncertainty of [others] and the world in a common, humanistic effort." This "third level" of Bonhoeffer's heroism was born after all from the conviction that [. . .] the battle between good and evil is conducted to a large degree in the darkness, and that "safe places"—just like "clean hands"—simply do not exist.[147]

Bonhoeffer also influenced more politically conservative activists. Stefan Niesiołowski, a leader in the Polish underground movement "Ruch," argues against questioning the motives of those who resisted Hitler simply because their resistance was ineffective. Bonhoeffer and the other major figures in the *Abwehr* conspiracy, he argues, acted primarily from moral conviction and not mere military expedience.

> The German opposition, as we know today from the documents, was active for many years. But in the face of the enormous disproportion of strength, and the authentic support that Hitler

---

146. Ibid., 24.
147. Ibid., 25.

enjoyed, they were unable to resolve the dilemma regarding in what manner they could return democracy to Germany. For this reason you can frame a charge of ineffectiveness, but you cannot question their intention.[148]

In a later article Niesiołowski concludes that Bonhoeffer and his fellow conspirators were patriots who resisted Hitler out of love for Germany, convinced that this was the only way to salvage her honor. He makes explicit his view concerning the Christian motives of the conspirators, writing "They acted above all from Christian inspiration, once again demonstrating that morality inspired by the Gospel is the fundamental value in the life of individuals and nations."[149]

Reconciliation

Understanding must precede reconciliation. Hence, as an advocate of Polish-German dialogue and reconciliation, Morawska explained to Poles in *A Christian in the Third Reich* why the German opposition movement seemed ineffective compared to their own resistance to Nazi aggression. She states that the "cult of the ruler" was well established, and notes the corresponding absence in German thought of a revolutionary tradition.[150] Furthermore, the weakness of democratic sentiments in society at large deprived potential opposition forces of an "ideological 'Archimedes point' in society . . . upon which a widely-based, effective opposition could be built."[151] The only realistic possibility was a "palace revolt" among members of the military elite whose resistance to Hitler, as Morawska argues contra Niesiołowski, was based more on the national interest than opposition to the moral outrages committed by the Nazi regime. Bonhoeffer's position stands in stark contrast. As he declared to Visser't Hooft in 1941, "I am praying for the defeat of my country. I think that this is the only possibility of paying for the enormous suffering that this country has brought into the world."[152] Morawska notes

---

148. Niesiołowski, "Z powodów moralnych," 16.

149. Niesiołowski, "Spiskowcy nowych Niemiec," 11.

150. Bethge writes of his fellow "confessing" seminary students: "As young Lutherans in 1934 we were totally unprepared for something like political resistance. We had neither the experience with nor conceptions of such activities." Bethge, *Friendship and Resistance*, 19.

151. Morawska, *Chrześcijanin w Trzeciej Rzeszy*, 140.

152. Ibid., 197.

the irony in this statement: "The sincere German patriot, who even in prison wrote with affection and love of his language and culture, who still thought with concern of a better and more honorable future, no longer had any path to defend the national honor except attitudes and actions that were everywhere named treason."[153]

Morawska's ground-breaking treatment of the German dilemma helped overcome Polish stereotypes of "bad Germans" and "good Poles."[154] Olschowsky and Duda suggest that her position as an outside observer gave her an advantage in analyzing the conditions leading to Germany's wide-scale acquiescence to Nazism. Prior to Morawska's work, they argue, the discussion in Poland of Germany during the Third Reich was often reduced to the two-fold question, "Why was a mass resistance movement lacking in Hitler's Germany, and why was the [movement] that did exist so ineffective in practice as to be unseen?"[155] The answer implied was simple: the Germans were either cowards or incompetents. This question, Olschowsky and Duda point out, assumes a "false analogy between the situation in occupied Poland and fascist Germany."[156] Germans resisting Hitler had to distinguish their nation's good from that of its fascist regime, accept being branded as traitors, and even consider their countrymen their enemies and their country's enemies their allies. In contrast, Poles who resisted the occupying German forces acted according to their political and cultural traditions, and enjoyed the support of a broad national consensus.[157] Olschowsky and Duda make the pregnant suggestion that a more appropriate basis for comparison with Nazi Germany would be Poland between the two world wars.

> To remain on a historically sensible level of comparison, one must ask about the attitude of the Polish Church to the anti-Semitic temptations of the National Democrats [*endecja*] or

---

153. Ibid., 198.

154. Melhorn concurs with the judgment that Morawska's biography of Bonhoeffer, together with her translation of his writings, "had breakthrough significance for a different view on the question of the anti–Nazi resistance movement in Germany." Melhorn, "Na marginesie recepcji Bonhoeffera w Polsce," 246.

155. Olschowsky and Duda, "Bonhoeffer a *inne Niemcy*," 1701.

156. Ibid.

157. Ibid., 1703.

ONR[158] prior to the war, about its stance towards the policies of the "Odrodzenie" movement and the *Sanacja*[159] party towards religious and national minorities ... just as in Germany, these matters were defended by a specific understanding of the good of the nation and the state. Only the answer to this question gives a basis for comparison. And one more small observation: if "to be German is to be Lutheran" is a nationalistic equation, what is the equation "To be Polish is to be Catholic"? We draw attention to this detail in order to point out a problem that is not resolved in the book, that is where should one draw the line between patriotism and nationalism in the attitudes of Germans, and are these criteria to apply as well to a characterization of Polish attitudes?[160]

Here the question of national identity and perceived national self-interest is related, not only to foreign military threats or invasions, but also to the majority's attitudes and actions towards religious or ethnic minorities, e.g., Protestants, Ukrainians, and especially Jews. The authors ask unsettling questions regarding the need for Poland to examine its own sins and demythologize its own recent history,[161] such as Poland's involvement in the "partition" of Czechoslovakia. When Hitler annexed the Czech "Sudetenland," the Polish Army occupied a small Polish enclave in the Zaolzia area, ostensibly to "protect" Poles from German exploitation. Although miniscule in scale with Nazi territorial aggression, there is no formal difference between these actions, as Hitler's spokesmen were delighted to point out. Arguably, Poland's moral complicity here consists in exploiting another nation's "misfortune," rather than standing in solidarity with the exploited. More to the point is the reluctance of many Poles to consider the presence of fascist tendencies in Dmowski's National Democratic movement,[162] or their influence

---

158. The ONR, or National Radical Camp, was founded in 1934. It was a nationalist-chauvinist movement, characterized by anti-Semitism and an anti-communist stance.

159. The *Sanacja* party governed Poland from 1926 until the German invasion of Poland in 1939. Until Józef Pilsudki's death in 1935, it resisted the rising tide of anti-Semitism. After 1935 it began flirting with the nationalist, anti-Semitic rhetoric and program that characterized the *Odrodzenie* (Renewal) movement.

160. Ibid.

161. Cf. Mac, "Nasze winy," 38–42.

162. Roman Dmowski, an ardent Polish patriot, was no Nazi. However, the ideological parallels between National Democracy and those strains of German nationalism which provided fertile soil for the Nazi propagandists are striking. Cf. chapter 8, "National Egoism," in Porter, *When Nationalism Began to Hate*.

on contemporary parties that draw on the *endecja* tradition. As documented above, the *endecja's* vision of "Piast Poland" defined "Polishness" in strict religious and ethno-linguistic terms, and set Poland in a never-ending survival-of-the-fittest conflict with other nations.[163] Though at a high cost, WWII cured many of such temptations. Although this brand of ethno-religious nationalism retains its appeal for a certain segment of Polish society, and political parties and rulers continue to appeal to it on occasion, it never became the dominant current in Polish politics and society.

Mazowiecki in turn declares that to understand the failure of German Christianity we must consider why Hitler's person and program were so attractive. "In one sense," he writes, "we cannot even speak here of a spiritual capitulation to Hitlerism; it was after all not so much capitulation as much as a way of rediscovering Germanness in Hitlerism." Yet at a deeper level than national identity, he argues that the conduct of Germans under the Nazis provides insights into human nature and into Christianity. To ask what makes us, as patriots, Christians, and human beings, susceptible to national, racial, and religious chauvinism requires taking a critical look at ourselves, our society, our church, and our nation.[164] Michnik, who agrees with Mazowiecki (and Bonhoeffer) that true patriotism demands such periodic "stocktaking," argues that it may also require speaking out against your own country, rather than defending it out of a misguided sense of solidarity. As patriots, says Michnik, "we should know the entirety of our history, but we should value and preserve only those parts that deserve to be preserved." In a respectful yet polemical response to Cardinal Wyższyński's warning against "the widespread tendency to 'dirty' our own history," he argues that "tough criticism," far from soiling the nation's history, gives "evidence of a noble and wise patriotism."[165] Michnik, in the spirit of Bonhoeffer's confession of the sins not only of Germany and also of his own Confessing Church, proceeds to enumerate several of Poland's own national sins.

To strengthen his plea for "honest patriotism," Michnik cites the wisdom demonstrated by the Polish bishops in their splendid letter to the German bishops. This letter, written forty years ago in 1965, contained

---

163. Many influenced by the legacy of the *endecja* are unaware of its roots in social Darwinism.

164. Mazowiecki, "Nauczył się wierzyć wśród tęgich razów," 9.

165. Michnik, *Church and the Left*, 151.

the famous phrase, "We forgive and we ask for forgiveness." Poland's Communist leaders were furious at what they saw as the "intervention" of the Church in Poland's foreign affairs. Many ordinary Poles were offended at the suggestion that Poland needed to apologize to Germany; Poles, they argued, were the victims, not the perpetrators of two world wars or the Holocaust. Yet it was this *pastoral* letter that initiated the process leading to Polish-German *political* rapprochement.

Thirty years after the Bishops' letter, at a Polish-German seminar commemorating the 1995 opening of the Dietrich Bonhoeffer House in Szczecin-Zdrój,[166] Bogusław Milerski took up the question of Polish-German reconciliation. Milerski argued that it was Bonhoeffer's Christological insights regarding this-worldly transcendence that drove his insistence that the place of Christians, and hence the Church, "is the world itself, even its center."[167] Because the Church is in the world, it must address its message to the nations as well as to individuals. This theological conviction, says Milerski, motivated Bonhoeffer's response to "the need of the hour," i.e., German nationalism.[168] Since the Church still has a responsibility to speak on crucial issues concerning politics and the nation, Milerski turns to the present "need of the hour." As recent conflicts in the Caucasus region and the Balkans show, belligerent nationalism remains a threat today. Yet there is also a "latent nationalism, present in all the countries of Europe," which can be found "sleeping in individual and social consciousness." Although latent nationalism finds its "unusual and spectacular" expression in attacks aimed at foreigners, it "lives on a daily basis, and this is far more dangerous, in the numerous phobias and stereotypes, which in turn map out directions for behavior, often [including] the global and fundamental [behaviors] of a given country."[169] Asking how the Church and Christians can responsibly address the question of Polish—German relations, Milerski contrasts nationalism, described as a sort of corporate egocentric narcissism, with a national culture that is open to others.

> Nationalism, as a concentration only on one's own interests, desires, imaginations, and fears is the greatest enemy of democracy, whereas it is precisely a model of society that is at once

166. I.e., Finkenwalde.
167. Milerski, "Kościół a narody," 9–10.
168. Ibid.
169. Ibid., 10.

open to others while not resigning from the roots of one's own national tradition that both Germany and Poland need, not only with respect to the interests of unifying Europe, but perhaps above all in light of the historically burdened neighborly relations between our nations.[170]

Milerski notes the danger in post-communist Poland of attitudes ranging from wariness, distrust or outright condemnation of "others," just because they are others. Those who succumb to such thinking blame others for the difficulties encountered in building a democratic society, and harbor a deep mistrust and rejection of all things foreign. Prime scapegoats include communism—the child of the East buried only surface deep beneath various socialist parties, and liberalism—the bastard offspring of Western culture. "Poland," these self-proclaimed patriots declare, "should tread its own path, not opening up excessively to that which is different and external." Such a stance fosters international conflict based on a revived social Darwinism. As Milerski explains, "The attempt is made in messianic fashion to set the Western 'culture of garbage' against Christianity—the Catholic culture of the Polish nation. In this way there is created the fatal blueprint, alternatively setting against one another not only national traditions but also the nations themselves."[171]

While chauvinistic nationalism does not represent the predominant attitude of the Catholic Church or its hierarchy, Milerski suggests that it is not a "marginal position" among Polish Catholics. His concern is not to critique a particular church or political party, but to work out "an ecumenical [position], for above all Church has a character that is supra-state and supra-national, and by this same token universal and ecumenical."[172] For direction in this quest Milerski quotes Bonhoeffer's speech in Fanö:

> In the face of nationalism and internationalism the ecumenical Christian community turns in the direction of its Lord and his directions. Nationalism and internationalism are questions of political necessity and possibility. Ecumenism on the other hand does not ask about these kinds of conditions but for the command for God, and not taking anything else into account,

---

170. Ibid. Milerski employs here the pejorative, Polish definition of nationalism.
171. Ibid., 11.
172. Milerski, "Kościół a narody," 11.

demonstrates the validity of these commands in the center of the world ... Peace on earth is not a subject to discuss, but the command given together with the appearance of Jesus Christ.[173]

Concerning this speech, Milerski writes that "In Bonhoeffer's opinion, it is the Word of God, which is not the property of some concrete entity or specific nation, but which nurtures the entire Universal Church as an ecumenical and supra-national community of various Christian fellowships, that authorizes both the objection of the Church to nationalism as well as its determined speaking out for peace and the peaceful co-existence of the nations." On these grounds, Milerski argues that theological rather than political or philosophical factors should determine the Church's position with respect to nationalism. The Church must follow Christ and obey his word, and stop posing as the defender of national traditions or serving as the representative of particular political interests. As he writes, "The Church can positively influence the matters of this world, only when it will in obedience put into practice the will of God, and not some concrete national, state or ideological interest."[174]

At Fanö Bonhoeffer called for an ecumenical council of all Christians, which could declare Christ's command of peace with one united voice, so that the world would hear and rejoice. Milerski suggests that this call went unheeded partly because Bonhoeffer's "program of the universal and ecumenical Church "living only by Christ" turned out to be over-idealized,"[175] citing as evidence *Sanctorum Communio*, where Bonhoeffer combined Saint Paul and the Hegelian formula "God existing as the church"[176] to identify ecclesiology with Christology. Longing for the Church to be empirical as well as a spiritual reality, Bonhoeffer blurred the boundaries between Christ and the Church, as a result of which the Church was endowed with Christ's power. But disillusionment soon set in and Bonhoeffer, still following Christ, turned to "worldly" political action, articulating his new understanding of the nature and role of Christ, and hence of the Church in the prison letters. It is perhaps ironic that by withdrawing the broad powers he had ascribed to the Church, he freed its members for responsible action in the real world. Milerski's description of Bonhoeffer's revised ecclesiology helps

173. Bonhoeffer, cited in ibid., 11.
174. Ibid., 11–12.
175. Ibid., 12.
176. I.e., *Gott als Gemeinde existierend*. Cf. Green, *Bonhoeffer*, 52 n. 91.

to explain the attraction of his Christian humanism for secular activists such as Kuroń.

> Bonhoeffer no longer understood the Church as *Christ existing* but as *existing in the pattern of Christ*. Jesus Christ was the one whose entire life could be characterized as *being for us (pro nobis)*, and this means that the Church must also be understood as existing as a community *being-for-others*. Bonhoeffer wrote: *Our relationship to God is not a "religious" relating to the highest, almighty and best being, . . . but is a new life in being-for-others, it is participating in the being of Jesus. Transcendence is not an unfinished and unreachable task, but the presently given and reachable neighbor. God in human form!* In other words: the Church is not a community being Christ, but a community that follows Christ into the center of the world, in responsibility for the world and for one's fellow human-being.[177]

Milerski declares that the Church testifies to the presence of Christ in the world through its openness to *others* in all their national, racial, and religious diversity. In a world where military conflict is often replaced by cultural colonization or the battle for market share, the Church's example shows the nations a way to overcome their respective superiority or inferiority complexes, and to meet other nations as partners rather than as potential victims or feared conquerors. "On one hand," he concludes, the Church "is the negation of nationalism, on the other it fosters the creation of an open society, and this not only in the perspective of a concrete nation but also in Europe in the process of uniting."[178]

In 2000, as the nations of Central and Eastern Europe prepared to join the European Union, Milerski noted that our mutual perception as individuals and nations is largely determined by our "self-understanding, stereotypes, and fears and phobias." Accordingly, he suggests that the educational policy of public institutions, including the Church, should be supplemented by a "pedagogy of reconciliation"[179] that takes its inspiration from Bonhoeffer's prison theology. While other institutions may adopt this for pragmatic reasons, the Church should accept it on theological principles, such as "Bonhoeffer's concept of God, "hiding

---

177. Ibid., 14.
178. Ibid.
179. Milerski, "Spotkać Boga w obcym człowieku," 31–32.

in" the face of another, so often a foreign person."[180] Similarly, the command "*be for others!*" entails an openness to those who are foreign and "other," which brings us closer to God.[181]

The Critique of Religion

Among Polish scholars two Lutheran professors have devoted the greatest attention to Bonhoeffer's critique of religion. Karol Karski considers Bonhoeffer's theology to represent a radicalization of the critique of religion initiated by Karl Barth, for Barth limited his critique to the realm of theology, whereas Bonhoeffer "draws from it practical consequences for the concrete historical situation."[182] Man has outgrown religion, and Christianity therefore must do the same, casting it off, not as something essential to its nature but like old clothes that it has now outgrown. As Karski writes, "For although God once filled the region of the entire world, today he has taken refuge on the altar where he lives like the spirit of every other religion. Therefore there is nothing left to do except resign from God as a working hypothesis of various regions of worldly life."[183]

Karski, who understands Bonhoeffer's quest to be the actualization of the Christian message for a world come of age, rather than the rejection or reduction of that message, points to Bonhoeffer's Christological center as the key to understanding the program of non-religious interpretation. As he explains, "Just as God entered into the world and suffered in it, even so Christians also must enter into the world, live in it in a worldly manner and suffer. Doing this, they participate in the suffering of God in the world: '*Jesus does not call us to a new religion, but to life.*'"[184] The *theologia crucis* moves Christians out of their religious ghettos into the fullness of life and worldly involvement.

Milerski, Karski's younger colleague at the Christian Theological Academy of Warsaw, approaches the thought of Bonhoeffer and Tillich as a response to the crisis in Western Christianity and Barth's critique of religion.[185] Arguing that the "main lack of the theology of crisis did

---

180. Ibid., 37
181. Ibid., 35
182. Karski, "Świeckie chrześcijaństwo Dietricha Bonhoeffera."
183. Ibid., 99–100
184. Ibid., 101–3.
185. Milerski, *Religia a Słowo*, 1994.

not consist in its concentration on Revelation, but in its failure to notice the necessity to mediate that Revelation," the author declares that what theological reflection requires is a "dialectical conception," which combines the critique of religion with a presentation of its positive contribution, since "Revelation is not only the annulment of religion but also its maintenance."[186] Milerski considers the theology of the cross, freed from the exclusivist equation "*either* Jesus Christ *or* religion," to be Bonhoeffer's major contribution to this dialectical conception. Tillich, stripped of his idealistic legitimization of the method of correlation, provides the "concept of symbolic mediation." Drawing on these insights, Milerski undertakes the "description of the reality of God without drawing on metaphysical and *a priori* terminology."[187] His formulation of the critique of religion as a "dialectic of religion and Word" is based on a "religious hermeneutical circle" of faith and symbol, and the experience of the divine presence (the Word of God) in the symbolic word: "In the human word, which is the necessary condition of every understanding, in the dialogical region 'in between,' the event of the real Word takes place."[188] Milerski closes by highlighting the potential this dialectic of religion and Word possesses for fostering meaningful dialogue on many levels. He concludes:

> The purpose of this thesis is not the presentation of some closed concept of the critique of religion, but the demonstration of its highly complex character. Perhaps expressing it in the form of "religion and Word" creates a possibility of dialog not only between different religions, Churches, and theological schools, but also between theology and the humanities. Let the conversation carry on ...[189]

The "critique of religion" took place at more popular level among Polish Catholics and secular activists. Michnik differentiates between *secularization*, defined as the "complete separation of church from state, complete separation of state from church, and complete civil rights for all," and *secularism*, understood as "the philosophical doctrine entailing the dissemination of a materialist and atheistic philosophy to all of

186. Ibid., 16.
187. Ibid., 300.
188. Ibid., 302.
189. Ibid.

society."[190] This distinction is used to argue that, contrary to its own propaganda, the Polish People's Republic (PRL) was no more secular than it was democratic. Since the PRL set secularism as its goal, the abolition of its political system was "the necessary condition for its secularization." As shown above, Michnik urged the "secular Left" to recognize that its liberal, humanist values have their source in Christianity. Neither should the Church equate the struggle for a secular society and civil rights with rabid anticlericalism. As Michnik explains,

> It took Communist totalitarianism to push the Left closer to the Church, as the Left began to realize that many common values were in jeopardy. For it turned out that there were common values between the Church and the left, something that both had denied. Today, probably, no one from the Church would deny that the Left defends such values.[191]

Michnik's expressed confidence in the Church's attitude towards the secular members of the opposition movement[192] is polemical but sincere. Though overstated, it was not unfounded, at least at the time. He points to the "noble and farsighted gesture" that the Polish episcopate made in coming to the defense of those, Catholics and liberals alike, who signed protest letters against the changes proposed in 1975 to the Polish Constitution. Michnik takes this as a sign that "just as in Bonhoeffer's analogy, *mother and children once again recognized each other.*" Now at last, Michnik dreams, the "rigid division into two camps, the Catholic and the Secular, might finally be overcome, replaced by the pluralistic unity of our culture." In contrast to the myth that only that which is Catholic is truly Polish, Michnik declares his belief that "the strength of our culture is its pluralism, its variety,"[193] and asks a probing question: "People of the Church must decide: do they seek to replace the official, totalitarian concept of 'socialist' culture with an equally fundamentalist doctrine of 'Catholic' culture? Or do they seek to create the conditions for the free development of the *entire* national culture?"[194] Michnik proceeds to clarify what he means by national culture:

---

190. Michnik, *Church and the Left*, 140.
191. Ibid., 147.
192. The same could be said of the left's confidence in the Church.
193. Michnik, *Church and the Left*, 153.
194. Ibid., 157.

> As religion, Roman Catholicism may inspire, and has inspired, cultural diversity. But culture is one. There is no Catholic culture, Protestant culture, or nonbeliever's culture; there is only Polish culture. And it is precisely this culture—pluralistic, yet understood as a unity—which we must defend.[195]

Polish Catholic writers have also conducted a Bonhoefferian-inspired critique of religion. Morawska, who describes Bonhoeffer's involvement in the Church struggle as a "long, tragic battle for the honor of German Christianity,"[196] asks why many Lutherans did not initially consider it collaboration to cooperate with Hitler's regime, and concludes that German Protestant theology contributed to the large scale failure of the Evangelical Church to resist Hitler. The nationalist equation, "to be German is to be Lutheran," matched by "the aspiration to be the *Church of the people*," led to compromise on fundamental principles in order to preserve the Church's freedom to preach and administer the sacraments. An overly individualized understanding of the Lutheran doctrine of justification by faith, bolstered by the cult of "order" and combined with an interpretation of the "two Kingdoms" doctrine that sharply separated the sacred from the secular, led to the ghettoization of the Church, and served to "anesthetize it to the moral message of actual social and political phenomena."[197] Although the Confessing Church noted no-little success in defending its internal purity and autonomy, few from its ranks joined Bonhoeffer in insisting that the church speak up in defense of the silent, helpless victims of the Nazi regime. For some, his statement about putting "a spoke in the wheel" bordered on treason, while his claim that "there is no salvation outside the Confessing Church," aimed at the "German Christians" who had bowed to Hitler, was perceived as sectarian.

In Morawska's view, the failure of the German churches impacted the whole of Western Christianity. "Those Churches," she writes, "did not rise to the level of the task, chauvinism blocked their most elemental ideals from their view, they looked above all to their own goals of self-preservation, or—in the heroic fraction—only the "purity of the ghetto," and considered the central ethical questions of their day to be-

---

195. Ibid., 157.
196. Morawska, *Chrześcijanin w Trzeciej Rzeszy*, 53.
197. Ibid., 56.

long to the secular realm that did not concern them."[198] Her description of the "ghetto mentality" of the German church spoke powerfully to Catholics seeking to break out of their own religious ghetto and engage in dialogue with other progressive forces in society.

Following her analysis of German Lutheranism, Morawska proceeds to critique the Roman Church. By defining the slogan, "To be German is to be Lutheran" as a nationalistic equation, she suggests that the parallel expression *Polak-Katolik* also bears nationalistic, perhaps even racist baggage. Furthermore, while the Reformation tends to confine religion to one's inner life with God, thus preserving it unstained but impotent, Catholicism's testimony on social issues was blunted by a highly concrete, institutional understanding of God's relationship to humanity. Therefore, where Bonhoeffer critiqued inwardness (subjectivity) and individualism, Morawska focuses on over-realized objectivity and institutionalism. As she writes, "an overly institutionally objectified God turned out to be almost as undemanding of a God, when it came to social testimony, as an overly 'other' or 'intimate' God."[199]

One might expect a radical interpretation of Bonhoeffer's late Christology from Morawska, who translated Robinson's *Honest to God*. Instead, she suggests a biographical approach to the prison letters: "One can look at them differently: not as a theological system . . . but as a record of very specific life experiences and psychological reactions. In them we meet, not only Bonhoeffer but his Christ—a Christ who continually calls on others to follow him on the costly road of discipleship."[200] Her description of Bonhoeffer's Christ leads her to reflect on his identity and the nature of his faith. How can one live "as if God did not exist" and remain "under the eye of God"? Can you reconcile solidarity with the world and the practice of "secret discipline"? What will the Church have to say when she speaks again after her long silence? These questions are real, declares Morawska, but so is the faith of the one who asked them. Reprising Anselm's *fides quaerens intellectum*, she reminds us that "Bonhoeffer's initial question was "Who is Jesus Christ for us today?" and therefore His presence and rule are assumed the whole time

---

198. Ibid., 78–79.
199. Ibid., 27.
200. Ibid., 220.

in advance."[201] Her critique of religion calls believers to follow Christ, and hence to active engagement in today's world.

Kłoczowski holds Bonhoeffer's task to be "confronting the world in the name of Christianity as a whole."[202] In a world come of age, the Church must recover a life of faith that is freed and transformed by grace. This requires putting aside the "religious" approach to Christianity, which Bonhoeffer described as metaphysical and individualistic. Kłoczowski understands "metaphysics" as doctrinaire thinking that reduces orthodoxy to adherence to a creed, and individualism as the view, present in Reformation theology and pietism, but also in Catholicism (e.g., quietism), that religion is a private, internal experience of God that is distinct and separate from involvement in other spheres. He notes that while Catholicism retained a better theoretical balance between the ultimate and penultimate (natural) spheres, "this does not mean that they have truly lived it," therefore Bonhoeffer's critique requires that all should reflect and act upon it. Jan Turnau,[203] who also understands "metaphysics" to mean "reducing the most essential and decisive content of Christianity to abstract speculations on the subject of various other-worldly matters and to correct formulas on this subject," declares that "Polish Catholics were ... confronted with the problem of "metaphysics" in this negative sense: what does it mean to be a Christian in the People's Republic of Poland?"[204] Both authors argue that while this "religious" Christianity proved itself powerless to resist Nazism, Bonhoeffer and his Polish readers moved haltingly yet inexorably towards responsible involvement in the "secular," political sphere. Kłoczowski adds that Bonhoeffer considered his move to "worldly" political involvement to be the fulfillment of the Christian gospel rather than its rejection. "Despite the fact that this led him to the fringe of organized "churchliness," this did not for a moment reduce the evangelical character of the inspiration of such activity."[205]

In 1995 Kłoczowski returns to "a man who is very important to me, Pastor Dietrich Bonhoeffer," to critique Catholic theology and spiritual experience. Paradoxically, Christ's passion turns his attention

---

201. Morawska, "Dietrich Bonhoeffer," 1361.

202. Kłoczowski, "Lekcja Bonhoeffera," 513.

203. Jan Turnau, (1933–), essayist, ecumenist, active in the Catholic Intellectuals Club, from 1951–1990 columnist for *Więź*, and from 1990 for *Gazeta Wyborcza*.

204. Jan Turnau, "Chrześcijanin w niewoli," 17.

205. Kłoczowski, "Lekcja Bonhoeffera," 517.

to the incarnation, as God's affirmation of the real world and the imperfect people who populate it. Kloczowski quotes "Ecce Homo" from Bonhoeffer's *Ethics*: "God loves the world. It is not an ideal man that He loves, but man as he is; not an ideal world, but the real world. What we find abominable in man's opposition to God, what we shrink back from with pain and hostility, the real man, the real world, this is for God the ground of unfathomable love, and it is with this that He unites himself utterly."[206] Arguing that "the Stations of the Cross arose out of the consciousness that we cannot go towards God while bypassing man, for the Christian is accompanied by the riveting conviction that God first became a man, before we found our way to God,"[207] Kłoczowski stresses that Christianity lives in the real world, not the arid regions of ivory tower theology, ecclesiastical ghettos or individualistic piety.

Mazowiecki's critique of religion develops the theme of this-worldly Christianity. He begins by observing that when Bonhoeffer joined the conspiracy he risked infamy as well as death. He accepted this double risk out of obedience to Christ's calls to follow him into the world. Mazowiecki writes, "Bonhoeffer matured to the understanding that it is possible and worthwhile to die for worldly values; the choice of his life path he now considered not as something that could merely be reconciled with Christianity but to be itself an act of Christian faith *par excellence*. As a theologian, Christian, and human being . . . he grew to the understanding that to participate in the powerlessness and suffering of Christ on the cross—this means to participate in the suffering of the world."[208] Such an understanding implies a marked revision of "worldly values." Mazowiecki argues that Christianity so-conceived implies "the radical crossing of the boundary between that which is worldly and that which is Christian. The paradox however of this radicalism is that this makes Christianity "unreligious" or worldly to the same degree as it makes that which is worldly Christian."[209]

As Mazowiecki notes, Bonhoeffer sought to liberate Christianity from the constricting boundaries of organized religion that shut matters of faith up within narrowly defined social forms and creeds, and he spoke against the demarcation of religious and worldly responsibilities

206. Kłoczowski, "Droga Krzyżowa—labirynt życia," 8.
207. Ibid.
208. Mazowiecki, "Naucyzł się wierzyć wśród tęgich razów," 16.
209. Ibid., 17.

that characterized his Protestant tradition. Negatively, this demands the rejection of a Christian ghetto mentality, or what Mazowiecki termed "smoke-screen thinking." Positively, it is "an affirmation of the autonomy of the world, of public life and culture, of the fact of the world's outgrowing of sacralized forms." Mazowiecki agrees with Bonhoeffer that in following Christ we become, not religious but human.[210]

Mazowiecki concludes by citing Morawska's question concerning the author of the prison letters: were these the reflections of Bonhoeffer the theologian or Bonhoeffer the man of faith? This question, Mazowiecki suggests, is problematic for the critic-theologian and the non-Christian reader of Bonhoeffer alike, for both must feel the genuine presence of God in the very life of the one who says we must live without God in this world. In the end it is this impression that prevents us from jumping to the hasty conclusion that "only one step was lacking for Bonhoeffer to deny his faith; can one not sense that it is precisely Bonhoeffer's faith, and that naked, powerless Christianity that is the content of this theology, which makes his understanding of human fate so authentic?"[211]

> The Christian is called to sharing with God His suffering. Perhaps above all Bonhoeffer is close today to many people through this, that he combines moral sensitivity with the prophetic thought of Christianity, solidarity with human fate . . . with the experience of God; not some formula of Him, but [God] Himself. At the very border, to which this thought reaches, it is as if the questioning of God through the formula *etsi Deus non daretur* runs hand in hand with the affirmation of Him in Christ; God reveals Himself through Christ in the gospel not as a "hypothesis," but as reality uniting division, as the redeeming and reconciling Word. The world is of age, but only through entering into the reality of the Cross of Christ is it freed from the ever renewed tendency to self-deification: worldliness as a value becomes Christian through the measure of humanity that Christ is for the world.[212]

Morawska, Kłoczowski, and Mazowiecki all argue that Bonhoeffer, in his critique of religion, was taking a stand against all forms of Christianity that compartmentalize life and thereby release Christ's followers from responsibility towards their fellow human beings. To the

210. Ibid., 18.
211. Ibid., 19.
212. Ibid., 19–20.

metaphysics, inwardness, individualism, and autonomy criticized by Bonhoeffer, they add the dangers of over-realized objectivity, institutionalism, and "smoke-screen thinking." In Mazowiecki's quote above, Bonhoeffer's dialectic of incarnation and crucifixion, the dialectic of God revealed in Christ, both affirms human dignity and guards it from the danger of self-deification. Yet the incarnate, crucified, and risen Christ is himself the reality that overcomes the division between secular and sacred, and who reconciles humanity with God. He is the ultimate reality that gives the penultimate its significance and worth, for "worldliness as a value becomes Christian through the measure of humanity that Christ is for the world."[213] Such a critique of religion presents a constant challenge for individuals and churches alike, a challenge to identify with Christ, and hence to solidarity with the world he reconciled and redeemed.

---

213. Ibid., 19–20.

Bonhoeffer on Christ, Providence, and Responsibility

Dorosz lists socialism, liberalism, Christianity, and Poland's own "tradition of national-liberation" as sources of inspiration for the Polish opposition movement (1968–1989).[1] Chapter 4 demonstrated how Bonhoeffer made a significant contribution to Christianity's influence; opposition intellectuals and activists, in creatively adapting these diverse traditions, discovered that Bonhoeffer spoke to their geopolitical situation.[2] Conversely, their reading of Bonhoeffer was shaped by the intellectual, cultural, and political history of Poland and Europe, including their own messianic legacy. Such a contextual reading is true to Bonhoeffer's dictum, that "we are placed objectively by our history into a particular context of experience, responsibility, and decision, from which we cannot withdraw without ending up in abstraction."[3] However, the *Sitz im Leben* of the Polish reception of Bonhoeffer, while stimulating a lively interaction with his thought, blunted its potential for a radical critique both of the messianic motifs underlying Polish thought and culture, and the opposition's own theory and praxis.

What the Polish reception of Bonhoeffer appears to lack from the perspective of his theology is deeper, sustained reflection on Jesus Christ. Furthermore, several key elements of Polish messianism, such as its penchant for historiosophy, its proposed theodicies, and its underlying epistemology, failed to receive systematic treatment in opposition

1. Dorosz, "Kuroń, Michnik, Lewica, Chrześcijaństwo," 142.

2. The major themes discussed below in the section of chapter 4 entitled, "The Polish Reception of Bonhoeffer: Selected Themes," also appear in chapters 5 and 6, as issues that occupy an important role in both the thought of Bonhoeffer and Polish messianism.

3. E: 100–101.

thought. While this latter observation in itself suggests that the opposition found messianism's values to be of more use in their context than its underlying presuppositions and worldview, given the power and longevity of Poland's messianic myths, messianism needs a hearty critique of its stance on these issues as well. Accordingly, chapter 5 will first examine Bonhoeffer's Christology along with his theology of sociality, then discuss his views on providence and history, before concluding with a section on human responsibility. Chapter 6 follows a similar outline, using Bonhoeffer to critique Polish messianism's central messianic ideas, its philosophy of history, and its view of responsibility.

Bonhoeffer on Christ and Community

Christ Existing as Community

In his doctoral thesis, *Sanctorum Communio*, Bonhoeffer introduced several themes that remained foundational to his theology. Responding positively but critically to Barth, he sought for the concreteness of revelation and the recovery of this-worldly, historical transcendence, which he grounded in the church. As Clements writes, "Bonhoeffer sets out to earth revelation in ecclesiology."[4] Bonhoeffer's point of departure is the concept of person, which he develops into a "theology of sociality." Marsh argues that "Bonhoeffer's christological description of life with others offers a compelling and unexpectedly rich alternative to post-Kantian models of selfhood."[5] Instead of the "subject-object" model of personhood characteristic of idealism, he posits an encounter of two subjects. The (potential) "I" reaches its "boundary" when it encounters the independent will of the "You." No longer may it define external objects as it pleases; the unsolicited address of another subject calls for an answer, and the ensuing interaction defines the identity of both subjects as social-ethical persons. Green notes that this construction is founded on the premise that "to be human is to be a person before God, and in relation to God,"[6] which by analogy suggests that human persons also exist in relation to other persons. This leads to the recovery of lost transcendence. Feil explains: "when the 'I' finds its boundary

---

4. Clements, "Community in the Ethics of Dietrich Bonhoeffer," 19.
5. Marsh, *Reclaiming Dietrich Bonhoeffer*, vii.
6. Cf. Green, "Human Sociality and Christian Community," 114–15.

in the "You" real transcendence is attained as ethical transcendence."[7] Bonhoeffer grounds this transcendence in God, who stands behind the You of the other person; otherwise, one human being would—ethically and socially speaking—"create" another. Bonhoeffer writes:

> One human being cannot of its own accord make another into an I, an ethical person conscious of responsibility. God or the Holy Spirit joins the concrete You; only through God's active working does the other become a You to me from whom my I arises. In other words, every human You is an image of the divine You.[8]

Bonhoeffer introduces the concepts of "objective spirit," "collective person," and "vicarious representative action," which contribute to a model of the church that is both "with" and "for" each other, which Bonhoeffer defines as "Christ-existing-as-community." He adopts the idealistic and romantic concept of "objective spirit,"[9] arguing that when two or more wills unite they create a "structure," perceived by those within and without the structure, which though existing only through its individual participants, has a "life" and "will" of its own that interacts with its members both individually and collectively.[10] Here Bonhoeffer distinguishes between a society and a community. While both have objective spirit, the former exists for an ulterior purpose, while the latter is also an end in itself.[11] Bonhoeffer's phenomenological description of objective spirit is eschatologically related to the community of God.

> Because of the eschatological character of community, which it shares with others, the deepest significance of community is "from God to God." This is the basis for the "holiness" of human community life, whether we think of the physical communities of blood and clan, historical communities like a nation, or life-shaping communities such as marriage and friendship.[12]

Bonhoeffer ascribes "personal character" only to community, not society. He distances himself from Hegel by insisting that individuals

---

7. Feil, *Theology of Dietrich Bonhoeffer*, 62.
8. SC: 54–55.
9. SC: 98.
10. SC: 98–100.
11. SC: 100–101.
12. SC: 101.

are not swallowed up into the community spirit.[13] Neither do "collective persons" possess their life autonomously, from the nation's "metaphysical depths," contrary to the concept of *Volk* already popular in Germany and soon to be invoked by Nazi ideology. Instead, collective persons arise in the same way as individual persons; initially through the encounter of individuals that form the community, then through the collective person's encounter with other collective persons.[14] Bonhoeffer cites the example of Israel, "which arose from being thus called by God, by the prophets, by the course of political history, by alien peoples."[15] God has a purpose in history for collective persons, including nations, friendships, marriages, families, and the church, as well as for individuals. Collective persons may share a collective "call," hence a collective responsibility, and they can bear collective guilt.[16] This is also true of humanity as a whole, which has been called by God in Jesus Christ. Here Bonhoeffer proposes the idea of corporate "humanity-in-Adam," which is composed of many individuals yet "sinned as a whole." This *peccatorum communio*[17] is "infinitely fragmented," and can be superseded only by redeemed humanity-in-Christ.[18]

This church-community is "with-each-other" and "for-each-other"[19] as the members of the community bear each other's burdens,[20] pray for each other,[21] and forgive each other's sins.[22] Thus the church is revealed as more than the sum of its members, to be truly "Christ

---

13. SC: 102–3.
14. SC: 103, 118.
15. SC: 118.
16. SC: 119.

17. Bonhoeffer rejects a "biological" understanding of original sin, together with approaches that argue from the individual act to universal culpability (Augustine *et al*) or deduce universal sinfulness from the sum of individual sins (Ritschl). Borrowing from Leibniz the concept of "monads," Bonhoeffer argues that each human individual "is also the human race," not biologically but socially, hence when the individual sins against God this becomes "the deed of the human race . . . in the individual person . . . each individual monad "represents" the whole world." SC: 115–16.

18. SC: 120–21.
19. SC: 178.
20. SC: 179.
21. SC: 188–89.
22. SC: 189.

existing as church-community."[23] This community is characterized by vicarious representative action (*stellvertretung*), "where one person bears the other in active love, intercession, and forgiveness of sins, acting completely vicariously."[24] Green explains that this concept is "best expressed by speaking of people who represent their communities and act vicariously on their behalf,"[25] though it would be improper to limit such vicarious action to unique, gifted individuals who occupy positions of influence.

Christ the Center of History

Compared to *Sanctorum Communio*, *Act and Being*, Bonhoeffer's *Habilitationsschrift*, presents a more developed Christology, which thereafter occupied the center of Bonhoeffer's theology. Whereas Barth countered liberal theology's anthropocentric tendencies by declaring that God is "totally-other" and "free-from-us," Bonhoeffer argued that the God of the covenant freely "chose to be bound to historical human beings ... God is free not from human beings but for them. Christ is the word of God's freedom. God is present, that is, not in eternal non-objectivity but ... "haveable," graspable, in the Word within the church."[26] This Christocentrism appears also in *Creation and Fall*, where he interprets the image of God socially, as a relationship between human persons that mirrors the relationship between divine persons in the Trinity, leading to the claim that "freedom is a relation between two persons. Being free means 'being-free-for-the-other.'"[27] Thus, as Green explains, "being-free-for-the-other-in-love images God's loving freedom for humanity."[28]

In *Christology*, Bonhoeffer moves beyond ecclesiology to make Christ the center of all reality: "The one who is present in Word, sacrament and community is in the centre of human existence, history and nature."[29] Asking "where" Christ stands in history, he answers firmly: "He

---

23. SC: 190.
24. SC: 191.
25. Green, "Human Sociality," 118.
26. AB: 90–91.
27. CF: 63.
28. Green "Human Sociality," 117.
29. C: 61.

stands *pro me*."³⁰ This *pro me* is related in time and space to all created reality: "He is the centre in three ways; in being-there for human beings, in being-there for history and in being-there for nature."³¹ As Chapman puts it, "The Mediator (Mittler) is the center (Mitte) of every part of existence. . . ."³² Christ's centrality to human beings relates to "being a person before God"; Christ neither replaces their personality nor occupies their entire consciousness. Interpreting his theology of sociality Christologically, Bonhoeffer states that human beings cannot fulfill the law, which constitutes a boundary³³ at the center of human existence that defines humanity individually and corporately. Christ, having fulfilled the law, now stands in the center as the boundary between the old and the new "I," between judgment and justification.³⁴ Bonhoeffer interprets history eschatologically, in light of the promise of Messiah. Just as the individual cannot fulfill the law, so history cannot fulfill the messianic promise, though it continually tries to do so "by glorifying itself in its own messiahs."³⁵ Bonhoeffer's brief comments on nature foreshadow his reflections on the penultimate and the natural in *Ethics*.

Bonhoeffer closed *Discipleship* with the image of Christ theme from *Creation and Fall*. His call for the church to follow Christ by obeying the Sermon on the Mount was an attempt at enabling the church to be the church in a world full of Nazis. Already we find that the church, by partaking of Christ, also partakes in humanity and acts on its behalf. He writes:

> Through fellowship and communion with the Incarnate Lord, we recover our true humanity, and at the same time are delivered from that individualism which is the consequence of sin, and retrieve our solidarity with the whole human race. Being partakers of Christ Incarnate, we are partakers in the whole humanity which he bore . . . we too must bear the sins and sorrows of others.³⁶

---

30. C: 61.

31. C: 62.

32. Chapman, "Bonhoeffer, Liberation Theology, and the 1990's," 301.

33. Here God is presumed to stand behind the law, and hence to be addressing the person.

34. A reformulation of the Lutheran dialectic of law and grace, and Luther's paradox of *simul iustus et peccator*.

35. C: 64.

36. CD: 272.

"Christ, Reality and Good," which opens the proposed reconstruction of *Ethics*,[37] clearly alludes to Nazi ideology, propaganda, and practice. Hitler's henchmen appear, albeit in the company of angels, as "villains and saints" once again walk this earth.[38] Yet Bonhoeffer began with Christ, not the ethical challenges of his day, which he considered the extreme expression of the general crisis of Western civilization. He states unequivocally: "The source of a Christian ethic is not the reality of one's own self, not the reality of the world, nor is it the reality of norms and values. It is the reality of God that is revealed in Jesus Christ."[39]

Christ the Reconciler of God and the World

Bonhoeffer based his ethics on Christ, the Mediator at the center of history, who reconciles God and the World.[40] In "Ethics as Formation" he writes that, "there is no more godlessness, or hate, or sin that God has not taken upon himself, suffered, and atoned. Now there is no longer any reality, any world, that is not reconciled with God and at peace. God has done this in the beloved son, Jesus Christ."[41]

Christ's incarnation affirms humanity and this-worldly life, his crucifixion is a sign of God's condemnation of this world, and his resurrection broke the power of death, bringing hope to a world reconciled with God. In counterpoint to the ancient Christian doctrine of *theosis*, Bonhoeffer declares that God became human so that human beings might become truly human.[42] The incarnation demonstrates God's love for real people. He writes, "God loves human beings . . . Not an ideal human, but human beings as they are; . . . God becomes human, and we must recognize that God wills that we be human, real human beings."[43] Jesus Christ confirmed God's love for us by taking on "the nature, essence, guilt, and suffering of human beings."[44] In contrast, Hitler is

37. Cf. E: 447–48.
38. E: 76.
39. E: 49.
40. Cf. Bonhoeffer: "All concepts of reality that ignore Jesus Christ are abstractions." E: 54.
41. E: 83.
42. Bonhoeffer writes, "God changed God's form into human form in order that human beings can become, not God, but human before God." E: 96.
43. E: 84.
44. E: 84.

characterized as the "tyrannical despiser of humanity" for whom "popularity is a sign of the greatest love for humanity."[45] In truth, the despiser holds in contempt the masses whose favour he curries. By affirming their meanest instincts, he leads to their progressive debasement; "he considers the people stupid and they become stupid; he considers them weak, and they become weak; he considers them criminal, and they become criminal."[46] Nevertheless, the masses declare the *Führer* a god, thus "contempt for humanity and idolization of humanity lie close together."[47] In Bonhoeffer's radio attack on the *Führer* principle, he concluded that leaders who "surrender to the wishes of their followers" become misleaders: "Leaders or offices which set themselves up as gods mock God."[48]

The God who affirmed humanity in Christ's incarnation also judged humanity in Christ's crucifixion. "*Ecce homo*—behold the one whom God has judged! [. . .] What happened to and in Christ happened to all of us. Only as judged by God can human beings live before God; only the crucified human being is at peace with God."[49] Bonhoeffer presents Christ as the Reconciler, who came under God's sentence by assuming our guilt. Here the social nature of his Christology and anthropology are clearly in view: "Only by executing God's judgment on God can peace grow between God and the world, between human and human."[50] In opposition to the crucified Christ, Bonhoeffer portrays successful individuals, who "stride on from deed to deed, win the future, and make the past unchangeable."[51] This description of Hitler, flushed with his recent military victories, nevertheless leaves Nietzsche's *Übermensch* lurking in the shadows. Following a critique of those who bowed to Hitler by idolising success or confusing the successful with the good, Bonhoeffer's parallel discussion of failure is a riposte to Nietzsche's view of Christianity as a mechanism of revenge and power-grabbing by society's losers. In response to both, Bonhoeffer rejects judging human

45. E: 86.
46. E: 86.
47. E: 86.
48. Bonhoeffer, "The Younger Generation's Altered View of the Concept of *Führer*," cited in Bethge, *Dietrich Bonhoeffer*, 260.
49. E: 88.
50. E: 88.
51. C: 88.

beings based on success or failure, for God's judgment falls on those who succeed and fail alike. Only those who are judged and reconciled to God in the Crucified One can stand before God. Though Bonhoeffer declares here that the cross, which represents vicarious suffering for others, may lead to historical success, not until *Letters and Papers from Prison* does he grant this principle normative status.[52]

After affirmation and judgment comes reconciliation. Drawing on his concept of corporate persons, Bonhoeffer declares that, "In Jesus Christ, the one who became human was crucified and is risen; humanity has become new. What happened to Christ has happened to us all, for he was *the* human being."[53] Christ has risen. Death is conquered by life, and humanity has a new start, for Christ's history has become our history, the history of the human race.[54] The miracle of Christ's resurrection stands in sharp contrast to the murderous rhetoric, policies, and actions of the Third Reich. Against the backdrop of humanity as renewed in Christ, Bonhoeffer debunks the eschatological claims of the "Thousand-year Reich," in which "big words are spoken of a new humanity, a new world, a new society that will be created, and all this newness consists only in the annihilation of existing life."[55] Hitler gambled everything in an all-or-nothing bid for world supremacy and the realization of his twisted vision. Bonhoeffer counters this blasphemous, over-realized "eschatology" with an inaugurated eschatology that dates its beginning from Christ's passion and resurrection, and looks to a fulfilment beyond death. Thus at midnight in Nazi Germany Bonhoeffer could proclaim with confidence, "The night is not yet over, but day is already dawning."[56]

Christ Taking Form in Our World

Reality as reconciled to God in Christ is not a formula that the world must conform to. Rejecting ideologies that impose utopian visions upon historical reality, Bonhoeffer proclaims: "Christ does not abolish human reality in favor of an idea that demands to be realized against all that is

52. E: 91.
53. E: 91.
54. E: 92.
55. E: 91.
56. E: 92.

real."⁵⁷ Christian formation is not conforming to Christian principles or implementing ethical systems. Formation is the process by which Christ forms us into His image;⁵⁸ it is becoming more like Christ in this life. While formation is God's doing, it requires active engagement on our part. "What matters," Bonhoeffer asserts, "is *participation in the reality of God and the world in Jesus Christ today....*"⁵⁹ This means that Christ's followers are to engage in what he is doing in their lives, community, and world. By reconciling God and the World, Christ overcame the need to choose between this-worldly relevance and other-worldly spirituality. The dichotomy of "being" or "doing" is overcome by renewed unity in the God-Man, Jesus Christ. Standing before God as those convicted and justified, Christ's followers are free to be themselves and free to be God's.⁶⁰ Since God became human and not an idea, Christ takes form "in real human beings, and thus in quite different ways."⁶¹

While formation is an individual matter, it is not individualistic. According to Bonhoeffer's formula, "Christ-existing-as-community," God forms those who take on Christ's form into a community.⁶² This community is not a fortress but a beachhead, not an exception but the new norm. As he writes, "[The church's] first concern is not with the so-called religious functions of human beings, but with the existence in the world of whole human beings in all their relationships."⁶³ The Church's walls must come down, for Christ entered the world to reconcile it with God. The Church is becoming what the whole world is meant to be; not "religious," but reconciled to Christ and conformed to him. The Church has the additional task of addressing "humanity in the light of its true form, which belongs to it, which it has already received, but which it has not grasped and accepted, namely, the form of Jesus Christ that is its own."⁶⁴

---

57. Cf. E: 99.

58. Contrary to Platonism, Bonhoeffer regards reality not as the idea of the perfect human being, but the historical person of Jesus Christ.

59. E: 55.

60. E: 94–95. Being yourself and being God's is the necessary foundation for "being-for-others."

61. E: 99.

62. E: 97.

63. E: 97–98.

64. E: 98.

Bonhoeffer rejects casuistry as too specific to be practical, and absolute principles as too general to be of any use. The need is to speak concretely "about how Christ may take form among us today and here."[65] In the following manuscripts[66] Bonhoeffer fleshes out the concept of "Christ taking form today" as a concrete ethic for "the West, the peoples of Europe and America who until this time have been unified by the form of Christ."[67] Ethics as formation takes place through the church, where Christ's form takes shape. Ethics as proclamation furthers the conformation of the church to Christ and empowers its witness to Christ among the nations.[68] This grounding of ethics in the church reflects Bonhoeffer's critique of individualism, his negative view of the conscience as an instrument of self-justification, and the theology of sociality that underlies his ethical reflections. With Barth, Bonhoeffer believed that God can speak his word into the concrete situation, and judged such a word necessary in the face of the Nazi threat. Bonhoeffer held the church responsible, not only to defend Christianity against Nazism, but to defend the humanist tradition of European culture and society.

Bonhoeffer waited in vain for the church to stand publicly with the Jews, or to bless those engaged in resistance activities. Bethge argues that Bonhoeffer joined the conspiracy following his disappointment at the Confessing Church's failure to defend the Jews. In his prison theology, Bonhoeffer's declared that the church had lost its voice by its non-participation "in the reality of God and world in Jesus Christ"; first it failed to proclaim "Peace!" in Christ's name, and later it defended its own privileges while ignoring the unlucky souls on the "outside." Therefore the Church must now "pray and do good" as it waits for new, non-religious words to proclaim Jesus Christ to a world come of age. Having proclaimed Christ without obedience, it must now obey in silence. Only when its deeds once again reflect Jesus Christ will its proclamation again ring with his power.

Both "Heritage and Decay," which develops Christian ethics for "normal" times,[69] and "History and the Good," which explores the need

65. E: 99.
66. I.e., "History and Good," and "Inheritance and Decay."
67. E: 101.
68. E: 102.
69. "Normal" here means post-Christendom. As Bonhoeffer argues at the end of "Heritage and Decay," "The Church must bear witness to Jesus Christ as living lord, and

in border situations for the free acts of responsible individuals, naturally follow from "Ethics as Formation." We will look first at "Heritage and Decay" to explore Bonhoeffer's view of providence and history, before returning to "History and Good" and the question of responsible freedom.

Bonhoeffer on Providence and Responsibility

Christ and the Church versus the "Abyss of Nothingness"

In "Heritage and Decay" Bonhoeffer bases his sweeping view of European history on the premise that Christ is the foundation of the West's "historical heritage," as expressed in the unity within Christendom (*corpus christianum*) of the Pope and the Emperor. The Reformation "shattered" the West's spiritual unity, while the Thirty Years' War destroyed its political unity.[70] The Protestant demarcation of reality into sacred and secular realms both "liberated" and "desacralized" society. The development of autonomous science, industry, and culture resulted in a mechanistic, rational world devoid of faith. Conscious class identity and conflict arose, as the nobility was challenged by the rising middle class, and then the masses who proclaimed the sovereignty of the people.[71] The anti-clerical French Revolution marked the birth of the "modern West," where human *ratio* and unbridled technology hold sway, and nationalism struggles to uproot kingdoms and establish new societies.[72] "Human liberation as an absolute ideal," concludes Bonhoeffer, "leads to the self-destruction of human beings,"[73] in revolutionary terror and nationalistic wars.

The unity of Christendom was replaced by the unity of Western godlessness.[74] Many still clung to Christian morality, but Nietzsche showed that Christianity cannot long survive the demise of the Christian God. Bonhoeffer declares that "deifying humanity is, properly understood, the proclamation of nihilism."[75] An alternative form of self-

---

it must do so in a world that has turned away from Christ after knowing him." E: 132.

70. E: 110–13.
71. E: 118–20.
72. E: 115, 122.
73. E: 122.
74. E: 122.
75. E: 123.

destruction is vitalism, defined as "life that makes itself absolute, that makes itself its own goal."[76] The Nazis' vitalism included race among life's inherent laws,[77] and for Bonhoeffer the quintessential expression of the West's denial of Christ was the expulsion of the Jews, by all means including the "final solution."[78]

Yet Bonhoeffer affirms the intellectual, technological, and social gains made during the process of secularization. The West owes to the Enlightenment an intellectual rigor and honesty, "which has ever since belonged to the essential moral requirements of Western humanity."[79] The use of reason led to the technological revolution, and the discovery of "eternal human rights . . . found in the birthright of every human being to freedom, equality of all before the law, and the common solidarity of all those who wear a human face."[80] Furthermore, alongside the hopeless godlessness of the West, "dressed up in religious-Christian finery" and hence as likely to be found within the church as outside its walls, there appears an anti-religious "promising godlessness," which by destroying false images of God and unmasking the errors and abuses of Christendom, clings to hope and prepares the way for the rediscovery of the true God and the true Church.[81]

The West's decay has brought it to brink of the "abyss of nothingness," described by Bonhoeffer in climactic, apocalyptic terms.

> Having lost its unity that was created by the form of Jesus Christ, the West is confronted by nothingness [*Nichts*]. Uncontrolled powers clash with each other. Everything that exists is threatened with annihilation. This is not just one crisis among others, but a conflict of ultimate seriousness.[82]

In his exposition of the abyss, Bonhoeffer critiques the Nazi's twisted eschatological claims, together with the slogans, policies, fears,

---

76. E: 178.

77. Cf. the editors' note [96], in E: 124–25.

78. E: 105. The reference is to the expulsion of the Jews from Spain, followed by the Inquisition, various pogroms and persecutions. Nevertheless, Bonhoeffer saw the looming Holocaust as culminating the West's efforts to purge itself of the Jews.

79. E: 115.

80. E: 117. The ideals of *liberté, egalité, fraternité* were the French Revolution's lasting contribution to Western civilization.

81. E: 124.

82. E: 127.

and aberrations of the Nazi era. He lists two things that can stop Europe from self-destruction: "the miracle of a new awakening of faith; and the power that the Bible calls the 'restrainer.'"[83] Reborn faith is God's act, accomplished in Christ and proclaimed by the church. Although Ballard identifies the restrainer as the "natural laws of history," by which evil carries within itself the seeds of its own destruction,[84] Bonhoeffer has in mind the state, which limits evil by the power of the sword.[85] Nevertheless, Pangritz and Clements[86] are surely correct when they argue that Bonhoeffer counts Germans opposed to Hitler and even the Allied armies among "the elements of order that still remain."[87] Facing the abyss, Bonhoeffer urged the church to "bear witness to Jesus Christ as living Lord" in a hostile world,[88] and to hold onto its eschatological hope, kept alive by the witness of a Church awaiting the *parousia*. In the interim, the church is to pass the heritage of the past on to the historical future. Anticipating the Tegel theology, Bonhoeffer considers the church's suffering for proclaiming Christ "infinitely more dangerous to the spirit of destruction than the political power it may still retain."[89]

"Church and World I" begins by observing that when faced with the evil of Nazism, the remaining forces of good and decency sought refuge "in the Christian domain, in the shadow of the Church."[90] The Church's orphans, "reason, culture, humanity, tolerance, autonomy,"[91] came home to their mother, sensing that only here, in the name of Jesus, was there power to stand against the antichrist. Bonhoeffer's reference to Soloviev's Antichrist, an allusion to Hitler,[92] gives an apocalyptic spin to the Third Reich. In response, Bonhoeffer appeals to Jesus Christ, not

---

83. E: 131.

84. This idea is found, not here but in: Bonhoeffer, *Letters and Papers*, 141–42. Note: if a date is not given, citations from LPP are from the 1959 edition.

85. E: 112.

86. Pangritz, "Sharing the Destiny," 268; Clements, "Integration, Conflict and the Ecumenical Quest," 238.

87. E: 132.

88. E: 132.

89. E: 132.

90. E: 341.

91. E: 340.

92. Bonhoeffer did not identify Hitler with "the" Antichrist; rather he perceived him as one of many antichrist figures (cf. 1 John 2:18).

religion, ethics, or a messianic philosophy of history. To stand against the abyss, one needs not messianism, but the Messiah. He writes:

> over against the Antichrist, only one will remain in force and endure, namely, Christ himself. Only that which participates in Christ can endure and overcome. Christ is the center and power of the Bible, of the Church, of theology, but also of humanity, reason, justice, and culture. To Christ everything must return; only under Christ's protection can it live.[93]

Many Poles who cited this passage acknowledged the need to base opposition on a transcendent foundation. Leaving the discussion of their views of transcendence for later, Bonhoeffer relates ultimate and penultimate "transcendence" alike to Jesus Christ, by juxtaposing Matthew 9:40 ("Whoever is not against us is for us") and Matthew 12:30 ("Whoever is not for me is against me"). Whenever and wherever someone calls on the name of Jesus, "there the power of Christ still has a sphere of influence; there one ought not to interfere, but allow the name of Jesus to do its work."[94] As Bonhoeffer explains, "This name provides safety for them and the noble values they defend. At the same time, this name claims both them and these values."[95] On the other hand, Bonhoeffer relates the discovery of the Confessing Church, which took its stand against the "abyss," that the claimed neutrality of those fell away was actually "hostility to Christ." Reduced in numbers, the confessing Christians discovered, ". . . an inner freedom and openness that protected it from all anxious efforts to erect boundaries. So it gathered people who had traveled from afar, and to them it could not deny its community and protection."[96] Bonhoeffer now brings these passages into harmony.

> Both sayings necessarily belong together, one as the exclusive claim, and the other as the all-encompassing claim, of Jesus Christ . . . it is the persecution of justice, truth, humanity and freedom that drove people, to whom these values were precious, under the protection of Jesus Christ and thus under His claim;

---

93. E: 341–42.
94. E: 342.
95. E: 342.
96. E: 344.

and this experience caused the church-community of Jesus Christ to discover the breadth of its responsibility.[97]

In Tegel prison Bonhoeffer could only trust that the Church would one day regain her voice. Here Bonhoeffer is still optimistic, declaring that the Church is drawing the world to itself through proclamation, through drawing near to Christ, and by renewing its own spiritual disciplines. Far more than a documentary account of a renewed, outward-looking, and involved Church, this constitutes a prayer of faith and an expression of hope for the future, for a new world after the Nazi storm, in which the Church of Jesus Christ would truly be the Church for others. De Lange also notes the "apologetic" character of this passage, writing that Bonhoeffer "wished to help the 'righteous' who no longer dared to call himself a Christian 'with much patience to the confession of Christ.'"[98]

Rusty Swords

Bonhoeffer, as Feil demonstrates, developed his position on the relationship of God to the world in opposition to the stance of cultural Protestantism, which had separated the two largely through a post-Kantian view of transcendence that left God with no place in world, and banished human knowledge and experience of God to the sphere of "inwardness."[99] Faith, understood by Bonhoeffer as a total response to God in the totality of life, was shut up within the increasingly narrow confines of "religion." This led to a heteronymous Christianity, which left the autonomous, secular world alone in exchange for its own limited domain.[100] Bonhoeffer describes the reaction to secularism's accommodation with the world as otherworldliness, which leads to rejecting the God-given though fallen world in favor of a "better" world created by human effort.[101] In contrast, Feil considers Bonhoeffer's understanding of the world to be "the most important of those contrapuntal themes" he developed against the *cantus firmus* of his Christology.[102]

---

97. E: 344–45.
98. de Lange, "Particular Europe," 90.
99. Feil, "Dietrich Bonhoeffer's Understanding of the World," 239–41.
100. Ibid., 240.
101. Ibid., 241.
102. Ibid., 242.

On several occasions Bonhoeffer catalogued the failed responses of religion and ethics to the world come of age. In the June 8, 1944 letter from Tegel prison, Bonhoeffer writes, "Man has learned to cope with all the important questions of life without recourse to God as a working hypothesis . . . As in the scientific field, so in human affairs generally, what we call 'God' is being more and more edged out of life, losing more and more ground."[103] Bonhoeffer argues that Christianity's opposition to human autonomy, its efforts to "prove to a world thus come of age that it cannot live without the tutelage of 'God,'"[104] have only made the modernist movement more anti-Christian. The "attack by Christian apologists upon the adulthood of the world" is pointless, because it seeks to return "mature" humanity to its adolescence, ignoble, because it amounts to a form of manipulation, and un-Christian, because it mistakes Christ for one stage of human religiousness.[105] Bonhoeffer displays his distaste for psychotherapy masquerading as theology, which preys on human weakness and fear, on death and guilt, in order to convince people that only the church can save them.[106] Pietistic and confessional attacks on modernism deny Christ as the "ruler of the entire world" by dividing the world into sacred and secular realms. Liberal theology accepts the shrinking place the world grants to the mysteries of faith. Barth correctly appealed to Christ against religion, "but gave no guidance, either in dogmatics or in ethics on the non-religious interpretation of theological concepts."[107] Bonhoeffer called this approach "a positivism of revelation,"[108] characterizing it as "take it or leave it."[109] His concern is that "the world is made to depend on itself and left to its own devices," whereas Christ is Lord of the whole world, not just the Christian ghetto. Bonhoeffer urged the church "to speak a word of reconciliation to mankind and the world at large."[110] The Confessing Church however "lapsed" even from Barth's promising but insufficiently developed approach into a "conservative restoration," preaching orthodox Christianity but failing to interpret it

103. LPP 1959: 106–7.
104. LPP: 107.
105. LPP: 108.
106. Cf. LPP: 107.
107. LPP: 109.
108. Cf. also Bonhoeffer's discussion of Barth in the April 30th, 1944 letter, LPP: 95.
109. LPP: 95.
110. LPP: 160.

for the modern world. Concluding that Bultmann's program of demythologization did not go far enough, Bonhoeffer insists that, "the full content... must be maintained... but the concepts must be interpreted in such a way as not make religion a pre-condition for faith." Earlier, on April 30th, he had written: "You cannot, as Bultmann imagines, separate God and miracles, but rather must interpret and proclaim *both* of them in a 'non-religious' sense."[111] Such an approach is contrasted to religious interpretation that is metaphysical, individualistic, and inward.

Prior to Bonhoeffer's "stocktaking" of Christianity surveyed above, he had found typical "ethical" responses to Nazism lacking. These reasonable people and ethical fanatics, others of conscience or duty, those who act in free responsibility or cultivate private virtue, represent individuals that Bonhoeffer himself observed, "good Germans" who fell to Hitler's lure, or failed in their resistance to his regime.[112] Their ethical weapons proved but rusty swords that shattered in the conflict with Hitler's radical version of the new, autonomous world of modernity. Here Bonhoeffer makes a tantalizing reference to "Don Quixotry":

> The perennial figure of Don Quixote has become contemporary, the "knight of the doleful countenance" who, with a shaving basin for a helmet and miserable hack for a charger, rides into endless battle for the chosen lady of his heart who doesn't even exist. This is the picture of the adventurous enterprise of an old world against a new one, of a past reality against a contemporary one, of a noble dreamer against the overwhelming force of the commonplace.[113]

Bonhoeffer's July 15, 1944 letter to Bethge adds one more strategy for resisting the world come of age. In a world where God is no longer needed as a working hypothesis in "morals, politics, science... religion or philosophy," "intellectual honesty" requires that all such hypotheses be dropped. Yet many find this hard to accept. He writes:

> At this point nervous souls start asking what room there is left for God now. And being ignorant of the answer they condemn the whole development which has brought them to this pass. Various emergency exits have been devised to deal with this situation. To them must be added the *salto mortale* back to the

111. LPP: 94.
112. Cf. footnote 10, E: 79.
113. E: 80.

Middle Ages, the fundamental principle of which however is heteronomy in the form of clericalism. But that is a counsel of despair, which can be purchased only at the cost of intellectual sincerity.[114]

The world has grown up, Bonhoeffer declares, and there is no way back to "the land of childhood." He characterizes the *salto mortale* as heteronomy, which as subordination to an outside law or institution,[115] attempts to deny the autonomy of the world come of age. The charge of intellectual dishonesty this entails recalls Bonhoeffer's April 30, 1944 letter, where he explains the implications for Christianity if the religious *a priori* no longer exists. He writes: "It means that the linchpin is removed from the whole structure of our Christianity to date, and the only people left for us to light on in the way of 'religion' are a few last 'survivals of the age of chivalry,' or else one or two who are intellectually dishonest."[116] Don Quixote represents the first group, which rejects the new age and "enters in the lists" against it. In the letter of July 15 we read that this *salto mortale* also comes at the cost of intellectual integrity.

Don Quixotry may attempt to deny the world's autonomy by returning to the pre-modernist synthesis.[117] It may apply ethical principles in a casuistic, absolute or abstract manner, rather than choosing to live in freedom and responsibility. Either way, Don Quixotry fights yesterday's battles with obsolete weapons, instead of engaging the modern world in its maturity and autonomy. Instead, as Bonhoeffer categorically declares, "we must replace rusty weapons with bright steel."[118]

The "World Come of Age"

Bonhoeffer increasingly differentiated between "the abyss," which he resisted, and "the world come of age," which he affirmed and embraced. To rehabilitate the world, he first redefined it, and then opened it up to the presence and promise of Christ. From the discussion above, we can characterize the abyss as the world of science and machines, ruled by unbridled reason and technology and devoid of faith. Reason, science,

114. LPP: 121.
115. Here, the institutional church and its clergy.
116. LPP: 91.
117. Today it might entail a retreat to modernism, or an uncritical embrace of postmodernism.
118. LPP: 80–81.

technology, and culture have become autonomous, and feel no need to appeal to God or transcendence to explain what remains unknown. Bonhoeffer refers to this as hopeless godlessness.

The world come of age is at once liberated and desacralized. Much good came out of secularization, including the benefits of technology, intellectual progress, social gains, and the formulation of basic human rights. Intellectual honesty and rigor have been established as "an essential moral requirement of Western humanity." Human beings have learned to cope without "God as a working hypothesis" in all areas of life. Although he considered it futile, manipulative, and un-Christian to deny the autonomy of the world, Bonhoeffer recognized a "hopeful godlessness," which by rejecting false concepts of God prepared the way for the true God of the Bible, revealed in Jesus Christ.

In an 1931 essay, Bonhoeffer distinguished between empirical science and a "scientific" worldview: "As far as science is a discovery of happening facts, theology is not touched . . . If science itself gives its own interpretation of the world, then it belongs to philosophy and is subjected to the critique of theology."[119] Thus Bonhoeffer grants science the freedom to explore the world, but denies its hegemony over the interpretation of its findings. Bonhoeffer also proposes an eclectic use of philosophical terms in theology. Acknowledging Barth's preference for Kant's terminology over Aristotelian/Thomistic and idealistic approaches, he notes Barth's reservations towards Kant and Neo-Kantianism. As Wüstenberg explains, "To Kant, God as he is in himself (*an sich*) cannot be recognized. Barth argues that God *an sich* cannot be recognized unless he reveals himself."[120]

Dilthey also influenced Bonhoeffer's conception of the world and worldliness, and his prison reflections on religionless Christianity. As Feil points out, Bonhoeffer's concern was "how the Word of God is to reach man in history."[121] Here Wüstenberg shows how Dilthey's critique of historical reason complemented Kant's critique of pure reason, with the result that the autonomy of man could be explained historically.[122]

119. Bonhoeffer, "Theology of Crisis," 96.
120. Wüstenberg, "Dietrich Bonhoeffer," 48.
121. Feil, "Dietrich Bonhoeffer's Understanding of the World," 243.
122. Wüstenberg, "Dietrich Bonhoeffer," 53. Wüstenberg goes on to show how Bonhoeffer's description of the growing autonomy of the world recapitulates this subject in Dilthey's *Weltanschauung und Analyse des Meschen seit Renaissance und Reformation*. Cf. Ibid., 54–55.

Accordingly Bonhoeffer, reading Dilthey, "began to articulate theological problems such as the criticism of religion within a historical framework. He stopped setting revelation over against religion (as Barth had done) but felt more fundamentally that the time of religion was over."[123] Wüstenberg notes in a later essay that Bonhoeffer's appropriation of Dilthey's historicism helped him move from Barth's critique of religion to his new program of nonreligious interpretation.[124] He writes:

> Adopting Dilthey's historical argument, that in modern times, that is, in the *Neuzeit*, human beings have come of age, [Bonhoeffer] combines it with a critique of religion. If the world came of age, religion would lose its meaning—a time of "religionlessness" would begin, in which Jesus could become "Lord of the world" anew.[125]

Bonhoeffer embraced the modern world and welcomed its achievements, without accepting it on its own terms. Instead, he interpreted the world through the person and work of Jesus Christ, who is not an idea or religion but a historical reality. Just prior to his arrest, Bonhoeffer wrote that "the cross of reconciliation sets us free to live before God in the midst of the godless world, sets us free to live in genuine worldliness."[126] Such worldliness' is defined as "the freedom and courage to let the world be what it really is before God, namely a world that in its godlessness is reconciled with God."[127] As Bonhoeffer explains, the cross has "overcome the divisions, tensions and conflicts between the 'Christian' and the 'worldly,'"[128] with the result that the world can give up its desperate attempts at self-deification, and simply be the world.[129] Significantly, the "godless world" here is no longer the "abyss of nothingness," but the place where human beings are called to live "genuinely worldly" lives before God. Here Bonhoeffer prefigures his statements

---

123. Ibid., 65.

124. Wüstenberg, "Bonhoeffer's Tegel Theology," 1997. Wüstenberg's argument is developed further in *A Theology of Life: Dietrich Bonhoeffer's Religionless Christianity*, 1998.

125. Wüstenberg, "Dietrich Bonhoeffer," 66-67.

126. E: 400.

127. E: 401.

128. E: 400.

129. The argument here assumes Bonhoeffer's reflections in *Ethics* on "The Ultimate and the Penultimate" and "Natural Life," to be discussed below.

from Tegel prison on being "for-others: 'To live as a human being before God, in the light of God's becoming human, can only mean to be there not for oneself, but for God and for other human beings.'"130

Although Bonhoeffer rejected Dilthey's positive appraisal of "inwardness" and "religion," his appropriation of Dilthey's "philosophy of life"131 enabled him to affirm human "autonomy" and the world come of age, not in general platitudes but real life, e.g., in ethics and law, whose "concepts are meaningful whether or not God exists."132 Bonhoeffer's famous quotation from Grotius, *etsi deus non daretur*, is in fact mediated by Dilthey, who wrote that "even if there were no God, the principles of natural law would maintain their independent and universal validity."133 Bonhoeffer takes Dilthey's philosophically ambiguous concept of life and makes it concrete in Christ, where it assumes the contours of Jesus' "being for others," which implies "participation in the sufferings of God in the world."134 Speaking non-religiously, such participation is what Bonhoeffer understood by faith. As Wüstenberg concludes, "In his 'Outline for a Book' Bonhoeffer describes the task of the church today in words that are easy to follow: the church must 'tell men of every calling what it means to live in Christ, to exist for others.'"135

Bonhoeffer avoided the twin dangers of the (neo)orthodox *salto mortale* that rejects or abandons the world come of age, and the liberal reductionism that capitulates to it, gratefully accepting temporary concessions granted by the world of science and machines. He combined a "theology of life" with the critique of religion and the *theologia crucis* to produce a theology that still instructs and challenges today. Perhaps more importantly, his theological method remains relevant, for it is not bound to a particular historical understanding of the world, whether pre-modern, modern, or post-modern. Instead, it critiques them all through the revelation of God in Jesus Christ.

130. E: 400.
131. E: 69.
132. E: 69.
133. Dilthey, cited in Wüstenberg, *Theology of Life*, 143.
134. Ibid., 70.
135. Bonhoeffer, cited in Wüstenberg, *Theology of Life*, 71.

Eschatology

Although Bonhoeffer, as Chapman points out,[136] devoted less time than some other twentieth century theologians to developing an explicitly eschatological perspective, this does not mean that he lacked an eschatology.[137] Bonhoeffer's views on history, providence, responsibility, and Christology reveal his fundamental eschatological orientation, while direct references to eschatology surface regularly throughout his work.

In *Sanctorum Communio*, Bonhoeffer describes the primal state eschatologically as "hope projected backward."[138] Declaring that social concepts such as person and community cannot be understood properly by studying humanity as it is, or by positing some primitive, untainted society, he argues instead for an eschatological basis for redeemed and reconciled humanity.[139] In between the creation and the *eschaton*, we live "within an intrinsically broken history," in which sin "infinitely alters the essence of things."[140] The "Christian concept of person," and hence of the church community, corresponds to the new humanity being formed in Christ, "which in hope overcomes the history of sin and death."[141] Throughout *Sanctorum Communio*, Bonhoeffer employs this theological "archetype" to guide his sociological reflections on the church by the governing perspective of revelation,[142] reaching the conclusion that philosophy of history will never yield a solution to history nor explain the essential nature of the church.[143] Instead, history must be understood as the conflict of two basic "tendencies," which are identified eschatologically as "*sanctorum communio* and Antichrist."[144] Bonhoeffer's holistic "eschatology of the church-community" deals with the church as a community of individuals as well as encompassing the "problems of the 'new world,' that is, the eschatology of culture, nature, and ecology.[145] Eternal death is understood as "the solitude of God's

---

136. Chapman, "Hope and the ethics of formation," 451.
137. Feil, *Theology of Dietrich Bonhoeffer*, 91.
138. SC: 61.
139. SC: 63.
140. SC: 62.
141. SC: 63.
142. SC: 64–65.
143. SC: 282.
144. SC: 283.
145. SC: 283.

wrath, that is to be alone in sin"; souls themselves choose death, for God will "respect the freedom of the will that ultimately remains defiant."[146] The redeemed will enjoy fellowship with God and his people, where they are "one in Christ, and yet all are individuals."[147] The thesis ends with a stirring expression of the church's eschatological hope.[148]

Act and Being ends with a discussion of infant baptism, which Bonhoeffer describes as "a call that can only be understood eschatologically."[149] Earlier, following Barth's understanding of revelation as "contingent," and "from outside," Bonhoeffer writes that the church is "constituted by the present proclamation of Christ's death and resurrection."[150] As Chapman points out, Bonhoeffer prefers spatial images of revelation to explain the way the transcendent God makes himself known, over the temporal images favored by others such as Moltmann.[151] Yet Bonhoeffer explains this "spatial image" temporally, arguing that the proclamation of the church becomes "present" by virtue of the future that is "coming to us." Bonhoeffer does not distinguish between "past" predestination and "future" eschatology, but employs both terms together to portray God's eschatological purpose to reconcile the world to himself through Jesus Christ, declaring that, "Christian revelation must occur in the present precisely because it is, in the qualified once-for-all occurrence of the cross and resurrection of Christ, always something 'of the future.'"[152]

In a moving passage from *Christology*, which to anticipate will sharply critique the over-realized eschatology of Polish messianism, Bonhoeffer argues that it is the promise of Messiah's coming, which lies at the heart of most philosophies of history, that gives history meaning.

> The promise of a Messiah is alive everywhere in history. History lives in and from this expectation. That is its meaning, the coming of the Messiah ... History has the promise only in a corrupt

---

146. SC: 286.

147. SC: 287. Speaking of this "dual outcome," Bonhoeffer does not rule out *apocatastasis*, with the caveat that this remains only a hope. Cf. AB: 301–2.

148. SC: 289.

149. AB: 159.

150. AB: 110.

151. Chapman, "Hope and the Ethics," 451.

152. AB: 111.

form. It lives from corrupted promises of "fulfilled time," its *kairos*. History must reveal itself and make its own centre visible. It is driven to glorifying itself in its own Messiahs. A messiah as the centre of history is a respectable conception for the philosophy of history. But this promise remains unfulfilled. History is hindered by the impossibility of fulfilling corrupted messianic promises. It knows of the Messiah at its centre, but comes to grief on it.[153]

History, Bonhoeffer declares, seems driven to realize the messianic expectation in its own way and time, which Ballard refers to as "storming . . . the gates of heaven."[154] History will never succeed at this task, for it needs the Messiah, not a philosophy of history or a self-appointed savior. Bonhoeffer's critique applies to all ideologies that promise the Kingdom of God on earth, that aim to make people good against their will, that seek to create—by force, if necessary—a better world. In Bonhoeffer's eschatological conception, the Messiah has already come in the historical events of Christ's incarnation, death, and resurrection. He writes:

> The Messiah Christ is at the same time both the destruction and the fulfillment of all the messianic expectations of history. He is their destruction in so far as the visible Messiah does not appear, but the fulfillment takes place in secret. He is their fulfillment in so far as God has really entered history and the expected one is now really there.[155]

In *Ethics* Bonhoeffer "eschatologizes" history by relating everything to the incarnate, crucified, and risen Christ. The Christ-event makes history "historical,"[156] establishes the Church, and reveals the new man (Christ) whose form is being realized in his followers and in the community to which they are called. The historical concreteness of revelation and formation has an eschatological foundation in the Christ-event, and the teleological goal of conformation to the image of Christ. This protects the real and the human from the tyranny of the ideal. Certain *Ethics* texts, including "Ultimate and Penultimate Things," are explicitly eschatological. Moltmann, interpreting *Ethics* "temporally and

---

153. C: 63–64.
154. Ballard, "Bonhoeffer on Providence in History," 274.
155. C: 64.
156. I.e., having a *telos*, a purpose and a goal.

eschatologically,"[157] recognized the intrinsic character of this passage,[158] which provides the theological foundation for affirming both the "natural" in *Ethics*, and "worldliness" in the prison letters. Bonhoeffer defines the natural as "that which, after the fall into sin, is directed toward the coming of Jesus Christ."[159] Feil also observes that Bonhoeffer defines the orders of preservation and later the mandates eschatologically.[160]

Eschatology does not play a large role in *Letters and Papers from Prison*. Feil argues that Bonhoeffer was concerned with life after the Third Reich, thus "to have busied himself with an (ahistorical) eschatology would have amounted to flight from the world and apocalyptism."[161] Nevertheless, the *Letters* contain a non-apocalyptic, historical eschatology. As Chapman notes, "'the world come of age' is paradoxically linked with a sense of Providence, in that the Lord of history summons human beings into partnership to fulfill his will in shaping the world."[162] De Gruchy, who called this Bonhoeffer's "dialogical character of providence . . . that speaks intelligibly to those who have 'come of age'"[163] holds that by combining belief in providence with human freedom and responsibility, Bonhoeffer avoids both "passive fatalism" and an all-inclusive view of sovereignty that attributes every event to God's prescriptive will. The Lord of history, who is free to work when and how he chooses, invites human beings to participate in making history. As de Gruchy summarizes: "Man is set free by God to make history *etsi deus not daretur* (i.e., as if God were not involved). There is no guarantee of success; it is rather a calling to accountability and deputyship."[164] This matches Bonhoeffer's own experience of providence and God's guiding hand, expressed in his moving declaration: "It may be that the day of final judgment will dawn tomorrow; in that case, we shall gladly stop working for a better future. But not before."[165]

---

157. Chapman, "Hope and the Ethics," 451.

158. E.g., the ultimate, *letztes*, is used temporally as well as qualitatively. Cf. E: 146, footnote [2].

159. E: 173.

160. Feil, *Theology of Dietrich Bonhoeffer*, 89.

161. Ibid., 89.

162. Chapman "Hope and the Ethics," 453.

163. de Gruchy, "Providence and the Shapers of History," 60.

164. Ibid., 62.

165. Bonhoeffer, LPP, 1971: 15–16.

Theodicy

If eschatology is a subterranean current running through Bonhoeffer's thought, which emerges at times into full view, theodicy as a theme rarely appears. Nonetheless, to start at the end, his famous phrase, "only a suffering God can help," alone warrants investigation of his approach to this issue.

In 1931 Bonhoeffer, defending Barth at Union Theological Seminary,[166] declared that God is not the God of philosophy, nor the world's ground of being, but its "free Lord and creator."[167] Yet the world has "fallen away from God," implying that the fault lies with humanity. Though God has overcome "death and evil and sin," this is presently visible only by faith. However, "at the end of everything" God will make it visible to all "by an act of his power."[168] Sin's ultimate origin is not discussed. Instead of explaining evil, Bonhoeffer proclaims God's eschatological victory over sin and suffering. He then turns the theodicy problem on its head, arguing that the issue is not how we are to justify God, but how God justifies the world. His answer can only be "in Christ," the Lord who is "*in* the world." He writes:

> Our thinking in terms of theodicy tries to justify God in the world. But for Christian thinking God justifies the world, and that has been done in Christ. Thus only through Christ do we see the Creator and the preserver and the Lord *of* the World *and in* the world. Only through Christ do we see the World in God's hands.[169]

In *Discipleship* Bonhoeffer relates Luther's cry of *sola gratia* to a holy God who establishes his sanctuary in a sinful world. Just as God once dwelt in tabernacle and temple, he is now present in the Body of Christ.[170] God's response to evil has become a reality in this world.[171]

In *Ethics* theodicy enigmatically appears in the context of a "thoroughly immanent optimism" based on the natural "basic will of life" that in the end prevails over the "unnatural" forces that act to undermine

---

166. Bonhoeffer, "Theology of Crisis," 85–97.
167. Ibid., 96.
168. Ibid., 96–97.
169. Ibid., 97.
170. CD: 245.
171. CD: 248–49.

it.[172] Bonhoeffer polemically attacks Nazi aberrations, such as vitalism, euthanasia,[173] and "social eudaemonism," which subordinate the individual to the good of the nation. Against these views, exploited by the Nazis in "explicitly ethnic and nationalist terms,"[174] Bonhoeffer asserts the rights of the individual, including the right to life. Arguing that God "stands up for these rights," often through "life itself,"[175] Bonhoeffer declares that "the problem of a theodicy that is implied here cannot be solved until later."[176] Rather than providing an answer, Bonhoeffer defines the question; while natural life eventually prevails, what may work out in the long run for the community provides little comfort and less benefit to the individual whose life is forfeit in the short run.[177] Bonhoeffer does not propose a theodicy of personal growth via suffering and martyrdom, much less through senseless pain and death. Nor does he justify God, nor explain why he fails to intervene in each individual case. The "solution" that was to come "later" was never written.

In "After Ten Years," Bonhoeffer proclaims Christ as the Lord of history who "bore all our human sufferings in his own body." Once again, instead of providing a theodicy he looks to Christ, who calls Christians to "act responsibly ... like free men," and thus display true sympathy for those who suffer.[178] Regarding suffering, Bonhoeffer writes:

> It is infinitely easier to suffer in obedience to a human command than to accept suffering as *free, responsible men*. It is infinitely easier to suffer with others than to suffer *alone*. It is infinitely easier to suffer as public heroes than to suffer *apart* and in *ignominy*. It is infinitely easier to suffer *physical death* than to endure *spiritual suffering*. Christ suffered as a free man alone, apart and in ignominy, in body and spirit, and since that day many Christians have suffered with him.[179]

Here human suffering is related to the suffering of Christ, which is both extraordinary and exemplary. Against the backdrop of Bonhoeffer's

---

172. CD: 176–77.
173. E.g., killing the mentally ill.
174. Cf. E: 183, footnote [45].
175. E: 184.
176. E: 185.
177. E: 184.
178. LPP: 144–45.
179. LPP: 145.

theology, this makes suffering as free, responsible human beings, who act for the good of others in vicarious representative action, the general pattern for those who would follow Christ into the world. This leads to a consideration of the "suffering God."

> Man's religiosity makes him look in his distress to the power of God in the world; he uses God as a *Deus ex machina*. The Bible however directs him to the powerlessness and suffering of God: only a suffering God can help. To this extent we may say that the process we have described by which the world came of age was an abandonment of a false conception of God, and a clearing of the decks for the God of Bible, who conquers power and space in the world by his weakness. This must be the start of our worldly interpretation.[180]

God is revealed not in power but in weakness. Yet God's "weakness" is neither passive nor helpless. Christ willingly suffered and bore our suffering in free responsibility and *Stellvertretung*. By allowing himself to be "pushed out of the world onto the cross," Christ became again the center of history, who reconciled humans beings to each other, to creation, and to God. Bonhoeffer's Christological approach to theodicy, together with his reflections on Christ's suffering, provide a necessary corrective to a theology of glory and power. A God who does not suffer, a Christ who did not go to the cross, would indeed be of no help. But does this imply that Christ can help only by suffering? As Bonhoeffer himself indicated, there is more to be said about theodicy. Moltmann, one of the earliest and most significant theological interpreters of Bonhoeffer, has gone helpfully beyond him in this area,[181] though one wonders if the "tyranny of the ethical" that Bonhoeffer warned against has not been replaced by a "tyranny of theodicy." Whether or not that is indeed the case, it does not excuse Christians today from wrestling with theodicy, any more than Bonhoeffer's warning excuses them ethical reflection and responsible action. For some, avoiding either ethics or theodicy may reduce to another form of cheap grace.

---

180. LPP: 122.
181. Cf. Chapman, "Hope and the Ethics," 453.

Bonhoeffer on Human Responsibility

Following Christ in the World

The *Ethics*' manuscripts discussed above laid the foundation for Christian ethics. In "Ultimate and Penultimate Things," Bonhoeffer moves to the constructive phase, to "concrete commandments and guidance ... for which obedience will be demanded."[182] Powerfully restating Reformation theology, Bonhoeffer describes the ultimate, i.e., the word of God, the good news of justification.[183] Jesus Christ justifies sinners by grace alone, thus freeing them for God and for others.[184] Yet justification is also by faith alone, a faith which "sets life on a new foundation ... the living, dying and rising of the Lord Jesus Christ,"[185] and which issues in love and hope.[186] Only now does Bonhoeffer move to discuss the penultimate. He rejects both radicalism and compromise. Radicalism believes in God the Judge and Redeemer. One is either for God or against Him, and those who will not be redeemed come under God's judgment and wrath. The compromise solution focuses on God as Creator and Preserver, thus freeing the penultimate from the demands of the ultimate. Both positions are extreme, because they "make the penultimate and the ultimate mutually exclusive," absolutizing either the idea of God's ultimate reality or of human penultimate reality, instead of affirming their unity in Jesus Christ.[187] To clarify the relationship between the ultimate and the penultimate, Bonhoeffer argues that an ethic built on only one Christ-event would end in compromise (incarnation), radicalism (crucifixion) or enthusiasm (resurrection).[188] He summarizes with this claim: "Christian life means being human in the power of Christ's becoming human, being judged and pardoned in the power of the cross, living a new life in

---

182. E: 102.
183. E: 146.
184. E: 146–47.
185. E: 147.
186. E: 148–49. Writing here in the third person, Bonhoeffer relates his own testimony as one who "lost his life to Christ, and now Christ became his life." Cf. footnote [9] on page 148.
187. E: 154–55.
188. E: 157.

the power of the resurrection. [. . .] Christian life is participation in Christ's encounter with the world."[189]

Bonhoeffer now describes the "preparing of the way." While the ultimate creates space for the penultimate,[190] the penultimate is also preparation for justification; only the living can hear and respond to the word of reconciliation.[191] Thus the penultimate must be "preserved for the sake of the ultimate," and Christ's followers are called to remove obstacles to the preaching of the gospel and establish conditions that foster its reception.[192] In an early example of non-religious interpretation, Bonhoeffer declares: "preparation of the way means repentance."[193] By alleviating suffering, establishing justice, defending the rights and dignity of the weak, and furthering the cause of peace, Christ's followers help prepare for His coming to individual lives and to society. Such actions are tied to providence: "Because we await Christ, because we know that Christ will come, therefore and only therefore do we prepare the way."[194] Recapitulating his remarks on the "abyss," Bonhoeffer notes that the West's rejection of the ultimate threatens the existence of the penultimate. The penultimate must be reclaimed for the ultimate or it will be lost. Yet Bonhoeffer declares that all that is "human and good" in the world is on Christ's side. The Christian's task is not to make faith in Christ the foundation of the state, economy, culture, etc. but to witness to Christ and be formed in his image. He therefore declares:

> It may often seem more serious to address such people simply as non-Christians and to urge them to confess their unbelief. But it would be more Christian to claim as Christians precisely such persons who no longer dare to call themselves Christians, and to help them with much patience to move toward confessing Christ.[195]

189. E: 159.
190. E: 159.
191. E: 160.
192. E: 160–62.
193. E: 164.
194. E: 167.
195. E: 169–70.

Freedom and Responsibility

In "History and Good" Bonhoeffer wrestles most directly with the theological basis for his involvement in the conspiracy. He argues that in extreme circumstances the need may arise for a "venture of free responsibility" that goes against accepted ethical norms. Once again rejecting casuistry and abstract ethical theories, he defines good as the "genuine decision in which the whole person, with both understanding and will, seeks and finds what is good only in the very risk of the action itself, within the ambiguity of the historical situation."[196] No longer torn between the "Christian" and the "worldly," which are reconciled in Christ, the Christian joyously responds to God's revelation in Christ, which is addressed to the total person and provides a Christological foundation for responsibility towards others.[197] Bonhoeffer defines such responsibility as "vicarious representative action" [*Stellvertretung*], which is based on freedom and the social bonds that tie one to God and to other human beings,[198] and is ultimately grounded in Jesus Christ.[199]

Responsible action is directed towards real people in the real world.[200] It relates to the world without making it absolute, for idolizing a cause, a nation, or an ideology leads to "destroying human beings by sacrificing them to the idol."[201] Instead, responsible action "reckons with the world as world, while at the same time never forgetting that the world is loved, judged, and reconciled in Jesus Christ by God."[202] Christ has overcome the conflict between the "worldly" and the "Christian," thus his followers live responsibly in the world, neither abandoning it to cultivate private virtue, nor seeking to establish the Kingdom of God in the place of fallen and redeemed creation.[203]

Responsible action takes into account the subject's own circumstances, knowledge, and motives, together with the potential outcomes of a given course of action.[204] It recognizes others as responsible per-

---

196. E: 248.
197. E: 252–53.
198. E: 257.
199. E: 258.
200. E: 261.
201. E: 260.
202. E: 264.
203. E: 264–67.
204. E: 267.

sons in their own right. No cause is absolute, but only a means to serve people, hence "the cause to which the ultimate personal sacrifice is made must, in this very act, serve human beings."[205] Furthermore, all things have their own intrinsic law derived from their origin, Jesus Christ,[206] which grows more complex the more closely a thing is connected to human existence. Here Bonhoeffer argues that the rules and conventions of statecraft have their use but also their limits. In the "extraordinary situation of ultimate necessities," responsible action is neither bound by reason and law, nor can it be turned into a new law.[207] When rules conflict with "the primordial facts of life," the case of *ultima ratio* arises where "one must decide as a free venture." [208]

Although the "free venture" affirms the law by acknowledging that the law is being broken,[209] no law can justify the free venture. Guilt is incurred regardless of whether or not one acts, therefore one "is able to live only by divine grace and forgiveness."[210] Bonhoeffer traces the guilt and freedom of responsible action[211] to the vicarious representative action of Jesus,[212] whose life shows that, "genuine guiltlessness is demonstrated precisely by entering into community with the guilt of other human beings for their sake."[213] Identifying with the individual or corporate guilt of others may entail confessing sin, enduring suffering, and acting in solidarity with and for them. It may also mean incurring guilt through law-breaking, as in the conspiracy against Hitler, whose members resorted to lying, deception, and violence.

If one's decision in the case of *ultima ratio* could be determined casuistically, or by applying a hierarchy of values that determines which principle takes precedence when multiple laws conflict, no law-breaking would be involved, and there would be no need for justification. However, in the real world, amidst conflicting laws and mandates that

---

205. E: 270

206. This counters Nazi claims that such rights are inherent in the nation, state, or "blood and soil."

207. Ibid., 273.

208. Ibid., 275.

209. E: 275.

210. E: 275–76.

211. E: 276.

212. E: 276.

213. E: 276.

only find their unity in Christ, the Christian's response becomes a venture of free responsibility. Since no law prescribes in advance what must be done, the choice of action implies the possibility of guilt. Bonhoeffer insists that in the case of *ultima ratio*, lying remains lying, killing remains killing, even though the law is being broken in order to restore the law. In defending Bonhoeffer, Lovin argues that he "stresses the guilt of those who choose violent resistance to point out that their choice is free and not inevitably forced upon them by circumstances."[214]

Though Bonhoeffer implies that one may sin despite obedience to Christ's command, he stops short of claiming that Jesus sinned through his solidarity with sinners and acts of free responsibility. If his law-breaking and guilt-bearing were not sin, may such acts be considered sinful for his followers?[215] And yet, Bonhoeffer refuses to import solutions from rejected hierarchical or casuistic ethical systems. By insisting that law-breaking always entails sin and guilt, even when chosen in obedience to God's perceived command, Bonhoeffer continues his crusade against cheap grace, which justifies sin instead of the sinner. Far worse than self-justification of responsible law-breaking is the refusal to "dirty our hands" through responsible action on behalf of others. Bonhoeffer preferred to entrust himself to God, who justifies and forgives sinners, not their sin. He writes, "Those who act out of free responsibility are justified before others by dire necessity; before themselves they are acquitted by the conscience, but before God they hope only for grace."[216] What Bonhoeffer claims here for the venture of free responsibility can also be said of "lawful" deeds, in which there is always an element of sin and guilt. It is only by grace that God counts the deed done in faith as righteous. In everything we do we must cast ourselves upon the grace of God in Christ Jesus.

Bonhoeffer observes that most Germans, raised in a society trained to obey authority, have lost the power of ethical freedom.[217] Yet one cannot escape from freedom, for responsibility is inherent in every

---

214. Lovin, "Christian and the Authority of the State," 43.

215. If breaking the law in obedience to God entails sinning, has not the law become once again an autonomous principle that stands in judgment over God's will and command?

216. E: 284.

217. E: 286–87.

ethical encounter with another person.[218] Arguing that obedience and freedom must not be separated, Bonhoeffer declares that "making obedience independent would lead to Kant's ethic of duty, making freedom independent to a romantic ethic of genius."[219] The individual's sphere of responsible action is described by developing the concept of "vocation." Whereas "cultural Protestantism" believed "in the sanctity of vocational duties and of earthly institutions" apart from the call of Jesus Christ, and the "monastic solution" sought to live responsibly by escaping from the world, Bonhoeffer declares that "conscience can be free only by fulfilling one's concrete vocation in responsibility to the call of Jesus Christ, that is, only from knowledge of Jesus Christ's becoming human."[220] The command to love one's neighbor extends the limits of responsibility to all humanity,[221] regardless of race, gender, class, marital status or vocation.[222] If Bonhoeffer in Tegel appears to limit responsibility by arguing that "nobody is responsible for all the suffering and injustice in the world,"[223] this is only to broaden and deepen it. He writes:

> We are not Christs, but if we want to be Christians we must show something of Christ's breadth of sympathy by acting responsibly, by grasping our "hour," by facing danger like free men, by displaying a real sympathy which springs not from fear, but from the liberating and redeeming love of Christ for all who suffer.[224]

Resistance

In 1933, following the issuance of the "Aryan Clause," Bonhoeffer broached the possibility of active resistance to the Nazis. He wrote:

> ... there are three possible ways in which the church can act towards the state: in the first place, as has been said, it can ask the state whether its actions are legitimate ... Secondly it can aid

---

218. E: 287.
219. E: 288.
220. E: 292.
221. E: 297.
222. E: 291.
223. Obedience to Christ defines the extent of our response to suffering, not the other way around. Few if any would claim responsibility for removing all suffering and injustice from the world; however, cf. the discussion in chapter 6 on "messiah complexes."
224. LPP: 144–45.

the victims of state action ... The third possibility is not just to bandage the victims under the wheel, but to put a spoke in the wheel itself. Such action would be direct political action (...).[225]

Bonhoeffer's involvement in the conspiracy would seem to follow naturally from this early position, had he not already been an outspoken advocate of non-violence. At the Ecumenical Conference in Fanö in 1934, he called on the Church to proclaim Christ's command of peace, declaring that Christ's word binds Christians of all nations together "more inseparably than people are bound by all the ties of common history, of blood, of class and language."[226]

Bonhoeffer drew his pacifism from Scripture, in particular his reflections on the Sermon on the Mount, published in 1937 as *Discipleship*. There he argues that to break the cycle of violence, someone must bear evil without retaliation.[227] Jesus, by instructing the disciples to give up the "right" of retribution, "releases his community from the political and legal order ... and makes it into what it truly is, the community of the faithful that is not bound by political or national ties."[228] Bonhoeffer appeals to the cross to affirm non-resistance and place commitment to Christ above loyalty to one's country: "Only those who there, in the cross of Jesus, find faith in the victory over evil can obey his command."[229] Whereas non-resistance foregoes retaliation, Christ's imperative, "Love your enemies" means to act positively in blessing.[230] Bonhoeffer reaffirms Christ as the source of vicarious, representative action, which by blessing, doing good, and praying, brings the enemy "closer to reconciliation with God."[231] Cultural Protestantism had diluted this extraordinary love for one's enemies into "patriotism, loyalty to friends and industriousness,"[232] which are expected of "heathen and Christian" alike. These values are not denied, but surpassed by the extraordinary love of Christ's disciples. In both the Fanö address and *Discipleship*, Bonhoeffer appeals for obedience to Christ's command of peace, and consistently

225. Bonhoeffer, "Church and the Jewish Question," 127.
226. Ibid., 142.
227. D: 133.
228. D: 133.
229. D: 136.
230. D: 139.
231. D: 141.
232. CD: 170.

places membership in the community of Christ over national ties. From the early 1930's, Bonhoeffer was consistently pacifistic and responsible, refusing to make either position into an absolute principle that functions apart from obedience to Christ. Instead, he called on the church community and individual Christians alike to discern Jesus' word of command in their concrete historical context.

Clements argues that the question Bonhoeffer faced in joining the conspiracy was "what possible grounds there were for *not* becoming involved with his close relatives, friends and others who seemed to represent the last possibility of retrieving Germany's name from total ruin."[233] Bethge affirms that Bonhoeffer's disappointment with the Confessing Church also played a major role in this decision.[234] Lovin agrees, adding that this influenced Bonhoeffer's move to make responsibility for others rather than obedience to authority the fundamental description of a Christian's life in this world.[235] Pursuing this theme, Lovin argues that Bonhoeffer recognized that in states such as Nazi Germany, which base their claims to authority on the "the will of the people," the issue is no longer one of obedience to legitimate authority but consent, either tacit or explicit, that legitimizes authority.[236] In such a situation, "not obedience, but deputyship, characterizes Christian life in the modern world."[237]

Bethge shows that Bonhoeffer's understanding of the church-for-others is based on Christ's role as reconciler, thus making it, like vicarious representative action, imperative for Christ's followers. Tracing the transition from confession to resistance, Bethge notes that he and his comrades initially defended the integrity and freedom of the church against Nazi inroads.[238] Only gradually die they realize that the *status confessionis* might propel them into political action. As he writes, ". . . none of our leaders, including Niemöller and Barth[239] had said anything

233. Clements, *Patriotism for Today*, 37.
234. Bethge, "One of the Silent Bystanders?," 58–71.
235. Lovin, "Christian and the Authority of the State," 39–41.
236. Ibid., 39–41.
237. Ibid., 43.
238. Bethge, *Friendship and Resistance*, 19.
239. Barth's 1938 pamphlet, "Justice and Justification," justified resistance theologically by identifying National Socialism as a religion. Few in Germany besides Bonhoeffer saw it until after the war. Ibid., 29 n. 7.

in public about co-responsibility that might involve changing the political system. Who at the time, in the face of the pogroms against the Jews, dared to appeal to our political co-responsibility?"[240] As Bethge relates, it was Bonhoeffer who taught the students at Zingst/Finkenwalde that speaking for the helpless, the powerless, the persecuted, and the disenfranchised is a necessary result of "our belief in Christ," and an obligation that may lead to political involvement.[241] Gradually it dawned on Bethge and others that "mere confession . . . meant complicity with the murders." He confesses, "And so it became clear where the problem lay for the Confessing Church: We were resisting by way of confession, but we were not confessing by way of resistance."[242] His conclusion is chilling:

> Between Barmen and Stuttgart the nameless millions lie buried. By leaving out the steps from confession to resistance, one ends up tolerating crimes, turning confession into an alibi and, in view of the injustice committed, an indictment of the confessors.[243]

From the beginning of the church struggle Bonhoeffer, still calling for peace, left open the possibility of political resistance, the "third way" in which the church can act towards the state. His political theology, theologically grounded in Christ, prevents a political ethic—any ethic—from being transformed from obedience to an ideology. The bottom line of Christian ethics is neither "peace" nor "justice," but "obedience to Jesus Christ."

Patriotism and Pluralism

Following Clements' *A Patriotism for Today*, this section focuses on patriotism and pluralism. Clements, who holds that Bonhoeffer's view of patriotism involves one's stance towards other religious and ethnic groups, economic classes, and nations, as well as the varied communities and nation to which one belongs, argues that patriotism springs from a clear vision of one's own nation, not from fear of the nation's enemies. Bonhoeffer, secure in his family roots and cultural heritage, broadened his perspective through experiences abroad, ministry among the poor

240. Ibid., 21.
241. Ibid., 24
242. Ibid.
243. Ibid., 28

and business classes, and ecumenical involvement. He purposefully cultivated relationships with those from other national, ethnic, and religious backgrounds. As de Gruchy comments, Bonhoeffer's German heritage and Christian identity "gave him the capacity to appreciate and learn from [others]."[244]

Being a Christian did not lessen Bonhoeffer's love for Germany, but placed it under obedience to Christ's call to come and follow. Bonhoeffer resisted attempts to use the Church as a tool of nationalism and racism.[245] His way of discipleship leads away from "nationalistic tribalism" to Christ, then back into the world to love and serve others, in particular the poor and oppressed.[246] Yet such "solidarity . . . had to begin with a solidarity with his own people,"[247] so Bonhoeffer returned to Germany in 1939 to "share the trials of this time with my people."[248] There he joined the conspiracy, standing with those who sought to save "Germany's name from total ruin."[249] De Lange declares that, "it was precisely in this anti-nationalism that he discovered true patriotism: choosing a Christian Europe really meant choosing for Germany."[250]

Bonhoeffer opposed those who sought to bolster the romantic concept of *das Volk* by appealing to the "orders of creation."[251] Rejecting the nationalistic claim that whatever exists is ordained by God, he argued instead that it is part of the sinful, fallen world.[252] However, as part of the penultimate world, it has meaning and purpose to the extent to which it is open to the coming of Christ. Bonhoeffer, barred from such "ultimate" actions as preaching, teaching, and publishing, understood his involvement in the conspiracy as solidarity with his nation and humanity in a penultimate way. To extend Clements' point, while many Germans sought to preserve the Church's legal freedom of proclamation by avoiding penultimate involvement, Bonhoeffer concluded that the church had thereby lost its spiritual freedom to speak, which must

---

244. de Gruchy, "God's Desire for a Community of Human Beings," 151.
245. Clements, *Patriotism for Today*, 30–31.
246. Ibid., 32.
247. Ibid., 33.
248. Bonhoeffer, cited in: ibid., 33.
249. Ibid., 37.
250. De Lange, "Particular Europe," 86.
251. Clements, *Patriotism for Today*, 46.
252. Ibid., 47.

be recovered following the war by a silent ministry of "prayer and good deeds"—the latter of a penultimate nature.

Christ loves real people, and a patriot loves the real nation, not its idealized caricature. As Clements notes, conservatism idealizes the nation as it is imagined to be, while radicalism idealizes the nation as it should be.[253] Bonhoeffer chose instead to love real people, helping them "to live more fully as human beings before God."[254] Accepting "responsibility for history,"[255] he demonstrated a positive but critical appropriation of his own national heritage.[256] While Bonhoeffer's words and deeds testify that one is first a Christian, then a citizen and patriot,[257] ecumenism is false if it becomes a way of escaping solidarity with and responsibility for the nation, its heritage, and its guilt.[258] Personally innocent, Bonhoeffer identified with Germany's crimes and the Confessing Church's failure to defend the Jews. In *Discipleship* Bonhoeffer argued that costly grace accepts the forgiveness of sins in fellowship with the suffering Christ. Thus "guilt can be faced and overcome through grace"; true repentance leads to renewal,[259] while unconfessed guilt distorts the past, denies present realities, and forfeits the ability to act responsibly for the future.[260] Accepting solidarity in corporate guilt requires approaching the guilty person, community or nation as one of the accused.[261] De Gruchy writes that, "The Church ... is called to confess both its own real guilt and that of the wider community,"[262] adding that a true confession of guilt includes a commitment to right wrongs and to change.[263]

Clements observes that every nation is faced with economic inequality and ethnic diversity, which undermines the notion of "the people" as a stable, homogeneous community,[264] and leads to the acceptance

253. Ibid., 67–68.
254. Ibid, 70–71.
255. Towards the past and the future.
256. Ibid., 87.
257. Ibid., 158.
258. Ibid., 159.
259. Ibid., 97–98.
260. Ibid., 105.
261. Ibid., 95.
262. de Gruchy, "Confessing Guilt," 43.
263. Ibid., 40.
264. Clements, *Patriotism for Today*, 132.

of pockets of poverty, oppression, and injustice.²⁶⁵ Bonhoeffer, a privileged, white European male, demonstrated his growing consciousness of socio-economic issues in his prison fiction, where members of different classes take their first, hesitant first steps towards understanding each other. In Bonhoeffer's theology of sociality, such encounters define one's own identity and require an ethical response. Thus de Gruchy declares, "Responsible openness to the 'other' is, then, a precondition of genuinely human relationships and the building of a sustainable community."²⁶⁶

Bonhoeffer considered the concept of the people to be racially inclusive, and denounced introducing race as a criterion of belonging to the people or the nation.²⁶⁷ In the Third Reich, to battle racism meant first and foremost to battle anti-Semitism. In the confession of guilt Bonhoeffer wrote for the Church, he declared: "The Church confesses that . . . it has witnessed oppression, hatred and murder without raising its voice for the victims and without finding ways of rushing to help them. It has become guilty of the lives of the weakest and most defenseless brothers and sisters of Jesus Christ."²⁶⁸ Bonhoeffer wrote in "Heritage and Decay":

> Western history is by God's will inextricably bound up with the people of Israel, not just genetically but in an honest, unceasing encounter. The Jews keep open the question of Christ; they are the signs of God's free, gracious election and of God's rejecting wrath; see the kindness and severity of God (Rom 11:22). Driving out the Jew(s) from the West must result in driving out Christ with them, for Jesus Christ was a Jew.²⁶⁹

These polemic texts are aimed squarely at Nazi ideology and practice. Once again Bonhoeffer, wielding his theology of sociality, insists that the West's ethical encounter with the Jews requires both a penultimate and ultimate answer. To drive the Jews out of Europe²⁷⁰ is a crime against fellow human beings, and a denial of Christ, in whom

---

265. Ibid., 135.

266. de Gruchy, "God's Desire," 149.

267. Ibid., 141.

268. E: 139.

269. E: 105.

270. As Clements writes elsewhere, "The route to Auschwitz began . . . in the widely diffused anti-Semitism which shamefully has been so much a part of European 'Christian' life and thought." Clements, "Liberation of Auschwitz," 7.

God speaks his word of judgment and reconciliation. Which "Christ" will be the center of history, the Nazi impostor that drove the Jews out, or the one that allowed himself to be driven out of the world onto the cross? De Gruchy, observing that Bonhoeffer proclaimed the crucified Christ, who "provides a radical critique" of power that dehumanizes and oppresses, concludes that, "the way in which the church responds to the "other" in the name of this Christ, and especially the way in which it responds to those it has oppressed and victimized in the past, will determine its future."[271]

Bonhoeffer's viewpoint on Europe as shattered *Christianitas* was perhaps obsolete even in his day. De Lange, who writes that, "In a profane, decolonized, and pluralistic Europe, the image of a united and Christian Europe can no longer be retained,"[272] suggests that Bonhoeffer, in citing Ibn Saud, the founder of Saudi Arabia, points the way to extend the West's encounter with the Jews to encounters with "others" from different races and religious traditions. Here Morin's argument that it was not Christianity but the confrontation of Europe with Islam that defined the West,[273] is consistent with Bonhoeffer's view of interpersonal, ethical encounters that shape both individual and corporate persons. De Gruchy also links Christ and a pluralistic encounter with the "other," when he argues that to answer the question "Who is Jesus Christ, for us?" we must first ask who is the "other" "through whom we are encountered and addressed by God, and to whom we are accountable?"[274] De Gruchy comments that our own identity and that of our community will be shaped in large measure by whether we perceive the other "as a threat or a gift."[275]

Barnett notes that while most Christian leaders within and without Germany believed that rebuilding Germany after the war would be based on rechristianizing society, Bonhoeffer foresaw a different role for the church in a secular, pluralistic world.[276] She writes,

> Bonhoeffer accepted the "world come of age" as a potentially liberating place for the church. This meant that the church had

271. de Gruchy, "God's Desire," 157.
272. de Lange, "Particular Europe," 93.
273. Morin, cited in ibid., 93.
274. de Gruchy, "God's Desire," 150.
275. Ibid., 151.
276. Barnett, "Communications Between the German Resistance," 69.

to affirm the world as it exists, not try to rechristianize it, and it put the church in a new position—"alongside other religions," as Bonhoeffer wrote.[277]

This is not to suggest that the church will cease to witness to Christ, but that it will do so by living in and for the world, not by claiming for itself the lost prerogatives and splendor of Constantinian Christianity. Concerning how Christians are to relate to those members of society who "feel a particular responsibility for the future of the country," De Gruchy writes, "It is not a question of reducing the gospel or Christian faith so as to make it more acceptable to humankind 'come of age,' but of showing how the tradition in fact relates to their experience and concern for society."[278] And while de Lange suggests that a theology of the trinity offers more for today's pluralistic Europe than a strongly Christocentric approach, he reaffirms Bonhoeffer's basic insight, that "a theology which neither maintains the incarnation as its basic intuition nor links it to the struggle of humanity for humanity is no longer either Christian or relevant."[279]

---

277. Ibid., 71.
278. de Gruchy, *Bonhoeffer and South Africa*, 59.
279. Ibid., 93.

6

Bonhoeffer and Polish Messianism

THIS CHAPTER ENLISTS BONHOEFFER'S THEOLOGY TO CRITIQUE POLISH messianism. First, Bonhoeffer's theology of sociality and the concept of "corporate persons" is used to critique messianism's view of Poland as the "Christ of the Nations." In addition, the romantic cult of the charismatic leader is compared to Bonhoeffer's attack on the *Führer* principle and his portrayal of Hitler as the "tyrannical despiser" of humanity. "Messianic Historiosophy and the Crisis of Modernism" employs Bonhoeffer's view of providence, modernism, and the world come of age to critique four Polish responses to the "abyss," and to address the related issues of romantic epistemology and the theodicy of Polish messianism. The final section, under the rubric of "Responsibility," evaluates the Polish tradition of patriotism, resistance, and national liberation against Bonhoeffer's theory and practice of responsible freedom in the Third Reich.

The "Christ of the Nations," and Polish Messiah Complexes

Polish messianism presupposed that nations possess a corporate identity or "national spirit." Behind this concept stood a personalistic view of the nation, considered metaphysically as greater than the sum of its parts. Nations enter into relationships with other nations and with God, who may entrust them with a mission in the world. As Szczypa explains, "every nation should seek to know its own purpose, in light of the ultimate cause which is God."[1] This is analogous to what de Gruchy

---

1. Szczypa, *Jan Paweł Woronicz*, 61.

describes as the German romantic view of history; each nation has a historical calling, destiny and mandate.[2]

Woronicz constructed his messianic philosophy of history based on the anachronistic knightly code of the Middle Ages. Within his hierarchical system of duty, honor, and loyalty, which embraces both divine and human reality, Christ became Poland's liege lord; the nation grounded its identity and its hope of future restoration in the Messianic King. Woronicz also cast Poland as an anti-type of the Lamb of God, who suffered innocently at the hands of wicked tyrants. Whereas this Christological element served Woronicz as a secondary basis for Poland's "resurrection," Mickiewicz made it his primary metaphor. Poland became the "Christ of the nations," an innocent victim crucified by the unfaithful nations.

In his day, Mickiewicz's sacramental images of Poland's sufferings were perceived as unconscionably utilitarian, if not heretical, by conservative Catholic circles. As late as 1981 Miłosz could repeat the charge: "To portray a nation as a collective Christ, as Mickiewicz did, is not only a contradiction but a blasphemy."[3] Mickiewicz may be acquitted of blasphemy; the "Christ of the Nations" theme is recognizable today as political theology, where Poland recapitulates Christ's political role as liberator. Nevertheless, in contrast to Bonhoeffer, who insisted on Christology's regulative function, both Mickiewicz and Woronicz employ an instrumental Christology to further the goal of national independence. Granting the legitimacy of a political reading of Scripture, they erred by placing the nation and not Christ at the "center" of history;[4] Poland's glorious and tragic history, not the historical Christ-event, provides the content of their historiosophical visions. In Bonhoeffer's words, Poland has been made into a "messiah as the centre of history."

Bonhoeffer's concept of corporate persons provides a sociological framework for describing a relationship between the nation and God, which helpfully critiques the personalist approach of messianism. Bonhoeffer stressed that nations are neither autonomous nor self-sufficient. Rather, as part of penultimate reality, they are called through their ethical encounters with each other to acknowledge their boundaries, admit they are not God, and respond responsibly to in-

2. de Gruchy, "Bonhoeffer, Calvinism and Civil Disobedience," 56–57.
3. Miłosz, *Land of Ulro*, 119.
4. This is especially visible in the *Books of the Polish Nation and the Polish Pilgrimage*.

dividuals and other nations. This helps to defend against those who would deify the nation or make it a law unto itself. If Woronicz's idea of a covenant between God and the nation is conceptualized sociologically instead of metaphysically, and further stripped of its feudalistic trappings, it can then be recast in terms of Bonhoeffer's view of the nation as a corporate person.

Another conceptual building block of messianism that can be rescued by Bonhoeffer's theology of sociology is Mickiewicz's notion of Poland suffering for the political sins of Europe. This idea compares favourably with Bonhoeffer's concept of vicarious suffering, which he held could apply to corporate as well as to individual persons. Examples from *Forefathers' Eve*, Part III include the vow taken vicariously by the prisoners on behalf of the nation to remember the martyrs and remain free, the vicarious suffering of the innocent youth of Żmudź, and Konrad's claim to "suffer for millions." These actions of (literary) Polish patriots on behalf of the nation were deliberately crafted to parallel the vicarious sufferings of Poland on the international level as the "Christ-of-the-Nations." Perhaps the most explicit and exalted expression of this idea is found in the *Books of the Polish Nation*, where Christ's vicarious sufferings become the model for Poland's suffering. However, those who would draw on Bonhoeffer to facilitate the present-day reception of Messianism's idea of Poland as the "Christ-of-the-Nations" must be careful to purge it of the metaphysical, organic concept of the nation that was held by both Woronicz and Mickiewicz in favour of Bonhoeffer's sociological view.

While Woronicz was constantly looking for a "man of God" to arise, the tension between a corporate and individual messiah becomes even stronger in Mickiewicz. In *Forefathers' Eve*, Part III, the messianic mantle passes from the youth of Żmudź, to Konrad, to Poland the "Christ of the Nations," to the "terrible man" who oscillates between an individual and corporate identity. This romantic cult of the charismatic leader, which expects the emergence of a champion of the people, who embodies its nature and expresses its aspirations, is a close cousin to the *Führer* principle that Bonhoeffer attacked. Like the *Führer*, charismatic leaders base their authority on the "will of the people" on whose behalf they ostensibly act. As Janion writes, "the measure of the greatness of the individual is his relationship with the feelings, dreams, and aspirations of the fellowship, with the thought of the 'people,' with the consciousness and memory of the nation."[5] However, when such leaders appear, they seem predisposed to abuse their power and manipulate the masses. Here Bonhoeffer's characterization of Hitler as "Antichrist" recalls messianism's identification of the Russian tsar as the "devil."[6] Ironically Mickiewicz's Konrad, who accused God of being a tsar, failed to recognize that in asking for the "rule of souls" he was the one acting like a tsar.

Mickiewicz himself suffered intermittently from a "messiah complex." In the so-called "Great Improvisation" he records his failed attempt to solve Poland's problems single-handedly, by storming the gates of heaven in the auto-biographical role of Konrad. As Bonhoeffer makes clear, the role of messiah is too great for anyone to fulfill, save for God who became a human being. Despite the tragic legacy of Nazism and Stalinism, the romantic leadership cult still has its followers, notably in Central and Eastern Europe where the difficult process of transformation and a lack of democratic traditions provide ripe conditions for "tyrannical despisers of humanity" to rise to power. Bonhoeffer's words censure contemporary Konrads, who suffer from their own "messiah complex":

> ... we are not Christs, we do not have to redeem the world by any action or suffering of our own. There is no need to lay upon ourselves such an intolerable burden. We are not lords, but instruments in the hand of the Lord of history.[7]

Bonhoeffer argues that good people may become "idealistic despisers" of humanity, by loving an idealized humanity instead of real people.[8] Against all contrary evidence, they believe in the innate goodness of humanity, overlooking, redefining or excusing the evil others do. Such illusions may appeal to God's affirmation of humanity in creation and incarnation, but ignore his judgment of sin on the cross. Konrad makes this error in *Forefathers' Eve*, Part III. Declaring his love for "Poland," he was nevertheless ready to destroy his fellow Poles if they refused to cooperate with his plan for their happiness. Thus Konrad, by seeking the "rule of souls" over an idealised nation, joined the ty-

---

5. Janion and Żmigrodzka, *Romantyzm i historia*, 21.
6. Kolbuszewski, *Literatura wobec historii*, 47.
7. LPP: 145.
8. E: 87.

rannical and idealistic despisers in one person. What about Konrad's alter ego, Mickiewicz? As argued above in chapter 3, the structure of *Forefathers' Eve* demonstrates Mickiewicz's capacity for self-criticism, and his affirmation of the call to love, live with, and struggle alongside real people. His inclusive, pluralistic view of Polishness is contrary to the chauvinistic, exclusive attitude of those who despise others who fail to satisfy their arbitrary religious, racist or political definition of the nation. Mickiewicz shows as well that there is hope even for erstwhile "messiahs" to lay down their unbearable burden, to take up the "yoke which is easy and the burden which is light," and follow the genuine Messiah at the center of history. As argued in chapter 3, this change took place for Gustaf-Konrad through a series of I-You encounters, through which he recognized "others" as real people, not as masses either to manipulate or to mold into conformity with some version of ideal humanity.

Poland has never yet succumbed fully to the lure of populism, thanks to its love for freedom, its democratic traditions reaching back to the original Commonwealth, and such remarkable individuals as Kuroń, who sought to free, empower, and ennoble people rather than to control, manipulate, and debase then. However, the poor and disenfranchised still long for a charismatic leader. In recent years, leaders of populist and nationalistic parties have openly demonstrated their disdain for the rule of law, or called on the legacy of the *endecja* without renouncing the national chauvinistic and anti-Semitic side of its pre-WWII ideology. The language of populism and demagoguery has once again entered mainstream politics.

In 2005[9] the Law and Justice Party (PiS) formed first a minority government and later a governing coalition with the support of the Self-Defense Party (Samoobrona) and the League of Polish Families (LPR). At that time this author wrote, "It remains to be seen whether the current government, formed with the support of such parties, succeeds in co-opting their radical electorate, or succumbs to their radical ideology." Today in 2008, both of these potential outcomes have taken place. In early elections held in 2007 following the breakup of ruling coalition, PiS not only captured the electorate of these smaller parties,[10] it also

---

9. This paragraph has been updated to reflect developments since 2005.
10. Neither Samoobrona or LPR are represented in the Polish Parliament today.

adopted much of their rhetoric and moved noticeably in the direction of the populism and nationalism that appealed to their voters.

PiS, Samoobrona and LPR all are (or were) led by strong, authoritarian leaders. Despite the real differences between them, underneath the surface of their appeal to the disenfranchised lies the cult of the charismatic leader, who is above the law and appeals directly to the people for authority. This is part of the legacy of romantic messianism that must be consciously articulated and rejected. Poles would do well today to heed Bonhoeffer's warning against both "tyrannical" and "idealistic" despisers of the people, and replace messianism's expectation of a political liberator or saviour with Bonhoeffer's Christ, the "man-for-others."

Messianic Historiosophy and the Crisis of Modernism

Woronicz: The Conservative Restoration

The disaster of the partitions compounded the crisis of modernity for Poles. Though as a catechist Woronicz acknowledged the challenges modernism presented to the church, as a poet and politician the national crisis took center stage. He judged the causes leading to Poland's downfall to be essentially spiritual, treating as secondary the obvious political, economic, and social problems that contributed to the weakening of the Commonwealth and its eventual loss of sovereignty. This reductionist diagnosis led to a reductionist program of national repentance and character development as the solution to the nation's problems. The renewal of Poland was cast in terms of the coming of the eschatological Kingdom of God, leaving important questions of a temporal and political nature unanswered.

Woronicz considered Poland's chief problem to be its loss or lack of religion due to the increasing secularization of society. His call to reaffirm orthodox doctrine, restore traditional values, and renew religious life remains the most common response of both the Catholic and Protestant churches in Poland to modernism.[11] In terms of Bonhoeffer's critique of religion, Woronicz's program for national renewal can be characterized as a conservative restoration, which "carries on the great concepts of Christian theology," yet without interpretation. Here the Church puts forth sustained efforts to retain its traditional forms

---

11. E.g., Szczypa finds much in common between the catechetical programs of Woronicz and the late Cardinal Wyższyński. Szczypa, *Jan Paweł Woronicz*, 134.

and expressions, but fails to enter into a critical engagement with contemporary culture, and is seen by society as increasingly isolated and irrelevant.

In a spirit quite foreign to Woronicz, certain circles within the Polish Church combine the call for a "conservative restoration" with a chauvinistic nationalism that crosses easily over into xenophobia, and a sharp rejection of modern (post-modern) culture that is expressed in a colorful variety of conspiracy theories.[12] As Porter notes, many Polish Catholics "feel themselves under siege by the amorphous dangers of modern culture, if not by a specific anti-Christian conspiracy."[13] One recognizes here the familiar contours of the struggle of religion against the crisis of the West. Porter cites Bishop Lepa, who in 1997 lamented a new "secular, leftist, libertarian" model of Polishness, spread by "manipulation (brainwashing), pornography, and advertising," noting that for Lepa, this "new model" is "a rejection of the nation as such."[14] Porter concludes that for those with this mentality "the 'Catholic nation' must reside in both an idealized past and a dreamed-of-future, but not to the chagrin of the clergy in today's secular, liberal, decadent world."[15]

While many proponents and supporters of conservative restoration attempts are sincere patriots and authentic religious leaders, not uncommonly their efforts mirror the nihilism they fear and oppose in two key respects. In the first place, conservative restorations, just like nihilism, tend to mythologize both past and future. By comparison, Bonhoeffer characterizes nihilism as a denial of the historical heritage of civilization. He writes, "There is no future and no past. There remains only the present moment rescued from nothingness and the desire to grasp the next moment . . . The burden of yesterday is shaken off by glorifying shadowy times of old; the task of tomorrow is avoided by talking about the coming millennium."[16] From this perspective, the difference here between the two comes in their attitude towards the present: nihilism has nothing left but to grasp the moment, while restora-

---

12. These attitudes are foreign as well to Cardinal Wyższyński, John Paul II, and the majority of both "progressive" and main-line Polish Catholics.

13. Porter, "Catholic Nation," 290.

14. Ibid., 290. Porter's critique should not be taken as an endorsement (e.g., of "advertising").

15. Ibid., 290.

16. E: 120–21.

tion movements deny the present by clinging to myths of better times. By contrast, Bonhoeffer sought by living responsibly in the present to pass the historical heritage on to future generations.

In the second place, many restoration attempts take the form of a "positivism of revelation," which to drastically oversimplify reduces to the assertion, "God!," in opposition to the exclamation, "*Nichts*," or "the *Übermensch!*"[17] On this level of "dialogue," or rather confrontation, the "winner" is the one who shouts longer and louder. The only options are to believe, or not. If the proclamation of God's word is rejected, one is left defenseless against the abyss. Bonhoeffer's project of "non-religious interpretation" is, among other things, an attempt to overcome the pitfall of the "positivism of revelation." The positivism of revelation can also take the form of proclaiming the nation as a corporate hero or *Übermensch*. In this light Woronicz's benevolent appeal to Poland's "vital force" is recognized as gentler but still dangerous parallel to Nietzsche's vitalism and Nazi appeals to the German national spirit, which Bonhoeffer countered with his appeal to Jesus Christ as the center of history, and the source of individual and corporate personhood.

Mickiewicz: Don Quixote and the Salto Mortale

In *The Prophetic Books*, Blake described the poetical-mythical land of Ulro, where fallen and estranged *Urizen*,[18] or "Reason," rules over a world of vegetable people.[19] Recalling Blake's vision, Miłosz in *The Land of Ulro* defines the "romantic crisis of European culture" as "the dichotomy between the world of scientific laws—cold, indifferent to human values—and man's inner world."[20] Appreciative of attempts by Goethe, Blake, and others to avoid the dichotomy and hold science and the human soul together, he argues that Mickiewicz, rather than attacking the enemy in open battle, "protected himself from the 'learned' . . . with 'faith and feeling.'"[21] Miłosz cites Niemojewski, who called *Forefathers' Eve* "the

---

17. As Bonhoeffer points out, these are just two ways of saying the same thing.

18. One of primordial mankind's four elements; the others are *Tharmas* (the body), *Urthona* (the Imagination) and *Luvah* (the emotions). Cf. Miłosz, *Land of Ulro*, 166.

19. Blake held that only "Imagination," denied by those scientists, artists, and churchmen who bow to the idol *Urizen*, can lead back to a full humanity where Body, Mind, Imagination and Emotions are again united. Cf. ibid., 168–72.

20. Ibid., 94.

21. Ibid., 106. Here Przybylski notes Mickiewicz's use of parody to discredit the

swan song of a great and vanishing age," and claimed that Mickiewicz drew on "beliefs that were the antithesis of modernity" to create—not a political drama, but a "drama of the Apocalypse."[22] Niemojewski, who understood that "all apocalypses are political," strove not to depoliticize but to spiritualize the drama, by casting Mickiewicz the believer as the enemy of enlightened humanity, fighting a brave but hopeless rearguard action against the onslaught of modernity.[23] According to this reading Mickiewicz is cast as what Bonhoeffer called a "survivor of the age of chivalry," a Don Quixote figure who attempted a romantic version of the *salto mortale*. His chosen weapons, "faith and feeling," may be placed alongside the "rusty swords" of Bonhoeffer's litany, as yet another futile attempt to hold back the abyss.

As a modern romantic, albeit a critical one, Miłosz shares in the romantic revolt against the arid world of rationalism. He has an agenda in interpreting Mickiewicz as a religious mystic. As Wiegandt explains, "[The identity of] Mickiewicz as a religious person and poet . . . is an argument for the main thought of the essay,[24] which is Miłosz's version of the wager of Pascal: one must believe in the Christian God, if one wants to rescue the meaning of human existence."[25] Dorosz demonstrates how Miłosz cites Mickiewicz's "faith and feeling," alongside Blake and Swedenborg's "Imagination," in order to "liberate them from the power of 'the objective truths of science,'"[26] and thus escape from the land of Ulro. However, as Dorosz rightly contends, this maneuver divides reason and imagination into an irresolvable dualism that, "inspired by a Manichean hatred for nature—condemns the imagination to soar in the clouds, deprived of points of contact with the earth, and as a result with reason."[27] The point, he concludes, is neither to condemn scientific research, nor to accept its all-inclusive claims, but to combat "the totalitarianism that the 'scientific worldview' introduces into the

---

Enlightenment's faith in science and reason. Cf. Przybylski, *Klasycyzm*, 409–15.

22. Ibid., 104.

23. Significantly, Niemojewski wrote in 1910 that the nineteenth century "marked the end of all traditional, religiously based civilizations." Niemojewski, cited in Miłosz, *Land of Ulro*, 103.

24. I.e., Ibid.

25. Wiegandt, "Gombrowicz i Miłosz o Mickiewiczu," 407.

26. Dorosz, "Wędrówki ziemię ulro," 147.

27. Ibid., 152.

region of human experience."[28] Bonhoeffer would agree. He rejected the dualism of reason and faith, of the natural and spiritual worlds, along with all forms of "two-spheres" thinking. Instead, he submitted exaggerated claims made on behalf of reason and the scientific method to a theological critique provided by God's self-revelation in Jesus Christ, arguing in effect that in Christ, human beings, nature, and the world come-of-age are released from the land of Ulro; all creatures and things are free to be themselves, without the unbearable, self-destructive urge to "be like god." Though they may not yet recognize it, their meaning and purpose is secure in Christ, their creator, redeemer, and reconciler.

Although Miłosz's basic characterization of Mickiewicz as a romantic Don Quixote is valid, there is substance to the claim that the latter's *salto mortale* was not a mere leap backwards to medieval *Christianitas*. Rather, it looked forward eschatologically to a new age of Christianity. Recognizing that Europe's old order was passing away, Mickiewicz anticipated a renewed and reformed Christendom, where the gospel would become an international ethic and the foundation of European society, and nations would live together in peace. According to this vision, in the *Books of the Polish Pilgrimage* he accepted the ideals of *liberté, egalité, fraternité* bequeathed to Europe by the French revolution, but insisted that they be applied in the spirit of love that will characterize revived Christendom. This is still a religious revival, and not a new form of Christianity for a world come of age. In contrast, Bonhoeffer increasingly came to realize that an appeal to Christ as the unity of the West is no longer viable in modern, pluralistic Europe. Accordingly, he sought to help the church find a new role in relationship to the state and society, which as de Lange suggests might draw on the resources of Trinitarian theology as a model for the church in a pluralistic society.

National Chauvinism: From Darwin to "God Is on Our Side!"

As discussed in the Introduction, Porter attributes the rise of Polish nationalism and anti-Semitism to the National Democracy (*endecja*) movement's rejection of eschatology. Since neither providence nor "progress" guarantees the future, the *endecja* was driven to first define,

28. Ibid., 158.

then create "Poland" along religious and ethnic lines, in order to secure its survival in the life-and-death battle between nations. Adopting Porter's thesis as a working hypothesis,[29] the next two sub-sections apply Bonhoeffer's view of providence to critique Polish national chauvinism in certain of its original and present-day forms, and to enquire whether Bonhoeffer helped Poland's secular revisionists retain their vision of an open, pluralistic society following their rejection of Marxism along with all philosophies of history that promise a future utopia.

To begin with national chauvinism, Bonhoeffer's 1944 essay "The First Table of the Ten Commandments" warns against invoking the name of a generic, amorphous, and undemanding "Almighty" to legitimize a nation's worldly ambitions of power and conquest, arguing that providence must be linked to God's self-revelation in Christ. As de Gruchy comments,

> A doctrine of providence without obligation to the God of history revealed in Jesus Christ ... can so easily provide legitimization for corrupt power and unbridled nationalism with the cry "God is on OUR side!" National-historical events, such as military victories, are clothed with a mythological significance and become the criteria for evaluating present history and anticipating the future.... [This temptation] is also exacerbated whenever those in power regard their policies and positions as ordained by God and beyond the prophetic critique of others.[30]

Poles have long mythologized their nation's history, for example by calling upon providence or the Virgin Mary to legitimize their political programs and aspirations. Velikonja, who calls this tradition a "kind of mytho-poetics, [whereby] political and military events are not merely explained but also justified and legitimized,"[31] cites several examples from Poland's history, such as Sobieski's 1683 victory over the Turks at Vienna, the 1655 victory over Sweden at Częstochowa,[32] and "the miracle on the Vistula" on Assumption Day, August 15, 1920, when General Pilsudski's forces defeated the Red Army outside of Warsaw. All

---

29. Note the theological support Bonhoeffer may provide for Porter's thesis (cf. p. 199–200 above); the Christ-event makes history historical, by providing it with an eschatological foundation and teleological goal.

30. de Gruchy, *Bonhoeffer and South Africa*, 54.

31. Velikonja, "Slovenian and Polish Religio-National Mythologies," 248.

32. The Częstochowa monastery houses the "Black Madonna" icon.

three cases have often been interpreted by Poles as evidence of divine providence, as well as the Virgin Mary's intervention.[33] Woronicz's glorification of past victories over enemy aggressors, enlisted as "proof" of God's blessing on faithful Poland, was fairly benign, given his pluralistic, inclusive view of the nation, and his view of Polish patriots as peace-loving defenders of the nation. However, as this section shows others have claimed God's blessing for their chauvinistic attitudes and nationalistic "policies and positions." De Gruchy's warning against separating providence from God's revelation in Christ calls for a close examination of the myths of Polish messianism, and of "Mary, Queen of Poland,"[34] as a basis for confidence that "God is on OUR side."

A more serious abuse of providence is the *mésalliance* between Catholicism[35] and the national-chauvinism and anti-Semitism of the National Democrats. Initially, the *Endecja* was anticlerical, for as Porter observes, the "Spencerian image of the *bellum omnium contra omnes*" allowed no transcendent law or ethical standards to stand above the "national creed."[36] Indeed, as social Darwinists, the *endecja* denied providence altogether. However, the crisis of modernity soon brought the *endecja* and Church closer together. In what Bonhoeffer would call a heteronymous *salto mortale*, the papacy condemned modernity, reasserted neo-Thomistic philosophy, and charged theologians with reconciling science with the teachings of the Church.[37] Nevertheless, other responses to modernism were attempted within the Catholic fold. Catholic modernism rejected Thomist epistemology and "argued for a clear distinction between reason and faith."[38] For Polish Catholics, the masses of dislocated peasants and workers represented a more widespread problem than the "alienation of the intelligentsia from an obscurantist, anti-modern Church."[39] Thus the Mariavite movement sought renewal of religious life in a non-hierarchical form, while Antoni Szech

---

33. Velikonja, "Slovenian and Polish Religio-National Mythologies," 249.

34. Velikonja and Davies speak of this tradition as *myth* in reference to its functional role in the formation of national identity.

35. Here Porter notes that the Church is neither monolithic nor dominated by such elements. Cf. Porter, "Marking the Boundary of the Faith," 261–85.

36. Ibid., 275.

37. Ibid., 266.

38. Ibid., 266.

39. Ibid., 268.

(Father Izydor Wyslouch) called for the clergy to "step forward bravely as the defenders of the people."[40] As well-intentioned as these varied attempts to avoid the abyss were, they potentially made the Church "one of many institutions," or agreed to submit its doctrine and practices to the modernist critique.[41] Many Catholics therefore sought an alternative approach, and allies who would embrace it. As Porter writes,

> As priests, Church officials and Catholic authors sought to penetrate the twentieth century's reconfigured public realm, they appropriated the concept of the nation as their point of entry. Ultimately, they redrew the boundaries of their faith so as to include within the fold a dynamic but dangerous political ally: the radical right.[42]

This alliance required both the Church and radical right to adjust their stance. Initially, the clergy saw the *endecja* as modernists who treated the Church "as a social institution, not as the sacred embodiment of the Kingdom of God on earth."[43] Neither was anti-Semitism promoted openly by the Polish Church. However, in a post World War I Poland, threatened by its own diversity as well as the growing military threat from Germany and the Soviet Union, for those prone to conspiracy theories the "enemy" began to take the form of a broad socialist-Masonic-Jewish plot against the Church.[44] By the 1920's anti-Semitic views appeared regularly in certain Catholic publications. Meanwhile, says Porter, the *endecja* rejected religious diversity in favor of the social cohesion of the "Polak-Katolik" myth, and advanced the Church from the status of a "national institution" to "the core of the nation's being."[45] This peace treaty between Christianity and chauvinism created a Polish version of "thinking in two realms," which made Christianity a private and family matter, but excluded it from business and politics. As Porter observes, "the modernists had tried to bring the Church down to earth, Dmowski and his colleagues allowed it to remain in heaven."[46] Certain Catholic authors, in turn "were increasingly drawn to the

40. Szech, quoted in ibid., 269.
41. Ibid., 272–73.
42. Ibid., 273.
43. Ibid., 276.
44. Ibid., 278.
45. Ibid., 280–81.
46. Ibid., 281.

endecja."⁴⁷ Porter paraphrases Ujejski's laundered account of National Democracy⁴⁸: since the nation is God's creation, "to sacrifice our personal good for the good of the nation was a great thing, and if we did so in the context of the international struggle for survival, then we were merely following a basic instinct for (collective) survival."⁴⁹ Such social Darwinism with a thin veneer of Catholic window dressing paved the way for rapprochement and cooperation. Porter concludes:

> Nationalism—now appropriately Catholicized—gave the Church a way of talking about mass politics, about social change and urbanization, and about Poland's place in a new Europe [...] Thus was born an entirely new form of Catholicism, one which pushed reformists like Szech outside the boundaries of the faith, but which had plenty of room for Dmowski and his many heirs.⁵⁰

This fatal alliance between Catholicism and National Democracy wed a nationalist ideology that excluded Christian morality from politics, with religious national sentiments derived from romanticism and the Polak-Katolik myth to cry, "God is on OUR side!" The parallels to fascist ideology and the German Christian movement are as obvious as they are taboo for many Polish historians. Today, certain Catholic circles still exhibit the anti-semitism, xenophobia, and national-chauvinism acquired via the *endecja*. Although few of chauvinism's modern proponents in Poland are perhaps aware of the *endecja's* ideological foundation in social Darwinism, the rhetoric of hate and exclusion, the credence placed in conspiracy theories, and the Spencerian battle of all against all, now rechristened as the struggle against the godless, pluralistic, liberal European Union, are alive and well. The renewed attempt by "conservative"⁵¹ politicians and their church allies in 2005 to harness the "dynamism" of radical parties right and left, together with their "radical projects, of more decisive, at times brutally presented postulates,"⁵² de-

---

47. Ibid., 282. This myth is alive and well in 2005.

48. Cf. Ujejski, *Nationalism as an Ethical Problem*, cited in Porter, "Marking the Boundary of the Faith," 282.

49. Ibid., 280.

50. Ibid., 282.

51. Many if not most of the self-proclaimed "conservatives" in Poland today are more aptly described as populist and nationalist.

52. Jarosław Kaczyński, leader of the Law and Justice Party (PiS), commenting in Parliament on the *exposé* or governmental program presented by the new Prime

mands a serious examination of what Porter dubbed this "Polish variant of Catholicism" and its historical baggage. It is high time for those bags to be unpacked, publicly renounced, and discarded. Perhaps then the patriotism and political savvy of the National Democrats can be saved from the wreck of its post-Spencerian ideology. In an ideal world, those who identify with the *endecja*, or consort with its present-day heirs and followers, would themselves critique its history, values, ideals, and presuppositions. For now, no such self-examination seems forthcoming. In this situation, Bonhoeffer's legacy presents a clear challenge to the Church to conduct a thorough stock-taking of the past and present flirtations with nationalism by some within its ranks. Brave, individual voices are raised, but the nation and the world still waits for the Church to speak Christ's word of command.

Citizens' Society: Promising Godlessness or Borrowed Transcendence?

If Porter's thesis is correct, the rejection of eschatology[53] by the former revisionists among the Polish opposition movement should have led them in the direction of nationalism and authoritarian rule. Whether or not his thesis holds true for Poles (or any others) during the second half of the 20th century, the fact remains that most of these former socialists did not become chauvinists. Several factors may have contributed to this. Theologically, the creation of human beings in God's image implies that, despite the sin they find themselves entangled in, all people retain their human dignity and at least a relative measure of residual goodness. Perhaps these particular Poles are just persons of the more decent sort? Another possibility is that socialism's humanitarian ideals managed for a time to survive their divorce from the historical progress promised by Marxist ideology. Then again, the ideological and genealogical links of many revisionists to the PPS, which had its own non-Stalinist version of socialism, suggests a "hereditary" aversion to national-chauvinism. Or perhaps it was the Nazi and Stalinist terror, the horrors of the Holocaust and the Gulag, which inoculated them against nationalistic, authoritarian ideology. While these and other factors all played a part, one more

---

Minister from PiS. Printed in *Gazeta Wyborcza*, (November 12–13, 2005), 4.

53. Including all philosophies of history, such as Marxism, which promise inevitable progress towards a utopian society.

possibility to consider is whether the discovery of "transcendence," acquired by many opposition members from reading Bonhoeffer and through their contact with the Catholic intelligentsia, helped to fulfill the role of missing "providence."[54]

Barańczak, in his appropriation of Bonhoeffer's phrase, *etsi Deus non daretur*, claimed that in Tegel prison responsibility towards the "other person" replaced God as the foundation of Bonhoeffer's ethics. But would Bonhoeffer indeed affirm that "after 'the death of God' the Decalogue need not die"? Such readings of Bonhoeffer were known in Poland, where Robinson's *Honest to God* was published in 1968. Yet Bonhoeffer argued that the penultimate both gains its significance from the ultimate and exists for the sake of the ultimate. If we deny the ultimate, i.e., God, Jesus Christ, justification, reconciliation, the Kingdom, we may yet lay claim to a high and noble humanism. But is this really what Bonhoeffer meant by non-religious Christianity? Can humanism sustain resistance to totalitarianism? Can it provide a viable foundation for natural life? Or is it the case, for Bonhoeffer at least, that if "God is dead," so is the Decalogue, and the abyss follows close behind?

The transcendence Bonhoeffer affirms in personal encounter, though genuine, retains its derivative nature. It cannot stand on its own, or be understood apart from Jesus Christ, who remained to the end the center and goal of Bonhoeffer's ethics, hope, and faith. Barańczak is honest and even courageous, for he makes his claim for responsibility in existential terms. In contrast, some of his contemporaries appear to have attached a borrowed transcendence to their humanism. Like their romantic forbearers, who employed messianic Christology to provide religious sanction for romantic historiosophy, they tended to sanction their vision of civil society with a radical reading of Bonhoeffer's prison theology, which replaced his Christology with a vaguely defined "transcendence." The result is not "non-religious Christianity" but "religious humanism" with a hefty dose of unfounded metaphysics; however we may evaluate the potential of such a position, it is hardly what Bonhoeffer had in mind. More promising is what de Gruchy termed Bonhoeffer's "dialogical" view of Providence, which grants human beings the privilege and responsibility of helping to make history, and

---

54. On the other hand, in certain cases the acceptance of "transcendence" by certain members of the Polish opposition led to their embracing, promoting and defending the chauvinistic version of Polish Catholicism ("God is on OUR side").

which was in practice appropriated by both the secular and Catholic wings of the opposition.

Historically, Barańczak's brand of humanism, founded on responsibility towards the other person, did indeed sustain many secular Poles in their courageous and costly fight for individual freedom and human dignity. Bonhoeffer himself argued for the reality of the transcendence found in one's fellow human beings, and rejoiced when others recognized it as transcendence. But he never rescinded his conviction that such penultimate transcendence has its true and necessary basis in the ultimate reality of Jesus Christ, the redeemer and reconciler of the world.

Critique of Religion: Romantic "Faith and Feeling"

In Mickiewicz's early poems, he declares that youthful enthusiasm will "Reach, where sight cannot reach, Break, what reason cannot break."[55] "Faith and feeling,"[56] rather than science and philosophy, are the epistemological instruments capable of discerning the "living truths" of the spiritual world, hence of replacing the dead world of matter with the world of the spirit. Here we must be clear what faith and feeling signify. W. H. Auden's otherwise excellent translation of "Romanticity"[57] renders "faith and feeling" as "faith and love," leaving a declaration as obvious as it is banal; telescopes and calculators can neither contain nor explain romantic love. This makes for a nice poem for sentimental Anglophone readers, but completely misses Mickiewicz's point. His "feeling" is not mere emotion, romantic or otherwise; it indicates spiritual intuition, insight, and inspiration, the "eyes of the soul" by which one experiences spiritual reality and truth directly. Faith on the other hand is belief in spiritual reality, which impinges upon this physical world, and can be experienced by those so gifted and inclined. In "Romanticity," the girl sees because she has feeling, the people believe she sees because they have faith.

Before submitting Mickiewicz's "faith and feeling" to Bonhoeffer's critique of religion, we may further clarify their meaning through

---

55. Mickiewicz, *Wiersze*, 15. Mickiewicz reprised this line in *Forefathers' Eve*, Part III when Konrad declares that "feelings will burn what reason cannot break."

56. Ibid., 29.

57. Cited in: Miłosz, *Land of Ulro*, 99.

a comparison with Schleiermacher's *Gefühl* and Otto's *Glaube* and *Ahndung*. Typical of romanticism as a movement of spiritual renewal over against materialistic and deistic forms of Enlightenment rationalism, Schleiermacher replaced Descartes' "I Think" and Kant's "I ought," with "I feel," making the subjective feeling of absolute dependence (*Gefühl*) the foundation of one's knowledge of God. In the *Addresses*, Schleiermacher posited a pre-cognitive moment when feeling and intuition are one, and he went on in *The Doctrine of Faith* to argue that religious feeling is direct knowledge or experience of God. Much like Schleiermacher, Mickiewicz used the word "feeling" or *czucie* to describe direct experience of spiritual reality that both precedes and supersedes all reflection, dogma, and evidence.

Moving on to Otto, Mickiewicz's advice to the old man in "Romanticity," "Have a heart, and look within your heart," expresses poetically what Otto meant when he wrote in *The Idea of the Holy* that, "Our [numinous state of mind] cannot, strictly speaking, be taught, it can only be evoked, awakened in the mind; as everything that comes 'of the spirit' must be awakened."[58] In *Forefathers' Eve*, Part 3, just prior to receiving the vision that revealed the meaning of Poland's suffering and foretold its future deliverance, Father Peter, praying in his cell, cries out:

> Lord! Who am I to come before You?
> Dust and nothingness;
> But having confessed to You my nothingness,
> I, dust, will talk with the Lord.[59]

This passage is a paraphrase of Genesis 18:27, where Abraham, pleading for God to spare the city of Sodom, declares: "Now that I have been so bold as to speak to the Lord, though I am nothing but dust and ashes . . ." Otto cites this same biblical text to illustrate the religious experience that he calls "creature-feeling," which he contrasts to Schleiermacher's "feeling of dependence." Schleiermacher erred, Otto explains, by confusing the individual's "self-consciousness" as a dependent—therefore created—creature with the deeper, original experience of the holy, "which has immediate and primary reference

---

58. Otto, *Idea of the Holy*, 7.
59. Mickiewicz, *Powieści poetyckie*, 185.

to [the numinous] object outside the self."⁶⁰ "Absolute dependence" is a subjective feeling within the individual, which only by inference can be traced to the external divine object that caused it; in contrast, "creature-consciousness" arises from the felt presence of the external numinous object. Father Peter's vision at best crosses over into the numinous by its aesthetic value, or the overabundance of religious feeling it provokes. However, his experience of being "dust and nothingness" is a clear example of what Otto would later describe as "creature-feeling." As Otto writes, "It is especially in relation to this element of majesty or absolute overpoweringness that the creature-consciousness ... comes on the scene as a sort of shadow or subjective reflection of it [...] there is the feeling of one's own abasement, of being but 'dust and ashes' and nothingness. And this forms the numinous raw material for the feeling of religious humility."⁶¹ Here it is worth noting that Mickiewicz's purposely contrasts Konrad's pride with the priest's humility, which made the latter worthy to receive the divine vision.

Kant's removal of religion to the realm of *noumena*, while placing it beyond the attacks of critics, helped to cement the dichotomy between knowledge and faith. Seeking religious knowledge, Otto adopted Fries' philosophical apparatus to describe the non-conceptual yet cognitive experience of the numinous. Fries posited a non-rational religious or aesthetic intuition, which he called *Ahndung*, in addition to *Wissen*, knowledge that results from science and logic, and *Glaube*, or rational belief.⁶² By distinguishing the religious from the moral and rational sense, and characterizing it as pure though non-conceptual reason, Otto made religious feeling autonomous, a source of knowledge in its own right. He advanced Fries' view by positing a religious *a priori*⁶³ defined as the sacred or holy. In the presence of the holy, one recognizes the numinous through the "faculty of divination."⁶⁴ This faculty allows one "to become consciously aware of [the holy] as an operational reality, intervening actively in the phenomenal world."⁶⁵ Otto identifies this

60. Otto, *Idea of the Holy*, 10–11.
61. Ibid., 20.
62. Cf. Ballard, *Rudolf Otto*, 46.
63. Otto, *Idea of the Holy*, 116 ff.
64. Ibid., 148.
65. Ibid., 147.

faculty with the testimonium Spiritus Sancti internum, Schleiermacher's Gefühl and Fries' Ahndung.[66]

Mickiewicz the poet intuitively believed in what Otto called the religious *a priori*. He would likely have found Otto's Friesien philosophy superfluous. Mickiewicz criticized German philosophers for practicing abstract, "school philosophy," which he contrasts to true philosophy that engages actively in the real world of ethics and politics.[67] Mickiewicz also accused German philosophers of hypocrisy, for proclaiming as truth in the church what they ridiculed in the classroom. He writes,

> Myriad pastors, who no longer believe in Luther, Calvin, or even Christ . . . threw themselves into abstract philosophy. In this way they relieved themselves of active work; it is undoubtedly more difficult to show what one should do in the religious life and how to do it, without ceasing to be a Christian, than it is to dream up a system, which releases us entirely from religious obligations.[68]

Otto's rational belief (*Glaube*), the doctrines of religion worked out rationally from the *a priori* concepts of God, immortality, and freedom, differs distinctly from Mickiewicz's understanding of faith as belief in spiritual reality and truth. On the other hand, "feeling" is a close equivalent to *Ahndung*, and functions much like Otto's "faculty of divination." Both Mickiewicz and Otto believed in direct, non-rational religious knowledge of spiritual reality, and Mickiewicz's works show evidence of his experience of the numinous. However, "feeling" bears a wider semantic range for Mickiewicz, who did not distinguish clearly between prophecy, visions, poetic inspiration, and direct religious experience. Otto would also have criticized Mickiewicz for including the moral in the religious sense, instead of developing it as an ideogram of numinous experience, or discussing it rationally as doctrine (*Glaube*).

Having thus clarified "faith and feeling," the critique of Mickiewicz's "religion" is fairly straightforward. Bonhoeffer would certainly agree with Barth, who attacked Otto for his "religious" approach, declaring that whatever the experience of the numinous was, it was neither an experience of God nor true transcendence. Bonhoeffer did not feel the need to comment directly on Otto's work, though in the 1931 address

---

66. Ibid., 149–50.
67. Mickiewicz, *Literatura Słowiańska*, 227.
68. Ibid., 213.

discussed above he noted Barth's critical stance towards the Marburg Neo-Kantians. Had he read Mickiewicz, he would likely have repeated the gist of Barth's critique of Otto; Mickiewicz's "feeling" belongs to romantic, religious experience, and not God's self-revelation. Bonhoeffer would also critique Mickiewicz's "religious" view of the relationship of the material and spiritual worlds, which impinge upon and influence each other. While this appears to agree with Bonhoeffer's cry of "no two spheres!", in reality it comes dangerously close to confusing ultimate and penultimate reality, instead of grounding penultimate reality on the ultimate reality of Jesus Christ. It also errs by granting spirit priority over matter, instead of affirming the concreteness of this worldly life. Furthermore, Bonhoeffer would turn attention back to the "reality of Jesus Christ"; and away from the fulfillment of poetic visions understood as "platonic ideas" and "prophecies" that must come to pass.

Messianic Theodicy

For many Poles, the national tragedy of the partitions appeared to link theodicy with history and providence. How could they trust in God when he had allowed them to lose their statehood? Woronicz answered that God had not forgotten Poland; one day His loving care for the nation would again be evident. Meanwhile, Poland had brought suffering upon itself, by breaking its covenant with God and proving unfaithful to its mission as the "bulwark of Christianity." Its suffering served to punish sin, as well as to cleanse and renew the nation. The nation had gone into captivity and exile, but if it would only repent from its sins, remember its identity, and return to its calling, God would restore its land and its freedom, along with its honored place among the nations. This Irenaean "soul-making" theodicy took precedence over the theme of suffering as national punishment.

Mickiewicz in turn drew primarily on New Testament images to present Poland as the "Christ of the Nations." Whereas Christ suffered to redeem the world spiritually, Poland's sufferings were redemptive morally and politically. Woronicz's suggestion that the partitioning nations bore the greater guilt laid the foundation for the romantic portrayal of Poland as the innocent Lamb of God, suffering at the hands of wicked kings and princes. This gave Poland the moral high ground, and served to ground the political-eschatological hope of national resurrection. *Forefathers' Eve*, Part III, marks the high point of Mickiewicz's theodicy. As argued in chapter 3, Konrad's accusations represent a theology of protest, where God, both indirectly as the source of Konrad's poetic inspiration, and directly in Father Peter's ensuing vision, joins Konrad in rebelling against and unmasking the deistic impostor who ignores his people's suffering, or cynically turns it to his own advantage. Father Peter's ensuing vision does not detract from or replace Christ's spiritual sufferings, but serves to ennoble and explain Poland's political sufferings; Poland's rebirth as a state will lead to the political and spiritual renewal of Europe and Christendom. Thus Mickiewicz aligns himself with the Augustinian tradition of "greater-good" theodicy.

Concerning method, Bonhoeffer would criticize both forms of messianic theodicy for a lack of theological control. Messianism interpreted suffering primarily in terms of Poland's past and future history, rather than in light of Christ, the redeemer and reconciler of the world. When it comes to content, Bonhoeffer chose to focus on how God justifies human beings, not how human beings can justify God. Rather than constructing an all-inclusive theodicy, he pointed to God who became incarnate in Jesus Christ. God did not remain aloof, as Konrad charged, but suffered in solidarity with and for us. Here Mickiewicz's protest theism keeps close company with Bonhoeffer's discussion of hopeful godlessness, which by clearing the decks of the Deistic God[69], prepares the way to recognize the "hidden God" who hangs on the cross in weakness, joining our protest against evil and suffering, and bearing our sin and solitude. In Mickiewicz's case, however, one must move backwards from the anti-type, i.e., Poland suffering vicariously for the sins of Europe, to get to Christ as the source and model of vicarious suffering. Nevertheless, the approach of both men is practical and pastoral rather than philosophical; God is against evil, which he resists and overcomes primarily by means of vicarious representative action, to which he also calls his followers. Those who undertake such action do not glorify or encourage suffering for its own sake, but are prepared to suffer when necessary for the social, economic, political, and spiritual redemption of others.

In *Ethics* Bonhoeffer declares that Christ crucified, together with the community of his followers, are signs to the world of God's judgment and love. He writes: "The body of Jesus Christ, especially as it is presented to us on the cross, makes visible to faith both the world in

---

69. Among other false or inadequate views of God and his work.

its sin and in its being loved by God, and the church-community as the company of those who recognize their sin and gratefully submit to the love of God."[70] By employing the concept of corporate persons, this sentence can be applied to Poland. In the theodicy of Woronicz, Poland was indeed portrayed as a nation that confessed its sins,[71] and submitted once again to God's love. If we thus combine the salient points of the theodicy of Mickiewicz and Woronicz, and bring the result down to human proportions, the messianic mantra of "Poland, the Christ of the Nations" reminds us today that Poland's suffering made visible the political world's sins of tyranny, injustice, and the suppression of freedom, and offered in their place a political gospel of freedom, justice, and the brotherhood of nations.

Responsibility

Providence, Freedom, and Responsibility

The doctrine of God's providence, especially as it relates to human freedom and responsibility, has a rich if turbulent history. In contrast to sincere but generally misguided attempts to understand and/or predict God's working in history, Bonhoeffer read history as the story of providence, not in order to identify what God is doing, but to discern what he would have us to do. His confidence that God is present and active in the world led him to responsible engagement with the world as a disciple of Christ, the "man-for-others." At the height of Hitler's power, Bonhoeffer wrote that while "success makes history . . . the Disposer of history is always bringing good out of evil over the heads of the history-makers."[72] The faith that God will overcome evil may lead to passivity, or free one from the paralyzing fear of personal failure. Here it leads directly to Bonhoeffer's appeal for this-worldly, historical responsibility. Instead of resisting "success" via heroic but fruitless gestures, or bowing to its power and allure, he encourages his friends to accept responsibility for "the molding of history, whether it be as victors or vanquished."[73] This idea was developed further in his prison poem, "Stations on the

---

70. E: 68.

71. Mickiewicz did so privately, and through his candid descriptions of literary characters he created in such works as *Master Thaddeus* and *Forefathers' Eve*.

72. LPP: 138.

73. LPP: 138–39.

Road to Freedom,"[74] which traces the road from discipline, through action and suffering, to death.

Bonhoeffer's perspective on providence and responsibility affirms certain aspects of Polish messianism. In a similar vein to "Stations . . .," Woronicz traced in his sermons the stages of a human life, from youth, through maturity, to death, the last of which includes what Bonhoeffer calls suffering. As Szczypa summarizes, "Youth was a time in 'which there were formed those character traits that made them true and not defiled persons.' In the age of maturity they were 'useful and not harmful citizens,' in the face of death they were shown to be 'living and not dead Christians.'"[75]

Nevertheless, both Woronicz and Mickiewicz read history to discover "what God is doing," grasping at any development that might lead towards Polish sovereignty. As we saw in earlier chapters, their haste in identifying potential national deliverers led them on numerous occasions to support rash undertakings and to place their hope in a variety of false messiahs. Bonhoeffer of course never promised that God would cause our efforts to act responsibly succeed, and the failure of specific "messianic" ventures does not in itself pass judgment on them or those who undertook them. Yet the bitter disappointments experienced in this regard by those who crafted Polish messianism and those acted upon its precepts and prophecies provides an powerful existential warning to those who would too readily identify a given individual, party or cause as God's chosen instrument of deliverance and renewal.

Many attempts at understanding providence go beyond seeking to understand what God is doing in history (i.e., identifying this or that historical event or person as part of God's sovereign plan and working), to using "God" to justify and bless one's own plans and actions. To counter this abuse of providence, de Gruchy cites Bonhoeffer's reading of Jeremiah with regard to the "hiddenness of God" within history, to argue against exploiting history to defend or justify one's country. Instead, we must allow Christ to judge our national as well as personal history.[76] De Gruchy adds that this leads us "to evaluate everything on the basis of the cross and the kingdom and in doing so to act as those

---

74. Bonhoeffer, LPP 1971: 370.
75. Rejman, *Jan Paweł Woronicz*, 164–65.
76. Cf. de Gruchy, *Bonhoeffer and South Africa*, 55.

whom God has set free for responsible action."[77] On this account as well, messianism is found wanting. Though the cross was not absent from his thought, Woronicz analyzed Poland's recent history primarily in terms of the covenant. The myth he created of Poland as God's faithful vassal[78] led to whitewashing its own political sins, especially towards the national, ethnic, and religious minorities that lived within its borders. This is offset only in part by his interpretation of Poland's sufferings as a sign of God's chastisement can be read as an attempt to let the kingdom judge the nation, though as noted above this reductionist theodicy had its theological shortcomings and practical drawbacks. However, by idealizing Poland's more distant past and sanitizing its history, he opened the door for Mickiewicz and others to undertake a full-scale use of history to justify "innocent" Poland. Similar attempts at self-justification are still prevalent in Poland today. To their credit, our messianic poets' purpose and practice was better than their theory; both aimed explicitly, as Bonhoeffer would wish, at encouraging Poles to work responsibly for the spiritual and political renewal of the nation and its citizens.[79] And contrary to the majority of those today who loudly and vigorously defend Poland's "virtue" against any and all accusations or suggestions of wrong-doing, the myth of Polish national virtue that they sought to promote was inclusive in nature, and sought to liberate and enfranchise not only the inhabitants of the Polish Commonwealth, but of neighboring nations as well.

In this regard the Polish opposition movement fares better than its messianic forebears. Its critical appropriation of Poland's heritage and history laid the foundation for citizens' society, which replaced the dilemma of "reform or revolution"[80] with a flexible ethic of freedom and responsible action that appealed directly to Bonhoeffer regarding the willingness to "dirty one's hands" on behalf of others. The opposition retained the messianic ideals of Christian humanism, while rejecting messianism's romantic philosophy of history that promised the vindication and success of the "Polish Idea," either by the upward course of

---

77. Ibid., 57.

78. That is, until it forget its calling and identity, and broke the covenant it had made with God.

79. The same is true of Mickiewicz.

80. Analogous to the choice between radicalism and compromise that Bonhoeffer condemns.

salvation history or by the apocalyptic appearance of a political messiah. Mazowiecki and others called for responsible action from the perspective of divine providence, while from the secular humanist position Kuroń and Michnik based the program of New Evolutionism on the penultimate transcendence found in interpersonal, ethical encounters. Both wings of the opposition steered clear of reading history "to discover what God is doing." As noted above, Bonhoeffer's dialogical view of providence and human responsibility helped these quite diverse circles to agree on and implement a common program, which in the ambiguous, hostile political climate of the Polish Peoples' Republic claimed an increasing area of public space in the name of freedom, truth, and humanity. Here, one aspect at least of messianic historiosophy can be rescued; messianism's eschatology may have been over-realized, but it was dialogical. For Woronicz and Mickiewicz, the God who guaranteed Poland's future called his people to join the struggle towards that goal. On the other hand, Bonhoeffer would reject messianism's appeal to primeval society,[81] insisting instead that one can only understand primal humanity eschatologically, in light of Jesus Christ and his present and coming Kingdom. The point then is not to recreate the past, but to be conformed to Christ.

If citizens' society consciously parted ways with Polish messianism in the area of historiosophy, Masłowski's recent demonstration of the compatibility of Mickiewicz's thought both with Catholic modernism and the Vatican II council[82] shows the extent to which the emphasis that the opposition movement placed on human responsibility was a continuation of the tradition of Polish messianism. Masłowski, noting Mickiewicz's extensive use of *The Imitation of Christ*, describes eight fundamental transformations of à Kempis by Mickiewicz in his approach to interpersonal relationships, ethics, and nature, which bring the romantic poet close to Bonhoeffer at many points.[83] Masłowski shows how Mickiewicz moved from the individualistic, inward, religious, and other-worldly ethic found in à Kempis, in the direction of what could be termed a proto-Bonhoefferian ethic of community and responsibility

---

81. Found in Woronicz's view of the immediacy of primeval society's contact with God. Mickiewicz explicitly calls on a primeval myth in the *Books of the Polish Nation*.

82. Masłowski, *Gest, Symbol i rytuały polskiego teatru romantycznego*, 1998.

83. The discussion below follows Masłowski's chart comparing à Kempis and Mickiewicz. Cf. ibid., 302. No independent critique of à Kempis is attempted here, as the interest is in Mickiewicz.

that affirms nature and demands an active faith that expresses itself in deeds.

To begin with, à Kempis stressed individual salvation, while Mickiewicz argued for "salvation through fighting for others and with others."[84] If anything Bonhoeffer's consistent rejection of individualism in favor of life in community intensified in Tegel prison, where he saw the Old Testament picture of "God in the center of the village" as the pattern for redeemed and reconciled life in this world, and declared that the church, like its master, must be "for-others".

Whereas à Kempis stressed obedience, Mickiewicz underscored the value of "promethean revolt,"[85] recalling Bonhoeffer's comments that the German nation had learned the freedom of obedience but not the freedom of responsible action. Admittedly, Mickiewicz's "promethean revolt" is akin to the "rusty sword" of one's "very own freedom."[86] Yet Bonhoeffer's editing of this passage[87] shows his recognition that the method he rejects is closely analogous to the deed of "free responsibility." Konrad's failure in his confrontation with God confirms that Mickiewicz concurs with the inadequacy of mere "promethean" action, which acts from autonomous pride instead of in true solidarity with the suffering God, or at least with the penultimate community.

Whereas à Kempis discouraged becoming overly familiar with others and argued for liturgical participation in the work of Christ that amounts to a religious interiorization of the spiritual life, Mickiewicz taught that familiarity with others "is a fundamental value funding the community," and demonstrated how individuals find their identity as members of the community through a process of "individuation and re-socialization" modeled on the incarnation.[88] This prefigures Bonhoeffer's insistence that individuals gain their identity in community, and his emphasis on Christ's affirmation of this-worldly life via the incarnation. Furthermore, à Kempis radicalized inwardness by expressing contempt for the world, and promoting a faith that is active in the "internal fight"

---

84. Cf. the discussion in chapter 3 of *Forefathers' Eve*, Part Three.

85. This promethean theme begins in "Ode to Youth." Notable promethean characters include Konrad Wallenrod and Gustaf-Konrad.

86. E: 79.

87. Cf. E:79 n. 11.

88. The ongoing transformation of Gustaf-Konrad illustrates the principle of individual self-realization through participation in and action for the community.

but passive in the world. Mickiewicz, in contrast, expressly affirmed the world,[89] and made the battle of faith a matter of activity in this world. The patriotic struggle required an ethic of self-sacrifice, and a lifetime of spiritual labor in and for this world. Believing in the power of the word, he was yet convinced of the need to move from word to deed, to act in the real world. Thus Mickiewicz anticipates Bonhoeffer's affirmation of "the natural," his rejection of inwardness, and his emphasis on active faith and costly grace.

Finally, à Kempis, by declaring conscience independent of the world, established "the autonomy of the spiritual individual." He also saw inspiration as "independent from life." This idealistic, a-historical approach promotes the autonomy of religion from the world instead of the autonomy of the world from religion. Mickiewicz transferred spiritual autonomy to the community, making inspiration "dependent on participation in the communal bond." While this autonomy has little to do with the autonomy of a world come of age, it is analogous to Bonhoeffer's insistence that the church is where the spiritual community hears God's word in order to proclaim it to the world by word and deed. Mickiewicz's Philomatic community, his sectarian Circle of God's Cause, and his Polish Legion were all intended to model the future Polish society. It is not far in principle to Bonhoeffer's vision of the Church as that place where the world can see Christ taking shape, indeed can see itself as it is called and meant to be.

Bonhoeffer insisted that obedience and freedom can only be realized together through responsible action. While his critique focuses more on the German tendency to make obedience independent of freedom, Mickiewicz tended increasingly towards the other danger of making freedom independent of obedience. Bonhoeffer describes this well, when he comments that, "making obedience independent would lead to Kant's ethic of duty, making freedom independent to a romantic ethic of genius."[90] Though Mickiewicz's fellow-poet and competitor for the "rule of souls" Słowacki provides a more crystalline example of the "romantic ethic of genius," Mickiewicz too is guilty of glorifying the role of his poetic and real-life messiah figures.

---

89. Cf. above all *Master Thaddeus*.
90. E: 288.

Resistance and Martyrdom

Bonhoeffer in *Ethics* rejected evaluating movements, ideas, or events in terms of "success" or "failure." This polemical stance, versus the success of Hitler's war machine on the one hand and Nietzsche's accusation that Christianity glorifies failure on the other,[91] was grounded theologically upon Jesus Christ, in whom God has judged and reconciled humanity with himself. Bonhoeffer's words warn against passing judgement on specific resistance efforts simply because they were unsuccessful. Here de Gruchy, in describing Bonhoeffer's dialogical view of providence whereby human beings participate in making history, adds the caveat that "There is no guarantee of success; it is rather a calling to accountability and deputyship."[92] One need not give blanket approval to all Polish demonstrations, conspiracies, and uprisings to question whether Solidarity's historical victory would have been possible without them.

On the other hand, Bonhoeffer as church activist and conspirator sought to make well-informed, intelligent decisions regarding the means of resistance and their potential outcome. The romantics' belief in the power of the spirit over matter, where matter took the concrete form of guns and weapons, did lead to many rash acts of resistance and uprisings. In contrast, the consistent choice of the Polish opposition movement to reject armed confrontation and violence, and to concentrate on building an independent civil society, was based on their pragmatic reading of past history and present geo-political realities. Through their efforts, the tradition of Polish messianism that recognized one's enemies as fellow human beings, and which sought if possible their joint liberation and not their death, bore fruit in the Round Table talks of 1989 that led to a negotiated replacement of Poland's communist regime by a free and independent government. As Michnik and Mazowiecki freely acknowledge, many mistakes were made along the way. Yet the story, for all its imperfect characters and less than ideal events, is still of mythical proportions.[93]

---

91. I.e., as a mechanism of revenge and power grabbing on the part of the weaker members of society.

92. de Gruchy, *Bonhoeffer and South Africa*, 62.

93. Praising the Round Table is politically incorrect in many Polish political salons today. Yet in this author's opinion, history will eventually judge in favor of Wałęsa, Mazowiecki, and Kuroń.

Bonhoeffer's reflections on success and failure helpfully critique the Polish martyr complex that glorified suffering and death, and which led at times to a passive attitude that bears suffering in this world in hope either for a messianic deliverer, or for a better life in the world to come. To what extent did messianism idealize suffering and foster passivity? A powerful expression of "romantic maximalism"[94] is found in Mickiewicz's poem, "To a Polish Mother," which exhorted Polish women to raise their children to know pain and suffering, which together with exile and death will be their patriotic lot. Sobolewski's story and Father Peter's vision in *Forefathers' Eve*, Part III, ennoble Poland's sufferings, raising them to the level of national sacraments through comparison with Christ's passion. In Father Peter's vision, hope comes not from acting responsibly in the world, but from the appearance of a messianic liberator. Mickiewicz and his epigones praised those who gave their lives for the nation and its freedom. Thus a cult of martyrdom developed, whose power is still felt today in the morbid pleasure Poles often display in recounting their history of suffering.

While Bonhoeffer knew that responsible actions may lead to suffering or death, he insisted that these are not be sought but rather accepted as the possible consequences of one's vicarious representative action. In the face of danger, prepared if need be for death, Bonhoeffer still longed to live, to be reunited with his family, friends, and fiancée, to finish his *Ethics*, and to contribute to the rebuilding of Christianity in Germany and throughout Europe. To be fair to Mickiewicz, while many have held the eschatological visions of *Forefathers' Eve*, Part III, to encourage passivity, this interpretation requires isolating these passages from the overall context and message of the book. As was argued in chapter 3, Father Peter's vision was intended to motivate and sustain responsible action, much as Bonhoeffer's faith in providence motivated him to live and work in the real world. Furthermore, it was argued above that at the end of the book it is Konrad who must learn how to live in this world, to love real people, and to struggle for justice alongside them. In support of this thesis is the poet's own insistence on the congruence of word and deed, which led him towards action to change the world, not towards escaping the world through quietism or mysticism.

The choice to engage in active resistance leaves open the question regarding the means of resistance. As Clements notes, Bethge's biogra-

---

94. Cf. Kolbuszewski, *Literatura wobec historii*, 47.

phy of Bonhoeffer raised some major ethical issues concerning one who had previously been seen as morally unambiguous. Did Bonhoeffer's "involvement in the 'great masquerade of evil'"[95] compromise the integrity of this modern "Christian martyr"? Polish messianism raised similar questions; e.g., does Konrad Wallenrod, with his dissemblance, assumed identity, and "betrayal" of the Teutonic Knights, provide a Christian model of resistance?

For generations Mickiewicz's works served as a crash course in resistance. "Ode to Youth," "A Pilgrim's Prayer," and the "List of Rules" call for "honorable" struggle on the battlefield, which had been codified and "Christianized" in the rules of knightly combat. Moral ambiguity appears in other works, as when Wallenrod resorts to deceit and treachery, when the representative "Polish Mother" raises her sons as conspirators, and when Gustaf-Konrad issues his vampire-like call for vengeance. Mickiewicz's Wallenrod clearly felt the loss of personal unity and the resulting experience of being torn between competing ethical demands. As Siwicka explains, "in the name of faithfulness, he must be unfaithful. It is a tragic conflict."[96] It would be anachronistic here to claim parallels in Mickiewicz's work to Bonhoeffer's appeal to recovered unity in Christ. Nevertheless, there are hints that point in that direction, for instance in Wallenrod's statement that "duty, despair and God's will drive me into the field."[97] Wallenrod felt that his recourse to deceit was both "cursed," and according to God's will. While he does not yet sense the recovered unity that overcomes the tension being competing loyalties and conflicting principles, he is not paralyzed by them, but chooses to act according to what he perceives to be obedience to God's will. This approaches Bonhoeffer's idea of the "deed of free responsibility." In *Sentences and Comments*, Mickiewicz sought to overcome the sacred-profane dichotomy through setting one's will towards God. As argued in chapter 3, this decision was the source of Mickiewicz's ethics and his patriotism.

Poles knew that those who lie may become liars, though who practice deceit may become deceitful, those who employ terror in the fight for freedom may become terrorists instead of free human beings.

---

95. Clements, *Patriotism for Today*, 19.
96. Siwicka, *Romantyzm*, 39.
97. Mickiewicz, *Powieści poetyckie*, 93.

Michnik recently summarized the ethical decisions faced by Poles from the time of Mickiewicz to the opposition movement of his own day:

> We constantly faced the dilemma: which police [documents] to sign, and which refuse to sign; whether to join a conspiracy or act legally; emigrate or remain in the country; get involved in conspiracies and uprisings or choose the path of conciliation or organic work; ostracize people on the other side of the barricade or continue to undertake hopeless attempts at dialogue? We asked each other: where are the limits of the cunning game with the enemy, and where are the borders of compromise? At different times we answered these questions differently. And we were often wrong.[98]

Bonhoeffer, who asked himself and his fellow conspirators: "Are we still of any use?," defended the need to make concrete choices, which cannot be determined casuistically, and which often require choosing between good and best, or even between bad and worse. Wallenrod accepted the responsibility to act, to actively resist evil and oppression. Perhaps he too entrusted his literary "venture of responsibility" to God who alone could judge him? Barańczak, commenting on Bonhoeffer's willingness to "dirty" his hands, considered this even more heroic than his defense of the independence and purity of the church community during the period of the "Church Struggle."

Pluralism, Dialogue, and Reconciliation

The pluralistic vision of Jagiellonian Poland, realized in varying degrees, included freedom of religion and equal rights for the gentry regardless of ethnic background. The May 3rd Constitution of 1791, which granted civil rights to city dwellers, also foresaw their gradual extension to the peasants. The progressive integration of society, including the Jewish population, continued until the fall of the January Uprising in 1863. Yet by today's standards there was much to be desired. Women were largely restricted to matters of home and family. Peasants had no legal rights, and many were little more than indentured servants. Civil war in the Ukraine left the Commonwealth vulnerable to the inroads of Germany and Russia. Following the golden age of tolerance in the fifteenth and sixteenth centuries, religious and ethnic minorities were increasingly isolated and ostracized. How did messianism shape attitudes towards

---

98. Michnik, "Rana na czole Adama Mickiewicza," 19.

cultural, ethnic, and religious pluralism in this complex society? Did it promote dialogue or impose ideology? Did it foster communication or incite confrontation? Did it seek social justice or support the rich and powerful?

Woronicz and Mickiewicz both match up favorably to Bonhoeffer's openness to ethnic and religious "others". Although Woronicz polemically idealized the Slavic peoples, his vision of Poland included Poles, Lithuanians, and other ethnic and national groups. Religiously, it incorporated Protestants, Orthodox Christians, and Jews along with Catholics.[99] Woronicz freely acknowledged the contribution of non-Catholic and non-ethnically Polish citizens to the nation's cultural heritage. However, his inclusive view of Polish society was undermined by the sacramental character of Poland's "covenant" with God, which appears theologically to exclude non-Catholics from the nation, or at best grants them status as "strangers and foreigners" in the land. Woronicz did not exploit this aspect of his system, but neither did he resolve the tension it introduced between pluralistic and sacramentally defined national visions. Bonhoeffer's theology of sociality avoids these shortcomings.

Mickiewicz's vision of Polishness was even more inclusive, and virtually free of nationalism, racism, sectarianism, chauvinism and anti-Semitism. He perceived Poland's struggle for independence as an effort to liberate all European nations from their oppressive rulers. Nevertheless, Mickiewicz did provide ample material for the forces of chauvinism to turn to their cause. His writings, especially the *Books of the Nation and the Polish Pilgrimage*, present Poland in highly idealized terms as the "innocent victim" of foreign treachery and aggression. Many of his readers transferred his attacks on unjust rulers to other nations as a whole, and came to perceive foreigners as hostile aggressors. Personally aware of Poland's many faults, Mickiewicz seldom expressed them in his poetry. His polemical reticence contributed to the defensive attitude displayed by many Poles today, who over-react to any criticism of their nation by foreigners, without asking whether it is well-founded or baseless. Michnik hits a better balance when he writes:

> In the biography of Mickiewicz there was the light of heroism and the shadow of one enslaved by the Czar's empire. In Polish

---

99. If asked, he would have likely included the few thousand Moslem Tatars, descendents of scouts and soldiers who were loyal to the Polish Crown.

history there was the brightness of heroism and the love of freedom, but there was also the darkness of enslavement, compromise and capitulation. For this reason reflection on the life and work of Mickiewicz is a look into the depths of Poland's heritage.[100]

Polish messianism envisioned radical social reforms, beginning with Woronicz, who campaigned actively for peasants to be granted full rights as citizens. Mickiewicz was even more insistent on the incorporation of the members of all classes into the socio-political nation. His "List of Rules" founded the future Poland on ethnic and religious pluralism, and granted equal civil rights to all.[101] He believed that since God was on the side of the poor and oppressed, Christians could not serve the interests of the ruling class. The major practical problem with the messianic program of integrating members of all social classes into one nation was that not enough nobles agreed with their vision, and not enough commoners believed in such "noble" intentions.

While Bonhoeffer's work in this area was limited, theologically in his prison fiction he sought to address issues of class and social justice through exploring the ethical encounter between privileged and working class members of society. This is significant, for according to Bonhoeffer it is through such I-You encounters that individuals become persons. These literary attempts bring to mind the sermons Woronicz addressed directly to peasants and workers,[102] thereby acknowledging them as persons, not an idealized or amorphous mass ("the people"). In *Master Thaddeus*, Mickiewicz proposed bringing equal rights to all, not by debasing the nobles but by ennobling the peasants.[103] The tradition of equal rights and social justice for all was continued by Poland's early socialist movement, and later found its expression among the Polish opposition movement and Solidarity. It is therefore ironic that the Polish Pope John Paul II oversaw the suppression of liberation theology. Like Bonhoeffer, his major attention, drawn in his case from the paradigm

---

100. Michnik, "Rana na czole Adama Mickiewicza," 18.

101. His sensitive treatment in *Master Thaddeus* of Jankiel, the Jewish inn-keeper provides one of many illustrations.

102. Cf. Szczypa, *Jan Paweł Woronicz*, 126

103. In contrast, the Soviet strategy was to bring even the petty bourgeoisie down to the level of the proletariat.

of Eastern Europe's battle with Soviet-style socialism, was directed towards freedom and civil rights rather than social justice.

If messianism has fostered national chauvinism, this is largely due to its reception by those who deny or twist its Christian and humanistic ideals. Yet messianism has many heirs who are true to its original spirit, who recognize with Mickiewicz that "Germans are also human." This is particularly evident when it comes to the practice of dialogue, and the process of national forgiveness and reconciliation. Selected examples are sufficient to demonstrate this claim. Chapter 4 documented the rapprochement between secular and Catholic intellectuals that began around 1968, and led to the rise of the Solidarity Movement. Out of this arose the "Round Table" discussions of 1989. Following the reunification of Germany, Prime Minister Mazowiecki formalized Polish-German rapprochement by signing the agreement recognizing the borders between the nations on the Oder River. In the first case Bonhoeffer's influence has already been shown. Regarding the second and third events, Mazowiecki acknowledges Bonhoeffer's influence on his own political thinking and decisions.[104]

Another singular event was the letter from the Polish Bishops to the German Bishops, which included the memorable phrase, "We forgive, and ask for forgiveness." This letter brought harsh criticism and reprisals from the Communist Government, but began the process of German-Polish reconciliation. This letter follows in the tradition of Woronicz's call for national repentance and his confession of the nation's guilt,[105] and Mickiewicz's rejection in *Forefathers' Eve*, Part III, of vengeance upon the nation's enemies. The Bishops' letter realizes the spirit of Bonhoeffer's own confession of the sins of his church and nation. Another case in point is Poland's public support for democracy and the right of Ukrainians to choose their own government during the 2004 "Orange Revolution" in the Ukraine. Polish demonstrations of solidarity, and mediation efforts by Polish leaders in Kiev and Brussels did much to reconcile the two nations. Here Poland lived up to its messianic ideals. Finally, since 1989 Poles have worked hard to come to grips with their nation's long but troubled relationship with its Jewish citizens, to

---

104. In a private conversation with this author. Note also his comments on non-political politicians, discussed in chapter 4.

105. Mickiewicz does not help here, for his vision of Poland denied national sin, and hence the need for confession and repentance.

apologize for the nation's own sins, and to keep alive the memory of the Holocaust perpetrated by Germany's Nazi regime on what is now in large measure Polish soil. Added to this are numerous conferences and publications, the annual "March of the Living" at Auschwitz, and public confessions of national guilt towards the Jews by Poland's President and Primate. Significantly, the late Polish Pope John Paul II, the first Roman Pontiff to enter a synagogue, confessed the sins of the Roman Catholic Church against the Jews, and made a historic bridge-building pilgrimage to Israel.

Patriotism and Nationalism

Virtually everything written about Poland in this book could be subsumed under the rubric of patriotism. For Poles, patriotism was not a separate value alongside others, such as human rights, freedom, or respect and tolerance for other human beings. Rather they incorporated these and other values into their understanding of patriotism. As Woronicz declared, "Patriotism is a collection, or I might say the essence of all exalted virtues."[106] Polish messianism in particular offered a pluralistic, inclusive vision of the nation. Its version of Polish patriotism did not seek conquest or vengeance, but liberation and dialogue leading to reconciliation and a world where all would live together in peace. Since these issues have been covered above, this section will focus on the distinction made by Poles between "patriotism" and nationalism, the latter being understood pejoratively as intolerant, aggressive, xenophobic, and chauvinistic.

Konrad Wallenrod illustrates the dilemma faced by Polish romantic messianism. His faithfulness to one community required betraying another. Loving his nation meant hating its enemies. Acting on the nation's behalf, he denied his identity as a Christian and husband. Is it possible, Mickiewicz here seems to ask, to be a Christian and a patriot? Mickiewicz wrestles with this question by exploring Wallenrod's attempts to be true to his rediscovered Lithuanian identity.[107] Before considering his answer, the analysis of the influences that shaped

---

106. Woronicz, cited in Szczypa, *Jan Paweł Woronicz*, 126.

107. A literary mask for Poland, as everyone but the Russian censor who was later punished for letting *Konrad Wallenrod* be published recognized.

Bonhoeffer's attachment to his country[108] undertaken by Clements to critique British patriotism serves also as a helpful framework to analyze Polish patriotism.

To begin with Poles, like Bonhoeffer, owe much to their family ties and cultural upbringing. Woronicz emphasized the family in his catechetical endeavors, while the family's inestimable role as the guardian of the nation's spirit and culture is captured in Mickiewicz's epic, *Master Thaddeus*, and praised in his political writing. More recently Morawska compared Bonhoeffer's relationship to German culture to that of the Polish intelligentsia, who as "people-at-the-crossroads" faced a similar task of reinterpreting and passing on their culture's legacy to the post World War II generation. Nevertheless, the desire to understand and learn from the world beyond one's own backyard was characteristic both of the Bonhoeffer family and the Polish romantics.

Woronicz and Mickiewicz placed their hopes for the renewal of Poland and Europe in a revitalized Catholic Church; as argued above, Woronicz looked for a conservative restoration and Mickiewicz a radically reformed Christianity. In contrast, Bonhoeffer did not found his vision for post-war society on a renewal of Christendom, but on a church that witnessed to Christ and lived "for-others" through its words and deeds. However, while writing as Catholic Christians, Woronicz and Mickiewicz acknowledged the past and future place in Polish society of Protestants as well as Jews. In light of the inclusive, pluralistic character of the messianic tradition, coupled with the warning contained in Bonhoeffer's claim that the expulsion of the Jews from Europe was the expulsion of Christianity, it is ironic that many of today's self-proclaimed Polish "patriots" are attempting once again to place exclusive ethnic and religious boundaries around the nation.

Clements, suggesting that Great Britain is suffering a loss of her "national story," cites Archbishop Runcie: "An historian told me the other day that we had somehow lost confidence in the story of England. There was no national story of destiny to sustain us."[109] As argued above, Woronicz and Mickiewicz considered it their task to craft a national story for the Poland of their day. The same is true of the creators of

---

108. Discussed above in chapter 5.

109. Dr. Robert Runcie, address to the National Free Church Federal Council Congress, *Free Church Chronicle*, Summer 1981, 20, quoted in Clements, *Patriotism for Today*, 11

Polish citizens' society. However, after 1989 Poland's national story fractured into several competing versions, few if any of which offered a clear vision of Poland's future. Following the parliamentary and presidential elections of 2005, nationalism appeared to be gaining in strength. Much like the end of the nineteenth century, when anti-Semitism entered the realm of polite conversation and public debate, the language of exclusion, xenophobia, and chauvinism was once again released into Poland's political and cultural mainstream. The dangers inherent in this trend are illustrated by British nationalist Enoch Powell, who as Clements notes appealed to "patriotism and national identity." He writes:

> It is Powell's constant use of the alien concept and the threat imagery which reveals the basis of his peculiar "patriotism" . . . To this, it can only be said that a "patriotism" which is based so largely on its emotive appeal to fear at the supposed threat, is utterly hollow at the centre . . . A true patriotism will speak first of what it believes the people to be.[110]

There are many Enoch Powells (as Clements portrayed him) today in Poland, who appeal to the frustrations of those left behind by Poland's transformation. The "threats" cited include politicians who have "stolen" Poland's wealth, post-communism and/or Western liberalism, secularization, the traditional threats to Polish sovereignty (i.e., Germany and Russia), and the godless European Union that threatens Poland's regained sovereignty. Given the recent political successes of these "patriotic" groups, their language of protest and popularity cannot be taken lightly. While many of the social problems they address are real, such parties are long on critique and short on constructive programs, and their respective visions of Poland are populist, reactionary, xenophobic, and at times racist. To answer their challenge requires more than proposals for how to improve the economy, reform health care, create more jobs, and win the next FIFA World Cup. More useful in this regard is a "national story" defining a modern, Polish nation, critically aware of its historical heritage, secure in its place in the world, and confident of its vision for the future. Clements' words, addressed to Great Britain in 1984, apply equally well to Poland in the twenty-first century: "We need to find our way to a love that can be both affectionate and critical,

---

110. Clements, *Patriotism for Today*, 1.

devoted and honest, avoiding equally a cynical indifference to our future, and the fantasies of archaic, imperialistic or racist patriotism."[111]

Although Polish messianism made love for the fatherland the greatest of all virtues, such patriotism was understood to flow out of one's love for God and to lead to love for other nations. As Woronicz wrote, "he who is not obedient to God cannot be faithful to the fatherland, his friends or the entire society."[112] As noted in chapter 2, his reversal of the pattern "person—citizen—Christian" leads one from Christ through love for one's country to a love for all human beings. Mickiewicz also considered the battle for political freedom for all the nations "the current fighting cause of Christianity."[113] The victory Father Peter was promised in his vision *Forefathers' Eve*, Part III, was over the kings, not the nations, and Mickiewicz's poem "To Muscovite Friends" shows his solidarity with their dreams of freedom and their sufferings at the hands of the Tsar. Furthermore, his rejection in the *Books of the Polish Nation* of "political parity," combined with his call for a federated Europe where individuals and nations would recognize each other as fellow human beings and work together as equals, recalls Bonhoeffer's declaration that peace cannot be secured by an arms race, or by a "balance of power" that seeks safety and "security" instead of true peace. For his part, Michnik considers "true patriotism" as one of the humanist values that discover their source in Christ.

There are other, rival forms of Polish patriotism, some of them quite dark. But the view of Brodziński, Mickiewicz, Michnik, Mazowiecki, and the Polish Episcopate boasts an ancient, unquestionably Polish pedigree. The brotherhood of nations is a homegrown vision, popularized and exported by Polish messianism, not an idea imported from abroad or smuggled into Polish political life by whatever "conspiracy" of Jews, masons, liberals and communists today's self-proclaimed "true Poles" care to fabricate. Instead, it is their own militant nationalistic vision that owes its genesis and persistent ethos to social Darwinism and the rise of European fascism. Today, a recovery of the inclusive Jagiellonian vision of Poland is needed, over against the exclusive view of Piast Poland that seeks to impose its "ideal" vision of Polak-Katolik on the pluralistic nation made up of real human beings. Those who rework Poland's

111. Ibid., 15.
112. Woronicz, cited in Rejman, *Jan Paweł Woronicz*, 166.
113. Kleiner, *Mickiewicz*, 240.

national myths to serve such ends falsely claim the mantle of Woronicz and Mickiewicz, or the blessing of the last great Polish romantic, Karol Wojtyła. As Mazowiecki wrote following the late John Paul II's funeral, "he managed to make the great values of the Polish culture, in particular the Jagiellonian tradition of tolerance and thinking in categories of openness and respect for others, an element of his mission that had a world-wide scope."[114] Archbishop Józef Życiński adds that "respect for human beings redeemed by Christ was something fundamental in the teaching of John Paul II . . . Therefore one needs to remind those attracted to populist slogans of the Pope's teaching, that you cannot build a civilization of love upon either a new form of the class struggle or the program of any party."[115] Polish messianism aimed, in its own way, at building such a civilization of love; Bonhoeffer, I believe, helps us see how it might be rightly conceived, which is a first step towards bringing it about.

---

114. Mazowiecki, "Głosy po śmierci Papieża," 1.
115. Życiński, "Bądźmy wierni papieskiemu stylowi," 19.

7

A Post-Messianic, Bonhofferian Polish Alternative to Secularism and Fundamentalism

ALTHOUGH MY AIM WAS NEVER TO PROVIDE A RUNNING COMMENTARY on Polish politics, the logic of this study in Polish messianism, including the use of Bonhoeffer to critique both messianism and the critical appropriation of its legacy by the Polish opposition movement between 1968 and 1989, led to a brief discussion of the Polish political landscape following the victory of Solidarity in the 1989 elections, influenced as it was for better and for worse by the persistent myths of romantic messianism. Much has taken place in Poland since my dissertation was completed in 2005, including the early parliamentary elections held in 2007 that led to a change of government. The original conclusion has therefore been expanded into a final, seventh chapter, which brings the story of messianism up to date, and proposes the building blocks of a post-messianic, Bonhofferian alternative to two current trends in Polish religious and political culture; secularism and fundamentalism.

Poland's recovery of national self-determination in 1989 brought both opportunities and challenges. In just a few short years, Poland has established viable democratic institutions, witnessed the development of a dynamic and diverse free press, reformed its economic and banking system, and become a member of NATO and the European Union. Such rapid political, social and economic transformation in a highly religious former member of the Soviet bloc makes Poland an important study in the process of secularization, which there goes hand-in-hand with fundamentalist reactions and the de-secularization of schools and public institutions.

The question, recently posed at the X International Bonhoeffer Congress in Prague regarding the potential and promise of a middle way or third road between secularism and fundamentalism is relevant to Polish society as a whole, but is of special urgency for Poles who seek individually and collectively to follow Christ in their concrete *sitz im Leben*. For Polish Christians and Christianity, the failure to respond to this question in a positive and constructive manner can only result in a self-imposed sentence of increasing irrelevance and isolation. One result of that failure is already visible, i.e., the emergence of the relatively new (to Poland) phenomenon of religio-political fundamentalism,[1] which in its own idiosyncratic way draws on the legacy of Polish messianism to further develop and promote the exclusive, "Polak-Katolik" vision of "Piast Poland." As will be argued, this new brand of Polish fundamentalism arose in part due to the failure by Christian communities in Poland to respond in an effective and engaging manner to the challenge of the rapid secularization of Polish society. As Father Michał Paluch wrote recently, "The future of the Church in Poland will depend in large part on the manner and extent to which it manages to participate in the process of modernization. The youngest generation will judge the Church stringently and ruthlessly in this area."[2] Tadeusz Bartoś adds in a similar spirit:

> We live in a civilization, in which the Church risks a great deal by resigning from change, On the one hand we have the liberal world, with freedom of speech and action, ease of movement, and against it there stands a centralized, almost military church structure. People who are children of this age won't find a place for themselves in this structure, they do not understand this mentality, they feel stifled in this environment. The Gospel does not deserve such negative advertising.[3]

Agreeing with Bartoś that the Gospel does not need such advertising, the lessons drawn here from the dialogue between messianism and Bonhoeffer are offered as resources to aid the efforts of the present-day heirs and practitioners, both "religious" and "secular," of the inclusive vision of "Jagiellonian Poland." They may also encourage those of other

---

1. *The Fundamentalism Project*, a massive five volume work edited by Martin Marty and R. Scott Appleby, and published between 1993–1995, found no significant phenomena or movement present in Poland at that time that met the criteria used to identify the diverse forms of fundamentalism studied throughout the world.

2. Paluch, "Are we the Titanic?" 17.

3. Tadeusz Bartoś, "I Am Not Leaving the Church," 25.

ethnic, religious, political, and national traditions who share similar convictions and commitments. Most of all though, they are addressed to those who would follow the incarnate, crucified and risen Christ where he lives in "the middle of the village."[4]

Fundamentalism and Secularism in Poland Today

The changing face of secularism in Poland

The secular segment of Polish society had its historic roots among the intelligentsia, who generally speaking shared the values of European humanism,[5] and the left side of the political spectrum, whose program and sympathies can be described for the most part as democratic socialism. Today, these traditional secularists find their ranks swelled by growing numbers of individuals with a secular mindset. The emergence of these new secularists can be explained only in part by appealing to widespread access to the internet and other media, the growth of consumerism, or the spread of "liberal" values. They are not characterized primarily by their relationship to the Church; while some would consider themselves agnostics or atheists, their ranks include large numbers of Catholics (and Lutherans and Baptists) who are just as likely to be practicing as non-practicing. In a country where nearly 2/3 of the population (over 60%) still attends church on Sunday, a study carried out in 1998 by Tomka showed that only one in five Poles (19.5%) considered themselves "deeply religious," whereas three out of four (77%) classified themselves more ambiguously as "religious to a certain degree," "neither religious nor non-religious," or "somewhat non-religious."[6] Neither is their political stance decisive, although on the opposite end of the spectrum a majority of religious fundamentalists are aligned with political groups on the far right. What most of these new secularists have in common is the sense that religion is irrelevant to their everyday lives; many "religious" people are thus in reality practical secularists, who rel-

---

4. LPP, letter of April 30, 1944, 282.

5. The "religious" intelligentsia in Poland was and remains a larger and more influential group than in most European countries. Among them are many who can perhaps be best described as Christian humanists.

6. Tomka, "Religion, Church, State and Civil Society in East-Central Europe," 45. For a more recent assessment of these trends, I await the data to be published this fall by Tomka and his colleagues from their recent sociological study concerning secularization and religion in Central Europe.

egate faith and spirituality to the sphere of private religious experience and/or public ritual.

The historic response of traditional religious and political authorities in Poland to secularism and modernity is an interesting study in its own right. As was argued in earlier chapters, the main reaction of messianism to the process of secularization was a reaffirmation of Christian orthodoxy, what Bonhoeffer would call a conservative restoration attempt. A few Don Quixotes preferred a romantic *salto mortale* back to an idealized pre-modern or revitalized Constantinian synthesis. A similar failure to proactively respond to modernism characterized Polish Churches, whether Roman Catholic, Orthodox or Protestant. During the interwar period, the most ambitious attempt to defend both nation and church against the inroads of modernism was the *mésalliance* between the political right, which embraced nationalism and flirted openly with anti-Semitism, and a certain segment of the Catholic Church. However, we must also note here the efforts of Christians to stand on the side of the poor and oppressed, and work for freedom and social justice, as documented by Bohdan Cywiński in his 1974 book *Rodowody niepokórnych*.[7]

Following the Second World War, Poland's communist regime adopted a secularist ideology, and embarked on a program for the progressive secularization of society. In this context, as Górniak-Kocikowska notes, "To battle communism meant, therefore, to battle the danger of secularization as well."[8] Paluch notes the Church's rational, apologetic response to communist ideology, but argues correctly that the most significant contribution it made in this period was to create a space where people could be free. In this way the Church won the good-will of the people.[9] In the context of a strong Roman Catholic Church, which made room for Polish cultural, artistic, intellectual and political expressions and aspirations, and which promoted and took part in dialogue between various groups within Polish society, secularization was perceived more as a political than sociological threat to religion.[10] This allowed plenty of room for non-fundamentalist

---

7. Cywiński, *Rodowody niepokornych*, 1974.

8. Górniak-Kocikowska, "Tensions in Poland," 12.

9. Paluch, "Are we the Titanic?" 19.

10 E.g., at Roman Catholic Parish of God's Mercy in Warsaw during the 1980's, there were art exhibits, film discussion clubs, literature and poetry readings, and explicitly political gatherings. Once I attended a religious meeting there, to learn that Lech

responses to the State's secularist program. Here indeed we might say that the Church heard and obeyed the concrete Word of God to his people.

Nor did religious fundamentalism arise immediately after the fall of communism. Secularization did not appear to be a big threat in 1989. After all, the Pope was Polish. In fact, de-secularization seemed to be the trend of the day. Religion was reintroduced into the schools, a reference to Christianity was inserted in the preamble to the Polish Constitution, and priests were called upon to bless newly opened bridges and shopping centers. Yet technological gains, growing media access, ease of foreign travel, and Poland's entrance into the European Union brought new secularizing pressures that could not be denied. Paluch notes the inadequate response of the Church to this challenge:

> Unfortunately, the Church succumbed to the temptation that appeared after 1989 to cash in the credits from the past; it did not embark quickly or consequently enough on the work of building an intellectual tradition that would be able to effectively engage with the currents of the modern and post-modern world.[11]

As Paluch goes on to add, "One who today must repeatedly achieve the choice to believe can rarely count on intellectual help within our churches." Such help seems just as rare within the Protestant community. Thus, over the past two decades it is not just secularization, but also the failure of Polish Christianity to engage proactively with (post)modernity, and to present a vital alternative to secularism, which has led certain prominent conservative religious and political leaders to embrace fundamentalism.

Space allows for only a brief description of Poland's new religio-political fundamentalists. In the discussion below it proved impossible to avoid reference to specific individuals and groups without falling into useless and unsupported generalizations. In particular, the Law and Justice Party (PiS) and *Radio Maryja* are identified as major players in the rise of Polish fundamentalism because they represent its mainstream, not its extremes. This choice does not imply that fundamentalism is confined to these organizations,[12] nor that this is the only or best paradigm suitable to describe them. It is not a blanket criticism of their

---

Wałęsa and his advisors were meeting in the room next door.

11. Paluch, "Are we the Titanic?" 19.

12. E.g., Protestant fundamentalists might support PiS, but would not identify themselves with *Radio Maryja*.

programs, policies or values,[13] nor is it an endorsement of Poland's other political parties. Nor does it claim that all politicians associated with PiS, all the clergy, employees and guests of *Radio Maryja*, together with all their supporters and listeners are fundamentalists. Rather it shows how closely attitudes, actions, and agendas that are characteristic of these organizations and their leaders correspond to major parameters employed by contemporary scholars to describe fundamentalism.

As with the rest of this study, this chapter is highly contextual, and reflects this author's own experience of living in Poland for the last twenty-seven years. Though it is hoped that readers in other contexts will find it informative and useful, they are cautioned against a hasty, uncritical or literal transfer of the terminology and concepts used to describe Polish fundamentalism to their own situation.

Moral Crusades; the End Justifies the Means

Poland's new fundamentalists see secularism as a threat to traditional Polish society and values, and even its national existence. For those who define Polishness ethnically and religiously, any perceived deviation from the "Polak-Katolik" myth is seen as a betrayal of and threat to the Polish nation. Apart from more serious consequences, this leads to such malicious pettiness as calling the late Czesław Miłosz a "Polish-language" poet, i.e., one who writes in Polish, but is not a true Pole at heart.

Poland's fundamentalist leaders, who have embarked on a crusade to defend both "morality" and "patriotism,"[14] wrap themselves proudly in the combined mantle of flag and cross. They believe they represent the truth both politically and religiously, and equate their own cause with that of the nation. Jarosław Kaczyński, the head of PiS, is a regular guest and speaker at the annual religious pilgrimage to Częstochowa of the followers of *Radio Maryja*. In 2007 he declared, "Today Poland is here!" In 2008 he was greeted with the words, "Welcome to this small patch of free Poland!"[15] The obvious implication of these remarks is that

---

13. In fact, little or no reference is made to their political policies and religious programs per se.

14. This does not imply that all or even most defenders of morality and patriotism are fundamentalists.

15. *Gazeta Wyborcza*, July 14, 2008, 11.

true Poland is under religious oppression and political occupation by those who do not sympathize with PiS and *Radio Maryja*.

Though PiS claims allegiance to the rule of law, their belief that they occupy the moral high ground serves to justify the means they choose to advance their aims, which include insinuations and personal attacks, as well as what appear to be unsupported criminal charges brought against their political opponents (or their spouses and grandfathers).[16] In a recent article Ludwik Dorn, once one of J. Kaczyński's closest advisors and still a member of PiS, but likely to soon be expelled from the party for his criticism of Kaczyński, explains this mentality.

> In opinion of [Dorn], over the last two or three years, and particularly since the election defeat, Jarosław Kaczyński underwent an evolution, that led him to a "completely mistaken intellectual-political analysis. For him the government and PO[17] are enemies of the Polish nation, therefore there is no possibility of conducting any kind of political maneuvering.
>
> If one defines the situation like Mr. Jarosław Kaczyński, this mobilizes the party, and through it the electorate, for a total war. According to this logic politically extreme unethical means, such as have been applied towards me, are justified."[18]

As one commentator wrote of the years that PiS spent in office, "instead of a crackdown on crime, we saw brutal tactics employed against court judges, the Constitutional Tribunal, and disobedient prosecutors."[19] The case of the Constitutional Tribunal is perhaps most revealing. During the days when PiS was in power, the Tribunal ruled that cer-

---

16. At this date, several charges against PiS officials over the misuse of power while they were in office are still in the courts. Regardless of how individual cases are resolved, many see an evident pattern of PiS officials and ministers bending the law to suit their purposes. In reply, PiS claims that these charges, as well as recent decisions by prosecuting attorneys and judges to drop cases initiated against their opponents when PiS was in power, are proof that the courts and prosecutors are now being used against them by the current ruling party. That may be the case, or perhaps it is just blustering to hide one's own political sins. Either way, it provides another example of the belief in the conspiracy theories that is noted below. While we await the verdict in these investigations, what is telling is that PiS officials know in advance who is guilty and who is not, and any court decision to the contrary is therefore treated automatically as proof of political manipulation by their opponents.

17. I.e., Platforma Obywatelska, the major political party in Poland's present ruling coalition.

18. Dorn, "PiS to nie Kaczyński."

19. Kurski, "Co nam dało państwo PiS."

tain bills passed by the Parliament were unconstitutional. The leaders of PiS suggested openly that since the court disagreed with them and their interpretation of the law, it should be changed. On one occasion, just two hours before a key verdict was to be issued, Jarosław Kaczyński expressed "his hope that the judges would not apply 'legal circus tricks,'" and implied that the Tribunal was plotting with the political opponents of PiS. Kaczyński had previously described the Tribunal judges as, "disgusting, cowardly opportunists," "just another bunch of wise men," and part of the "sham-elite,"[20] who looks out for their own interests instead of defending the laws of the nation. This time, he threatened, "it will be necessary to consider very seriously a new structure of the Tribunal." When the constitution and court gets in his way, the head of the Law and Justice Party wants to dismantle the established legal system of government checks and balances. As Kurski comments on this incident,

> One cannot qualify the words of the Prime Minister differently than as an attempt to exert political pressure on the independent constitutional court. Not the first attempt, but another in a series of attempts. The Prime Minister is accustoming us to the fact, that he undermines the legal culture of the state. We must not agree to this.[21]

Two qualities that were shared by messianism and Bonhoeffer, and which Poland's modern moral crusaders appear to have lost or forgotten, include a sensitivity to the complexity of life's moral choices and dilemmas, and the acute awareness that the means chosen to promote one's cause has a deep and often lasting impact both on one's own character and integrity, as well as on the reception of one's values and ensuing support for one's cause by others. When respect for the law is promoted by religio-political sheriffs who take the law into their own hands and bend it to fit their personal or political needs, when justice is demanded without a willingness to extend grace and forgiveness to the penitent, when truth is defended by those who fail to display love and humility, there law, justice, and truth are devalued, and their errant knight-defenders discredited.

---

20. Orig. *łże-elita*, lit. "lying-elite," a term coined by J. Kaczyński and used by PiS to describe politicians and members of the intelligentsia whose arguments and program, in their opinion, consist mainly of lies and propaganda.

21. Kurski, "Trybunał Konstytucyjny niewygodny dla premiera."

To be truly set free from the ghosts of the past, Poles who want to know the truth about their history, their nation, their party, their church, or themselves must be willing to surrender the moral high ground claimed by Mickiewicz, even though this claim is bolstered by Poland's recent history as a victim of foreign aggression and totalitarianism. Like Woronicz and Bonhoeffer, they should remember and honor the best of their nation's high ideals and remarkable history, but also be ready to confess its failures, and especially the times it was on the side of tyranny and oppression. The same is true of individuals and churches. The gospel, political or no, rings truer and cuts deeper when it flows from the heart of a fellow (repentant) sinner than from the mouth of a self-righteous neighbor, preacher or politician.

The Mixture of Politics and Religion

During the Polish transition from communism to representative democracy, apart from a few missteps early on, the Roman Catholic Church has refrained from the temptation to support one political party, or to forge a formal alliance between cross and crown. Nevertheless, certain influential members of the clergy, including those identified with *Radio Maryja*, have closely aligned themselves with Poland's political conservatives and their more radical allies, and regularly promote attitudes that are nationalistic, populist, xenophobic, and even anti-Semitic in character. Despite being warned by the Polish Episcopate and the Vatican to avoid further political agitation and party politics, *Radio Maryja* continues its support for one political option.

Rather than criticizing such attitudes or shunning such support, officials of the recent ruling coalition led by PiS regularly appeared on *Radio Maryja* and its television station *Trwam* throughout their two-and-a-half years in power. Now, occupying minority seats in Parliament, they continue to court the support of *Radio Maryja*, to appear on its airwaves, and to attend its public gatherings as honored guests. As Kurski wrote just prior to the 2007 elections, "the alliance between the PiS and Radio Maryja continues . . . at the price of the government's consent to the radio station's anti-Semitism,"[22] adding a few lines later, "this

---

22. The leaders of PiS are not anti-Semites. Yet they continue to appear on *Radio Maryja* without criticizing or condemning its periodic anti-Semitic statements.

[i.e., PiS] government uses the altar for its own purposes without scruple."[23]

The way in which political leaders solicit and accept such support is as disturbing as the decision on the part of clergymen and influential representatives of the religious media to engage openly in party politics. Ironically, in 1992 it was J. Kaczyński who declared that the quickest way to a secular society in Poland was to establish a Christian Democratic Party. Fifteen years later he has accomplished just that, and his words are proving prophetic. His "moral crusade" is both foreign to what Bonhoeffer would consider authentic Christianity, and counterproductive of its own stated goal, i.e., to defend religion and public morality. This *mésalliance* of so-called conservative[24] politics and fundamentalist religion is turning the young and educated of society away from Christianity. Their reaction typically is, "If this is what it means to be a Christian, I want nothing to do with it." Many see no viable alternative but to embrace secularism.

The marriage of politics and religion is also expressed in the vision PiS shares with some Polish clergymen that Poland's calling is to aid in the re-Christianization of Europe. This *salto mortale* back to the medieval synthesis of Constantinian Christianity is a reincarnation of the messianic myths of the 19th century, and the tradition that called Poland the bulwark of Christianity. Górniak-Kucikowska concludes,

> As you can see, the Polish Politicians who try to "re-convert" Europe to Catholicism have some historic reasons for doing it. From their perspective, this is what Poland should be all about; and it should be Poland's current mission to save Europe from secularization.[25]

The issue here is not morality per se, nor religious leaders who speak to significant ethical issues and related government policies. Neither is it patriotism, nor even citizens and politicians who express clear views on public morality. The problem is legalistic, overbearing moral crusades, combined with a form of religious nationalism (or nationalistic religion) that identifies too closely the roles and responsibili-

23. Jarosław Kurski, "Co nam dało państwo PiS."

24. In many ways much of what passes as conservative or right-wing politics in Poland has more in common with populism, expensive social programs, high taxes, and governmental economic paternalism.

25. Gorniak-Kucikowska, "Tensions in Poland," 13.

ties of church and state, or even tries to resurrect the project of European Christendom, where power is shared and maintained by a coalition of mutual support and privilege between cross and crown. Here, it is fair to say that messianism, with its belief in the nation's divine calling and mission, and its vision of a Europe spiritually renewed and politically reunited, is responsible to no small degree for the blurring of the lines between faith and party politics, between church and state.

Yet along with its grand myths, the authors and architects of messianism called for morality in politics, and urged the Church to take a stand on pressing social and ethical issues. Bonhoeffer would concur on the Church's responsibility to speak and act, not just to defend its own privilege and integrity, but on behalf of human beings in general, and in particular those deprived of freedom, dignity and social justice. With regard to the government and politics, he held that the Church's role is to remind the state both of its responsibilities towards its citizens, and that it is not God.

The Cult of the Leader; the Politics of Fear; Conspiracy Theories

Poland's new fundamentalist groups are all built around a strong or charismatic leader.[26] Recently, a supporter of *Radio Maryja* was heard to exclaim, "Thank God for Father Rydzyk. Now that the Pope is dead, he is all we have left."[27] On the political side, fundamentalist leaders do not hide their disdain for the intelligentsia,[28] who for the most part find their attitudes, actions, and choice of political allies highly offensive. Yet like all leadership cults, they also patronize and disdain the common people whom they purportedly represent. One member of PiS is reported to have said about a smear campaign he was conducting prior to

---

26. I.e., Father Rydzyk of Radio Maryja, the Kaczyńscy brothers of PiS, Andrzej Lepper of the Self-Defense Party (Samoobrona) and Roman Giertych of the League of Polish Families (LPR). Giertych has since resigned (at least for now) from an active role in politics. Lepper should perhaps be classified more as a populist than fundamentalist, though he shares certain traits with the others.

27. The fact that there is a Pope today, albeit one of German descent, seems to have escaped her attention.

28. With the exception of course of those on the right side of the political spectrum, who support or sympathize with their party and program.

the last election, "The dimwitted plebs will buy it."[29] Their rhetoric often portrays the disadvantaged as helpless victims of ruthless exploitation, who need a modern-day Robin Hood, in the form of populist leaders and parties, to give back to them what the rich have taken. They proclaim "solidarity" with the disadvantaged, but rather than doing much to help them, dedicated the bulk of their time in office to exposing former communists and informers, or attacking their political opponents, many of whom were once fellow members of Solidarity and the Polish opposition movement.[30] Some seem driven by a personal desire for power, or are quick to remember every slight, real or imagined, which they have ever received. In what is not a minor fault, they take their image far too seriously, and seem unable to laugh at themselves. Rival leaders and legends of the anti-communist opposition, such as Lech Wałęsa or Adam Michnik, must be discredited. In the end, leaders who feel so threatened by other strong figures that they must attack and discredit them only reveal their own inferiority complexes and pettiness.

The practice of politics and religion by Poland's religio-political fundamentalists is based in large measure on fear, ranging from the fear of change and economic hardship to xenophobia. Their appeal to a variety of implied threats to the nation suggests their "patriotism" has indeed moved decisively in the direction of nationalism, albeit of a defensive rather than aggressive kind. There are many such threats available to chose among, both from without, where such traditional enemies as Germany and Russia do well for starters, and within, where current favorites include crypto-communists, liberals[31], masons, and of course Jews. This fear of others helps to explain the enthusiasm with which Polish fundamentalists subscribe to conspiracy theories. Of course, there are the venerable Jewish/Masonic/Socialist plots to control the world, or at least the Polish housing market, banking system and

---

29. Orig, "Ciemny lud to kupi." Although Jacek [not to be confused with Jarosław Kurski of PiS denies he said this, several reputable journalists report this statement as being accurate.

30. The unfinished business of lustration and mountains of secret police files promise new insinuations and "revelations" for years to come. Unfortunately, Poland did not have its own version of South Africa's "Truth and Reconciliation" Commission. By separating the two, both opponents and proponents of various forms of lustration have undermined the potential to deal constructively with the painful truth about the past and move on.

31. Who are actually fiscal conservatives.

private media. Another popular version is the decadent, cosmopolitan, libertinian West, known for short as "liberalism" or the European Union. These are combined and recombined in novel ways, as in the recent appeal by *Radio Maryja* to its followers, to oppose "the unprecedented attack of leftist and libertinian forces."[32] To this has been added Poland's own home-grown, all-ubiquitous "Network" (*układ*). During its years in power, and now as the largest opposition party in parliament, PiS has made the task of unmasking and dismantling the Network to be its primary *raison d'être*.

The "Network" as envisioned by PiS is a sort of omni-present matrix, created by communists and certain members of the opposition movement, who it is claimed joined forces over the ruins of the Soviet satellite state to rule the nation and divide up its wealth.[33] It includes prominent politicians, businessmen, academicians, media representatives, those in the legal professions (lawyers, judges, and prosecutors), a not insignificant portion of the clergy, and of course the Polish underworld or "mafia."[34] Frequently it appears that anyone who does not belong to or support PiS, or who critiques and opposes its policies, is by definition a member of the Network. Such suspicions leave no one safe from suspicion or attack. "The current government," accused J. Kaczyński recently, "is acting as if its plan was to weaken the nation, to destroy its unity and identity."[35] Members of the Network and independent media are suspected of working either for the Zionists or Liberals. During *Radio Maryja's* recent pilgrimage, a cameraman from the television station TVN was attacked by the station's supporters, one of whom shouted, "Private Television? We know! You are from Israel!" A day earlier Fr. Rydzyk had exclaimed, "We know who controls the media!" The crowd responded on cue, "The masons!" This was clearly the expected reply, for no correction was forthcoming.

32. *Gazeta Wyborcza*, July 14, 2008, 11.

33. E.g., on Wałęsa's 65th birthday, as he attended a gala at the Royal Palace to celebrate the 20th anniversary of his receiving the Nobel Peace Prize, the Polish news agency PAP reported that, "President Lech Kaczyński believes that Lech Wałęsa was the leader of the fight for independence in the 1980's, nevertheless later, 'rather than finish the Solidarity revolution, build a new state, a real Third Commonwealth,' he rested his power on part of the old communist party apparatus." PAP, "Wałęsa brutalnie i grubiańsko naruszał cześć moją i brata."

34. Many individuals from these circles did benefit, legally or illegally, from the process of transformation.

35. *Gazeta Wyborcza*, July 14, 2008, 11.

Polish fundamentalists apply a form of the "second-degree separation" practiced by some American religious fundamentalists, who studiously avoid not only real or suspected liberals, but otherwise conservative Christians who associate with them, e.g., in a Billy Graham crusade or local community service projects. Poland's religio-political fundamentalists not only refuse to forgive communists and their collaborators,[36] they also reject opposition figures such as Michnik and Mazowiecki, who in evaluating those accused of collaboration take into consideration the complexity of individual and historical circumstances, and who are willing to acknowledge and grant absolution for sincere efforts to repent of one's mistakes and to atone for them by years of labor on behalf of others.

Poland's social problems and challenges are real. While the majority of Poles have benefited from the modernization and transformation of the economy and society, others have been left behind. The anxiety the latter feel over the rapid pace of change is understandable, while the economic and social pain they experience is both real and tragic. However, for self-proclaimed leaders to manipulate people's fear and suffering in order to build a power base, raise money, and win elections is not on the list of appropriate responses.[37] Instead government officials, involved citizens, and the Christian community should initiate and engage in concrete efforts to help those who can't help themselves, and help those who can to become responsible for themselves and for others.

Freedom of the Press; the Use of Modern Technology and Media

For such a young democracy, Poland's private press and media are well-developed and thriving, and its better representatives easily hold their own against their counterparts in Western Europe. Nevertheless, many who work in the industry identify with the broader culture and ideals

---

36. The rare exceptions are for those former communist supporters or collaborators who have "seen the light" and joined the ranks of the fundamentalists.

37. Seldom perhaps are leaders completely calculating and cynical about their appeal to the disenfranchised. Neither is there sufficient evidence to declare this to be the case in Poland. Accordingly, no moral or psychological judgment is offered here concerning the character or motives of Poland's fundamentalist leaders, rather the observations here concern their observed political culture and public behavior.

of European humanism, both Christian and secular, and frequently find themselves at odds with the attitudes and agenda of Poland's religio-political fundamentalists. This leads to frequent criticism of what they perceive as the fundamentalist rhetoric and actions[38] of PiS, *Radio Maryja* and others.

Many fundamentalists in turn are so convinced that they represent true Poles, that they seem mystified and offended by the fact that the majority of their fellow citizens do not recognize them as their natural religious and political leaders. In their black and white world, either you are for them, hence for God and country (as they understand these concepts), or you are against them. Since according to one of messianism's most persistent myths the Polish common people are by definition good, this leads them to conclude that there must be a campaign of lies and treachery being conducted against them, and that Poland's private media has joined an organized attack against them. We have already touched on the attitude of *Radio Maryja* and its listeners towards the media. Recently, PiS declared a boycott of the major independent television station TVN and its associates, claiming they are biased and unprofessional. This was self-evident to them, since TVN dares on occasion to disagree with "the truth" as they see it. Commenting on this decision, J. Kaczyński argued that "reporters should at least feign neutrality." In what amounts to verbal blackmail, he said that the boycott will last, "until TVN comes to the conclusion that it needs to change its way of operating. It must be communication, and not writing yourself into a certain operation directed against us."[39] Similar insinuations are regularly made, e.g., that the media serves the Network, or that it is under foreign influence, most probably German or Jewish.

But much like many of their counterparts in other countries, for all their criticism of the media Poland's new fundamentalists recognize its power and make good use of it. Polish public television and radio, which to date has fallen prey to successive governments, is at the present time still under the control of PiS, which has fought to keep its political control intact. When the Governing Board of Polish Radio (PR)

---

38. Here, the reference is to criticism of specifically fundamentalist rhetoric and actions. Critique of more concrete political programs and policies, or of specific political and pastoral views and practices, is another matter. Part and parcel of fundamentalist mentality seems the inability to distinguish the difference.

39. *Gazeta Wyborcza*, July 18, 2008, 2.

attempted to suspend the PiS appointed Chairman and Vice-Chairman of Polish Radio for, among other reasons, their politicizing of Poland's public radio stations, the PiS appointed chairman of the National Board of Radio and Television (KRRiT) intervened with "his (i.e., PiS) members" of the PR board[40] to block this action against the PiS Chairmen.[41] It is to be hoped that the present government, perhaps with the support of the socialists that is needed to override Lech Kaczyński's Presidential veto, lives up to its commitment to reform Poland's public media and place it beyond the control of all political parties. Time will tell.

Along with its normal religious programming, including catechetical and pastoral programs as well as religious music, *Radio Maryja*, together with its related newspaper (*Nasz Dziennik*), and television station (*TV Trwam*), conducts regular talk shows, lectures, interviews, and auditions, and which take a consistently anti-liberal,[42] anti-European Union stance. The problem, however, is not the radio station's views on the economy, or of the relative advantages or disadvantages of Poland's belonging to the European Union, but rather the tone and content of these programs, which engage overtly in party politics, identify the political and religious views espoused by *Radio Maryja* with the cause of Christianity (or at least its understanding of Polish Catholicism), and appeals to xenophobia and anti-Semitic themes. In his efforts to influence and control the media, Fr. Rydzyk has also established a college, the "School of Social Culture and Media," in order to train a generation of reporters and announcers both how to proclaim "the truth," and to see through the "lies" and falsehoods presented by politicians and other news media.

Although the reactionary, integrist views of the circles associated with Radio Maryja do not represent the stance, either of the progressive wing of the Roman Catholic Church in Poland, nor the position taken by the Polish Episcopate, there is enough support from its listeners,

---

40. The law governing the KRRiT clearly states that it cannot interfere in the decisions of the Governing Board of Polish Radio, whose members, once appointed, are independent.

41. Kublik, "Jak prezes Kołodziejski wypełniał w nocy swoją misję."

42. It should be noted that the definitions of "liberal" and "conservative" employed by fundamentalists in Poland differs significantly from the understanding of those terms in Western Europe or the United States. "Liberal" for example can refer to theological, ethical, political or economic "liberalism." The same is true of "conservative." The confounding of categories is bewildering.

priests, and certain bishops to render it seemingly invulnerable to criticism and calls to reform. Repeated warnings from the Polish Episcopate and even from the Vatican have resulted in promises to avoid further political action, all of which were promptly broken. The Episcopate established a committee to investigate and influence the radio station, but it has so far proven singularly ineffective at regulating the radio, holding it accountable financially, or limiting its political involvement.

A Word on Anti-Semitism in Poland Today

The important and highly complex subject of Polish anti-Semitism has been touched on at several places throughout this study. It is perhaps enough here to state that there is no place for anti-Semitism in either the high ideals of Polish messianism, or the legacy of Dietrich Bonhoeffer. Yet a word is in order, for just as it is throughout Europe and beyond, the struggle against anti-Semitism as well as other forms of ethnic, national and religious bigotry and hatred, is still going on within Poland. Many conferences have been held, and many books and articles published on Poland's efforts to deal with its long relationship with its Jewish citizens. Here, two pieces of anecdotal evidence will suffice to illustrate.

Not many Poles today are active anti-Semites, and while passive anti-Semitism is a much greater problem, it still touches a decided minority of the population. Poles are not genetically determined anti-Semites, nor are either active or passive Polish anti-Semites deprived of opportunities to change their views. Yet tragically, certain political and religious leaders, who identify themselves as both Polish patriots and Christians, tolerate or even promote such activities and attitudes. To cite just one example, Jerzy Robert Nowak, an author and speaker associated with *Radio Maryja*, travels around Poland speaking to crowds in Catholic parishes about the threat of the Jews and masons, to the dismay of many Poles, including both Catholics and secular humanists. Unfortunately, he is not alone, and has numerous supporters among both the laity and clergy.

Yet despite such phenomena, the image often held outside the country, i.e., that the majority of Poles are anti-Semites, is widely inaccurate. Michnik shows the progress that has been made in this area in an article that is worth quoting in some length. In it he responds to charges by Elie Wiesel (whom both Michnik and this author greatly respect) that the response to a lecture Wiesel delivered in Poland revealed his critics' anti-Semitism. Michnik writes:

> Wiesel's review conveys the image of a country unable to confront the plague of anti-Semitism. Several years ago, following the publication of Gross's book *Neighbors* about the destruction of a Jewish community in Jedwabne, Poland became the stage of a broad debate that was ignored by neither the Polish president nor the primate of the country's Catholic Church. There is probably no other country in East Central Europe that would be accounting for the dark chapters of its own history with such seriousness and honesty. That debate was as important as the publication of Gross's book.
>
> A couple of weeks ago rabbi Michael Schudrich was assaulted by a hooligan on a Warsaw street. This was probably not the only case in the world of a hooligan assault on a rabbi. Poland, however, is likely the only country where on the next day the president ostentatiously invited the rabbi to meet him and in front of the cameras expressed his solidarity with the victim of the assault. Anyone who writes about anti-Semitism in Poland and ignores those facts, falsifies—even if unintentionally—the truth about Poland.[43]

In the face of Poland's rich, but troubled and at times dark relationship with its own Jewish community, it is imperative that both political and Church leaders of all denominations continue to reassert the principles of dialogue and mutual respect for others that characterized Polish messianism and the Polish opposition movement. Bonhoeffer too developed this theme both practically and theologically, and in Poland as elsewhere his thought has helped to facilitate reconciliation and cooperation between of "people of good will" in this and other areas. One local Polish example is the "District of Mutual Respect," which for years has promoted dialogue and cooperation between Roman Catholic, Orthodox, Protestant and Jewish communities in Wrocław. One of the most important benefits of such initiatives is simply the chance to get to know "the others" with whom we share our journey through this world. This too is a building block of a Polish alternative to fundamentalism.

---

43. Michnik, "Elie Wiesel Accuses Poland—commentary by Adam Michnik."

A Polish Post-Messianic, Bonhoefferian Alternative to Secularism and Fundamentalism

A Polish Post-Messianic . . .

This study, which began with an examination of the romantic myths of Polish Messianism, has led to my own selective retelling of those myths, as well the more modern myths that arose around the Polish opposition movement and the Solidarity trade union. As was argued in the Introduction, Poland today needs its historians and myth-makers, who can help the nation to recover its forgotten memories and chart a course for its future. However, as Davies notes, not all Polish myths are healthy, and if the best ones are not retold or new ones created, then other, darker myths are likely to take root.[44] As this study has shown, two major visions have vied for supremacy as the Polish meta-story: the myth of Jagiellonian Poland as an inclusive, pluralistic society, and the exclusive myth of Piast Poland defined in sharply ethnic and religious terms. Porter, an open admirer of Polish messianism's inclusive myths,[45] in calling for their reexamination suggests we follow Zweig in admitting "that our fathers served "delusions" while recognizing that they were wonderful and noble delusions, full of potential for formulating a national politics for the modern world."[46] While this author shares Porter's appreciation for Polish messianism, and his belief in its lasting promise and potential, this statement raises some serious questions regarding one's choice of delusions. Is it truly advisable to build a "national politics for the modern world" that is founded on delusions? What criteria, if any, may be established for judging delusions to be "noble" or "full of potential"? Why, for example, should I prefer my inclusive delusions to your exclusive delusions?

To answer in brief, as Porter would surely agree, the very process of recognizing the degree to which myths have become delusions allows us to appropriate them in a new manner. Subjected to a thorough historical, sociological, and theological critique, myths can then be reworked and incorporated as part of a conscious construction, which reflects on

---

44. Davies, "Polish National Mythologies."
45. Naturally, Porter is therefore also a critic of the exclusive myths of Piast Poland.
46. Porter, *When Nationalism Began to Hate*, 238.

the past to help explain the present and suggest a path for the future.[47] Since history and myth intertwine to form the meta-stories that provide identity for social entities such as nations, we may apply Alves' words on history as the recovery of forgotten memories to these myths as well. Alves writes:

> "The historian is someone who recovers forgotten memories and disseminates them as a sacrament to those who have lost the memory. Indeed, what finer community sacrament is there than the memories of a common past, punctuated by the existence of pain, of sacrifice and of hope? To recover in order to disseminate. The historian is not an archaeologist of memories. The historian is a sower of visions and hopes."[48]

"Sowers of visions and hopes" aptly describes Woronicz and Mickiewicz, who together helped create the myth of Jagiellonian Poland. As the use of Bonhoeffer to critique Polish messianism demonstrates, their noble "delusions" included romantic epistemology, an instrumental and reductionist Christology, an over-confident and simplistic theodicy, an over-realized eschatology, and the marvelously naïve belief that the Christian gospel can become an international ethic among the family of nations. While one can admire or at least respect the grandeur of such delusions, the point is not to return to them via a romantic *salto mortale*. Rather, we may free messianism of its "noble delusions" in order to reaffirm its even nobler values: cultural, ethnic and religious pluralism; social justice; public and political morality; human dignity and freedom; civil responsibility; patriotism that leads to reconciliation and harmonious cooperation with other nations rather than to national-chauvinism. As this chapter has shown, further resources that may be rescued from messianism and reissued today include a commitment to dialogue instead of confrontation, the readiness to confess our own personal and corporate sins, whether they are of a spiritual, social and political nature, while forgiving the sins of others, a respect for other human beings that rejects anti-Semitism along with all forms of ethnic, religious and national prejudice and bigotry, and a replacement of the romantic cult of the leader with servant-leaders and public servants who seek to en-

---

47. Such myths should no longer be described as delusions, though unless they are subjected to ongoing reflection and critique, they will lapse back into delusion.

48. Alves, "Las ideas teológicas y sus caminos por los surcos institucionales del Protestantismo brasileño," 363.

noble and empower those they serve rather than patronize and exploit them. While I believe my account of these myths and the values they transmit is both historically accurate and faithful to the spirit of their authors, I have made conscious choices concerning the selection and interpretation of the individuals, literary works, and events discussed. I make no apology for this. I like the story of messianism that emerges; others are free to retell the myths in their own fashion.

... and Bonhoefferian Alternative ...

Bonhoeffer once aided the Polish opposition in its selective, contextual appropriation of messianism, and hence in its struggle for freedom, the dignity of the individual, social justice, and national self-determination. Yet as my friend John Matthews once remarked to me, coming to grips with Christ and the modern world is not a one-time event. Rather, each new generation must come of age. Today there is a renewed interest in Bonhoeffer's legacy. Poles are reading his works to see what he offers for their present situation. That offering is substantial. As was argued in chapter 6, Bonhoeffer's legacy points the way to a replacement of messianism's romantic epistemology with a Christocentric biblical realism founded on God's self-revelation in the incarnation, life, death, and resurrection of Jesus Christ. Bonhoeffer's dialogical view of providence and human responsibility, in which God invites human beings to share responsibility for history, finds a close analogy in citizens' society whose strategists, like Bonhoeffer, rejected the over-realized historiosophy that characterized messianism, together with ideologies that seek to impose their vision of a better world on reality.

Although Bonhoeffer's theodicy of solidarity with those who suffer, which leads to vicarious action on their behalf, is far less ambitious in scope than the Irenaean or Augustinian solutions proposed by Woronicz and Mickiewicz, it retains and respects the full "pathos" of human suffering that is often undermined in all-encompassing approaches to theodicy. His life-long belief in and commitment to the Church, his growing affirmation of the world, and his call for a thoroughgoing Christological critique of both remain relevant and necessary today. Does he also point the way forward to new and renewed expressions of Christianity, which through the practice of "prayer and righteous actions" will both learn a new language to speak of Jesus Christ, and earn a voice in contemporary society? Specifically, can

Bonhoeffer's words on costly grace, his theology and praxis of life in community, his Christological ethics, and the worldly Christianity of his prison theology stimulate and advance the efforts of efforts of Post-Messianic Poles to realize the ideals of Jagiellonian Poland. Can they help Polish Christians and the Churches they belong to conceptualize, practice and articulate their faith in Jesus Christ in a society marked by growing secularism and a vigorous fundamentalist reaction?

. . . to Secularism and Fundamentalism

As was suggested at the start of this chapter, one of the main conditions that has promoted the rise in recent years of religio-political fundamentalism in Poland was the failure of its Christian community to provide an attractive alternative to secularism. Although the political and religious situation in Poland is dynamic and fluid, it seems likely that secularism as well as fundamentalism will continue to exert significant influence in coming years, regardless of how the church and society reacts to new developments that may markedly affect the course of events. Yet this should not lead Christians to despair or passive resignation, but instead to proactive engagement with the society and world they live in. How then are Polish Christians doing on this count? Apart from a few local exceptions, which are happily becoming more frequent, Protestant churches and individuals have yet to enter the public sphere, speak out on social and ethical issues, or otherwise make their presence noticeably felt in society. The so-called open or progressive wing of the Roman Catholic Church, which has a real presence and voice, and whose publications are read as well by numerous Protestants and secular humanists, represents perhaps the most thoughtful and consistent attempt to respond to the challenges of modernization and secularization faced by Polish society today. Although its original leaders are aging, their place is being taken by younger clergy and laypersons, many of whom however find the Church hierarchy too constricting or slow to react. It is this circle that has been in the forefront of calling for a truly Christian response to secularism. One example of this call came in the series of articles published in the Catholic weekly *Tygodnik Powszechny*, and entitled "Three Processes."

In this series Węcławski, in his article of the same name that initiated the series,[49] called for a theological discussion of "fundamental matters" facing the Polish Church and Polish society. In an account that roughly parallels Bonhoeffer's description of the world-come-of-age, Węcławski describes how to this day many keepers of the Christian tradition continue to cultivate a religious *residuum* that long ago ceased to interest the major currents of our technological, information-rich society.[50] Bortnowska, in her contribution to the ensuing debate, argues that a theological discussion in Poland of fundamental matters requires undertaking and completing the long-overdue analysis of and response to modernism. Nevertheless, she wonders if such an analysis won't muddy the air "with a black cloud that will be difficult to find one's way through?"[51] Bartoś in turn cites Schillebeeckx to the effect that Polish Catholicism has not yet undergone a confrontation with the Enlightenment tradition. As Bartoś elaborates:

> Busy with other matters, such as the XIX and XX century struggle for independence, deprived for decades of its own religious, academic, and theological institutions, [Polish Catholicism]—more messianic than rational—did not have the opportunity, desire or ability to confront the ideas of modernism.[52]

As readers of this study will recognize, Bartoś refers here to the legacy and ongoing influence of Polish messianism, which not only supplied the parameters for the nineteenth and to a somewhat lesser degree twentieth-century debate over Polish national identity, but also established paradigms for the response of the Polish Church and nation to the "crisis of modernism." Bonhoeffer's positive yet critical approach to modernism can help the Polish churches—and more broadly Polish society—find a path through the "black cloud," i.e., to critically engage not only with modernism, but also its heir and successor, postmodernism, as well as what comes after.[53] As argued above, a Bonhoefferian analysis of messianism shows how Woronicz's "conservative restoration" leaves the world outside the church "to its own devices," while

---

49. Węcławski, "Trzy procesy," 1, 19

50. Ibid., 19.

51. Bortknowska, "Wigilia z teologiem (dziennik)," 17.

52. Bartoś, "O możliwości debaty teologicznej dzisiaj," 8.

53. I write Polish *churches*, for an inadequate response to modernism also hinders theological discussion of fundamental matters among Polish Protestants.

Mickiewicz's *"salto mortale"* back to the worldview of a previous era is as colorful and futile as Don Quixote's tilting at windmills. These "rusty swords" may be replaced with Bonhoeffer's affirmation of and engagement with a world come of age, understood (by Christians) not on its own terms but through God's self-revelation in Christ. In this vision, Christians individually and corporately follow Christ into the world, where they regain their voice as they serve others through prayer and good deeds. Incorporated into this vision, the ideals of Polish messianism, reaffirmed and restated by the architects and engineers of Polish citizens' society, and further corrected and deepened by a critical engagement with Bonhoeffer's theology, truly remain "full of potential for formulating a national politics for the modern world." The result will likely resemble what Bonhoeffer scholar John de Gruchy, in his recent personal reflections on a life of theological thought and praxis, has called "Christian humanism."[54]

One further proposal I find intriguing was suggested recently by Harvey. In his plenary paper at the X International Bonhoeffer Congress,[55] he drew on Bonhoeffer's use of the Old Testament to call on Christians to reconfigure ourselves as a church in exile. Is this possible in Poland? As one who comes from a free-church tradition, I can certainly visualize that. And I am not alone. There are those in Poland who think this way, or at least are asking questions that lead in this direction. Nevertheless, the way will not be easy. At the Congress I asked my Polish colleague, a Catholic priest and theologian, and fellow-member of the Polish Section of the International Bonhoeffer Society, if he could envision the Catholic Church re-inventing itself as an exilic community. His answer was "yes, but this is very difficult." The same is true for Protestants in Poland. Perhaps what we should hope for and work towards in the near future is the emergence in Poland of Christian humanistic, exilic communities, of various Church traditions and in dialogue with each other, that seek to live for and witness to Christ both within their own confessions, the broader Christian community, and society at large. That such engaged and engaging Christian communities could arise would in itself be a powerful sign of grace and the reality of Christ in this world.

---

54. de Gruchy, *Confessions of a Christian Humanist*, 2006.
55. Harvey, "Life in Exile."

Bonhoeffer described how in his day the Church's "lost children," i.e., the values of European humanism and human rights that were also held by Polish messianism, found their way back to their "mother" (the Church) and to the "source—Jesus Christ." Today as then, some of the "faithful brothers" of these returning "prodigals," who themselves never left home, seem less than enthusiastic to see their long-lost siblings, and even remain a bit uncomfortable in their presence. Today as then, it is high time for the Church, with all of its sons and daughters, to go looking for the children who are still "lost," not simply to drag them into the Church again, but to proclaim that Christ truly is what he claimed to be, the "Lord of the whole world," and not just the Christian ghetto. Why then are we so slow to start, why are our footsteps so tentative? Perhaps we who remain inside the Church's walls hesitate to undertake such an adventure because we ourselves have wandered away from the source?

Węcławski describes the many individuals in Poland who identify faith with a religious organization, with the institutional church, with larger or smaller fellowships, with the confession that "Jesus is Lord," or with Mary, the "Queen of Poland." Nevertheless, Węcławski declares, "these same people, when asked if they identify with the death and resurrection of Jesus as the beginning of their Christian calling, stand helpless."[56] Post-messianic Poles, who want to overcome such helplessness, who invite others to share in their reflections on the incarnate, crucified and resurrected Christ, who gladly welcome those who join them in following the one who is "God-for-us," "the Suffering God," and "the-man-for-others," who would follow right into "the middle of the village"[57] and "the open air of intellectual discussion,"[58] in order to engage with those they meet there in praxis that feeds on and nourishes such reflection and discipleship, such travelers as these will find a friend and fruitful dialogue partner in Dietrich Bonhoeffer.

Myths may serve to shape the future as well as to explain the past. In a world where oppression and injustice are still present in abundance, the messianic myth of "Poland, the Christ of the nations" can be positively recast as a call to follow the example of Christ, "the-man-for-others," by standing in solidarity with the suffering, by speaking out in their behalf, and by working responsibly with other nations "for your

56. Węcławski, "Trzy procesy," 1.
57. LPP, letter of April 30, 1944.
58. LPP, Letter of August 3, 1944.

freedom and for ours." Such a post-messianic, Bonhofferian vision of Polish religious and political life recognizes that it is not the State's job to Christianize the world. Neither is this a realistic or desired political goal for the Church. Rather than engaging in nostalgic longing and ardent labor for a revival of Christendom, the Church today is called to take its place in a pluralistic society, and there to share Christ's love and truth by attitudes and actions that match or even surpass the purity of its doctrine and the power of its preaching, remembering that deeds speak louder than words. When the world sees a Church that is becoming the Church-for-others, as Christ was the man-for-others, it may indeed recognize what it means to be, not merely "religious," but fully and truly human.

Bibliography

Alves, Rubem. "Las ideas teológicas y sus caminos por los surcos institucionales del Protestantismo brasileño." In *Materiales para una historia de la teología en América Latina*, edited by Pablo Richard. San José, Costa Rica: DEI, 1981.
Anderson, Benedict. *Imagined Communities*. London: Verso, 1983.
Ballard, Steven. *Rudolf Otto and the Synthesis of the Rational and the Non-Rational in the Idea of the Holy*. Frankfurt: Lang, 2000.
Ballard, P. H. "Bonhoeffer on Providence in History." *Scottish Journal of Theology* 27 (1974) 268-86.
Barańczak, Stanisław. "Dlaczego nie całkiem jestem Chrześcijaninem." *Aneks* 13/14 (1977) 125-32.
———. "Notatki na marginesach Bonhoeffera." In *Etyka i Poetyka: Szkice 1970-1978*, 9-25. Paryż: Instytut Literacki, 1979.
Barnett, Victoria. "Communications Between the German Resistance, the Vatican and Protestant Ecumenical Leaders." In *Religion im Erbe: Dietrich Bonhoeffer und die Zukunftsfähigkeit des Christentums*, edited by Christian Gremmels and Wolfgang Huber, 54-71. Gütersloh, 2002.
Barth, Karl. *Protestant Theology in the Nineteenth Century: Its Background and History*. Grand Rapids: Eerdmans, 2001.
Bartnik, Czesław. *Teologia narodu*. Dzieła zebrane vol. 9. Częstochowa: Tygodnik Katolicki "Niedziela," 1999.
Bartoś, Tadeusz. "Nie odpuszczam Kościoła." *Gazeta Wyborcza* (2007) 25.
———. "O możliwości debaty teologicznej dzisiaj." *Tygodnik Powszechny* 5 (2006) 8.
———. "Ostatni wielki romantyk." *Gazeta Wyborcza* (2005) 17-18.
Batowski, Henryk, editor. *Legion Mickiewicza: Wybór źródeł*. Wrocław: Zakład narodowy im. Ossolińskich, 1958.
Baum, Gregory. *The Church for Others: Protestant Theology in Communist East Germany*. Grand Rapids: Eerdmans, 1996.
Bethge, Eberhard. *Bonhoeffer, Exile and Martyr*. Edited by John W. de Gruchy. London: Collins, 1975.
———. *Dietrich Bonhoeffer: A Biography*. Revised and edited by Victoria J. Barnett. Translated by Eric Mosbacher et al. Minneapolis: Fortress, 2000.
———. *Friendship and Resistance: Essays on Dietrich Bonhoeffer*. Grand Rapids: Eerdmans, 1995.
———. "Living in Opposition." In *Reflections on Bonhoeffer*, edited by Geffrey Kelly and John Weborg, 25-31. Chicago: Covenant, 1999.
Bonhoeffer, Dietrich. *Act and Being*. Translated by Reinhard Knauss and Nancy Lukens. Edited by Clifford Green. Dietrich Bonhoeffer Works English 2. Minneapolis: Fortress, 1996.
———. *Christology*. Translated by John Bowden. London: Collins Fontana, 1971.

———. "The Church and the Jewish Question." In *Dietrich Bonhoeffer: Witness to Jesus Christ*, edited by John de Gruchy, 124–30. Minneapolis: Fortress, 1991.

———. "The Church and the Peoples of the World." In *Dietrich Bonhoeffer: Witness to Jesus Christ*, edited by John de Gruchy, 131–33. Minneapolis: Fortress, 1991.

———. *The Cost of Discipleship*. Rev. ed. New York: Collier, 1963.

———. *The Cost of Discipleship*. Translated by R. H. Fuller. London: SCM, 1959.

———. *Creation and Fall*. Dietrich Bonhoeffer Works English 3. Minneapolis: Fortress, 1997.

———. *Discipleship*, Dietrich Bonhoeffer Works English 4. Minneapolis: Fortress, 2001.

———. *Ethics*. New York: Macmillan, 1964.

———. *Ethics*. Dietrich Bonhoeffer Works English 6. Minneapolis: Fortress, 2005.

———. *Letters and Papers from Prison*. New York: Fontana, 1959.

———. *Letters and Papers from Prison*. New York: Macmillan, 1967.

———. *Letters and Papers from Prison*. New York: Macmillan, 1971.

———. *Life Together and Prayerbook of the Bible*. Dietrich Bonhoeffer Works English 5. Minneapolis: Fortress, 1996.

———. *Sanctorum Communio*. Dietrich Bonhoeffer Works English 1. Minneapolis: Fortress, 1998.

Borowy, Wacław. "Poet of Transformation." In *Mickiewicz: Poet of Poland*, edited by Manfred Kridl, 34–56. New York: Columbia University Press, 1951.

Bortknowska, Halina. "Wigilia z teologiem (dziennik)." *Tygodnik Powszechny* 4 (2006) 17.

Chapman, G. Clarke. "Bonhoeffer, Liberation Theology and the 1990's." In *Reflections on Bonhoeffer*, edited by Geffrey Kelly and John Weborg, 299–314. Chicago: Covenant, 1999.

———. "Hope and the Ethics of Formation: Moltmann as an Interpreter of Bonhoeffer." *Studies in Religion/Sciences Religieuses* 12 (1983) 449–60.

Chlebowski, Bronisław. *Literatura Polska Porozbiorowa jako Główny Wyraz Życia Narodu po Utracie Niepodległości*. Warsaw: Wydawnictwo Zakładu Narodowego im. Ossolińskich, 1923.

Chmielewska, Anna. "List do Przyjaciół." *Aneks* 12 (1976) 83–107.

Cieśla-Korytowska, Maria. *O Mickiewiczu i Słowackim*. Kraków: Universitas, 1999.

Clements, Keith. *A Patriotism for Today: Dialogue with Dietrich Bonhoeffer*. Bristol: Bristol Baptist College, 1984.

———. "Community in the Ethics of Dietrich Bonhoeffer." *Studies in Christian Ethics* 10 (1997) 16–31.

———. "Integration, Conflict and the Ecumenical Quest." In *Religion im Erbe: Dietrich Bonhoeffer und die Zukunftsfähigkeit des Christentums*, edited by Christian Gremmels and Wolfgang Huber, 225–41. Gütersloh: Kaiser, 2002.

———. *What Freedom: The Persistent Challenge of Dietrich Bonhoeffer*. Bristol: Bristol Baptist College, 1990.

Cywiński, Bohdan. *Rodowody niepokornych*. Kraków: Znak, 1974.

Czerniawski, Adam. "A Poetical Political History." In *New Perspectives in Twentieth-Century Polish Literature*, edited by Stanisław Eile and Ursula Phillips, 6–23. London: Macmillan, 1992.

Davies, Norman. "Polish National Mythologies." In *Myths and Nationhood*, edited by Geoffrey Hosking and George Schöplin, 141–57. London: Hurst, 1997.

de Gruchy, John W. "Bonhoeffer, Apartheid and Beyond: The Reception of Bonhoeffer in South Africa." In *Bonhoeffer for a New Day*, edited by John de Gruchy, 353–65. Grand Rapids: Eerdmans, 1997.

———. "Bonhoeffer, Calvinism and Christian Civil Disobedience in South Africa." *Scottish Journal of Theology* 34 (1981) 245–62.

———. *Bonhoeffer and South Africa: Theology in Dialogue*. Grand Rapids: Eerdmans, 1984.

———. "The Catholic Church and Democracy in Poland: Reflections of a South African Observer." *Journal of Theology for Southern Africa* 96 (1996) 34–43.

———. "Confessing Guilt in South Africa Today in Dialogue with Dietrich Bonhoeffer." *Journal of Theology for South Africa* 67 (1989) 37–45.

———. *Confessions of a Christian Humanist*. Minneapolis: Fortress, 2006.

———. "The Freedom of the Church and the Liberation of Society: Bonhoeffer on the Free Church, and the 'Confessing Church' in South Africa." In *Bonhoeffer's Ethics: Old Europe and New Frontiers*, edited by Guy Carter et al., 173–89. Kampen: Kok Pharos, 1991.

———. "God's Desire for a Community of Human Beings." In *Religion im Erbe: Dietrich Bonhoeffer und die Zukunftsfähigkeit des Christentums*, edited by Christian Gremmels and Wolfgang Huber, 147–63. Gütersloh: Kaiser, 2002.

de Lange, Frederik. "A Particular Europe, a Universal Faith." In *Bonhoeffer's Ethics: Old Europe and New Frontiers*, edited by Guy Carter et al., 81–96. Kampen, The Netherlands: Kok Pahros Publishing House, 1991.

———. "Waiting for the Word." In *Bonhoeffer for a New Day*, edited by John W. de Gruchy, 94–111. Grand Rapids: Eerdmans, 1997.

———. *Waiting for the Word: Dietrich Bonhoeffer on Speaking about God*. Grand Rapids: Eerdmans, 1995.

Dorn, Ludwik. "PiS to nie Kaczyński." *Politbiuro*, October 1, 2008. Online: http://politbiuro.pl/politbiuro/1,85401,5754557,Dorn__PiS_to_nie_pan_Kaczynski.html.

Dorosz, Krzysztof. "Kuroń, Michnik, Lewica, Chrześcijaństwo." *Aneks* 37 (1985) 137–51.

———. "Wędrówki ziemię ulro." *Aneks* 20 (1979) 129–58.

Drawicz, Andrzej. "Bonhoeffer w zasięgu ręki." *Znak* 474 (1994) 26–29.

Eile, Stanisław. *Literature and Nationalism in Partitioned Poland, 1795–1918*. London: Macmillan, 2000.

Elshtain, Jean Bethke. "Caesar, Sovereignty and Bonhoeffer." In *Bonhoeffer for a New Day*, edited by John W. de Gruchy, 223–35. Grand Rapids: Eerdmans, 1997.

Feil, Ernst. "Dietrich Bonhoeffer's Understanding of the World." In *A Bonhoeffer Legacy: Essays in Understanding*, edited by A. K. Klassen, 237–55. Grand Rapids: Eerdmans, 1981.

———. *The Theology of Dietrich Bonhoeffer*. Philadelphia: Fortress, 1985.

Fisher, Joschka. Interview with Adam Michnik. *Gazeta Wyborcza*, June 3–4, 2000, 22–24.

Falk, Barbara. *The Dilemmas of Dissidence in East-Central Europe*. New York: Central European University Press, 2003.

Glenthøj, Jørgen. "Dietrich Bonhoeffer's Way between Resistance and Submission." In *A Bonhoeffer Legacy*, edited by A. J. Klassen, 170–77. Grand Rapids: Eerdmans, 1981.

Górniak-Kocikowska, Krystyna. "Tensions in Poland over Ecumenical Dialogue." *Religion in Eastern Europe* 28 (2009) 12.
Green, Clifford. *Bonhoeffer: A Theology of Sociality.* Rev. ed. Grand Rapids: Eerdmans, 1999.
———. "Ethical Theology and Contextual Ethics." In *Religion im Erbe: Dietrich Bonhoeffer und die Zukunftsfähigkeit des Christentums*, edited by Christian Gremmels and Wolfgang Huber, 255–69. Gütersloh: Kaiser, 2002.
———. "Human Sociality and Christian Community." In *The Cambridge Companion to Dietrich Bonhoeffer*, edited by John W. de Gruchy, 114–15. Cambridge: Cambridge University Press, 1999.
Grzywna-Wileczek, Anna. *I jest więcej prawd w Piśmie.* Lublin: KUL, 1994.
Harvey, Barry. "Life in Exile, Life in the Middle of the Village. Dietrich Bonhoeffer on a Post-Christendom Ecclesiology." Plenary paper read at the X International Bonhoeffer Congress in Prague, July 2008. Publication pending with other Congress materials.
Havel, Vaclav. "The Power of the Powerless." In *Open Letters: Selected Writings 1965–1990*, 125–214. New York: Vintage, 1992.
Holoubek, Gustaw. "Byłem Konrad." Interview by Piotr Stasiński. *Gazeta Wyborcza*, April 4–5, 1998, 10.
Janion, Maria, editor. *Reduta: romantyczna poezja niepodległościowe.* Kraków: Wydawnictwo Literackie Kraków, 1979.
Janion, Maria, and M. Żmigrodzka. *Romantyzm i historia.* Warsaw: Panstwowy Instytut Wydawniczy, 1978.
Jedlicki, Jerzy. "Polish Concepts of Native Culture." In *National Character and National Ideology in Interwar Eastern Europe*, edited by Ivo Banac and Katherine Verdery, 1–22. New Haven: Yale Center for International and Area Studies, 1995.
Karski, Karol. "Świeckie chrześcijaństwo Dietricha Bonhoeffera." In *Teologia Protestancka w XX Wieku*, 93–107. Warsaw: Wiedza powszechna, 1971.
Kelly, Geoffrey, and C. John Weborn, editors. *Reflections on Bonhoeffer: Essays in Honor of F. Burton Nelson.* Chicago: Covenant, 1999.
Kleiner, Juliusz. *Mickiewicz.* Vol. 2, part 1. Lublin: Towarzystwo Naukowe KUL, 1997.
———. *Sentymentalizm i preromantyzm.* Kraków: Wydawnictwo Literackie, 1975.
Kłoczowski, Jan. "Lekcja Bonhoeffera." *Znak* 4 (1971). Reprinted in *Gazeta Wyborcza* 17 (1990) 512–17.
———. "Droga Krzyżowa—labirynt życia." *Gazeta Wyborcza* 90 (1995) 8.
Kolbuszewski, Jacek. *Literatura wobec historii.* Wrocław: Wydawnictwo Uniwersytetu Wrocławskiego, 1997.
Kołakowski, Leszek. "Głosy z kraju o Chrześcijaństwie, socjalizmie, Kościele i polityce: Słowo wstępne." *Aneks* 12 (1976) 60–64.
———. "What is Left of Socialism." *First Things* (2002) 42–46.
Kosian, Józef. *Chrześcijaństwo jako "Istnienie dla Innych: Antropologia teologiczna Dietricha Bonhoeffera.* Wrocław: Wydawnictwo Uniwersytetu Wrocławskiego, 1992.
———. "Dietrich Bonhoeffer—w poszukiwaniu modelu Chrześcijańskiego przyszłości." In *Filozofia nadziei*, Akta Universitatis Wratislaviensis 1951, 139–61. Wrocław: Wydawnictwo Uniwersytetu Wrocławskiego, 1997.

———. "Miejsce etyki w Bonhoefferowskim modelu Chrześcijaństwa bez religii." *Acta Universitatis Wratislaviensis*. Wrocław: Wydawnictwo Uniwersytetu Wrocławskiego, 1972.
Kozicki, Stanisław. *Dziedzictwo polityczne trzech wieszczów*. Warsaw: Wydawnictwo S. Arct, 1949.
Kridl, Manfred, editor. *Mickiewicz: Poet of Poland*. New York: Columbia University Press, 1951.
Król, Marcin. *Romantyzm. Piekło i niebo Polaków*. Warsaw: Fundacja Res Publica, 1998.
Kublik, Agnieszka. "Jak prezes Kołodziejski wypełniał w nocy swoją misję." *Gazeta Wyborcza* (2008).
Kuroń, Jacek. "Chrześcijanie bez Boga." In *Polityka i odpowiedzialność*, 17–33. Londyn: Aneks, 1984.
———. "Lewica—prawica. Bóg." In *Wiara i wina*, 336–38. Wrocław: Wydawnictwo Dolnośląskie, 1995.
———. "Duma i Wina." In Andrzej Romanowski, *Ludzie tamtego Czasu*, 171–84. Kraków: Wydawnictwo Krakowskie, 2000.
Kurski, Jarosław. "Co nam dało państwo PiS." *Gazeta Wyborcza* (2007). Online: http://wyborcza.pl/1,76842,4467465.html.
———. "Trybunał Konstytucyjny niewygodny dla premiera." *Gazeta Wyborcza*, March 14, 2007. Online: http://wyborcza.pl/1,76842,3985638.html.
Levy, Armand. *Adam Mickiewicz, Poet of Poland: A Symposium*, edited by Manfred Kridl, 238–39. New York: Columbia University Press, 1951.
Lipski, Jan Józef. "Etos Komitetu Obrony Robotników." *Aneks* 29/30 (1983) 30–46. Also in Jan Józef Lipski, *KOR: A History of the Workers' Defense Committee in Poland, 1976–1981*, 62–78. Berkeley: University of California Press, 1985.
Lisicki, Paweł. "Nie–ludzki Bóg." *Znak* 2 (1992) 101–16.
Long, D. Stephen. "Ramseyian Just War and Yoderian Pacifism: Where is the Disagreement?" *Studies in Christian Ethics* 4 (1991) 58–72.
Lovin, Robin. *Christian Faith and Public Choices: The Social Ethics of Barth, Brunner and Bonhoeffer*. Philadelphia: Fortress, 1984.
———. "The Christian and the Authority of the State: Bonhoeffer's Reluctant Revisions." *Journal of Theology for Southern Africa* 34 (1981) 32–48. Also in *Ethical Responsibility: Bonhoeffer's Legacy to the Churches*, edited by John Godsey and Geffrey Kelley, 103–30. New York: Edwin Mellen, 1981.
Lutosławski, Stanisław. "Filozofia narodowa." In *Spór o charakter narodowej filozofii polskiej*, edited by Stanisław Pieróg. Warsaw: Wydział filozofii i Socjologii Uniwersytetu Warszawskiego, 1999.
Mac, Jerzy Sławomir. "Nasze winy." *Wprost* 24 (2000) 38–42.
Makowski, Stanisław. "Watykan wobec powstania listopadowego." In *Kordian Juliusza Słowackiego*, 121–26. Warsaw: Cytelnik, 1973.
Marsh, Charles. *Reclaiming Dietrich Bonhoeffer: The Promise of His Theology*. New York: Oxford University Press, 1994.
Masłowski, Michal. *Gest, Symbol i rytuały polskiego teatru romantycznego*. Warsaw: Wydawnictwo Naukowe PWN, 1998.
Maver, Giovanni. "Adam Mickiewicz in Rome in 1848." In *Adam Mickiewicz: Poet of Poland*, edited by Manfred Kridl. New York: Columbia University Press, 1951.
Madziarski, Wojciech. "Księdza się pamięta." *Gazeta Wyborcza* (1999) 16.

Mazowiecki, Tadeusz. "Czuj się wolny." In *Druga Twarz Europy*. 91-99. Warsaw: Biblioteka "Więzi," 1990.
———. "Druga twarz Europy." In *Druga Twarz Europy*, 100-108. Warsaw: Biblioteka "Więzi," 1990.
———. "Żywioł i człowiek." *Zeszyty Literackie* 4 (2004) 92-93.
———. "Głosy po śmierci Papieża." *Tygodnik powszechny* 15 (2005) 1.
———. "Naucyzł się wierzyć wśród tęgich razów." *Myśl Protestancka* 1 (2001) 3-20. First published in *Więź* 12 (1971) 5-21.
———. "Powrót do najprostszych pytań." In *Druga Twarz Europy*, 49-56. Warsaw: Biblioteka "Więzi," 1990.
———. "Zapiski." In *Druga Twarz Europy*, 125-36. Warsaw: Biblioteka "Więzi," 1990.
———. Speech delivered at the Catholics Intellectuals Club of Wrocław on November 5, 2004.
McGrath, Alister. *Historical Theology*. Oxford: Blackwell, 1998.
Melhorn, Ludwig. "Na marginesie recepcji Bonhoeffera w Polsce." *Teologia Polityczna* 1 (2003-2004) 246-50.
Michnik, Adam. *The Church and the Left*. Chicago: University of Chicago Press, 1993.
———. "The Dispute over Organic Work." In *Letters from Prison and Other Essays*, 223-48. Berkeley: University of California Press, 1985.
———. "Elie Wiesel Accuses Poland—Commentary by Adam Michnik." *Gazeta Wyborcza* (2006). Online: http://wyborcza.pl/1,75546,3448941.html.
———. "George, fajny chłop." *Gazeta Wyborcza* (2000) 1.
———. "Kłopot i błazen." *Aneks* 51-52 (1988) 4-22.
———. "Anti-authoritarian Revolt." In *Letters From Freedom*, 29-67. Berkeley: University of California Press, 1998.
———. "New Evolutionism." In *Letters from Prison and Other Essays*, 135-48. Berkeley: University of California Press, 1985.
———. "The Prague Spring Ten Years Later." In *Letters from Prison and Other Essays*, 155-59. Berkeley: University of California Press, 1985.
———. "Polska na zakręcie, Gazeta na zakręcie." *Gazeta Wyborcza* (2004) 12-14.
———. "Rana na czole Adama Mickiewicza." *Gazeta Wyborcza* (2005) 19.
Michnik, Adam, Józef Tischner, and Jacek Żakowski. *Między Panem a Plebanem*. Kraków: Znak, 1995.
Mickiewicz, Adam. *Dzieła poetyckie*. 4 vols. Warsaw: Czytelnik, 1983.
———. "Księgi narodu polskiego i pielgrzymstwa polskiego." In *Dzieła poetyckie* 2. Warsaw: Czytelnik, 1983.
———. *Dziady*. In *Dzieła poetyckie* 3. Warsaw: Czytelnik, 1983.
———. *Konrad Wallenrod* in *Dzieła poetyckie* 2. Warsaw: Czytelnik, 1983.
———. *Literatura Słowiańska: Kurs Trzeci*. In *Dzieła wszystkie* 10, 202-28; 259-83. Warsaw: Czytelnik, 1998.
———. "Mickiewicz as Journalist: Summary and Excerpts." In *Adam Mickiewicz, Poet of Poland: A Symposium*, edited by Manfred Kridl, 94-105. New York: Columbia University Press, 1951.
———. *Pan Tadeusz*. In *Dzieła poetyckie* 4. Warsaw: Czytelnik, 1983.
———. "Pilgrim's Litany." In *Dzieła poetyckie* 2. Warsaw: Czytelnik, 1983.
———. *Wiersze*. In *Dzieła poetyckie* 1. Warsaw: Czytelnik, 1983.

Milerski, Bogusław. "Dietrich Bonhoeffer." In *Leksykon wielkich teologów XX/XXI wieku*, edited by Józef Majewski and Jarosław Makowski, 30–39. Warsaw: Biblioteka "Więzi," 2003.

———. "Etyczna orientacja chrześcijaństwa w ujęciu Dietricha Bonhoeffer." In *Nauka, Kościół, Ekumenizm*, 81–82. Karol Karski, Warsaw: Semper, 1994.

———. "Kościół a narody: Ekumenia w obliczu nacjonalizmu i internacjonalizmu," *Studia i dokumenty ekumeniczne* 11 (1995) 9–15.

———. "Religia a kultura." *Rocznik Teologiczny Chat* 34 (1992) 175–91.

———. *Religia a Słowo. Krytyka religii w ujęciu Dietricha Bonhoeffer i Paula Tillicha*. Łódź: Wydawnictwo Ewangelickie św. Mateusza, 1994.

———. "Rewizja chrześcijaństwa w listach więziennych Dietricha Bonhoeffer." In *Z problemów hermeneutyki protestanckiej.*, 43–56. Łódź: Wydawnictwo Ewangelickie Św. Mateusza, 1996.

———. "Spotkać Boga w obcym człowieku. Od teologii Dietricha Bonhoeffera do pedagogii pojednania." *Rocznik Teologiczny ChAT* 1 (2000) 31–37.

Miłosz, Czesław. *The Land of Ulro*. New York: Carcanet, 1981.

Modras, Ronald. *The Catholic Church and Antisemitism: Poland, 1933–1939*. Chur, Switzerland: Harwood Academic, 1994.

Moltmann, Jürgen. *On Human Dignity: Political Theology and Ethics*. Minneapolis: Fortress, 1984.

Morawska, Anna. *Chrześcijanin w Trzeciej Rzeszy*. Biblioteka Więzi. Kraków: Znak, 1970.

———. *Bonhoeffer, Exile and Martyr*. London: Collins, 1975.

———. "Dietrich Bonhoeffer." *Znak* 29 (1968) 1340–64.

———, edited. *Wybór Pism*. Biblioteka Więzi. Kraków: Znak, 1970.

Müller, Hanfried. *Von der Kirche zur Welt: ein Beitrag zu der Beziehung des Wortes Gottes auf die societas in Dietrich Bonhoeffers theologischer Entwicklung*. Leipzig: Koehler & Amelang, 1961.

Napiórkowski, Andrzej. *Dietrich Bonhoeffer Bonhoeffer i jego wizje kościoła*. Kraków: Wydawnictwo Naukowe PAT, 2004.

Nation, Mark. "Discipleship in a World Full of Nazis: Dietrich Bonhoeffer's Polyphonic Pacifism as Social Ethics." In *The Wisdom of the Cross: Essays in Honor of John Howard Yoder*, edited by Stanley Hauerwas et al., 249–77. Grand Rapids: Eerdmans, 1999.

———. "Pacifist and Enemy of the State: Bonhoeffer's Straight and Unbroken Course from Costly Discipleship to Conspiracy." *Journal of Theology for Southern Africa* 77 (1991) 61–77.

Niesiołowski, Stefan. "Z powodów moralnych." *Gazeta Wyborcza* 231 (1992) 16.

———. "Spiskowcy nowych Niemiec," *Gazeta Wyborcza* 167 (1999) 11.

Norwid, Cyprian. "O Juliuszu Słowackim w sześciu publicznych posiedzeniach." In *Dzieła wybrane* 4. *Proza*, 235–89. Warsaw: Państwowy Instytut Wydawniczy, 1968.

Olschowsky, Heinz, and Walter Duda. "Bonhoeffer a inne Niemcy." *Znak* 210 (1971) 1700–1705.

Otto, Rudolf. *The Idea of the Holy*. London: Oxford University Press, 1923.

Paluch, Michał. "Are We the Titanic?" ("Czy jesteśmy Titanicem?") *Więź* (2008) 17.

Pangritz, Andreas. "Sharing the Destiny of His People." In *Bonhoeffer for a New Day*, edited by John W. de Gruchy, 258–77. Grand Rapids: Eerdmans, 1997.

———. "Theological Motives in Dietrich Bonhoeffer's Decision to Participate in Political Resistance." In *Reflections on Bonhoeffer*, edited by Geffrey Kelly and John Weborg, 32–49. Chicago: Covenant, 1999.

Polska Agencja Prasowa (PAP). "Wałęsa brutalnie i grubiańsko naruszał cześć moją i brata." In *Gazeta Wyborcza*, September 30, 2008. Online: http://wyborcza .pl/1,75248,5752069.html.

Pfeifer, Hans. "Ethics for the Renewal of Life: A Reconstruction of Its Concept." In *Bonhoeffer for a New Day*, edited by John W. de Gruchy, 137–54. Grand Rapids: Eerdmans, 1997.

Pigoń, Stanisław. "Fundamenty ideowe legionu." In *Zawsze o Nim*. 225–43. Kraków: Wydawnictwo literackie, 1960.

Porter, Brian. "The Catholic Nation: Religion, Identity, and the Narratives of Polish History." *Slavic and Eastern European Journal* (SEEJ) 45 (2001) 289–99.

———. "Marking the Boundary of the Faith: Catholic Modernism and the Radical Right in Early Twentieth Century Poland." In *Studies in Language, Literature, and Cultural Mythology in Poland: Investigating 'The Other,'* edited by Elwira Grossman, 261–85. Lewiston, NY: Mellen, 2002.

———. *When Nationalism Began to Hate*. Oxford: Oxford University Press, 2001.

Przybylski, Ryszard. *Klasycyzm, czyli prawdziwy koniec Królestwa Polskiego*. Gdańsk: Wydawnicto Marabut, 1996.

Przybylski, Ryszard, and Alina Witkowska. *Romantyzm*. Warsaw: Wydawnictowo Naukowe PWN, 1997.

Przybył, Jan. "Romantyzm, Katolicyzm, antyklerykalizm." *Rocznik Teologiczny ChAT* 44 (2002) 81–97.

Przychodniak, Z. "Walka o rząd dusz. O strategii i stylu artykułów politycznych w Pielgrzymie Polskim." In *Księga Mickiewiczowska*, edited by Zofia Trojanowiczowa and Zbiegniew Przychodniak, 135–61. Poźnan: Wydawnictwo naukowe, 1998.

Rasmussen, Larry. *Dietrich Bonhoeffer: His Significance for North Americans*. Minneapolis: Fortress, 1990.

———. "The Ethics of Responsible Action." In *The Cambridge Companion to Dietrich Bonhoeffer*, edited by John W. de Gruchy, 206–25. Cambridge: Cambridge University Press, 1999.

Rejman, Zofia. *Jan Paweł Woronicz: Poeta i Kapłan*. Chotomów: Verba, 1992.

Ruszkowski, Janusz. *Adam Mickiewicz i ostatnia krucjata: studium romantycznego millenaryzmu*. Wrocław: Wydawnictwo Leopoldinum, 1996.

Samsonowicz, Henryk. *O "historii prawdziwej."* Warsaw: Novum Orbis, 1997.

Schroeder, Steven. "The End of History and the New World Order." In *Theology and the Practice of Responsibility*, edited by Wayne Whitson Floyd and Charles Marsh, 21–35. Valley Forge, PA: Trinity Press International, 1994.

Segel, Harold. *Polish Romantic Drama: Three Plays in English Translation*. Ithaca, NY: Cornell University Press, 1977.

Shelley. "A Defense of Poetry." In *Shelly: Selected Poetry, Prose and Letters*. London: Nonesuch Press, 1951.

Siemieński, Lucjan. *Religijność i mistyka w życiu i poezyach Adama Mickiewicza*. Kraków: Drukarnia Władysława Jaworskiego, 1871.

Siwicka, Dorota. *Romantyzm: 1822–1863*. Warsaw: Wydawnictwo Naukowe PWN, 1997.

Smaszcz, Waldermar. *Rozum i wiara*. Warsaw: Pax, 1999.

Stefanowska, Zofia. "O Dantejkości trzeciej części *Dziadów*." In *Próba zdrowego rozumu: studia o Mickiewiczu*, 65-70. Warsaw: Państwowy Instytut Wydawniczy, 1976.

———. *Historia i profecja: studium o Księgach narodu i pielgrzymstwa polskiego*. 2nd ed. Kraków: Wydawnictwo Literackie, 1998.

———. "Mickiewicz „śród żywiołów obcych"." In *Próba zdrowego rozumu*, 316. Warsaw: Rytm, 2001.

———. "Wielka—tak, ale dlaczego improwizacja?" In *Próba zdrowego rozumu: studia o Mickiewiczu*, 71-86. Warsaw: Państwowy Instytut Wydawniczy, 1976.

Szadek, Jadwiga. "1968: Dziesięc lat później." *Aneks* 20 (1997) 119-28.

Szczypa, Józef. *Jan Paweł Woronicz, kerymat narodowy i patriotyczny*. Lublin: Redakcja wydawnictw Katolickiego Uniwersytetu Lubelskiego, 1999.

Tischner, Józef. *Polski kształt dialogu*. 1980. Reprinted, Kraków: Znak, 2002.

Tödt, Heine Eduard. "Conscientious Resistance: Ethical Responsibility of the Individual, the Group, and the Church." In *Ethical Responsibility: Bonhoeffer's Legacy to the Churches*, edited by John Godsey and Geffrey Kelly, 17-41. New York: Mellen, 1981.

Tomka, Miklós. "Religion, Church, State and Civil Society in East-Central Europe." In *Church-State Relations in Central and Eastern Europe*, 45. Kraków: Zaklad Wydawniczy, 1999.

Trojanowiczowa, Z. "Organizator narodowej wyobraźni." In *Księga Mickiewiczowska*, edited by Zofia Trojanowiczowa and Zbiegniew Przychodniak, 9-24. Poźnan: Wydawnictwo naukowe, 1998.

Jan Turnau. "Chrześcijanin w niewoli." *Gazeta Wyborcza* 84 (1995) 17.

———. "Jakby Boga nie było." *Gazeta Wyborcza* (2005) 15.

Velikonja, Mitja. "Slovenian and Polish Religio-National Mythologies: A Comparative Analysis." *Religion, State & Society* 31 (2003) 233-60.

Van Hoogstraten, Hans Dirk. "The Enemy and Righteous Action." In *Bonhoeffer for a New Day*, edited by John W. de Gruchy, 175-89. Grand Rapids: Eerdmans, 1997.

———. "Europe as Heritage: Christian Occident." In *Bonhoeffer's Ethics: Old Europe and New Frontiers*, edited by Guy Carter et al., 97-111. Kampen: Kok Pahros, 1991.

Walicki, Andrzej. "National Messianism and the Historical Controversies in the Polish Thought of 1831-1848." In *Culture and Nationalism in Nineteenth Century Eastern Europe*, edited by Roland Sussex and J. C. Eade, 128-41. Columbus, OH: Slavica, 1985.

———. *Philosophy and Romantic Nationalism: The Case of Poland*. Oxford: Oxford University Press, 1982.

Wajda, Andrzej. Interview in *Gazeta Wyborcza* (2000) 2.

Weigandt, Ewa. "Gombrowicz i Miłosz o Mickiewiczu." In *Księga Mickiewiczowska*, edited in Zofia Trojanowiczowa and Zbiegniew Przychodniak, 399-418. Poźnan: Wydawnictwo naukowe, 1998.

Weintrub, Wiktor. *The Poetry of Adam Mickiewicz*. S-Gravenlage: Moulton, 1954.

Węcławski, Tomasz. "Trzy procesy." *Tygodnik Powszechny* 51 (2005) 1, 19.

Wędzel, Jolanta. "*Egzystencjalna orientacja teologiczno-etycznej myśli Marcina Lutra i Dietricha Bonhoeffera*." In *Rocznik Teologiczny* 35 (1993) 189-245 and 38 (1996) 127-98.

Wojtyła, Karol. "Homilia Jana Pawła II podczas Mszy św. W Sopocie." In *VII piełgrzymka Jana Pawła II do ojczyzny*, 25. Olsztyn: Wydział Duszpasterski Kurii Metropolitalnej Warmińskiej, 1999.

Woronicz, Jan Paweł. *Jan Paweł Woronicz: Pisma wybrane*. Warsaw: Open, 1993.

———. *Sybilla, Hymn Polski* Lwów: Nakład wydawnictwa mrówki, 1869.

Wüstenberg, Ralf. "Dietrich Bonhoeffer on Theology and Philosophy." *Anvil* 12 (1995) 45–56.

———. "Religionless Christianity: Dietrich Bonhoeffer's Tegel Theology." In *Bonhoeffer for a New Day*, edited by John W. de Gruchy, 57–71. Grand Rapids: Eerdmans, 1997.

———. *A Theology of Life, Dietrich Bonhoeffer's Religionless Christianity*. Grand Rapids: Eerdmans, 1998.

Wybicki, Józef. "Mazurek Dąbrowskiego." In *Reduta*, edited by Janion, 103–4. Kraków: Wydawnictwo Literackie, 1979.

Zerner, Ruth. "Dietrich Bonhoeffer's Views on the State and History." In *A Bonhoeffer Legacy*, edited by A. J. Klassen, 147–50. Grand Rapids: Eerdmans, 1981.

Życiński, Józef. "Bądźmy wierni papieskiemu stylowi." *Gazeta Wyborcza* 4 (2005).

www.ingramcontent.com/pod-product-compliance
Lightning Source LLC
Chambersburg PA
CBHW050621300426
44112CB00012B/1605